women in development

a resource guide for organization and action

ISIS women's international information & communication service

foreword by Boston Women's Health Book Collective

new society publishers

Inquiries regarding requests to republish all or part of **Women in Development** should be addressed to New Society Publishers, 4722 Baltimore Avenue, Philadelphia, PA 19143.

ISBN: 0-86571-040-6 Hardbound
      0-86571-041-4 Paperback
Printed in the United States. (Previously published as a European edition ISBN 2-88116-000-x.)

Design and layout: Liz Mackie and Ximena Charnes
Cover design: Dion Lerman and Nina Huizinga
Cover photograph: Maggie Murray

New Society Publishers is a project of New Society Educational Foundation and a collective of Movement for a New Society. New Society Educational Foundation is a non profit, tax-exempt foundation. Tax deductible contributions can be made to any of its projects. Movement for a New Society is a network of small groups and individuals working for fundamental social change through nonviolent action. To learn more about MNS write: Movement for a New Society, 4722 Baltimore Avenue, Philadelphia, PA 19143. Opinions expressed in this book do not necessarily represent agreed-upon positions of either the New Society Educational Foundation or Movement for a New Society.

foreword

The idea linking women to development issues is scarcely two decades old. Since Esther Boserup's critical reflections first appeared in 1970, economists, planners and other internationalists occupied with development have gradually been forced to "discover" that women should be included in their planning. The flow of rhetoric began, and will doubtless continue after the United Nations Decade for Women Conference in Nairobi in 1985. Meanwhile, women researchers and activists fighting for recognition and participation in the planning process have understood once again that economic justice remains central to any improvement in the status of women, here or in the third world. Furthermore, mere "inclusion" in development projects conceived by traditional male planners in either the developed or developing countries is almost universally not in women's interests. Not only must there be genuine partnership for women in the development process, but the whole concept of development itself must be changed before it can work in the interests of any third world peoples.

The ISIS **Women In Development** guide is one of the few resources linking these issues. Written from women's perspectives and rich with the voices and photographs of third world women themselves, the Guide offers a systematic and scholarly exploration of the relationship between women and multinationals, rural development, health, education, migration, etc. The range of documentation and resources is superb. But unlike most academic efforts, **Women In Development** also presents concrete tools for activists who recognize that to wait for "trickle down" development for women, or for enlightenment about women's needs from the policy-makers and international agencies, is probably to wait forever. By working together, there are steps women can take now, and the Guide directs us to those groups and programs that are making a difference.

This is the single best text we have seen for incorporating international and development issues into Women's Studies Programs anywhere in the world. But more than that, it is the resource every women's group needs to understand the inescapable connections between our work here in the West and the struggles of women and people everywhere in the third world. It is a must for every woman concerned with the future course of world development and how that development will affect us all."

Judy Norsigian   *Norma Swenson*

Judy Norsigian, Norma Swenson
for the Boston Women's Health Book Collective

contents

introduction

Two parallel trends have gained momentum in the past two decades: one is the women and development debate and the other is the feminist movement and the great upsurge of women mobilizing and organizing around the world, continuing a centuries-old struggle of women to liberate ourselves from oppression and subordination in society. Until very recently, there has been little dialogue between the two, or effort to relate one to the other.

Yet the experiences of women in these struggles have led to new insights about the nature of the attitudes and institutions which create and perpetuate domination and inequality of women and about how these are intertwined with structures of economic domination and inequality. A feminist perspective is very relevant to development and development issues; that is, to issues such as supplying people's basic needs — food, water, shelter, health and education. And development is or should be of important concern to feminists.

Development planners and policy makers, however, generally consider feminism as irrelevant to development. At best, they view feminism as a luxury for better-off women in industrialized countries. And we in the women's movement, especially in industrialized countries, have often concentrated on organizing around a limited number of issues directly affecting women in our own countries: child care, reproductive rights, violence against women, discrimination. We have put our energies into these because it is precisely these areas which are neglected or considered secondary by other movements, parties or unions. On the other hand, we have often ignored issues of international politics and economics.

This is beginning to change. Women are addressing issues of food, water and economic exploitation from a feminist perspective. This book examines the insights this perspective brings to some of the main trends and issues of development. It explores how feminists are challenging the assumption that "integrating women into development" will solve problems caused by development plans and policies which have neglected or been detrimental to women. Not an in-depth study or analysis, this book is meant simply to be a guide to recent thinking and literature about women and development and to the feminist critique of these.

We have tried to pick out of the enormous amount of material produced on women and development those resources we feel are really relevant to women and to identify gaps in research and materials. We also list some of the groups actively involved in mobilizing and organizing around the world and record some of their experiences as a resource for others and to facilitate contact between existing groups.

the scope of the guide

Since it is impossible to cover all areas of development and feminism in one book, we have chosen to focus on certain areas: multinationals; rural development and food production, including appropriate technology and income generation; health, migration and tourism, education and communication.

The introductory article "Rethinking Women and Development" places these areas in the overall context of the various theories and trends of women and development and the feminist perspective on these. "Women and Development Literature: A Survey" gives a general overview of some of the main contributions to present thinking on women and development.

We have chosen to look at multinational corporations first because of their determining impact on development in all parts of the world, and on women workers, consumers and transmitters of culture in both industrialized and developing countries.

The chapter on rural development examines the main trends in development policies over the past few decades and their effects on women, especially food producers. It raises questions about attempted solutions to problems in rural areas and about appropriate technology and income generating projects.

Health is a major area affecting women as bearers of children and as those primarily responsible for the health care of themselves and their children. In examining the health care systems in developing and developed countries, this chapter raises questions about the control of health care, population control and pharmaceutical industries.

Migration and tourism are issues which development planners usually examine only marginally, if at all. Yet development policies directly affect the growth of migration and tourism and these in turn affect women in particular ways. This chapter examines how women are mobilizing around these issues.

The chapter on education and communication raises questions about the role of education as a means of socializing women and as a means to gain greater self-determination. It examines how communication and information systems are often used to the detriment of women and speaks of the importance of women gaining access to them and shaping them to serve our own needs.

Other important issues we would have liked to deal with, but could not due to lack of space, are funding, aid, evaluation of projects and national liberation struggles. Areas that we have touched on only briefly are sexuality, marriage structures and relationships. Other issues such as violence against women and sexual harassment and their impact on women's potential for self-determination run throughout all the chapters. Although we would have liked to examine in more detail the potential and limitations of different political and economic systems, the questions feminists are raising are directed at all types of systems.

resources for research and organizing

Selected resources follow the overview articles in each chapter. We have tried to assess the usefulness of the materials from the governmental, intergovernmental and better known development agencies and to highlight some of the less well-known sources, especially materials produced by women, action-oriented groups and organizations and feminists who are bringing a feminist perspective to development and trying to break the gap between theory and practice.

We have not included every development journal, agency, and institute in the world, nor every feminist group or organization. We list academic studies only in exceptional cases and refer the reader to universities for this kind of material. We have chosen to describe groups, organizations and institutions at greatest length and to assess the books, periodicals and other materials they produce. Listings of materials quickly become dated, but groups working on the issues are likely to continue producing and updating resource materials.

We have made every effort to make this resource guide as accurate and up-to-date as possible. However, some groups change addresses often and it is possible that we have made some errors. We would very much appreciate your calling to our attention any changes or inaccuracies as well as any material we may have left out or missed that you feel is important.

acknowledgements and credits

The idea of this Resource Guide was first developed at the very beginning of ISIS by two of the founding members, Jane Cottingham and Marilee Karl. Anita Anand joined us in the work in 1980 and played an important part in giving the guide its final shape. Over the years, as we worked on collecting the material and discussing the contents and format, it has been enriched by the input of many, many people from all corners of the world. It would be impossible to list by name every person, group or organization who supplied materials, advice and support and who shared the ideas and experiences which have gone into this guide. Although the authors of the articles and chapters take the final responsibility for the content, this guide is the result of the contributions and work of many. We would like to thank those individuals, groups and organizations who provided the materials in the ISIS Bulletins which were used as a basis for this book, and those who supplied the resource materials listed in this guide. We would also like to thank Saralee Hamilton of the Women and Global Corporations Network for her contributions to the chapter on multinationals; the Boston Women's Health Book Collective, especially Judy Norsigian and Norma Swenson, the Dispensaire des Femmes, especially Rosangela Gramoni and Patricia Schultz, and the participants of the Third International Women and Health Meeting for their contributions to the Health chapter.

We thank all the members of the ISIS collective, other women working at ISIS, and the ISIS Associates for their advice and support.

Photographs by Maggie Murray are taken from the book *Our Own Freedom*, published by Sheba Feminist Publishers, with kind permission from the author.

We have tried to credit graphics wherever we could, but they were often unsigned or we could not find the original source. Our apologies to the artists; we would welcome your contacting us to put this right for the future.

a note on terminology

None of the terms used to describe the world is entirely satisfactory. Arguments can be presented for and against using developing and developed countries, third world, industrialized world, North-South and so on. Since these are all we have at the moment, however, we have used various of them throughout the book. We emphasize that all countries are developing in one way or another and that development links and concerns us all.

a final note

Our hope is that the shared insights, ideas, experiences and resources in this guide will contribute to developing a new theory and practice of development which includes a feminist perspective.

Isis

The members of the ISIS collective are: Rossana Cambi, Maria Teresa Chadwick, Gabriela Charnes, Ximena Charnes, Roxanne Claire, Jane Cottingham, Ana Maria Gómez, Marilee Karl, Elizabeth Mackie, Monica v.d. Meden-Niebergall, and Valsa Verghese.
Other women working at ISIS are Christina Georgeff and Maria Antonieta Saa.

The ISIS Associates are: Olga Amparo Sanchez, Colombia; Anita Anand, India; Marie Assaad, Egypt; Brigalia Bam, South Africa; Nita Barrow, Barbados; Jacqueline Berenstein-Wavre, Switzerland; Jessie Bernard, USA; Kamla Bhasin, India; Peggy Billings, USA; Elise Boulding, USA; Violet Coomarasamy, Malaysia; Miranda Davies, England; Akke van Eijden-van Dam, Netherlands; Annette Kaiser, Switzerland; Sister Mary John Mananzan, Philippines; Magaly Pineda, Dominican Republic; Nawal El Saadawi, Egypt; Adriana Santa Cruz, Chile; Marie-Angélique Savané, Senegal; Geertje Thomas, Netherlands; Ah Fong Chung, Mauritius; Karin Himmelstrand, Sweden; Boston Women's Health Book Collective, USA.

rethinking women and development

Anita Anand

Over the last two development decades, there has been much evidence to show that the situation of women in developing countries has deteriorated. As we enter the third development decade, there are several questions to be raised regarding the nature of development, and the role of women in such development. To understand why women have been left out of the development process, a brief historical review of development is essential.

Development has meant different things to different people, based on what influences their thinking. It is helpful to look at the work of Karl Mannheim who defines two basic modes of thinking based on one's class interest — ideological and utopian — that shape one's perception of reality. Sheldon Gellar applies these two modes to the thinking that influences development theory and models.

Ideological thinking asserts the worldviews of ruling groups, supports the status quo, and sees change taking place largely within currently established structures. Most mainstream development models and work are based on the ideological mode of thinking. Models based on such thinking view development as an administrative problem, the solution to which lies in the transfer of vast amounts of capital and technological resources from the rich to the poor nations. Utopian thinking reflects the opinions of certain oppressed groups, believes in the transformation of the existing structures by overthrowing the status quo, and sees change through destruction of structures responsible for exploitation and oppression of the masses. Models based on the utopian modes are generally marxist or nationalist in orientation, rejecting the existing power relationships between the "haves" and the "have-nots" and call for basic change in the system. In these models, underdevelopment is not defined as a problem of lack of resources or technology, but one of exploitation and poverty caused by capitalistic expropriation.

Gellar also cites a third model of development, based on moralist-idealist thought. The moralist-idealists are those who believe in the "good society" defined in terms of justice, freedom and liberation, rather than the GNP, industrialization, or public ownership of the means of production. They remain utopian in nature in that they identify with the poorest of the poor and call upon the dominant classes to cast aside their affluence. However, much of their effort is spent working with the very institutions which the utopians claim have created the suffering of the masses.

1960-1980: from then to now

During the first development decade (1960-1970), the world's gross international product increased by one trillion dollars. Of this, 80 percent went to the industrialized nations (average annual increase: 1000 dollars) and 6 percent to poor nations (incomes less than 200 dollars). At the end of the first development decade, an annual growth rate of 5 percent had been achieved by most developing countries. Also increasing were rates of unemployment, population growth and the disparity in people's incomes. By this time it had become clear that in spite of rising GNP, the essential needs of people were not being met.

At the same time, developing nations were being depleted of their natural resources at an alarming rate — either in the form of direct imports to developed nations, or as raw material for production of potentially exportable commodities. The development strategy in the 1960s had concerned itself with increased food production to meet increasing population growth. With technological revolutions such as the Green Revolution, this had been achieved, yet food shortages were acute. Massive population control programs were promoted, yet the real reasons why people had children were never fully understood by the population experts.

With the increasing militancy of the developing nations, a more palatable form of development had to be devised. So new concepts were developed by the experts. With the use of terms such as "basic human needs," "new directions," "meeting the needs of the poorest of the poor," and more

A development scheme employing poor peasants to improve water supplies in a drought-prone area of India.

recently "growth with equity," a whole new development jargon emerged. The developing world retaliated with the New International Economic Order (NIEO), demanding a fairer share of the world's resources, fairer trading patterns, and more input into international decision making. Currently, the two sides maintain these positions with the developing countries pushing for the NIEO, seeing BHN (Basic Human Needs) as a ploy to avoid dealing with structural issues. The developed countries continue to talk of human rights, land reform, technology transfer without admitting the need for real change in their own economic practices.

During these two decades, women working on development issues were suffering the same fate as women in general. They were considered marginal to the process of the highly intellectual development debate, and were treated as such. In the early 1970s several European and North American women began advancing the concept of "integrating women into development." Their work pointed out that development had actually harmed women, that many women in developing countries were worse off than before. More studies were conducted by social scientists, political scientists and other academicians, confirming these findings.

In 1975 the International Women's Year conference declared a decade that would concentrate on women the world over. Since then, at national and international forums, women's role in the economic process has been a major component, and the race for "women in development" was on. Education, vocational/technical training were seen as essential prerequisites for women to move into the development process. Having women in decision-making positions, allocating funding for women's projects and initiating legislation on the prerequisites would further hasten this integration process. The theory was that, as women's work was not recognized

as part of the national economy, sufficient opportunities should be made available to women to move into the market economy. This would ensure income generation for them and a sense of self-confidence to participate in the development process.

integrating women into development: a pseudo-feminist myth

The definition of integration is "to form into a whole"; "to incorporate into a larger unit," "to end segregation of and bring into common and equal membership in society or an organization" (Webster). In the case of "integrating women into development," if the "whole" is development then we can assume that bringing women into development would end an essentially sexist process of progress. However, when the literature and theories about women in development were being propagated, the nature of development, as it existed, was never questioned. The proponents of such thinking were in basic agreement with mainstream development thought. The only quarrel with it was that women had been left out. Even to this day, the most ardent proponents of integrating women into development have not realized that neither mainstream nor marxist models have room for women, as neither group has addressed the problem of patriarchy. Society's acceptance of male-domination has pervaded development work. Though much lip service has been paid to the equal participation of women in the male-dominated development circles, this has remained by and large "integration" without much thought or attempt towards genuine power sharing with women.

income generation: no questions asked

For mainstream development models, development has meant the "integration" of developing countries into the international market system, whereby the notion of "growth" was to be manifested in increased economic production. Towards this end, education and employment were considered a means for income generation. Therefore, it should come as no surprise that common indicators used to determine women's involvement in development have been employment and education. When most women live in rural areas and in a non-market economy (70 to 80 percent are involved in subsistence work), these indicators have little validity. As women make up 60 to 90 percent of the agricultural labor force and produce 44 percent of all food, why is it crucial to talk of income generating projects? Rather, would it not be better to recognize women's current productivity? Most developing economies have moved or are moving from agrarian-based to industrial-based economies, in spite of what their governments may claim. During this process, the structure of agriculture has suffered. With growing emphasis on cash cropping and non-food crops, subsistence farming has suffered a major setback.

This has had serious repercussions on women and the rural communities. Through subsistence farming, most of a rural family's and community's needs were met. Excess edibles were sold or bartered in local markets for commodities such as soap and clothes. With increasing numbers of women having to shift to cash cropping, and with meager economic returns, the family's needs are not being met. Nutritionally this has taken a heavy toll on the health and well-being of rural communities. Former food-producing communities are now growing cash crops or non-food crops for export to urban, national and international markets. Whereas once they were somewhat self-sufficient, they now mostly rely on government handouts or foreign aid. Income generating projects may be a godsend to women, with few opportunities for subsistence farming and few or no skills for alternative work in a limited job market, who have been forced into non-farm work. However, it further exacerbates the problem of vanishing subsistence farming and food dependence on foreign markets.

Enlisting women in new jobs, largely for manufacturing export items, often requires their migration to urban areas. Skills that women are taught are "female-prone" — a term used to describe skills which women are supposedly best at, such as sewing, knitting, embroidery, and which are low-skilled, low-paid and easily replaceable. Local and multinational industries such as textiles, electronics and agribusiness have capitalized on this shift and preferentially hire women. Paying low wages for long hours in unhealthy and hazardous working conditions, these industries claim they are liberating women. Multinationals have been keen advocates of this transfer of women's work from self-sufficient to market-oriented types. The industries well realize the gold mine they have struck with women who are usually the most willing to work, the easiest to fire and the least likely to unionize. Income generation advocates little realized the complexity of issues when they suggested this. With little or no protection for wages, benefits and work, women are the most abused section of the formal labor force.

education: literacy or critical consciousness?

Education, along with income generation capacity, has been perceived as the key to the golden door of success and equal participation of women in the development process. It is true that women need education to be able to participate in society, but the nature of this education has not been sufficiently questioned.

In industrialized societies or urban areas of developing countries, education can be a stepping stone to economic self-sufficiency. However, the educational systems in most developing countries are relics of their colonial past, and irrelevant to the needs of most people, especially women. The education is either highly specialized (in which case women have to compete in a narrow job market) or too general (in which case women have access only to the lowest paid jobs). Economically, even such education is beyond the means of most people. If a child has to be educated, preference is given to the male child, who is a better asset in terms of financial returns. For the affluent, educating women is an exercise that will increase their price in the marriage market.

If education is to have any value for women, it must be a means to raise their consciousness about the oppressive structures that keep them in positions of powerlessness. Most educational systems do not provide a climate for such thinking skills to develop. In developing societies, most educated women — the leaders, academicians, professionals in establishment organizations — perpetuate the status quo. The reasoning behind this is that if the patriarchal system has worked for them, it should work for all women. Demands for traditional

education from third world women and others come from a lack of perspective of what this limited privilege can be used for.

When a woman is relatively powerless and has little control over what is happening in her environment, education for literacy is meaningless. What she craves is knowledge of why she must bear so many children, work endless hours without respite, be beaten and raped, have an alcoholic husband, and go hungry. Existing educational systems have not provided women with the tools to understand and analyze the true nature of social, political and economic systems that govern their lives and oppress them, and this is why they have failed. If women are to be change agents in their societies, the education offered them must be a tool for consciousness raising and action. This end result cannot be brought about by learning the three Rs or being drilled in nutrition and family planning.

appropriate technology: appropriate for whom?

Transfer of technology has been a major ingredient of mainstream development work. This transfer has filled the coffers of many multinational corporations that manufacture and export heavy equipment, has supported highly specialized and largely intellectual research and development institutions, and has meant large investments for developing countries. It has proved an expensive and futile exercise and developing countries are now demanding technologies that meet the needs of their budgets and projects.

Taking off from the "small is beautiful" ideology, the con-cept of appropriate technology emerged. Developed countries rushed into developing ones with new designs and innovations that would revolutionize the developing world. Recognizing that women do back-breaking work for long hours, the women in development community sought solutions once again in technology. Instead of examining why women, after hard work in the fields and markets, have to return home to cook, care for children, gather fuel and water and take care of animals, the development planners seized upon appropriate technology. Smokeless stoves, grinders, seed hullers, weeders, hoes and suchlike were invented and improved upon to cut the time spent in these tasks. The inherent sexism in permitting men to return from the fields, bathe, eat and go visiting with friends has never been questioned. Job sharing of "women's work" is unheard of.

Similar questions can be raised regarding technical innovations that have supposedly eased the burden of women's work in developed societies. Have the vacuum cleaner, dishwasher, blender, ice maker enabled a woman to have a more equal relationship with a man? Equality cannot be achieved as long as women are seen as marginal to the existence of men, society or development.

The new directions in technology suffer from the same malady as development. They are male-dominated, designed mostly in developed societies, and often involve resources alien to the local environment. Even when the appropriate technologies are locally developed, they are often done in research laboratories and academic institutions with little input from the women and men in the field who will be utilizing the technologies.

health

Most of the health care focus around women has been in family planning and nutrition. While it is important for women to have access to information and services to control their fertility, much of the help offered has been misguided and controlled mainly by population specialists and family planning agents, who are usually men. Reproduction information and services made available to women are largely male and establishment-controlled, and unsuited to the lifestyles and bodies of the women receiving them. Additionally, services such as regular checkups and pre and post-natal care are rarely available. Efforts by the overzealous and insensitive population community (with help from the pharmaceutical industry and national governments which work hand in hand with these organizations) have been based on the premise that it is better to have reduced fertility at any cost than over-population. Who makes this decision is quite clear — certainly not the women on the receiving end of these programs. In spite of the known dangers of synthetic contraceptives, the women in development community has further pushed for these programs.

A similar situation exists in the area of nutrition. The popular thinking is that most people in developing countries do not have sufficient know-how to balance their diets and need to be educated. However, it can be said that development has done more to undermine the possibility of achieving a balanced diet than to help it. Development strategies, supported by international food politics, have pushed for the boost in food production of items for export (to earn foreign exchange for sophisticated technology and research), as well as non-food items. Towards this end, land once producing food to meet the needs of the community is being used for cash-cropping and income generation.

To alleviate this problem, solutions are being proposed and implemented such as food substitutes (e.g. soymeal) which are alien to the diet of the local people and, therefore, rejected. Questions relating to the overall structures of agriculture, of land ownership, crop priorities, etc., are hardly ever raised. If they are, it is in the light of reformist measures such as land reform or water reallocation.

If a society were committed to maintaining a fair standard of health for its people, it would devise and implement systems of agriculture and health care that would make the goal possible. As long as foreign exchange earnings and modernization are higher priorities for most developing societies, basic health care will remain an illusion. Research and development emphases will be on diseases which affect mainly the elites (e.g. cardiovascular diseases), with little attention to the politics of malnutrition and reproduction. Development experts, unwilling to question the power and control of medicine and researchers will continue to ignore the role of women in the health and planning process, except as a means to serve the experts' ends.

women in development: a long-distance affair?

Since its conception, much of the mainstream women in development work has been like a long distance affair. Largely defined by western women and their elitist counterparts in developing countries, it has fallen prey to the same assumptions that development work has; i.e., development is an

Upper Volta.

overseas problem. All societies are developing societies. While it is true that most people in less developed countries live more precariously than their western counterparts, it is also true that marginalized sections of developed societies have much in common with their counterparts in developing countries. This relationship, a critical one if development were viewed as a class issue, has been ignored by the experts. It is easier to deal with something which is not too close to home and which is also more exotic.

At the same time, this long distance strategy excuses governments of developed countries from dealing with issues of deprivation at home. With increasing internationalization of capital and human resources as well as raw materials over the last decade, it has become detrimental to development work not to establish this link. As a result, the strategies in the past, as well as the ones being proposed for the future, lack validity. Case in point: the marginalization of women in developing societies (so well elucidated in the women in development literature) cannot be overcome without examining the roots of marginalization, which is the patriarchal system, not only in the developing societies but in the developed ones as well.

That some percentage of women in developed societies enjoy a certain level of economic independence must not be equated with the achievement of equality in the power structures that control their societies. This is evident in examining the position of the majority of women in developed societies, who are the poorest, most oppressed, overworked and marginalized sections of their society.

Decisions made in any country regarding women in the

garment industry affect women in the USA, Mexico, Britain, Italy, India, Sri Lanka, Korea, Taiwan and many other countries. Flight of capital and the internationalization of trade has brought these women together — either to lose or gain from such investments or to collectively organize against the single-purpose of the multinational corporations: maximization of profit.

Women working in the mainstream development community have largely failed to address these issues — at home or overseas. It is easier to propagate reformist measures such as income generating projects, job skills, nutrition education, welfare and the like than to examine the root causes of overt sexism, agricultural displacement, and the marginalization of women in any society. If ever the issues of power and powerlessness are brought up at a national/international forum, it is only at the theoretical level — with little pragmatic followup.

Women in development can have real meaning when the vital links between the local and global situations are made. For example, women in the USA must look at the struggles of women in their rural communities, women in Appalachia, Native American women, farmworker women, working class women. Many of the problems these women are facing are similar to those being faced by their sisters overseas. As most

women in the USA fall into the marginalized categories, the women in development community in the USA has gravely shirked its responsibility in neglecting these issues and failing to relate them to the marginalization of women overseas.

toward a theory of women and development

For women to become a vital force in their societies, change will have to be based on a new theory of development which embraces feminism. Feminism poses some challenges to development theory and praxis that must be addressed if any effective and inclusive work on bringing about a new order is to be done. It questions the artificial barriers between the political, social and economic aspects of society, and how individuals relate to these orders. Feminism asserts that the personal is political and personal change is a prerequisite to societal change ... the internalization and subjectification of being a change agent. It insists that the experience of women be recognized and validated in all work related to change. Examples of how this theory can be developed already exist, in progressive women's movements all over the world that are challenging the power of patriarchy. Women are organizing, speaking out against injustice in the home, workplace and society. These struggles are not restricted to upper and middle class women (as we are often told), but evident in working class and peasant women's groups, who have a long history of struggle against oppression.

At the same time, the struggle against patriarchy and economic oppression cannot be separated from the struggle of those who are poor and powerless. Progressive women's movements can be separate, and part of all those who work to bring about a just, participatory and sustainable society.

strategies for change: reform or radical?

There is no one strategy that will ensure equitable development for all. However, there are several directions that such strategies can go which could enable equitable development. If change were to be categorized in two broad areas — reform and radical — each category would have certain strategies that would enable change to be brought about.

Reformist strategies are those which are devised to alleviate problems (e.g., food stamps for the hungry, unemployment compensation for the unemployed) without much attention to the cause of the problems. Radical strategies are devised by examining the root of the problem, and proposing alternatives to presently existing structures that are responsible for creating the problems.

Whether strategies are reformist or radical in nature, they can go hand in hand, especially in societies where a total transformation of the political, social and economic system is not in sight, but there must be understanding of the means and the end.

The US 1980 Democratic Political Convention illustrated the need for such awareness. Political reforms meant that for the first time, women were half of the delegates to the national convention. However, as a columnist Richard Reeves pointed out, "Women, even when they share floor space at a convention, may never truly share political power of change politics. The game has rules made by men and they have a life and momentum of their own." Such reforms are important, but should not alone be taken as necessarily representing a real shift toward equality in decision making.

Both reformist and radical movements share a common goal for change. The underlying ideologies of the two are different, but reforms rightly integrated can become steps to more long-term change.

helping shape this future

Individuals and institutions interested in building this new just order need first of all to do more intentional thinking about the kind of political, social and economic order that will meet the needs of all people. Towards this end, development must mean the production, distribution and consumption of goods and services in the most equitable manner possible, with maximum participation of all people. For those in the developing and developed world it means study, consciousness raising, dialoguing and brainstorming about how people can gain control over their economies, no matter where they are. It means concentrating on the problems locally, state-wide, nationally and internationally.

A feminist approach to this future would require that this process happen before "development" is planned. It would also require the participation of women in every step of the way.

And finally, women — and men who are concerned about development — must learn to stand fast. Too long the theory has prevailed that when other more pressing issues of politics and peace are dealt with, then humankind will be able to turn to the needs of women. The challenging idea of our times is a determination to build a world less divided between rich and poor, the weak and the powerful. In moving to this goal, the old theory can no longer hold. True development, just development, cannot happen when the needs, talents, and potentialities of half of the world's population are seen as secondary and marginal. That is why feminism is not a frivolous concern. It deals with work, with struggle, and above all with the dream of a new day for all peoples.

Women at work, Australia

women and development: a survey of the literature

Mary Roodkowsky

Change and progress in the computer age happen fast. As recently as 1960, the development establishment paid little attention to women and could safely ignore the women who protested. Today, planners' desks are piled high with "women-and-development" papers, books and monographs, and development bureaucrats have, by and large, learned that they may not refer to farmers as only "he."

How much difference do all those words make? Reading some of them can give us an idea about what women expect from development, and how well the planning structures have responded in the past two decades. The following survey covers some of the most important papers, books and documents on the topic, criticizing them from the basis of someone who believes that development should serve – not use - women.

During the 1950s and 1960s, a few conferences on development issues discussed the involvement of women in the development process, albeit rather tangentially. The most important pioneering work on the subject appeared in Ester Boserup's *Woman's Role in Economic Development*. It documented and discussed in detail the negative impact of the development process on women. Boserup showed how colonialism and the forms of modernization it brought lowered women's status while raising men's, by imposing new patterns of sex roles on farming and trading, and by carrying such inequalities to the new industrial and urban sectors.

When Boserup wrote this book, she could truthfully begin with these words: "In the vast and ever growing literature on economic development, reflections on the particular problems of women are few and far between." Boserup's own work is a first step toward rectifying that problem, both through its own analyses, and by serving as a cornerstone for numerous further works and projects. Many of the topics introduced or elucidated by Boserup have become major themes in the women and development movement.

Woman's Role in Economic Development pointed out the ways in which modern agricultural methods hurt women. New implements and instruction about new techniques were available to men only, raising their productivity and their perceived worth in the society. Women's productivity and perceived social worth decreased by comparison. Their workload often increased, for often when men grew cash crops they were unavailable for, or unwilling to do, their traditional farm chores. In addition, many women lost informal rights to the land they farmed; in Boserup's words, women's role changed from that of a decision-making cultivator, to that of a "family aid" or "hired hand." Other economic changes affecting women include the transition from a subsistence economy – in which, in some parts of the world, women have a great deal of autonomy – to a cash economy, which usually replicates the industrialized world's patterns of male domination.

Boserup advocates greater roles for women in these modern industrial work forces, and calls for greater educational opportunities to facilitate such employment. She disagrees with a strain of development thinking prevalent at the time she was writing, which argued against policies to give women better employment, on the theory that they would be taking jobs away from men (who really needed them) in areas of high unemployment. Boserup claimed that women's working would create opportunities for other avenues of development.

Boserup writes as a planner and economist, who sees development as a process benefitting national economies through modernization. When development excludes women from full participation, it denies its benefits to women and it functions far less effectively. Planners should increase women's involvement and productivity in the modern sector, and provide women with the necessary education. Boserup's confidence in the planning process, and in the necessity of fitting women into that process so as to increase their status, presages one main trend in women and development thinking today, which calls for an "integration of women into the development process."

the development of the issue

Throughout the 1970s, as women organized for their rights, the development bureaucracy began to respond. International meetings made a point to mention the impact on the status

Facing page: ILO

Women are already engaged in most essential social tasks.

Africa of the United Nations, for example, had a meeting in March 1969 entitled The Regional Meeting on the Role of Women in National Development, followed by more specific meetings in Rabat and Addis Ababa during the following two years. By 1973-74, a number of action programs sponsored by the ECA had begun, especially in home economics and other traditional "women's" fields.

Concurrent with these developments was growing awareness of the impact of development on women in the United Nations. As early as November 1967, the General Assembly passed a Declaration on the Elimination of Discrimination Against Women, which promoted greater "economic participation of women" in order to promote the integration of women in development. By 1972, International Women's Year (which was originally suggested by a group of women's non-governmental organizations) was proclaimed for 1975, by the General Assembly of the United Nations, with the three themes of equality, development and peace.

Two special conferences that took place that year confirmed and energized the women and development movement. In July of 1975, both an official IWY conference and a dynamic public Tribune met for two weeks in Mexico. Two booklets are available from the United Nations describing each conference and their proceedings.

Together these conferences form a turning point in the movement to bring a new relationship between women and development, by providing the impetus, the networks, the energy, and the validity for a worldwide movement. In fact, most of the documents and many of the projects dealing with the issue owe their existence to these conferences — either directly (as preparatory or follow-up documents) or historically, being inspired by the conference or conference follow-up.

For the purposes of this survey, the body of literature on women and development will be divided into three general categories, which, taken together, can give a comprehensive picture of what kinds of statements have been and are being made about women and development:

- Descriptions of the negative impact of development on women, or about the status of women in developing nations.

- Organizational documents and reports, and development agency literature on the topic.

- Policy recommendations and critical analyses of the women and development movement, and feminine approaches to solving the problem.

As with any categories, these overlap each other, some of them considerably, especially because so much of the material is anecdotal.

what does development mean for women?

Materials on women and development produced since the 1975 IWY conference range from interviews to statistical tables and comprise diverse political perspectives.

Much of the literature takes the form of interviews or reports of interviews with third world women, which reflects a bias of the women and development movement — that development comes from the people involved. Some of the

of women of whatever it was they discussed. The United Nations Conference on Population in 1977, for example, recognized the close connection between the role of women and population growth, especially with respect to the close correlation between rises in women's labor force participation and education, and declines in birth rates.

That same year, those who wished to involve women and women's needs in development planning, achieved a minor victory in United States policy. The Percy Amendment added to the Foreign Assistance Act called for United States representatives in international agencies "to encourage and promote the integration of women" into the economies of the nations involved, and into policy-making positions in those organizations, "thereby improving the status of women."

As a result, "women and development" became an official part of official development efforts in the United States. A Women in Development office was organized at the U.S. Agency for International Development, and agencies ranging from the World Bank to the non-governmental private voluntary organizations began to encourage special women's programs.

Meanwhile, in the field, development projects had already begun special programs to "involve women more in development" by the early 1970s. The Economic Commission for best materials of this genre, naturally enough, come from third world groups themselves.

One magazine, published in West Africa, while not exclusively about women, carries some of the finest articles about and for women. *Famille et Développement* has covered such topics in the past few years as agriculture and women's work in the field; has run a major set of articles entitled "La polygamie est-elle un mal nécessaire?" ("Is Polygamy a Necessary Evil?") which discusses the economic and historical factors involved in that practice, including interviews with women married to polygamous men; and even dared to publish on a previously undiscussed and taboo subject, clitoridectomy and infibulation. *Famille et Développement* reaches grass-roots development workers, and just plain folks throughout francophone Africa. The magazine has succeeded in doing in its pages what the women and development movement should be all about — women's concerns are not only treated separately where appropriate, but the needs of women are treated as a prominent concern within whatever topic is being discussed — whether it is tourism, and the growth of prostitution it generates, or housing and water problems, and what these mean to women.

Another French magazine, a quarterly published in the Ivory Coast, *AGRIPROMO,* devoted one issue to *Le Travail de la femme (Women's Work).* There are interviews with a woman from Burundi, "Si je ne travaille pas tout le temps je serai méprisée" ("If I Don't Work All the Time, I Will be Scorned") and, even more telling, interviews with men from Togo, "Ma femme m'aide, mais je ne l'aide pas" ("My Wife Helps Me, But I Don't Help Her") and "Ma femme ne fait pas du vrai travail" ("My Wife Doesn't Do Real Work"). In addition, there are charts of the differing workloads of women and men, as well as discussion guides, all written in simple French.

A fascinating pair of books report and analyse a series of talks with women in six developing countries: Tunisia, Egypt, Sudan, Kenya, Sri Lanka, and Mexico. Perdita Huston, the author, an American journalist and development planner, sought over 150 women's opinions on the ways the modernization process has affected their lives. Huston used an unstructured, open-ended approach in her interviews, without attempting to fit the women she talked to into a predetermined set of questions — and a predetermined set of assumptions. She met with women where they gathered in groups, in the fields, markets, or health care facilities and talked with them informally. From these groups she asked for volunteers for individual, in-depth interviews, lasting one hour or more, which Huston began with the question, "How does your life differ from that of your mother and grandmother?"

One of these books, *Message from the Village,* recounts portions of these discussions, edited heavily for their content on women's views of family planning (for which Huston's study was funded) and on personal autonomy. The interviews are presented country by country, with short introductions and descriptions of the women and the context of the interview. There is a short concluding chapter suggesting ways to improve family planning programmes. Huston calls for measures to change men's attitudes, and to deal with male dominance, which Huston believes is the strongest barrier to family planning. She also emphasizes the need for women's leadership and stronger women's organizations.

The second book, based on the same set of interviews, *Third World Women Speak Out,* includes conversation about a wider range of topics, especially on the ways in which women see the social and economic changes in their lives,

Maggie Murray

Men meet - women work.

in their families, in education, health care, and politics. It also recounts interviews with professionals such as health care workers, political leaders and academics.

Huston finds out that women's opinions about the modernization of their societies are mixed: "The changes most often mentioned by rural women I interviewed as characterizing the 'new times' were increased dependence on cash and the newly available educational opportunities. The first of these factors "makes life more difficult"; the second offers to their children advantages that were not available to previous generations". Not only were some of the economic changes seen as harmful in themselves, but also as they alter family relationships. For instance, one woman from Kenya commented that men had wrongly used their extra money, staying away from home and finding women elsewhere.

Particularly interesting are the women's comments on family planning, desirable family size, and the constraints that prevent women from using contraceptives; the discussion of "female circumcision" or infibulation, which well portrays the dilemmas women face; and discussions with women about the education they desire for their daughters.

A commentary at the end of the volume analyzes Huston's interviews from standard social science approach. It adds some numerical data: in a third of the statements about the relationship between economic problems and the household situation, women complained that men spend what they earn on themselves, not sharing it with the family. This part of the text reports a fact that should help to dispel any residual notions

Open-air market, Upper Volta.

that people in developing areas are passive victims: women mentioned solutions to economic problems more frequently than they mentioned economic problems themselves.

A great deal of other literature has appeared describing the problems women face in development. In her new book, *The Sisterhood of Man,* Kathleen Newland discusses the status of women in seven major areas: legal systems, educational systems, the labour market, the family, politics, the mass media, and health systems. Unlike many analysts, Newland refuses to neatly slice the realities of women's societies into first and third worlds according to nations. Thus we find mention of progressive, feminist magazines like *Famille et Développement* from Senegal and *Femme* in France juxtaposed with discussions of the images of women in journals like *McCalls* from the USA or romance novels in Latin America. What emerges is a picture of women's status determined mostly by sex roles, no matter where in the world one searches.

Newland's work details numerous facts, written with a consistently pro-woman vocabulary. Newland supports many of the changes brought about by the women's movement, and includes a very short chapter on the empowerment of women at the end of the volume. One only wishes that such a lucid thinker and fine writer as Newland might delve deeper into these policy changes on which she only touches.

For an excellent collection of popularly written articles

surveying the status of women in third and first worlds, one might look toward the *New Internationalist*'s issue, "Women Hold Up Half the Sky". One article is an interview with a Bangladeshi woman, talking about her early marriage and her husband who beats her ("Oh, sister, I have so many problems"); another is an interview with a South African woman, and yet another by an African, on women in Guinea Bissau. An introductory article by Maggie Black describes some of the ways in which the development process has excluded women.

The *Handbook of International Data on Women* provides a completely different sort of information on women and development — numerical. It is an indispensable volume for anyone needing statistical information about the status of women across the globe. The authors, Elise Boulding, Shirley Nuss, Dorothy Lee Carson and Michael Greenstein, used data collected by various agencies of the United Nations and the Institute of Behavioral Sciences at the University of Colorado at Boulder. The data, ranked by nation, detail the participation of women in numerous industries and forms of employment; by birth, marriage, reproductive and death information; and about political structures as they affect women. The authors developed two new terms to describe their way of presenting the information. One is the "index of femaleness" which shows the proportion and the number of those engaged in certain activities (such as an occupation or a level of education) who are women. The other is the "distribution index" which shows what percentage and number of women are involved in a subgroup of a larger category of women (for example, a table showing what percent of all live births that have been recorded by mother's age, were to women in a given age group).

The authors remind us about the difficulties in obtaining regular and reliable figures on women which both result from the undervaluing of women, and cause further inattention to women's needs. Yet, they say, even these inadequacies in the data paint an accurate picture of the problem facing those who want to write about women.

what do the official agencies say?

The large planning agencies have, of course, said much on the topic of how development relates to women and to women's concerns. This section reviews, very briefly, several pieces of popular promotional literature on this topic, coming from international and non-governmental agencies.

From literature produced by several of the international aid agencies it is possible to discern something about how such agencies think about women and development. For example,

the Food and Agriculture Organization of the United Nations has issued a booklet called *The Missing Half*, a slick, illustrated 48 page pamphlet. With short text, large graphic designs, and numerous photographs, it could serve as a good introduction to the problems of women and development.

Some of the most powerful discussion of the issues takes place through its pictures. Most show women at work – sowing, harvesting, winnowing, pounding, and serving food; driving a tractor, caring for children. One particularly moving picture shows a mother nursing her baby as she sits in the marketplace, her face staring blankly, perhaps as she muses about the chores that await her.

The narrative takes a stab at development programs, commenting that "the first people needing to be developed are the developers themselves." Unfortunately, sometimes the language slips into a somewhat condescending perspective (many family planning programmes have failed "because of the incapacity of uneducated women to adapt themselves to abrupt changes") and once, despite all the booklet has said about women as agricultural producers, the text refers to a "farmer and his wife." One of the best paragraphs comes at the very end, where it discusses the relationship between development programmes and women: "Women's participation in development should not, however, be considered solely in terms of their contribution to the society and the economy. It is a goal in its own right."

Another booklet from the United Nations Development

Danois/UNICEF

Vietnam.

WE FULLY RECOGNIZE THE IMPORTANCE OF INTEGRATING WOMEN INTO DEVELOPMENT!

THEY'RE MUCH CHEAPER THAN MEN!

Liz Mackie/Sourcream

the unions to which they do belong, prevents women from earning what they should. Other parts of the book are genuinely sympathetic to the double workload women face, and critical of programs that have not recognized that burden, as for example, a study of the impact of water programs in Kenya that showed "when water was made more accessible, women received less assistance from other family members in fetching it. Without supporting programmes, such as improving the efficiency of the water-carrying system, improved access to water may hold no benefits for women".

What this booklet lacks is not a coherent analysis of the problems facing women but rather the dynamism of third world women. One has the sense — not only in the title — that the developing world is still one that needs to be acted *upon* by external agents of change. The World Bank explains what its projects are *doing for* women overseas, with little sense of women's presence in these projects. This, of course, characterizes the structural problem of the World Bank style of development itself, and one that most assuredly affects its attitudes toward women in their projects.

analysing the developers - what are they planning?

The following sections survey some documents discussing the various approaches to women and development, and proposing options for the future. It includes both papers that are somewhat theoretical and a sampling of reports of projects and conferences that analyze the woman/development relationship and prescribe new programs. Only one book is reviewed here, and unfortunately there are none by third world women. Virtually all of the rest of the important work on the topic is found in a few key collections of works, either in book, report, or magazine form.

Since it is generally agreed by now that the development process has excluded women, the differences occur in the solutions proposed by the agencies, planners and theorists. By now, the phrase "integration of women into development" has become a code word used in many, many different ways. Some people using the phrase agree with its utilitarian meaning: women can be a legitimate *means* for reaching certain development goals; others use it less deliberately, or try to give it new meanings.

Much literature promoting the "integration of women into development" comes from the large planning agencies.

One relevant report — for what it omits, as well as what it includes — is a compilation of preparatory papers for a January 1978 conference called The International Conference on Women and Food. It was held in the United States and sponsored by the Consortium for International Development and the US Agency for International Development, to focus on the United Nations World Food Conference resolution on *Women and Food*. However, the preparatory papers, taken as a whole, do not emphasize women's role. Of the ten papers included, half are by men, half by women. Each one of the five essays by women deals directly with the problems of women and development, either from an overall perspective (such as Elise Boulding's "Women, Peripheries and

Programme, by Ester Boserup and Christina Liljencrantz, is *Integration of Women in Development*. The first third of its text is devoted to a short presentation of "the nature of the problem," pointing out a number of ways in which the modern economic sector excludes women. The second section deals with some of the changes the authors call for in order for women to become a fuller part of that modern industrial sector: changes in attitudes toward the marriage and reproductive cycle; literacy and job training, including giving women the tools for nontraditional, better-paying jobs; policies to hire women in both the public and private sectors. The final section calls for legislative programs that give and publicize women's rights, and also calls for programs that provide training facilities that will help both men and women to raise their productivity. The text itself is dry and uninspired, neither numerous hard facts on the one hand, nor anecdotes, are included. And, although at the very beginning and at the very end, the authors reassure us that development exists for the benefit of people, much of the body of the text urges women to accommodate themselves to the development system.

The World Bank has also brought out a pamphlet called *Recognizing the "Invisible" Woman in Development: The World Bank's Experience*. The title itself reveals a great deal — women invisible to whom? Only to those whose self interest blinds them to the women whose work sustains societies around the world.

The text of the book presents a variety of development themes, some of the problems facing women, and what measures the World Bank has been taking to alleviate them. The presentation deals with both the theme of justice for women and the interests of women. Some of the sections discuss the need for women to have control over their work:

Failure to recognize the economic contribution of women implies failure to consider the factors affecting their contribution, the ways in which they are prepared for their tasks, the tools and techniques they use, and the efficiency of their efforts. The support by society, which women may need, is also ignored, as is the question of whether they control the proceeds of, or rewards from, their efforts.

The text also suggests that the low participation of women in unions, and the inability of women to exercise power in

Women workers share many of the same problems, whether in the third world or highly industrialized countries. Croydon, England.

Food Production") or with reference to a particular region or topic (like Kathleen Cloud's "Sex Roles in Food Production and Food Distribution in the Sahel"). Of the five papers by men, one (by Douglas Caton, reviewed below) deals in depth with women; the others do not, being concerned with strategies for increasing food production and with analyses of food systems — with occasional reference to women.

Perhaps some authors felt that women had already achieved equality in the development process, so there was no need for specific mention of their needs.

One paper aware of the exclusion of women in development planning was written by Douglas Caton of AID. "Elements of the Food Production/Distribution System: An Overview on How Women can Contribute" is the only one in the collection by a man to discuss the role of women in development.

From the title, one can discern what Caton means by "food system." It could not be the small plots that women farm throughout much of the developing world, for there women contribute enormously to their families' food needs. In fact, it is the modern capitalist, cash-oriented system to which Caton refers.

Part of Caton's paper discusses the various operations of a food system, which he describes in part as follows: "Agricultural production activities are composed of a set of individual farm input-output production function relationships."

Progress — for women and for the economy — depends upon women's greater involvement in this sector: "Lessening women's work burden, such as getting water and firewood, or working in the fields, has no pay-off for women, and for the nation, unless it is accompanied by a complementary effort along the road to full economic integration, such as training in modern production practices, and crop intensification or diversification."

Caton selects Taiwan as one example of successful integration of women into the modern economy, that could serve as a model for integration in agriculture. He enthusiastically describes the ways in which the Taiwanese Government has pulled women into technical occupations, because there "women were explicitly dealt with as a national resource." Caton heralds in particular the involvement of women in the electronics industries, where "foreign investors, under the cited agreements with the Chinese (*sic*) government, established labor compounds consisting of a manufacturing plant, dormitories, food, health and recreational facilities, and training facilities."

Even if it does not already sound like the "company store" all over again, some comments made by Rachael Grossman will illustrate another side. In her article "Women's Place in the Integrated Circuit", she shows what the involvement of women in Southeast Asian electronics industries has meant. Young women leave home to work in factories producing electronic components for calculators, computers, etc. They are often housed in barracks-like accommodations, earning less than a dollar a day. They peer through microscopes for long hours and deal with potent chemicals. Many of them develop such severe eye problems from this work that by their mid-twenties they are retired, with few or no transferable skills, no savings, and alienated from their traditional culture.

A very different understanding of the "integration of women into development" comes from development planner and writer Barbara Rogers. Beginning with a discussion of how different cultures assign roles according to gender, *The Domestication of Women* then describes how male-dominated Western biases have affected development planning. The book points out the structural sexism of planning agencies, notably in two divisions of the United Nations, the Food and Agriculture Organization and the UN Development Programme. That sexism brings harm to women through the development program it sponsors: Rogers shows in detail how data gathering and project implication have a negative impact on women. She points out that even the phrase "status of women" implies a very passive attitude toward women's role, an attitude that continues to see women as objects rather than subjects of development. As a result, Rogers places heavy emphasis on the need for much greater inclusion of women in leadership roles within planning agencies.

One main theme throughout Rogers' work is that women already are included in development, and must not be perceived as tangential to it. Separate women's projects only ghettoize women and leave unchanged the power relationships within the planning agencies. What is really needed is for women to be integrated into projects as full, equally powerful members of the planning process.

While Rogers so firmly – and rightly – insists that women must have more power in planning, she never goes a next step, to ask about and to comment on the structures that have so assiduously excluded women. At the beginning of the book, Rogers states that she will not be discussing motives but only the impact of certain policies. But, will not the same mistakes be repeated if another question is not asked: what structures and priorities in mainstream development have permitted it, until now, to exclude women? If women, and all people, are to be subjects and authors of their development, it is not only the sexism of the planning bureaucracies that needs to change but their entire structure, perspective and even function.

women who slice the knot differently

The phrase "integrating women into development" means different, almost opposite, things to different people. For some like Catón, it means including women more and including more women, in the modern agriculture and industrial sectors. For others, like Rogers, it means that women must have equal power in development planning structures, so that they may make development meet their needs.

The longer the development bureaucracies call for "integration of women into development," the more many women are criticizing what that has meant and will mean for women. The point, they say emphatically, is *not* to increase women's role in the modernization process that the developing world is undergoing. Rather, when the reasons *why* women have been excluded are examined, it will become apparent that what is needed is an overhaul of the entire development process and economic structures. For them, participation of women means direction of that process by women; in fact, by all those involved.

African Achola Pala provides one such critique of efforts to include women in a short, lucid essay "Definitions of Women and Development: An African Perspective." (This appears in an essential volume for those interested in the topic, *Women*

Handloom weaver, India.

and National Development: The Complexities of Change).

Pala argues that the problems of women in African absolutely cannot be considered apart from "the wider struggle by African people to free themselves from poverty and ideological domination." Many of the studies, she says, that show that women have been denied the fruits of the development process, neglect the reality that that process has not really helped men either. In fact, she writes that African women are already well-developed into their economies; the problem actually facing them is that those are dependent economies.

Pala argues that the problems of women in Africa absould not be considered; but that, rather than being considered just in comparision to African men's status, it be studied with respect to the social and economic situation in which they live. "What we must look for, then, is not how African women lost their development opportunity during colonial or contemporary neocolonial periods... but, rather, the differential impact of such socio-economic conditions on men and women." Her recommendations, building on this analysis, call for, among other things, emphasis on development priorities "as local communities see them." That will be the effective way to bettering African women's load and to making change work for them.

Another perspective on the movement to "integrate women into development" is provided by Ingrid Palmer. In an article "New Official Ideas on Women and Development," Palmer approaches several new policies or ideas from the perspective of what they can be expected to do for women. For example, the Basic Needs Approach calls for development strategies that address the needs of the very poorest people; that emphasize production increases that provide the essentials the poor need; and that include greater participation of people in decision making. Palmer brings a feminist critique which shows that the BNA will not and cannot help women without prior mobilization of women; "until woman's direct access to resources is specified, there can be no real realignment of economic opportunities and of rights of appropriation over the returns to those opportunities between the sexes." Furthermore, specific application of BNA policies to women would be needed. Even some of the basic components of the BNA do not address women's needs. For example, where it

Noi Donne

calls for higher productivity, new employment, this may bring far more benefits to men who form the larger part of the unemployed Women — already busy — may lose further ground Palmer states "there may thus be a case for giving priority to changing women's present inadequate employment into adequate employment, even at the cost of retaining some male unemployment."

Palmer reverses the usual priorities. She demands something of development *for* women, rather than claiming that women must serve development for their own good.

****

Much more has been written, and should be written, on development and women — how women have been told they should "join development efforts" and how development really could better women's lives.

What is currently available is still inadequate. The reams of paper used for discourses on the subject often·repeat themselves or provide variations on a theme We need a greater number of incisive analyses especially written by women, and by third world women, we need to seek it out, encourage it, read it, and promote the policies that will support women. And that, in the end, will transform development in some very basic ways.

multinationals

This chapter gives an overview of multinational corporations and their impact on women as workers, consumers and transmitters of culture. It also looks at the ways women are organizing against the negative effects of multinationals. The resources for research and organizing provide information about materials, groups and organizations actively working on these issues.

This chapter was written by Marilee Karl. Special thanks go to Anita Anand and Saralee Hamilton of the Women and Global Corporations Network for their help both in writing the overview and in compiling the resources.

integrating women into multinational development?

Marilee Karl

Multinational corporations have an enormous impact on economies and on the lives of people in both industrialized and developing countries. They affect women as workers, consumers and transmitters of culture in particular ways. Over the past decade, the rapid growth of export-oriented multinational enterprises in developing countries has had a decisive influence on the type of development taking place. Yet most work on development issues continues to concentrate on agriculture and rural areas. Policy-makers and planners concerned with women and development have responded to the challenge of global corporations with little more than a call to increase women's integration in the waged labor force.

Today it is more urgent than ever to examine the impact of multinational corporations on development. Because of their increasing size and wealth, multinationals are capable of imposing a model of development based on economic growth and profit maximization rather than on a more just and equitable distribution of goods and services. They are thus an issue for all who want to promote the kind of development which benefits all people and enables them to develop their potential and take power over their lives. Those working in particular for the improvement of women's lives cannot ignore the implications of multinationals for women.

Multinationals demonstrate the interrelatedness of development in industrialized and developing areas of the world through their global scale and impact. It is possible to deal effectively with them, and the situations and problems they create, only in a global way.

Feminists, for the most part, have not been in the forefront of research and action around multinationals. Yet they have a particular contribution to make: feminism brings a holistic approach to the issues, seeking the economic, political, social and sexist (i.e., discrimination against women because they are women) causes of the oppression of all. A feminist perspective on multinationals as a development issue can thus bring some new insights to the complex phenomenon.

the global nature and power of multinationals

A multinational or transnational is a business firm with activities in several different countries.[1] The great majority of multinationals are incorporated in and have their decision-making bodies and top management in North America, Japan and Europe. They also repatriate most of their profits to their country of origin. Their size and wealth enables them to locate where it is most profitable, where their investments will yield the highest returns. They also have the ability to organize and manage global markets.

No effective international rules or regulations govern multinationals. Many of them have greater power and wealth than some of the countries where they operate. The decisions of a multinational may effect the economy, the foreign policy and the political and social life of a country as well as the daily lives of workers and consumers. Their power makes it possible for them to avoid labor unrest or improvement in wages and working conditions. A multinational can close down a plant and move its operations to a country where workers can be paid less and where governments will ensure a more docile labor force. Because multinationals have factories in many different countries, they can allocate production processes in such a way that a strike or the closing of one factory will not harm their operations.

export-oriented development

Since the 1960s, multinational investment in developing countries has been increasingly promoted as a model of rapid economic development. This export-oriented industrialization is replacing an earlier model of import substitution manufacturing; that is, rather than encouraging local industries to produce for domestic consumption, such industrialization promotes production of goods and crops for export. Governments of industrialized countries and international financial institutions support export-oriented development not only because it brings more profits to the countries of origin of the multinational corporations and the banks, but also because this type of development binds the third world countries more tightly into the international capitalist system.

development and growth for whom?

Many third world countries promote such development. They see export-oriented investment as a source of quick capital which should allow the country to generate its own growth and to earn foreign exchange to meet balance of payment deficits. However, only a small elite benefits in any substantial way. This type of growth widens the gap between the rich and the poor and, by permitting an elite to control virtually all industry, allows politically repressive regimes to consolidate and extend their power.

Developing countries often compete to attract investment by multinational corporations, offering incentives such as free exploitation of natural resources, favorable tax situations, subsidized utilities, lax health and safety standards, free trade zones[2] and especially a cheap labor force. In many countries, political repression ensures that this labor force will remain unorganized and not demand higher wages, benefits, or better working conditions. Often strikes are prohibited by law and unions are either forbidden or government-controlled.

The hoped-for benefits for the developing countries – increased employment, transfer of technology and skills, and foreign exchange earnings – have been minimal. Most production processes located in the third world require low skills and have made only a small dent in the unemployment situation. Foreign exchange earnings have been minimized by tax concessions and subsidized services.

international development banking

Multinational banks and international financial institutions such as the World Bank and the International Monetary Fund (IMF) encourage and support export-oriented industry and agriculture in the world.[3] In order to attract multinational investments, developing countries have had to invest capital in infrastructure and in developing the energy sources required for the establishment of factories, and in military equipment needed to control the political situation of the country. This has meant loans from international banks and consequent spiraling debt. This in turn has had adverse effects on the population, especially the poorest. It has meant devaluation of currency, rising costs of living, unemployment, scarcity of goods and services.

The benefits of internationally financed and developed energy sources are often not distributed equitably but enhance the position of the multinationals and a small local elite at the expense of the majority of the population and of local farmers and businesses who cannot compete with the multinational corporations.[4]

the effects on industrialized countries

Multinational corporations also play a major role in the economies of the industrialized countries in which they are based. Richard Barnet, co-author of *Global Reach: The Power of Multinational Corporations*, writes: "The U.S. economy is now the North American division of the world economy. Because there are no effective world public authorities, no community-based planning in the United States, the managers of the multinationals in their daily operations have by default become the principal planners for the U.S. economy."[5] The size and power of the multinationals, which makes it possible for them to locate plants wherever conditions are most favorable, undermines the efforts of workers and unions in industrialized countries to achieve better wages and working conditions and of environmentalists to control pollution and the disposal of toxic substances.

Small businesses and farms in industrialized countries, as

THE FREE TRADE ZONE

CARROT

FOR FOREIGN COMPANIES

Cheap labour

No customs duties

No import quotas

No foreign exchange controls

Unlimited profits repatriation

Long tax holidays

Cheap loans

Subsidised utilities

No local provincial taxes

Anti-strike laws

100% foreign ownership

Voices/Christian Conference of Asia Urban-Rural Mission

Automation in the textile industry, Germany.

in developing ones, are being squeezed out of existence by the competition of the big enterprises.

women on the assembly line

Many export-oriented industries, particularly agribusiness (food processing, preserving and harvesting) and light manufacturing such as electronics, textiles, toys and shoes, preferentially hire women.[6] As a result, enormous numbers of women have been brought into the money economy, many of them for the first time, as wage earners.

Integrating women into the labor force has been seen as a way of promoting women's economic independence and power and thus "integrating" them into the development process. Employment by multinationals has not resulted in any substantial gains for women, however. On the contrary, women are super-exploited by these enterprises whose main motivation for hiring women is the higher profits derived from paying women lower salaries.

The exploitation of and discrimination against women in export-oriented industries in the third world is linked to that of women in the labor force in already industrialized coun-

tries. Almost everywhere women receive lower wages than men for the same work, receive fewer benefits, are more easily laid off or fired. This is justified by the argument that women are only supplementing family income and the father or husband is the main earner in the family. This myth continues in spite of the fact that a large percentage of women in the work force of both developing and industrialized countries either head their families or support themselves and other members of their families. However, in many of the export-oriented industries in Asia and Latin America, women are paid bare subsistence wages.

Maternity leave and benefits are also used to justify paying lower wages to women because of the costs to the company of providing benefits. Very often, however, maternity leave and benefits are simply not provided. Many industries hire young, unmarried women and lay them off after a few years, or even a few months. In this way, they avoid paying not only maternity benefits but also higher wages to more experienced or senior workers. A large pool of young women available for employment enables companies to do this. Moreover, the fact that these women are new to the formal labor force offers the multinationals the advantage of employees who are unorganized and who have had no experience in organizing.

Women are also considered best suited to the monotonous, unskilled work involved, in particular, in the electronics and

Production line in a television factory in Japan.

textile industries – work requiring patience, willingness to work hard, and the "nimble" fingers of young women.

On top of this, women carry a double burden of work: in the field or factory and then in the "reproduction of the labor force" at home, caring for the house, the meals, the clothes, the children and the other needs of the family. Where there are few or inadequate social services – and this is the case generally in both industrialized and developing countries – women's burdens are even heavier. They are usually left with finding individual solutions for caring for children, the sick and the old. Exhaustion and its detrimental effects on physical and mental health are added to those of unhealthy conditions at the workplace. The electronics, textile and agribusiness industries which preferentially hire women are among those with the highest health and safety hazards.

Sexual harassment and exploitation are other hazards commonly found in the workplace. Male supervisors often demand sexual favors from women in return for hiring them, keeping them on, promotion or raises, or simply because they are in positions of authority over women and have the power to intimidate them. Male co-workers also harass women. This hazard is found in both developing and industrialized countries and has its root causes in sexist attitudes towards women.

electronics

Electronics is a relative newcomer to the multinational scene, and one of the most rapidly growing. This industry produces the components – the integrated circuits – which are used in computers, calculators, digital watches, electronic games, military systems, word processors and the like. The production processes involved are carried out literally on a "global assembly line," stretching from California, USA, halfway around the world to East and Southeast Asia. In the United States in 1975, 40 percent of the 11 million electronics workers were women and women made up 90 percent of the production workers. It is estimated that nearly half a million women are employed by the same industry today in East and Southeast Asia, comprising more than 85 percent of all electronics workers in this region. Many of the largest corporations have their head offices in the United States, in the Santa Clara Valley of California. The trend to move the labor intensive parts of the production process to Latin America and Asia began in the 1960s and increased in the 1970s, to take advantage of the large and cheap labor force. The management, engineering and highly skilled processes remain in the industrialized countries. Production processes are allocated in such a way that the factories in the various countries perform only a part of the process. This is possible in the electronics industry because the component parts are tiny, lightweight and easily transportable. This global assembly line enables the multinationals to make use of their workers at will. When workers in California, for instance, press for safer working conditions, the companies can threaten simply to move to Malaysia, and in fact have done so. Today electronics plants are found in Hong Kong, Taiwan, South Korea, Singapore, Malaysia, Thailand, Philippines, Indonesia and Mexico. The early 1980s, however, have begun to see some movement back to the richer countries because of the increasing automation of some of the formerly labor-intensive production processes.

Electronics factories create a high number of serious health and safety problems for their workers, in spite of the superficially "clean" appearance of neat rows of uniformed workers and air conditioning – which are provided for the protection of the equipment, not the comfort of the workers. Workers peer through microscopes the whole day attaching hundreds of minute wires to silicon chips. After several years of work, many of them find their eyesight deteriorating, at which point they are no longer capable of performing the job and find themselves out of work. Other workers are occupied in dipping the chips into toxic acids, or coating them with silicon which can cause a fatal lung disease. High work quotas force women to work under intense pressure, and under the threat of losing their jobs to the thousands of other women looking for employment or to another plant of the same

Living conditions on a banana plantation, Philippines.

multinational. Workers are often set in competition with workers in another plant of the same company. Breaks are short and sometimes insufficient to eat properly and even visits to the toilet are often considered privileges.

The management of multinationals have devised a number of subtle techniques to control workers. Companies foster a paternalistic family spirit and encourage women workers to take up western consumer habits and values, by such things as promoting beauty contests and selling cosmetics and western-style clothing on their premises. They try to sell women the idea that "freedom" or "liberation" from traditional societies can be gained through spending earnings on western-style consumer goods. Many women, however, have been driven to seek employment in the cities because of the decline of the rural areas and are a major means of support for their families left behind in the countryside. They are caught between two worlds.

In some places companies house women in dormitories, with several women sharing the same room and even the same bed, taking turns sleeping during the different shifts. The company becomes virtually their whole world.

On the other side of the globe, microelectronics is having a great impact on the quantity and quality of jobs, especially those which traditionally employ many women, such as office work. Women are finding themselves replaced by computers and word processers or moved from secretarial positions to the more alienating word processing pool.[7]

textiles

The textile industry is much older than electronics and has been a traditional employer of women for more than a hundred years. There are many similarities between the electronics and the textile industries in terms of wages, working conditions and social control of workers. Many factories of the multinational textile industry, however, closed down operations in industrialized countries and regions and "ran away" to areas and countries with cheaper labor forces much earlier.

In the United States, the southern states provided the raw material, cotton, for the manufacturers of the north who employed large numbers of women, many of them immigrants, in sweatshop conditions. As labor became organized, the garment plants picked up and moved first to the south, and then to Mexico, Latin America and Asia. When economic conditions warrant, the plants simply move back or on to yet greener fields. Because this affects mainly women's jobs, there has been little of the hue and cry now being heard over plant closings and runaways in fields such as the auto and rubber industries which primarily affect men's jobs.

Japanese and European multinationals have expanded into cheap labor areas of Asia, such as South Korea, Taiwan and Indonesia. In Europe, an influx of migrant workers from Asia, Africa, the Caribbean and southern Europe forms

Lunch break in a garment factory in the Philippines.

Banana

Banana, Asian Social Institute, Manila.

These pictures are from the slideshow *Banana*, which shows how giant agribusiness firms, like this one in the Philippines, drive the peasants from their land to make way for large plantations growing export crops.

Many women have no choice but to work on the plantations, at often exploitative wages and in unhealthy conditions.

Virtually the same pictures could have been reproduced from many other countries in Asia, Africa and Latin America, where the same process is in operation.

Liz Mackie/ISIS

another source of cheap labor at home. Some textile companies, especially in Europe and Australia, simply parcel out garment sewing to piece workers, women who work at home and are paid by the piece, without any benefits such as minimum wage, insurance, or sick-leave. One of the main reasons women resort to this type of employment is that it is the only way they can earn money while caring for children and the home.

Piece work is used as a means to keep wages low. When workers begin producing so much that they earn more, the company may lower the pay per piece. Where piece work has been replaced by a daily wage, workers are usually required to fulfill a quota, often so high that it is necessary to skip meal breaks and work overtime.

As the electronics industry, textiles has its health hazards, one of the most serious being fiber dust which can cause lung disease.

agribusiness

Agribusiness is the corporate control of food production and processing. Increasingly over the past two decades, multinational corporations have come to determine what is grown, where and how, how it is processed and where it is distributed. They have been buying up vast tracts of fertile land in third world countries and converting it into plantations for cash crops, usually a single crop meant primarily for export. Agribusiness is also flourishing in countries such as the United States where more and more small farms have been put out of business or swallowed up by these giant corporations. Some of these corporations are "vertically integrated"; that is, they control all the processes in the production of food, from planting and harvesting to processing, packaging, storing, transporting and marketing.

In many developing countries, agribusiness has taken large areas used for producing food for local consumption and turned them over to the production of cash crops for export. This negatively affects agricultural self-reliance and many countries once completely or nearly self-sufficient in food have become importers of basic foods.

Agribusiness repeats a common pattern in many countries: it draws men into the money economy, employing them in cash cropping and giving them – when needed for the work – technical know-how and equipment. Women are left to continue subsistence farming to supply the family's food needs under even more difficult circumstances than before. They are not provided with equipment to lessen the burden and are often deprived of the best land and the labor of men who traditionally performed some of the tasks involved in food production.

Agribusiness also exploits the labor of women. Depending on the crop and the area of the world, women are employed in planting, growing and harvesting. They are often hired as cheap seasonal labor for some of the most monotonous and difficult jobs such as weeding and picking. While women work in all aspects of food production, they are found especially in the food processing and packaging sectors. Whether they are Mexican migrant laborers in the onion fields of Arizona or Filipinas cleaning bananas on the plantations of Mindanao, they are subject to the same health hazards of pesticides and toxic chemicals, the same low wages and job insecurity. Where people find the land on which they were growing food crops taken over by multinationals, they have little choice but to seek employment in them, no matter how exploitative the conditions, or to migrate to the cities. Agribusiness contributes to driving women off the land to seek jobs in the cities in the textile, electronics or other industries.

the global supermarket

Multinational corporations have a great and growing impact on what people consume in nearly every part of the world.[8] Through their decisions and power to control what is produced and where it is distributed, and through their multimillion dollar advertizing compaigns, they have created a "global supermarket," reaching into the remotest areas and competing with small businesses, local products and markets. Women, as primary providers of food, health care, clothing and the household needs of their families, are prime targets of these campaigns.

Multinationals claim they are offering people more "freedom of choice" with their wide range of products. Is this really so? We have seen how agribusiness causes a decrease in the production of food crops for domestic consumption by converting large areas of land for production of export crops. Through their control of the seed industry and through seed patenting, they are also dramatically decreasing the variety of seeds and plants available. Their high-powered advertizing campaigns create new needs and desires in both industrialized and developing countries. Local products in developing countries cannot compete with the imported goods of multinationals and are pushed off the market. The same is true for goods produced by small businesses in the home countries of the multinationals as well. Consumers may actually have less choice because of the activities of multinationals.

Since multinationals are concerned mainly with profit,

not the well-being of people, their advertizing and promotional activities do not necessarily have positive effects on consumption patterns. A glance at the media suffices to show how multinationals create aspirations for a certain kind of materialistic lifestyle, desires and needs for non-essential goods. The impact of the food and drug industries on people's lives and health is even more serious.

The food processing, packing and distributing industries spend enormous amounts developing, producing and promoting processed foods such as colas and soft drinks, processed cheese, sweetened breakfast cereals, highly refined bakery goods, artificially flavored snack foods, powdered milk and infant formula, candies, instant coffees and teas, and so on. In industrialized countries such as the United States, many people are poorly nourished because of their high consumption of "junk" foods – snacks and other highly refined and sweetened food and drink. In developing countries, more severe nutritional problems often arise. Convinced by sophisticated advertizing that imported goods, colas and snacks are better, healthier, more desirable and attractive than local products, women will spend scarce money on less nourishing food and drink for their families. Very often, however, they have no choice. Nothing else is available on the market.

This can create absurd situations: for instance, people living in citrus producing countries may have difficulty finding fresh citrus fruit drinks and must choose between artificially flavored soft drinks or powdered orange drink. In the meantime, the citrus fruit is shipped to colder climates where agribusiness can make more profits from the demand for year-round fresh tropical fruit they have helped create.

The pharmaceutical industry sells everything from medicines to pesticides, to infant formula, cosmetics and soap. Where government controls and regulations are lax, which is the case in some third world countries, corporations are able to sell products banned in their home countries. They may fail to provide adequate labeling or information about medicines and the potential side-effects of these and other products. Governments, medical professionals and development agencies bear part of the responsibility for the lack of control in the sale and use of medicines and other products. This is clearly the case where they promote the use of contraception which is still in the experimental stages or without informing women of the side-effects and enabling them to make an informed choice of the kind of birth control they want to practice.

Manufacturers of infant formula – many of which are well-known food or drug companies – lead aggressive advertizing and promotional compaigns for their products in third world countries. These practices include the distribution of free samples through clinics and hospitals, funding research and conferences, and giving grants to clinics and medical personnel. Non-governmental organizations have been instrumental in bringing worldwide attention to the effects of these

Canning meat in a Thai factory. Women predominate in the food processing and packaging industry all over the world.

Cape Verde Islands.

practices on children.

The World Health Organization (WHO) points out: "Breastfeeding is ideally suited to the physiological and psychosocial needs of the infant everywhere. In adverse socioeconomic and environmental circumstances breastfeeding has considerable advantages over artificial feeding because of such factors as the possible use of contaminated water for mixing feeds, the lack of facilities for the proper preparation and storage of breastmilk substitutes, and lack of information about their proper use."[9]

effects on culture

In managing the global supermarket, multinationals have profound effects on culture, creating new needs and desires,

The global supermarket advertises in a Filipino mountain village.

changing eating and living habits, determining what food and goods are available. They play a prime role in spreading throughout the world a homogenous culture, holding up western-style goods as the ideal and replacing locally produced products with more expensive processed and synthetic goods. These changes represent an abrupt break with or disruption of culture in many places, rather than an evolution. On the other hand, multinationals often reinforce some of the worst sexist aspects of societies, especially in sex roles and division of labor.

Dominating the world's mass media and communication systems through ownership and financing them through advertisements, multinationals promote a consumer society and images of women and women's roles most profitable to themselves. They target women especially in the whole genre of women's magazines, radio and television programs. Educational materials are also increasingly concentrated under their control.

Multinationals play a major role in affecting patterns of migration from rural to urban areas. We have seen how agribusiness squeezes farmers off the land. Multinationals also force small merchants out of business. These people, many of them women, are forced to seek employment in the cities. Some find jobs in multinational industries such as electronics and textiles, others join the ranks of the unemployed or turn to prostitution. This massive migration to urban areas has contributed to the great spread of slum dwellings in the cities.

The tourism industry, largely controlled by multinational interests, also affects culture. "Through tourism, developed nations export their politics, trade and lifestyle to give them both economic and political gain. Materialistic and money-oriented political systems are reinforced, thus undermining the heritage and destroying the human dignity of the in-

Women demonstrate against government intervention in labor unions.

digenous people and leading to the violation of human rights."[10]

The tourist industry exploits women in particular as sex objects to attract tourists and as workers. It employs women as waitresses, barmaids, "hospitality girls" and masseuses. As the phenomenon of sex tourism increases, more and more jobs entail prostitution.

Women play an important role in transmitting the effects of multinationals on culture. As mothers and educators of the young, women pass on these images, needs, desires and reliance on the products of multinationals to their children. More often than not, women have little or no choice in the matter, so profoundly have the multinationals affected their living situations and the products available.

development agencies and multinationals

Development agencies and international bodies are not doing a great deal to counteract the negative effects of multinationals.[11] On the contrary, many of them actively promote the development of agribusiness and export-oriented industries. International financial institutions such as the World Bank give loans to develop the infrastructure needed. Development agencies of industrialized countries, such as the United States Agency for International Development (USAID), and United Nations agencies, such as the United Nations Industrial Development Organization (UNIDO) and the Food and Agricultural Organization (FAO), give loans, grants and technical assistance for the promotion of multinationals' investment in developing countries.

The commissions and agencies of the United Nations

giving attention to the problems created by multinationals often neglect the specific situation of women. Notable exceptions are the World Health Organization (WHO) and UNICEF which have taken up the issue of the sale of infant formula and a code of conduct with recommendations about the promotion of baby foods by multinationals. The United Nations Commission on Transnational Corporations, charged with drawing up a code of conduct for multinationals, has involved few women, however. The draft code makes no mention of the specific discrimination and exploitation of women by multinationals. Only a few of the non-governmental organizations researching and taking action against the detrimental effects of these corporations give more than cursory attention to the particular situation of women workers.

women organizing

The power of multinationals and the problems they create are enormous. Combatting the negative effects of multinationals is an enormous task but, while it is very difficult, it is not impossible. People are organizing around the issue of multinationals on many levels, in factories and communities as well as nationally, regionally and internationally, in various kinds of groups and organizations. Women are active on all these levels.

In spite of the risks of organizing, in spite of repressive working and living situations, women are not passively accepting their exploitation and oppression. From the fields of New Mexico to the sweat shops of South Korea, from the office workers of Boston to the textile workers in free trade zones, women are organizing strikes, educating themselves and each other about their rights and researching the activities of multinational corporations. They are also organizing consumer education, information and action compaigns. Some of these actions are described in the following reports.

sugar workers organize in the Philippines

The stories of Flora and Della are taken from *No Time for Crying* by Alison Wynne. This book is a series of "stories of Philippine women who care for their country and its people." It is available in English from the Resource Centre for Philippine Concerns, C.P.O. 2784, Kowloon, Hong Kong. Dutch, Italian and German versions are also available (see Resource listings).

Flora

I worked in a hacienda of seventy-two hectares with workers. In 1972 the workers elected me as their leader. We heard on the radio that all workers should receive a minimum wage of 7 pesos (US.95) per day and yet we received only 3 pesos (US.41). We decided to take our complaint to the local constabulary. When we arrived the commander told us to go to the National Labour Relations Commission. We went there, thirty-eight of us, asking for the minimum wage, medical benefits and other things the government said we should receive. A hearing was set for a future date, then it was postponed and scheduled for another time, and this treatment went on and on for months. During this time the union member workers were locked out and had no work. I was surprised that the management locked us out simply because we complained and asked for the benefit which was ours by government decree. We were very angry because we had no money and our families were going hungry. Even when we received the back-to-work order the hacienda owner would not take us back.

One evening, all of us who were out of work discussed what we could do. We decided to go to the owner of that hacienda and explain what we wanted. We simply wanted work so that our children would no longer be hungry. He told us, "Go away. You are rebels." That is how we are regarded when we are no longer ignorant of our situation as workers.

We travelled from one hacienda to another, but could find no work because we were known to be union members. Sometimes we would go secretly to a hacienda to organise the workers and talk with them in the evenings so that they could learn their rights. One time two people were sent to tell me, "Stop your work or you will be stockaded." But I ignored the threats...

May first rally of the independent KMU (May First Movement) labor union, Philippines, 1982.

I hold district meetings of the sugar workers in several areas once a week. We sit and talk, and plan how to solve the problems which arise among the workers. Every time I go to places for meetings I am harassed. The police follow me all the time, but I am not afraid. I give thanks to God that I can still do my work and help people to stand up and feel more human. Now that I have discovered my rights I am determined to pass on this knowledge to others. The minds of the workers are very closed. The workers are afraid to stand up for themselves. I want all of them to say, "I am a person, like you. These are my rights that I am demanding." We must unite to achieve our demands. We cannot do it alone because of the forces of oppression which are against us.

Now the hacienda owners are becoming afraid. They say to me, "Why are you disturbing my workers and causing trouble?" Before the workers were afraid of the owners. Now the workers are getting strong and the owners are becoming afraid.

Four years ago a friend of mine was killed because of his educational activities among the workers. Many citizens have been held in the stockade for periods of three months to a year, simply for talking to the sugar workers. I have received numerous warnings — "Stop work or we will kill you." But I don't stop. My husband and son were both held for a week at one time, but so far I have not been held. When I began working I was afraid, but now I have no more fear because knowledge has taught me my rights, and I am happy to be free and working for a better society. I am called the tiger woman because I am not afraid. I will not be intimidated.

Della

Ever since I can remember I have known poverty. Most days we had very little food. If there was no work we lived on tapioca and camote. I worked in the hacienda from the age of nine, weeding the sugar canes...

At the age of sixteen I married one of the hacienda workers. He joined the union, and so was locked out. Once you are marked, no plantation will give you work. We would go from one place to another and work for a while until our names were discovered on the list of union members which the hacienda owners have compiled and share with each other.

For two months we had no money and could only manage to give our baby a little food once a day. For ourselves, we had only water or coffee. One day in desperation we went to the priest who gave us 10 pesos (US$1.35). We used this money to travel to the city and tell our plight to the National Federation of Sugar Workers. It was there that we heard about this community project, and were glad to have the chance to come and live here. At least here we have a roof over heads. We have simple food to eat each day, and there is plenty of work to do in planting the lands, and there is hope...

This communal farming project was begun two years ago by some community workers who wanted to help unemployed people. They knew the land was available for renting, so signed an indefinite lease for ten hectares. Thirty-seven people began the project, and after a while they all dispersed to their own communities, leaving the project for landless, locked-out union workers like us to carry on. We are four families – fourteen persons in all. These three nipa huts are divided into separate living quarters for each family. We have three carabaos, and are farming tapioca, rice, camote, ginger and vegetables. We are raising chickens, pigs and rabbits. We are working towards self-sufficiency but at the moment the project is subsidised with funds from an agency. As we bring more of the land into production we will be able to support a greater number of families.

More and more people are becoming unemployed and homeless as the hacienda owners turn to mechanisation. This experiment in communal farming is hoped to be a model which will help others to find some means of supporting themselves and their families. There are several small areas of unused lands available for renting. If people can see that it is possible to make this venture work, then perhaps agencies will fund other groups to set up communal farms like ours.

solidarity with women workers of Conel, Peru

In February 1980, the feminist group Acción para la Liberación de la Mujer Peruana (Alimuper) made an appeal for international solidarity with women factory workers in Peru. They wrote:

Forty women workers of the Consorcio Electronico who took over the factory in December 1979, to defend the stability of their jobs, are asking for support and solidarity to continue their struggle and to take over the administration of this enterprise.

The managers of CONEL decided to close the factory, alleging that they were in a difficult economic situation. This maneuver was encouraged by the authorities of the Ministry of Labour. For ten months the women workers – most of them mothers of families – have not received their salaries. They are living in a precarious situation: sleeping on

Peasant women defending land rights and cooperatives in Peru.

Asociación Amauta, Peru

mats or in the factory yard, not knowing if there will be food from one day to the next. On 3 January 1980 they were attacked by fifty thugs sent by the director of the factory. They defended themselves courageously.

The decision to remain inside the factory was taken in order to prevent the owners from removing the machinery. CONEL is a business which makes replacements for electrical appliances and which mainly employs women. The workers have verified that the owners have established new businesses with the profits of CONEL.

The forty women remain inside the factory, ready to face renewed violence from the thugs and the police, in spite of an eviction order. Among them are two mothers in late stages of pregnancy, as well as children of two, three and four years.

ALIMUPER is requesting letters to be sent to President General Morales Bermudez, demanding the end of violence against the women workers and that they be permitted to exercise their right to work.

The appeal was taken up and passed on to women all over the world through the International Feminist Network. Letters supporting the women workers arrived from Denmark, England, Belgium, Japan, Netherlands, Mexico, Sweden, the United States and other countries. Feminist publications in many countries wrote articles about the Peruvian women's occupation of their factory, while feminist groups and union women in the Netherlands helped sponsor a trip of one of the Peruvian women workers to meet with women's groups and the media in Europe. In Peru, feminist groups joined mass demonstrations in support of the workers.

The women of Conel were able to continue their occupation for well over a year. During this time, they strengthened their consciousness as workers and as women and developed their organizing ability. The international support and solidarity they received from feminists, unions and women's organizations played a significant role in this.[12]

campesinas meet

This article by Anita Anand and Saralee Hamilton appeared in the Fall 1980 issue of AFSC *Women's Newsletter* of the Nationwide Women's Program, American Friends

The same women buying and selling in the market.

Service Committee, 1501 Cherry Street, Philadelphia, Pennsylvania 19102, USA.

During a three day event last spring (1980) in El Mirage (Maricopa County) Arizona, campesinas spoke to one another about their lives, their work and their struggles. They shared personal testimonies of their efforts to decrease the precariousness of their lives and those of their families. Many of these women had participated in farmworker struggles in the Southwestern US and Mexico. Many declared how these experiences revolutionized their lives. They now see themselves as "having a purpose beyond the immediate roles of wives, mothers and workers." They described how they now see themselves as equals with men on picket lines, as women who can win victories by being outspoken, organized and determined. They were unified in feeling capable of making changes in their lives.

Appeals were made to defend basic rights to obtain work, minimum wages, equality in fields and home, access to essential services like health care, child care and information about other farmworker struggles.

Slide presentations of onion workers in the Southwest and Mexico vividly pointed out the similarities and differences between farm labor situations in the two countries whose economic and agricultural structures are intensely interlocked. A slideshow, *A Day in the Life of a Campesina* has been compiled.

Virginia Rodriguez observed, "We lived with no knowledge of what was happening in the rest of the world. An 80 day onion strike of 3000 workers in 1978 changed my life forever. The strike woke me up. I started to become active in the world around me."

Adela Serrano, Director of Centro Adelante Campesino, traced the idea for this regional gathering to experiences of three campesinas from Maricopa County while attending the Women and Global Corporations Conference in Des Moines in October 1978. She stressed that they wanted to organize a similar event put together and organized entirely by women farmworkers. Adela has worked on other aspects of follow up to the Des Moines conference and is active on the steering committee of the Women's Network on Global Corporations. The Network provided technical assistance in fundraising and literature resources at the request of the Arizona women.

subdued women can also strike back

Malay women workers in the Free Trade Zone of Bayan Lepas, Penang describe a few experiences of their "attempts to secure some degree of just wages for the work that we do." These are recounted in *Struggling to Survive: Women Workers in Asia*, published by CCA-URM, 57 Peking Road, 5/F, Kowloon, Hong Kong.

It all started at Advanced Micro Devices (AMD) where we produce electronic components. In September (1980) our hopes soared when we received a memorandum informing us of an increase in wages.

Alas, we rejoiced too soon. Staff members earning over $200 monthly got a $60 raise, but we, the backbone of the factory, earning well below $200, got only a mere $5 extra. But we are the tools and the machines that make the factory run. Without us, there will be no production!

A wave of spontaneous anger at this injustice swept over us. Management was taken by surprise to find that the subdued and frail women whom they thought were easy prey for their exploitation could down their tools in angry protest.

We slowed down our production and when the afternoon shift workers came, we rallied together, and by nightfall, a full strike was on.

Luckily for us, the bus drivers who bring us back and forth to work, supported our action and refused to obey management's command to take us home, on the pretext that it was risky for fear their vehicles might be damaged.

Management was stunned and tried to identify the leaders but even we ourselves did not know who the real courageous leaders were. Perhaps our feelings were aroused simultaneously by the gross injustice and as the message was passed around by word of mouth, we all rose up together to defend our rights and to take concerted action.

Although we were ignorant and exploited, our spontaneous strike impressed management who grudgingly offered an increase of $40.

Our success in this factory inspired many other downtrodden workers to take similar action. However, not all of them met with the same degree of success.

Management always managed to outwit us by wily methods. For example, on paper we were entitled to a $30-50 increase monthly but the actual increase came to less than $10.50 a month.

In Intel, workers also fought for a more adequate wage but failed through lack of support from the whole work force. Management was quick to capitalize on this weak point and dismissed their claims with a $40 increase, not in their basic pay but in the cost of living allowance, which means in actual fact that whenever a public holiday, overtime, or bonus occurs, there is no increase in wages at all, since no allowance is ever given on those occasions.

Another factory, RUF Malaysia, owned by Germans, producing transistor radios and electronic components, also met with some reactions from their 850 exploited workers.

On September 19, the entire work force — 90% female — stopped work to ask for an increase of $2-3 daily, free transport, subsidised food and reduced working hours.

Management flatly refused to consider their claims, pointing out that they just had had a raise on July 1. But it was precisely this mockery of a pay increase that led the deceived workers to take industrial action...

Riot police were called in to disperse the workers who were reminded that it was illegal to form groups of more than five for any purpose. Management then sacked all the workers. Later, all were allowed to return to their former jobs but with the pay they had before the strike.

Thirteen workers who had been more active in the strike were dismissed. Even the two newspaper reporters who covered the story at the request of the workers were also detained by management.

The only good thing that came out of the strike was that management recognized the need to meet with the workers and at least to listen to their grievances...

the international infant formula campaign

One of the biggest and most effective campaigns beyond the local level is the international infant formula campaign, which has brought the issue to international attention and forced some changes in corporate practice.

In the early 1970s, European non-governmental organizations such as War on Want in England and the Third World

Action Group in Switzerland began researching and publicizing the sometimes disastrous effects of the aggressive promotion of infant formula in the third world by large multinationals. One of these corporations, Swiss-based Nestle, brought a lawsuit against the Third World Action Group for defamation. While the verdict upheld Nestle's claim, it also admitted that advertizing practices could endanger people's health.

During the two-year court case the publicity campaign about the use of infant formula and the advertizing practices of multinationals grew in both industrialized and developing countries. Groups and organizations in the third world used written and audio-visual materials to demonstrate the possible danger to life and health of using formula where people lack the hygienic conditions and money necessary for its proper use. They also collected documentary evidence about the multinationals' promotion and advertizing practices.

This evidence was used by groups in the home countries of the multinationals to bring a number of actions against these companies. In the United States the Interfaith Center for Corporate Responsibility (ICCR) and the Infant Formula Action Coalition (INFACT) were in the forefront of organizing many activities including negotiations with corporations, shareholder actions against companies, presentations before Congressional committees, and a national boycott of Nestle products.

An international coalition, International Baby Food Action Network (IBFAN), was set up with offices in Switzerland. The issue has also been taken up in numerous publications of feminist groups, churches and non-governmental action, research and consumer groups.

These activities and campaigns brought the issue to international attention. In 1979 the World Health Organization (WHO) and UNICEF organized an international meeting

Hands off textile jobs in Calabria. Women march, Italy 1978.

bringing together representatives of governments, industry and the non-governmental organizations involved in the infant formula campaigns. After a two-and-a-half-year process, the World Health Assembly adopted, in May 1981, a Code of Conduct with recommendations to member nations to adopt legislation regulating the promotion and sale of infant formula. The Code was adopted by a vote of 118 to one. The United States cast the sole negative vote with Argentina, Japan and South Korea abstaining.

The campaign can claim some significant successes with the adoption of the Code and some concrete changes in corporate practice. Nevertheless it is far from ended. Continued vigilance, publicity and action are needed. Feminists, in particular, are beginning to point out that the issue of infant formula and breast feeding cannot be seen in isolation from "the organization of society as a whole, which perpetuates the poverty of certain social groups and which also does not provide the conditions necessary to enable women to fulfil, without undue difficulty, their roles as workers, mothers, wives and citizens while still enjoying their rights to education and rest."[13]

international solidarity

Because of the global nature and power of multinational corporations, international solidarity and organization are needed to combat effectively the negative effects of multinationals. This is vital since corporations try, and often succeed, in dividing workers, pitting the employees in the factories of one country against those in another. In addition to the essential organizing and consciousness raising of women workers in local plants, there are a number of things which could and are being done. Some of these are:

— forming networks and communications channels to share information and research, organizing international solidarity for local struggles and activities;
— working for national legislation to curb the power and exploitative activities of multinationals, for health, safety and environmental regulations, and to prevent the exportation of pollution and the dumping of unsafe products abroad;
— pressuring United Nations agencies to include women in any codes or negotiations dealing with multinationals;
— monitoring the enforcement of national legislation and international codes;
— researching the activities of multinationals and of development agencies, international financial institutions and United Nations organizations in regard to multinationals;
— pressuring non-governmental organizations researching and organizing around multinationals to take seriously the exploitation of women and to include a feminist perspec-

tive in their work;
- organizing local, national and international campaigns against the negative effects of multinationals, such as the infant formula campaign;
- providing workers in local factories with information about the activities of the multinational elsewhere;
- questioning the model of development promoted by multinationals and the concept of integrating women into the labor force at any cost;
- providing alternatives to employment by multinationals.

Women must ensure that they and their problems are taken seriously and are an integral part of these activities, not relegated to secondary or peripheral positions. Feminists have often neglected the issue of multinationals in the past, but they can make an important contribution by bringing a feminist perspective to the analysis of multinationals and the oppression of women. This oppression ties women together globally and must be fought globally and in solidarity around the world.

Footnotes

1 The following description of multinationals and export-oriented development is based on material listed in the resource section of this chapter. For a more detailed analysis and examples, see especially: Richard J. Barnet, *Global Reach: The Power of Multinational Corporations* (New York: Simon and Schuster, 1975); Barnet, "Multinationals: A Dissenting View," *Saturday Review*, February 7, 1975; Barnet, "Are Multinationals and Development Compatible?" *Engage Social Action Forum*, 56, November 1979; Barbara Ehrenreich and Annette Fuentes, "Life on the Global Assembly Line," *MS Magazine*, January 1981; "Free Trade Zones and Industrialization of Asia," *Ampo: Japan-Asia Quarterly Review*, vol. 8 no. 4, vol. 9 nos. 1-2, 1977; Rachael Grossman, "Women's Place in the Integrated Circuit," *Southeast Asia Chronicle*, no. 66 and *Pacific Research*, vol. 9 nos. 5-6; Linda Y. C. Lim, "Women Workers in Multinational Corporations," *Michigan Occasional Paper*, no. IX, Fall 1978; *Minangkabau! Stories of People vs TNCs in Asia* (Hong Kong: Urban Rural Mission – Christian Conference of Asia, (URM-CCA), 1981); "Multinational Corporations and Global Development," *Hunger*, no. 24, July 1980; Lenny Siegel, "Microelectronics Does Little for the Third World," *Pacific Research*, vol. X no. 2, 1979; Siegel, "Orchestrating Dependency," *Southeast Asia Chronicle*, no. 66; Holly Sklar ed., *Trilateralism* (Boston: South End Press, 1980).

2 A free trade zone is an enclave within a country that is partially or totally exempt from customs and tax levies and other laws and decrees of the country. For a good brief description of a free trade zone, see "Free Trade Zones: A Capitalist Dream," *Race and Class*, vol. 22 no. 2, Autumn 1980. A detailed analysis of free trade zones and their effects in Asia is found in "Free Trade Zones and Industrialization of Asia," *Ampo*, 1977.

3 See especially "The International Monetary Fund and the Third World," *Hunger*, no. 22, February 1980; Cheryl Payer, *The Debt Trap* (New York: Monthly Review Press, 1974); Howard M. Wachtel, *The New Gnomes: Multinational Banks in the Third World* (Washington: Transnational Institute, 1977).

4 Examples of this can be seen in the hydro-electric projects along the Chico River and Mindanao in the Philippines. These are described in: Joel Rocamora, "Agribusiness, Dams and Counter-Insurgency" and Martha Winnacker, "The Battle to Stop the Chico Dams," *Southeast Asia Chronicle*, no. 67, October 1979.

5 Barnet, "Multinationals: A Dissenting View." This article gives a good overview of the effects of multinationals on industrialized countries.

6 The material in this section and in those following on women in electronics, textile and agribusiness industries is based on the docu-

mentation in the resource section of this chapter. For a general overview of women workers and for statistics on numbers of women workers, wages and the division of labor among men and women, see Ehrenreich and Fuentes, "Life on the Global Assembly Line," *MS*; Ofelia Gomez and Rhoda Reddock, "Multinationals and Female Labour in Latin America," *Scholas Journal*, no. 1, 1979, pp. 60-80; "Maquiladoras," *Boletín Informativo*, no. 9, November, December, January 1979-1980, pp. 11-14; Kathleen Newland, *The Sisterhood of Man* (New York: W.W. Norton and Co., 1979) pp. 129-134; Newland, *Women, Men and the Division of Labor* (Washington: Worldwatch Institute, May 1980); Soon Young Yoon, *The Halfway House - Mncs, Industries and Asian Factory Girls*, (UNAPDI, 1979); and *Struggling to Survive: Women Workers in Asia* (Hong Kong: CCA-URM, 1981).
On the electronics industry, see especially: "Electronics Factories: Hazards and Harassment," *Majority Report*, January 6, 1979; Maria Patricia Fernandez, *Francisca Lucero*, (Philadelphia: American Friends Service Committee, 1978); Susan S. Green, *Silicon Valley's Women Workers* (Honolulu: East-West Center, July 1980); Grossman, "Women's Place"; Mary Alison Hancock, *Electronics: The International Industry* (Honolulu: East-West Center, 1980); Lim, "Women Workers"; "Microcomputers: Big Profits from Tiny Chips," *Dollars and Sense*, February 1978, pp. 3-5; Diana Roose, "Asia's Silicon Valley," *The Nation*, August 25 - September 1, 1979; "Delicate Bonds: The Global Semiconductor Industry," *Pacific Research*, vol. XI no. 1, January 1981; Siegel, "Fairchild Assembles an Asian Empire," *Pacific Research*, vol. IX no. 2, January-February 1978; A. Sivanandan, "Imperialism in the Silicon Age," *Race and Class*, Autumn 1979; Robert T. Snow, *The New International Division of Labor and the U.S. Workforce* (Honolulu: East-West Center, 1980); Christina Tse, *The Invisible Control: Management Control of Workers in a US Electronic Company* (Hong Kong: Center for the Progress of Peoples, 1981).
On the textile industry, see especially: *Asian Women's Liberation*, no. 2, April 1980; "Capital's Flight," *NACLA's Latin America and Empire Report*, vol. XI no. 3, March 1977; Michael Flannery, "America's Sweatshops in the Sun," *AFL-CIO Federationist*, May 1978.
On agribusiness, see especially: *Alternative News and Features*, no. 10, July 1981; Joyce N. Chinen, *Cigars and Support Hose* (Honolulu: American Friends Service Committee, 1977); Susan George, *Feeding the Few* (Washington: Institute for Policy Studies, 1979); George, *How the Other Half Dies* (New Jersey: Allenheld, Osmun and Co., 1977); Sally Hacker, "Farming Out the Home: Women and Agribusiness," *Science for the People*, March-April 1978; "Transnational Poisoning," *IDOC Bulletin*, no. 7, July 1981.

7 On the microelectronics revolution, see especially Michael Goldhaber, "Politics and Technology," *Socialist Review*, no. 52, July-August 1980; "The Microelectronics Wave," *IDOC Bulletin*, nos. 1-2, January-February 1981; Colin Norman, *Microelectronics at Work* (Washington: Worldwatch Institute, October 1980).

8 On the global supermarket and its effects on culture, see the material listed above under agribusiness (footnote 6).

9 *Infant and Young Child Feeding: Current Issues* (World Health Organization, Geneva, 1981), p. 7.

10 *Minangkabau! Stories of People vs TCNs in Asia* (Hong Kong: URM-CCA, 1981), p. 28.

11 See especially, *Alternative News and Features*, no. 10, July 1981; Ehrenreich and Fuentes, "Life on the Global Assembly Line," *MS*; *Minangkabau!*, pp. 109-112; and Anita Anand and Ann Fraker, "Women and the U.N. Code of Conduct on Multinationals" (Washington DC: United Methodist Church) 1980.

12 For a history and description of the struggle of the women workers of CONEL, see *Mujer y Sociedad* no. 2, December 1980 and no. 3, June 1981.

13 Marie-Angélique Savané, "Yes to Breast Feeding, but... How?" *Assignment Children*, no. 49/50, Spring 1980, p. 86.

multinationals

resources for research & organizing

The Resources for Research and Organizing have been selected with the aim of providing essential information and addresses especially for those engaged in action, organization and conscientization about multinationals as well as in action-oriented research. In this section of the Guide, we are listing groups and organizations first and describing the written and audio-visual resources and other services they provide. Most of these groups and organizations are engaged in ongoing work on multinational corporations, and will be producing further materials in the future. Following the groups and organizations, the resources are arranged by periodicals, books and pamphlets, and audio-visuals.

Resources on the pharmaceutical industry are listed under the Health section. A special section of this guide deals with migration and tourism.

resource centers

Asia Monitor Resource Center (AMRC)
2 Man Wan Road 17-C, Kowloon, Hong Kong and 464 19th Street, Oakland, California 94612, USA.

The AMRC, established in the Fall of 1976 in Hong Kong, has built up an impressive data base on the activities of multinational corporations in Asia. It systematically surveys the most important daily papers in East and Southeast Asia and publishes a quarterly magazine **Asia Monitor**, covering trends and developments in each country of Asia in the field of foreign investments, economic development patterns and transnational enterprises. The **Asia Book Monitor**, a supplement to the **Asia Monitor**, is a quarterly review of books about Asia and related economic, political and social issues. In-depth reviews, prices and ordering information make this a valuable resource. Subscriptions: US$ 18 surface mail personal; $ 30 for libraries and non-profit organizations.

In 1976, AMRC published **America in Asia**, vol. 1, a research guide on US economic and military activity in Pacific Asia. Vol. 2, a handbook on facts and figures on US economic and military activity in Pacific Asia, is in preparation.

AMRC also has a special project on **Occupational Safety and Health in Asia's Chemical Processing Industry**. In 1980, it launched a research and publication project on the US military presence in Asia.

In late 1982, the AMRC produced a **Primer** and a **Case Study** on problems of health and chemical hazards in the electronics industry. Especially useful for health workers and labor organizers, the easy-to-use and graphic **Primer** combines detailed information on jobs, health hazards and appropriate protective measures. It details the hundreds of chemicals used in electronics industries, how they are used, their effects and what workers can do to protect themselves. The **Case Study**, which is also available in Chinese, describes the action taken by a community health center in Hong Kong in an attempt to deal with health hazards in the electronics industry. While these books focus on Asia, much of the information is applicable worldwide.

Asian Social Institute
1518 Leon Guinto Street, Malate, Manila, Philippines.

Among the numerous slideshows produced by the Institute on the situation of the Philippines, there is one of particular interest in the area of agribusiness: **Saging (Banana)**. This is an analysis of the condition of workers in the banana industry, the injustices and exploitation committed against them by the company and their helplessness against an enemy which has not only power and money but the government on its side.

Center for the Progress of Peoples
48 Princess Margaret Road 1/F, Kowloon, Hong Kong.
Tel: 3 - 7145123-4

Among the activities of the Center for the Progress of Peoples is a study on women workers in electronics factories in Asia being carried out by Sr. Christina Tse. The first part of the study, already completed, focused on the mechanisms used by the electronics industry to control workers in factories in Hong Kong, particularly Fairchild. An important part of the study was conducted by involving the workers themselves in the research project. The aim was not merely to get a better and more reliable way to gather facts, but also to help the workers reflect on their work experience and environment and initiate a conscientization process. The report of the study entitled **The Invisible Control** is available from the Center. Price US$ 2.40. Discounts for third world and bulk orders.

Another book by Sr. Christina Tse is **Reflections on Japanese Management: Letters to a Woman Worker** (1982). Written in letter form, the book relates the author's insights into the manipulation of workers, especially women, in Japanese firms, gained through interviewing women workers. Price: US$ 2.50 plus postage.

The Center also helps to link up workers and organizers in multinational corporations, particularly in Asia, by passing on requests for assistance from workers in one factory to others working for the same corporation elsewhere. It prepares reports on working conditions in the factories which can be used by organizations of workers.

The Center's newsletter, **Asia Link**, published six times a year, contains short news items on workers' struggles and on the Center's activities. Subscription rates are: outside of Asia US$ 3, Asia $ 1.50, Hong Kong $ 1.

Centre de Recherche sur L'Amérique Latine et le Tiers Monde (CETRAL)
35 rue des Jeuneurs, 75002 Paris, France.

A research center on Latin America and the third world, CETRAL has produced a number of studies on agribusiness, including "Le Lait et Nestlé en Columbie" (69 pages); "La Production du lait au Brésil. Le Cas Nestlé" (135 pages); "L'Agroindustrie de la viande au Honduras" (106 pages); "La Structure agro-industrielle au Venezuela" (109 pages). Most of these studies are also available in Spanish from CEESTEM — Centro de Estudios Economicos y Sociales del Tercer Mundo, Co. Porfirio Diaz 50, San Jerónimo-Lidice, Mexico 20 D.F., Mexico. CETRAL also produces a quarterly journal **Amérique Latine** on the political and economic situation of that continent as well as on transnationals. Price per copy for the journal and the studies: 30 francs in France, 35 abroad.

The Centre on Transnational Corporations
Room BR-1005, United Nations, New York, New York 10017, USA.

"The Centre on Transnational Corporations is an autonomous body within the United Nations Secretariat that serves as a focal point for all matters related to transnational corporations, and acts as secretariat to the Commission on Transnational Corporations. The objectives of the work program are to further the understanding of the nature of transnational corporations and of their political, legal, economic and social effects on home and host countries and in international relations, particularly between developed and developing countries; to secure effective international arrangements aimed at enhancing the contribution of transnational corporations to national development goals and world economic growth while controlling and eliminating their negative effects; and to strengthen the negotiating capacity of host countries, in particular the developing countries, in their dealings with transnational corporations." The Centre on Transnational Corporations publishes **The CTC Reporter**. Price US$ 3 per issue.

It also publishes studies such as the 242 page report on **Transnational Corporations in Food and Beverage Processing** showing the extent and impact of these industries in developing countries. Thoroughgoing and documented in detail. Price: US$ 17.

Christian Conference of Asia – Urban Rural Mission (CCA-URM)
57 Peking Road 5/F, Kowloon, Hong Kong.

Actively involved with workers and their organizations in Asia, the CCA-URM office in Hong Kong has a great deal of information available on women and multinationals in Asia. It has also produced some excellent books on the issue including **Minangkabau! Stories of People vs TNCs in Asia**, a 154 page book which intersperses recent case studies of multinationals in Asia with a clear and concise overview of the issues. It covers areas such as the reasons why corporations are investing in Asia, the myths of benefits to the third world countries, the mechanisms for dominating the economy, and actions people are taking to combat the negative effects of multinationals. Price: US$ 2.

Struggling to Survive: Women Workers in Asia is another valuable and highly interesting book. This is a 162 page compilation of actual stories of the struggles of women workers in various countries of Asia. It gives details about their working conditions and treatment and recounts their attempts to organize for their rights. Besides description, the book gives background and statistical information as well as analysis and suggestions for organizing. Price: US$ 1.

Tea and Poverty (1980) by Nawaz Dawood is a study of the tea "plantations and the political economy of Sri Lanka." It documents the growth and development of this industry which employs great numbers of women in often extremely exploitative conditions. Price: US$ 5. **From the Womb of Han: Stories of Korean Women Workers** (1982) is a collection of historical articles, interviews and stories, many of them told by the women workers themselves. Price: US$ 1.50.

Christian Conference of Asia – Urban Rural Mission (CCA-URM)
2-3-18 Nishi-Waseda, Shinjuku-ku, Tokyo 160, Japan.

The struggles of the women workers at the Dong-Il textile factory in Inchon, South Korea have been supported and documented by the CCA-URM in their newsletter **Voices** and in other publications. The **ISIS International Bulletin 10** on "Women and Work" reprinted several documents on the case of these women who, when they attempted to organize and elect women to the leadership of their union, were brutally attacked by management and by male workers. They appealed for and received international publicity and support for their struggle which spans several years of educational and organizing work as well as strikes, occupation of the factory and direct confrontation with management. The experiences they share, both their victories and their failures, clearly illustrate the problems of organizing in repressive economic and political situations.

Citizens' Alliance for Consumer Protection
P.O. Box 3153, Manila, Philippines.

This local consumers' union has several study/action groups: energy and public utilities, health and medical services, food and nutrition, entertainment and tourism, finance. It is an example of what local action groups are doing.

Consumers' Association of Penang (CAP)
27 Kelawei Road, Penang, Malaysia.

CAP is a local consumers' union. It publishes a monthly paper **Utusan Konsumer** containing news and features on health, food, complaints, prices, environment, and other vital consumer issues. Recent issues focused on sex tourism and on infant formula.

Contemporary Archive on Latin America (CALA)
1 Cambridge Terrace, London NW1 4JL, England.

CALA's **Data Bank Project** aims at monitoring and exchanging information about the activities of multinational corporations in Latin America. Information from relevant press and other sources is systematically monitored, clipped and cross-indexed by centers throughout the region, and the final indexes and clippings are brought together in a publication.

Corporate Data Exchange (CDE)
198 Broadway, room 706-7, New York, New York 10038, USA.

CDE investigates economic concentration and corporate control. It serves as an information clearinghouse for public interest groups, labor unions, churches, community activists and others who attempt to study or influence corporate behavior. The CDE has published so far a series of stock ownership directories (agribusiness, transportation industry, energy, etc.), a handbook on US bank loans to South Africa, and a report on the pension fund investments in the US.

Counter Information Services (CIS)
9 Poland Street, London W1, England.

CIS publishes regular "anti-reports" with company profiles or trend descriptions in the various industries. Its issue on **The New Technology** is particularly interesting, dealing with the devastating social impact of the use of microprocessing in the industrial and white collar sectors, affecting job opportunities especially for women. The report also discusses the corporations' profits and state promotion of this new technology.

Data Center
464 19th Street, Oakland, California 94612, USA.
Tel: (415) 835-4692.

The **Corporate Profiles Project** of the Data Center documents the activities of industrial and financial corporations in the USA and abroad. Each profile covers a wide range of aspects on a particular corporation. The Data Center has extensive documentation on labor, human rights, foreign investment and multinationals and provides a search service for information. Contact the Center for prices.

Earthwork/Center for Rural Studies
3410 19th Street, San Francisco, California 94110, USA.

This is a clearinghouse of information and resources on land and agricultural issues with books, periodicals, films, slide-shows and video tapes available. Of particular interest is the slide/tape show **Guess Who's Coming to Breakfast?**, which examines the multinational corporation Gulf and Western and its involvement in agricultural exploitation in the Dominican Republic. 35 mins. 1976.

LAWG Newsletter/Canada

East-West Center
1777 East-West Road, Honolulu, Hawaii 96848, USA.

The Culture Learning Institute of the East-West Center, a national educational institution established by the US Congress in 1960, sponsored a research project on the "Impact of Transnational Interactions" in 1979 and 1980. The research concentrated on the electronics industry and its impact on women workers and a number of useful working papers are available from the Center on this issue. These are: **Silicon Valley's Women Workers** by Susan S. Green; **Electronics: The International Industry** and **The Electronics Industry in New Zealand** by Mary Alison Hancock; and **The New International Division of Labor and the U.S. Workforce** by Robert T. Snow.

In her paper, subtitled "A Theoretical Analysis of Sex-segregation in the Electronics Industry Labor Market," Susan Green attempts to examine in a more profound way than has been hitherto done, the international division of labor by linking it to the sexual division of labor. She also briefly reviews the contributions of socialist feminist labor market theory to the issue and questions the assumption that the employment of women breaks down their traditional roles and gives them power.

In her first article on the international electronics industry, Mary Alison Hancock gives an overview of the US firms operating in Southeast Asia. Her second paper examines the dependence of the electronics industry in New Zealand on the international industry and the sexual division of labor and exploitation of women within that industry.

Robert Snow's article deals with the effects of the new international division of labor on the US workforce and asserts that "the question must be posed much more specifically: who are the workers who have gained or lost jobs as a result of corporate decisions to move production overseas?" All of these papers are accompanied by bibliographies, tables and statistics.

In addition, the Institute has produced a 46 page bibliography compiled by Mary Alison Hancock on Women and Transnational Corporations. Unfortunately, it is not annotated, nor are addresses given.

IDOC – International Documentation and Communication Center
Via Santa Maria dell'Anima 30, 00186 Rome, Italy.

IDOC is an important source of information and documentation on current international issues such as multinational corporations, human rights, liberation movements and people's struggles both in the third world and in industrialized countries. An independent organization founded in 1962, it specializes in alternative research and information. Its extensive collection of these materials is indexed in a manual system, using computer logic, OASIS. From this collection, it is able to answer information requests and compile bibliographies on request.

IDOC publishes a monthly **IDOC Bulletin** in English and occasional books. On the issue of multinationals it has published "The Microelectronic Wave" Bulletin no. 1-2, January-February 1981 with overview articles and an excellent annotated bibliography of materials in English, French, Italian and Spanish (28 pages). "Rural Conflicts" Bulletin no. 5-6, May - June 1979 with articles on agrarian reform, agribusiness and development, and an extensive, annotated bibliography on these issues (50 pages). An updated bibliography on agribusiness (April 1981) is available on request. **The Corporate Village**, 1977, a 236 page book, deals with transnational control of communication systems. Price: US$ 8. Bulletin subscriptions: $ 12 per year, airmail postage $ 4 extra.

Infant Formula Action Coalition (INFACT)
1701 University Avenue SE, Minneapolis, Minnesota 55414, USA.
Tel: (612) 331-2333.

An information and action coalition, INFACT monitors the promotional activities of the baby food corporations, promotes and coordinates campaigns and actions on the infant formula issue and provides a wide range of uptodate informational materials on the industry and on actions of non-governmental organizations and the United Nations. In addition to press releases and occasional papers, it produces a monthly newsletter. Also available from INFACT is a one-half hour, three quarter inch video cassette entitled **Formula Factor**, produced by the Canadian Broadcasting Corporation. Rental US $ 20. INFACT is part of the International Baby Food Action Network (IBFAN) and acts as the US clearinghouse for this.

INFACT

Diego Rivera, The Militant/LNS

Institute of Development Studies (IDS)
University of Sussex, Brighton BN1 9RE, England.

As part of its ongoing studies on the subordination of women, IDS has produced a number of highly useful materials on women and development and on women, work and multinational industries. It has also been active in organizing seminars on these issues. Among its publications are two excellent bibliographies. **Women in Social Production** by Adrienne Cooper and Kate Young covers feminist and non-feminist literature on women's work, both waged and unwaged. It was prepared for a study seminar on Women in Social Production in the Caribbean, in July 1980. **Women Workers in Export-Orientated Industries in Southeast Asia** was prepared by Diane Elson for a seminar on this issue in Sri Lanka, November 1981. Both are compiled and annotated from a feminist perspective and are interesting and highly useful.

Institute for Food and Development Policy
2588 Mission Street, San Francisco, California 94110, USA.

The Institute for Food and Development Policy monitors agribusiness activities, especially as these influence the peasant communities in the third world. Recent publications include monographs on Chile and on Bangladesh; the **Food First Resource Guide** (documenting the roots of world hunger and rural poverty and discussing the causes of inequality in control over food producing resources and the solutions to world hunger); **World Hunger: Ten Myths** by F. Moore Lappé and J. Collins, co-authors of **Food First** (discussing the ten myths of "scarcity, over-population, production solutions, food versus environment, rich world versus poor world, foreign aid and passive poor" in describing the causes and solutions to world hunger). **Aid as Obstacle** by Lappé, Collins and Kinley is subtitled "Twenty Questions about our Foreign Aid and the Hungry" and deals with the way official development assistance is actually hurting rather than helping the poor and the hungry, 1980.

Instituto Latinoamericano de Estudios Transnacionales (ILET)
Apartado Postal 85-025, Mexico 20, D.F., Mexico.

ILET is an international, non-governmental organization with programmatic aims to increase the empirical and theoretical understanding of the transnational phenomena, under the following sections: the foreign capital sector; communications industry complexes; the state and TNCs; global studies; political power and processes of change. ILET publishes books, monographs and reports. Of special interest is the book **Compropolitan: El orden transnacional y su modelo feminino** by Adriana Santa Cruz and Viviana Erazo. A study of the women's magazines in Latin America, this book shows how multinationals use the media to promote an ideology and image of women which they can exploit for their own interests.

Interfaith Center on Corporate Responsibility (ICCR)
475 Riverside Drive, Room 556, New York, New York 10115, USA.

The ICCR is "an organization of church and religious institutional investors concerned about the social impact of corporations and the application of social criteria to investments." It monitors the social performance of American corporations and produces a wide range of informational materials. ICCR members are also involved in a number of activities such as shareholder resolutions, public hearings and boycotts. The ICCR has been particularly active in the infant formula campaign and has excellent information available. In its monthly newsletter **The Corporate Examiner** which includes an **ICCR Brief** highlighting a particular social area and focusing on one or more corporations, the ICCR provides uptodate resources and information about action options for issues studies. Subscription: US$ 25, per year.

In 1978, the ICCR published the **Agribusiness Manual: Background Papers on Corporate Responsibility and Hunger Issues** (231 pages), an important resource for understanding the growth of US-based giant corporations that control food production, processing and marketing around the world, and for getting involved in supporting actions to counter their power. Price: US$ 6.

International Baby Food Action Network (IBFAN)
European Clearinghouse: P.O. Box 157, 1211 Geneva 19, Switzerland.
US Clearinghouse: 1701 University Avenue SE, Minneapolis, Minnesota 55414, USA.

IBFAN provides an international network coordinating and sharing among groups and organizations the research gathered in monitoring the promotional activities of the baby food industry. It promotes international actions and campaigns on the issue of infant formula and more appropriate infant feeding practices. IBFAN publishes a newsletter and has much useful information and resource material available.

The International Organization of Consumers Unions (IOCU)
9 Emmastraat, 2595 EG The Hague, Netherlands.
IOCU Regional Office for Asia and the Pacific: P.O. Box 1045, Penang, Malaysia.

The IOCU links the activities of consumer organizations in more than 50 countries, promoting worldwide cooperation in consumer protection, education and information and the comparative testing of consumer goods and services.

The IOCU Regional Office for Asia and the Pacific published in 1980 a booklet entitled **Consumer Action in Developing Countries**, dealing with such varied topics as drugs, sweetened condensed milk and the relevance of consumer movements to less developed countries. It also propagandizes a **Consumer Action Charter**, pinpointing five principles as the basis for consumer actions and campaigns: critical awareness, involvement or action, social responsibility, ecological responsibility, and solidarity.

The booklet **Appropriate Products** is an 80 page report of the IOCU Seminar on Appropriate Products held in Penang in March 1982. Before looking at particular cases of appropriate and inappropriate products, there is a discussion of the concept of appropriate product within the framework of appropriate technology.

One of IOCU's action projects is **Consumer Interpol**, a network which alerts people and takes action against the marketing of hazardous products, the dumping or exporting of dangerous goods by multinationals in the third world and health hazards in the workplace. IOCU also publishes **Consumer Currents**, a monthly digest of information on consumer issues. This is restricted to members of IOCU in the Asia and Pacific region. Of international interest is **HAI News**, published by IOCU for Health Action International. This network is described in the resources of the Health section of this Guide.

WITH THANKS TO PICASSO

Interreligious Taskforce on US Food Policy
110 Maryland Avenue NE, Washington, DC 20002, USA.

An ecumenical organization, the taskforce publishes **Hunger** and **Food Policy Notes.** While most of these brief overviews of food issues deal with US domestic policy, some are of wider interest. In 1980 **Hunger** no. 22 dealt with "The International Monetary Fund and the Third World." no. 24 with "Multinational Corporations and Global Development," and no. 25 with "Which Way the Third Development Decade?" while **Food Policy Notes** no. 29 gives a bibliography on the International Monetary Fund. These are all short, concise, clear and critical looks at the issue. Good background material for study groups.

Joanna Vogelsang

ISIS – Women's International Information and Communication Service
Via Santa Maria dell'Anima 30, 00186 Rome, Italy and P.O. Box 50 (Cornavin), 1211 Geneva 2, Switzerland.

A Women's International Information and Communication Service, ISIS has, among its wide range of resources, a great deal of information and material on women and multinational corporations, sexual harassment on the job and occupational health and safety. It is also in contact with networks, groups and individuals researching and taking action on these issues, and is able to provide information about resources, actions and research. In addition to this Resource Guide, ISIS has published two issues of its quarterly **ISIS Women's International Bulletin** on women and multinationals. "Women and Work," no. 10, focuses on women organizing in their place of work in all continents. "Women and New Technology" (no. 24 in English) looks at the impact of the microelectronics industry on women in both the industrialized and developing world. Both bulletins emphasize the interrelatedness of women's exploitation and of their attempts to organize in all parts of the world. Both contain a rich selection of annotated resource listings. Price per issue: US$ 4.50 for individuals and $ 6.50 for institutions, surface; $ 6, individuals and $ 8 institutions, airmail. Bulk rates available on request.

ISIS has also produced **Bottle Babies: A Guide to the Baby Foods Issue** by Jane Cottingham on the medical, marketing and socio-political aspects of the issue. It includes a section on the action undertaken in industrialized countries and substantial resources. Price US$ 3. English, French and German.

Mexico-U.S. Border Program
American Friends Service Committee, 1501 Cherry Street, Philadelphia, Pennsylvania 19102, USA.

This program has a number of materials available on multinational corporations on the United States-Mexico border including two unpublished manuscripts by Maria Patricia Fernandez. These are 1) "Francisca Lucero: A Profile of Female Factory Work in Ciudad Juarez," a 15 page overview and personal examination of the employment of women in "maquiladoras" – partial assembly plants of multinational corporations on the border; 2) "Mexican Border Industrialization, Female Labor Force Participation and Migration," a 26 page examination of the connections among gender, class, family structure and occupational alternatives for both men and women along the Mexican border in the context of its recent industrialization.

Mexico-U.S. Border Program
Mexican Friends Service Committee, Ignacio Mariscal 132, Mexico 1, D.F., Mexico.

This program monitors the working conditions at the Mexico-U.S. border which since 1965 has been undergoing a rapid process of development known as the "Border Industrialization Program" or BIP. Encouraged by foreign investments incentives, electronics and textile industries established themselves on the Mexican side. These industrial sectors have traditionally been considered "women's work" both in Mexico and in the U.S.

The Mexico-U.S. Border Program of the Mexican Friends Service Committee publishes a **Boletín Informativo** in Spanish and in English about developments at the border. It also sponsors two research projects: "Women and Transnationals in Ciudad Juarez," by Jorge Carrillo V., and "The Reality of the Maquiladoras," by Patricia Fernandez Kelly ("Maquiladoras" are assembly plants). Of interest also is the "Testimony" submitted by Luisa María Rivera, director of the program, to the California legislature in October 1980. This 4 page paper describes the exploitation of women in the "maquiladoras".

National Action/Research on the Military Industrial Complex (NARMIC)
1501 Cherry Street, Philadelphia, Pennsylvania 19102, USA.

NARMIC is a research group within the American Friends Service Committee with a major focus on the corporations which participate in and profit from military involvement in third world countries. Recent NARMIC studies include: **Nuclear South Africa, The Philippines, Arming the Third World, Investors in Apartheid.** The group has also produced a slide tape show **Sharing Global Resources: Toward a New Economic Order** which examines the role of US multinational corporations in the development and exploitation of natural resources in the world, particularly in Chile, Jamaica and Appalachia. 25 mins. Price: rental US$ 10; sale $ 50.

Another slideshow **Acceptable Risk?** gives an overview of the production of nuclear arms and power with a focus on the corporations which produce them and the people who are affected. 35 mins. Price: US$ 60. Also available as filmstrip. Price: $ 50.

Nationwide Women's Program

American Friends Service Committee, 1501 Cherry Street, Philadelphia, Pennsylvania 19102, USA.
Tel. (215) 241-7160.

The Nationwide Women's Program has as one of its major focuses the issue of women and global corporations, particularly agribusiness and the textile and electronics industries. In October 1978, the Program convened a conference on "Women and Global Corporations: Work, Roles and Resistance," out of which has come a wealth of resource material. This conference brought together over one hundred women workers, organizers and researchers from the United States and three other countries to examine the role of global corporations, actions and organizing to challenge corporate power, and ways to build communication and support among women working on these issues. The **Women and Global Corporations Network** grew out of this conference.

In addition, the Program has several excellent and indispensable resources for organizers and researchers. These are:

Study Packet of 24 reprints and articles used as resources and background for the conference, focusing on basic information about global corporations, women's jobs and the textile, electronics and agribusiness industries. It is appropriate both as an introduction to the issue and for deepening understanding of the dimensions of multinationals' impact on women. It can be used for a wide range of women's groups, union groups and classes. Price: US$ 4.

Directory of Resources, both printed and audio-visual, with a listing of conference participants, networks and groups focusing on women and global corporations, particularly electronics, textiles and agribusiness. This 95 page directory is an extremely useful resource with its selected, annotated listings of books, periodicals, articles, films and slideshows. Information on price and how to obtain the resources is included. Price: US$ 4.50. For postage and handling for both of the above, add 25% of purchase price.

The quarterly **AFSC Women's Newsletter** contains a special section on "Women and Global Corporations" with information and news about resources, conferences, campaigns and actions. It is an excellent source of information on what women are doing on the issue of multinationals and highly useful for networking among women. In addition, the program has a wide variety of uptodate and useful informational materials, both written and audio-visual, including **The Corporate Slide Show**, a hardhitting look at the advertizing and employment practices of corporations, particularly in relation to women.

Through the Looking Glass

North American Congress on Latin America (NACLA)

151 West 19th Street, 9th Floor, New York, New York 10011, USA.

NACLA publishes bi-monthly a magazine of in-depth studies, the **NACLA Report on the Americas**. Each report analyzes a particular aspect of the effects that giant banking and corporate investors — with strategic support from the US government — have had on the direction of Latin American development. Recent reports have increasingly emphasized the links between issues of popular concern in the US and conditions in Latin America, demonstrating the need for working class struggles in the US to incorporate demands that are international in scope.

Full issues have been devoted to the apparel, electronics, asbestos, auto and steel industries on a global scale, as well as multiple issues on agribusiness. Corporate studies have included the Rockefeller empire, particularly Chase Manhattan Bank, Cargill, Del Monte, W.R. Grace, among others. In 1980 NACLA devoted many of its issues to understanding the roots of the struggle in Central America.

The September–October 1980 issue is devoted to "Latin American Women." Subtitled "One Myth — Many Realities," it explores the nature of women's work and the sexual division of labor in Latin America, the largely female labor force in the US-Mexico border industries and how the Latin American women's movement is dealing with issues of women's oppression. Price: US$ 2.50. Subscriptions: $ 13 per year for individuals and $ 24 for institutions; airmail postage extra.

AFSC Womens Newsletter

Pacific - Asia Resources Center (PARC)

P.O. Box 5250, Tokyo International, Japan.

The PARC was begun in 1969 to communicate to peoples abroad the struggles in Japan against US-Japanese collaboration in the military domination of Asia, particularly Vietnam. Since then, PARC has expanded to include reports and analyses on the economic and cultural as well as political and military role of Japan in the world, particularly the third world.

PARC publishes **AMPO, Japan-Asia Quarterly Review**, which continues to be one of the most significant and informative English language publications from the Japanese left (one year 4 issues, surface mail: US$ 12 for individuals, $ 20 for institutions).

In 1978 PARC began a five-year action-oriented research project on Japanese Transnationals and their Impact on the Third World, the **PARC TNE Project** (Transnational Enterprises). The results of the research are published in AMPO as they are completed in order to make them available for use by action groups and people concerned, particularly victims of the activities of transnational enterprises. Study units have been formed and the subjects of study have been defined according to both industrial and geographic criteria. There is also a unit working on women workers and TNCs, centering on the textile industry.

PARC has produced two excellent audio-visuals. **Who Owns the Sky**, a 25 minute slideshow with English narration, is subtitled "Kawasaki Steel at Home and Abroad." It examines the case of this Japanese multinational's exportation of polluting plants from Japan to the Philippines. Price: US$ 70 or 20,000 yen. **They Will Never Forget**, a 8 mm color film with English narration, of 30 minutes, was produced with the People's Film of Thailand. It depicts the women workers' takeover and collective operation of the Hara Jeans factory during the short-lived period of democracy in Thailand. Price: US$ 350 or 80,000 yen, airmail postage included.

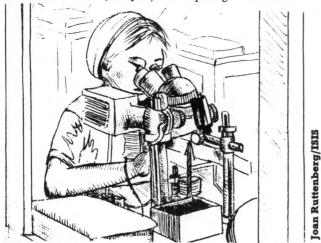

Joan Ruttenberg/ISIS

Pacific Studies Center
222B View Street, Mountain View, California 94041, USA. Tel: (415) 969-1545.

The Pacific Studies Center is a non-profit activist oriented information center, operating since 1969. It publishes a quarterly, **Pacific Research**, which focuses on US foreign and military policies, multinational corporations, and the political economy of Asia and the Pacific. It also maintains a library and information files on these subjects. This material is accessible through an **Information for Hire** service. The Center has recently created the **Global Electronics Information Project**.

Issues of **Pacific Research** which are particularly useful for research on the electronics and textile industries include:

"Fairchild Assembles an Asian Empire" by Lenny Siegel and Rachael Grossman, vol. IX no. 2, January – February 1978. This eight page article traces the growth and expansion of Fairchild Semiconductor in the United States and Asia. As one of the leaders in the electronics industry, Fairchild is representative of many other global corporations which bring huge benefits to stockholders and managers in their home countries at the expense of workers at home and abroad. The article gives detailed and documented information on how such corporations operate.

"Philippines: Workers in the Export Industry" by Enrico Paglaban, vol. IX, nos. 3 and 4, March — June 1978. This 31 page study focuses on the garment and electronics industries in the Philippines, giving a profile of the industries, examining the conditions of the workers and the particular exploitation of women, and a history of the workers' movement in the Philippines. In addition to statistics, the article is documented by statements from workers and management of various textile and electronics firms.

"Changing Role of S.E. Asian Women," vol. IX, nos. 5 and 6, July - October 1978. Published together with **Southeast Asia Chronicle**, this 32 page issue is subtitled "The Global Assembly Line and the Social Manipulation of Women on the Job." Rachael Grossman's excellent article, "Women's Place in the Integrated Circuit," reports on the electronics industry and its impact on women in Southeast Asia and the United States, examining corporate policies and control. This issue also contains an article on the growth of tourism and prostitution in the Philippines and one entitled "Orchestrating Dependency" by Lenny Siegel, showing how export-oriented industrialization is being promoted as a development model by the US government, global corporations, and financial institutions such as the World Bank, the International Monetary Fund and the Asian Development Bank.

"Microelectronics Does Little for the Third World" by Lenny Siegel, vol. X, no. 2, 1979. This six page essay gives an overview of the export-oriented electronics industry in Asia.

"Delicate Bonds: The Global Semiconductor Industry" by Lenny Siegel, vol. XI, no. 1, first quarter, 1980. This thoroughgoing 26 page study summarizes and analyzes the growth of the semiconductor industry in the USA and abroad.

"Mattel: Not So Swell" by Linda Robbins and Lenny Siegel, vol. XI, no. 2, second quarter, 1980. This good description of the activities of the "runaway" Mattel industry also relates how women's groups have effectively organized pressure on a multinational to improve conditions. The issue also contains an article on competition between the US and Japanese electronics industry and a good bibliography.

Individual subscriptions to **Pacific Research** cost US$ 10 ($ 12 foreign surface mail) for eight issues (two years). Institutional subscriptions cost $ 22 ($ 24 foreign). Airmail subscriptions can be arranged at cost. Copies of single issues may be ordered at US$ 1 apiece ($ 1.50 for vol. IX, no. 3 and following) by individuals and $ 2.20 each ($ 3.30) by institutions.

Global Electronics Information Project. The project has three key goals: 1) To establish an international network of researchers, journalists, and activists concerned about global production in semiconductors and other similar industries. The project intends to link up labor, human rights, and women's groups on an international scale. 2) To produce a pamphlet documenting the structure of the semiconductor industry and its global implications. 3) To develop a program of policy alternatives designed to make the electronics industry more responsive to the needs of workers in rich and poor countries alike. The **Global Electronics Information Newsletter** is a four to eight page monthly which serves the network of the project. It provides data and short news items about the industry and about research and action. Newsletter subscribers are asked (not required) to donate US$ 5 ($ 10 foreign airmail).

Data Center/USA

Southeast Asia Resource Center
P.O. Box 4000D, Berkeley, California 94704, USA.
Tel: (415) 584-2546.

The Southeast Asia Resource Center is a major source of information on current developments in the countries of Southeast Asia, and on US involvement there. The Center follows and interprets events in the new societies of Vietnam, Laos and Kampuchea (Cambodia), and also covers Thailand, the Philippines, Malaysia and Indonesia. The Center maintains a mail-order service specializing in hard-to-find books and pamphlets on Southeast Asia. A free catalogue is available on request. The Center publishes the **Southeast Asia Chronicle** six times a year. Of particular interest is the issue on "Changing Role of S.E. Asian Women," no. 66, January - February 1979, published together with the Pacific Studies Center, with an excellent article by Rachael Grossman on "Women's Place in the Integrated Circuit" and others on tourism and export-oriented industry. This issue offers a documented look at new corporate strategies for social control on the job, and the attempt to orient every facet of employees' lives around the company's plant. It is a first-hand report featuring interviews with women in Hong Kong, Malaysia, Indonesia and the Philippines, who talk about the impact of these policies on their lives and about their efforts to resist them. It is an excellent resource for organizing and educational work.

Subscriptions: US$ 8 regular; $ 6 low income; $ 12 institutions; $ 10 foreign surface mail; $ 15 foreign airmail and $ 20 sustaining.

The Third World Studies Center
Room 3134, Faculty Center, College of Arts and Sciences, University of the Philippines, Diliman, Quezon City, Philippines.

The Third World Studies Center is formed by a group of economists and sociologists of the University of the Philippines. They publish regular reports and studies in the series, **The Philippines in the Third World Papers**. Those already published include:

"Foreign Investment and the Multinational Corporations in the Philippines";
"Philippines Studies on Transnational Corporations: a Critique";
"Multinational Corporations: a Sociological Perspective";
"The Politics of Major Japanese-Filipino Joint Ventures: a Sociological View."

Transnational Information Exchange (TIE)
c/o Transnational Institute, Paulus Potterstraat 20, 1071 DA Amsterdam, Netherlands, or c/o IDOC, via S. Maria dell'Anima 30, 00186 Rome, Italy.

TIE is a network of research organizations and action groups whose work is European-based and who are gathering information or promoting campaigns on the growing influence of transnational corporations in the world economy. It began in 1978, and in 1979 held a Consultation on the Auto industry in Europe which brought together members of action and research groups and representatives of workers' organizations from seven European countries. A consultation on the Telecommunications industry following the same pattern was organized in June 1980.

TIE's aims are defined as follows:
1. to enable the exchange of information and experience between action and research groups working on TNCs, mainly in Europe, but also between Europe and the rest of the world.
2. to develop a similar dialogue between such groups and workers' organizations and trade unions in order that the type of information produced may be of most help to those whom it most affects, and that the contacts between workers' representatives from TNC subsidiaries in different countries may be strengthened and more fully informed.
3. to promote discussion and debate on the effects of growing corporate power, both within Europe and in other parts of the world, with a view to exploring the most effective forms of countervailing power.

The network is formed by more than fifty groups throughout Europe, all of them involved in research and/or action on TNCs. Two among them have a permanent task in the network: the Transnational Institute in Amsterdam which produces the **TIE Bulletin** (US$ 10 per year, $ 3 per copy) and IDOC in Rome which coordinates the documentation work. The Bulletin regularly lists resources on women and corporations.

The Transnational Corporations Research Project
University of Sydney, Faculty of Economics, Sydney, Australia 2006.

This research and publications project focuses on the impact of transnational corporations in Asia and the Pacific and on Australian responsibilities in the region. It publishes books, occasional papers and research monographs. Current work is concerned with: transnational corporations in fisheries in the South Pacific; agribusiness in Australia; transnational corporations in Malaysia; advertizing and politics in S.E. Asia; Japanese transnational corporations in Australia; etc.

E. Fernandez/Philippines

The United Nations Commission on Transnational Corporations
United Nations, New York, New York 10017, USA.

The UN Commission on Transnational Corporations is charged with negotiating a code of conduct which is expected to contain comprehensive and generally acceptable standards regarding the behavior of TNCs and the treatment of TNCs by home and host governments. These standards would require TNCs *inter alia*, to respect national sovereignty, adhere to economic and social objectives, respect human rights, and abstain from interference in internal political affairs and intergovernmental relations. In addition to these general principles, specific standards would deal with the behavior of TNCs regarding ownership and control, balance of payments and financing, transfer pricing, consumer and environmental protection. In the matter of employment and labor, the standards would refer to the ILO Tripartite Declaration. The Working Group is also developing standards regarding disclosure of information by TNCs to the public, governments and trade unions and other representatives of employees.

Women, and particularly feminists, are beginning to criticize the lack of participation of women in the formulation of this code and to analyze the impact or lack of it that this code will have on the lives of women.

JR/ISIS

The United Nations Industrial Development Organization (UNIDO) Program for Women
Vienna International Centre, P.O. Box 300, A – 1400 Vienna, Austria.

The UNIDO Program for Women was presented in July 1980 at the World Conference of the UN Decade for Women in Copenhagen. It upholds the view of "involving females in development planning," highlighting "constraints on women in taking a more active part in industrialization," recommending "remedies and pinpointing areas where they could make major economic contributions."

Women and Global Corporations Network
American Friends Service Committee, 1501 Cherry Street, Philadelphia, Pennsylvania 19102, USA.
Tel: (215) 241-7160.

Focusing on women in agribusiness, electronics and textiles, the Women and Global Corporations Network brings together people, information and resources in order to break down the isolation of local groups and strengthen individual efforts to combat the negative effects of global corporations on women's lives. The network is:

— Building links among groups in the United States and abroad concerned with the impact of corporations on women.
— Creating a growing store of information and analysis of the ways global corporations touch women's lives.
— Bridging the gap between researchers and activists.
— Offering information and support for women organizing against corporations in their own communities.

The Network members provide resources and are actively working with groups on research organizing and analysis. Some of the areas of work are the electronics workers in the Santa Clara Valley, California; the computer industry; data compilation on multinational activity in Latin America; a strike by textile workers in Texas; electronics workers on the US-Mexico border; women farmworkers in Arizona. The Network is establishing contacts with labor unions and women's organizations in the United States and other countries.

The Network is an important source of information, resources and technical assistance in the areas of agribusiness, electronics and textiles. Groups and individuals wishing to participate in the network are invited to make contact.

Women and Work Hazards Group
c/o British Society for Social Responsibility in Science (BSSRS), 9 Poland Street, London W1, England.

A good source of information and materials on occupational health and safety hazards, this group has a number of publications available including a **Health and Safety Information Packet**. They contribute to the **Hazards Bulletin**. The Politics of Health Groups of the BSSRS has produced a pamphlet **Food and Profit – It Makes You Sick** which examines the food industry and how this contributes to ill-health in society. Price: 35 pence each.

Women's Occupational Health Resource Center
School of Public Health, Columbia University, 60 Haven Avenue, B-1, New York, New York 10032, USA.

A good general resource for literature on many aspects of women and occupational health including the hazards of housework, this center can provide a list of publications on this issue. While it is US oriented, much of the material has wider application.

World Council of Churches (WCC) Program on Transnational Corporations
World Council of Churches, 150 route de Ferney, 1211 Geneva 20, Switzerland.

The World Council of Churches has an ongoing program of research on transnational corporations. "Struggling for the Sharing of Wealth and Power," or simply **Sharing**, is the title of the news bulletin about the developments of this program. A permanent feature of the Bulletin is different sections reflecting on churches' actions on multinational corporations and workers' opinions on the same subject. There are also reading suggestions and presentations of alternatives (alternative ways of relating to TNCs and alternatives to the TNC's model of development).

The purpose of the bulletin is to create links between churches, church councils and conferences, grassroot communities, research groups, labor organizations, peoples' movements and individual Christians on the issue of transnational corporations and their impact on the life of people.

The program has also produced a packet of reports and studies dealing with **Transnational Corporations: A Challenge for Churches and Christians**, February, 1982.

World Health Organization (WHO)

Maternal and Child Health, Division of Family Health, 1211 Geneva 27, Switzerland.

WHO has a number of publications, many of which were produced together with UNICEF, on infant feeding and the marketing of infant formula. **Infant and Young Child Feeding Current Issues**, published in 1981, deals with the issues of breastfeeding, appropriate weaning practices, appropriate marketing of breast milk substitutes and provides background information on nutritional requirements in infancy, human milk, breastfeeding, supplementation and weaning. It contains the recommendations of the Joint WHO/UNICEF Meeting on Infant and Young Child Feeding of October 1979 and the World Health Assembly resolution of May 1980 on Infant and Young Child Feeding.

Also published separately, the recommendations cover: the encouragement and support of breastfeeding, promotion and support of appropriate and timely complementary feeding practices with the use of local food resources, strengthening of education, training and information on infant and young child feeding, development of support for improved health and social status of women in relation to infant and young child health and feeding, and appropriate marketing and distribution of infant formula and weaning foods.

periodicals

Other periodicals dealing with multinationals are listed under the organizations which produce them.

Aegis

P.O. Box 21033, Washington, DC 20009, USA.

This quarterly "magazine on ending violence against women" is an excellent resource for information about sexual harassment on the job. It lists books, periodicals, audio-visuals on this issue as well as groups and organizations. While most of the information is from North American sources, **Aegis** also provides news and resource listings from other countries. One of the groups publishing this magazine is the Alliance Against Sexual Coercion (AASC), a US action and information group working on this issue.

Alternative News and Features (ANF)

4A Bhagwan Dass Road, New Delhi 110001, India.

"A counter-information service from the third world," this monthly service, begun in 1980, aims to respond to the information needs of alternative networks and institutions within and outside India. Among the issues it deals with is the role of multinationals in India.

Asian Women's Liberation

Asian Women's Association, Poste Restante, Shibuya Post Office, Shibuya, Tokyo 150, Japan.

This English version of a Japanese newsletter is produced by the Asian Women's Association, a group of women whose goals are "to liberate ourselves from the oppressive forces in Japanese society and to respond to the desperate cries from other Asian countries." One of their main areas of concern and study is the involvement and impact of Japanese corporations in other countries of Asia and the exploitation of women workers by these corporations. The April 1980 issue contains several reports on Japanese multinationals in South Korea, Thailand, Taiwan, the Philippines and Indonesia as well as on the working conditions of women in Japan itself. It is an effort to build links and solidarity among working women. Price per issue: US$ 2.50 plus postage (Asia and USA $ 1, elsewhere $ 1.50).

BALAI Asian Journal

P.O. Box S.M. 447, Sta. Mesa, Manila, Philippines.

A quarterly Asian journal produced by a team of researchers, **BALAI** analyzes and presents in popular form issues relating to transnationals and the control of natural and human resources in Asia. Issues include: oil (December 1980), minerals (March 1981), marine wealth (June 1981), forestry (September 1981) and women workers (December 1981).

Food Monitor

350 Broadway, Suite 209, New York, New York 10013, USA.

This by-monthly magazine critically examines rural development and food aid programs, agricultural policy and the problems of world hunger.

Ibon

P.O. Box S.M. 447, Sta. Mesa, Manila, Philippines.

Ibon's distinctive feature is popularization of economic data. It is a fortnightly newsletter aiming at presenting in clear and simple terms which the majority of the people can understand, basic data about the economic situation of the Philippines and its dependence on foreign interests and how this affects the daily life of the people.

Glynn Gomez

Multinational Monitor
P.O. Box 19312, Washington, DC 20036, USA.

This monthly magazine examines the role of multinationals in the global economy, with an emphasis on corporate power in the developing world. Issues include: US export of hazardous industry, foreign investment, women's labor, commodities trading, US foreign policy impact. Each issue contains concise reports on new developments, interviews with activists and corporate managers, relationships between host countries and multinationals; notes on new publications, organizations and in-depth reviews. Subscription: 12 issues US$ 15.

Newsletter of International Labour Studies (NILS)
Galileistraat 130, 2561 TK The Hague, Netherlands.

This newsletter serves to facilitate an exchange of information among scholars concerned primarily with the working class of Latin America, Africa, Asia, the Caribbean and the Middle East. Concerned mainly with transnational capital, the international division of labor, and working conditions in third world countries, the newsletter gives information about the struggles of workers in the third world and links these with struggles in the rest of the world.

The July 1980 issue is devoted to the issue of women and wage labor. It includes a detailed report on a study of women workers and their struggles in South Korea, an extensive bibliography on women and wage labor, and information about research and projects on this issue. Subscription: individuals US $ 10; libraries $ 35, for 10 issues.

Off Our Backs
1841 Columbia Road NW, Washington, DC 20009, USA.

A women's news journal with a feminist perspective, **Off Our Backs** has been covering news and providing information and analyses for the past ten years. It appears monthly. It regularly covers women organizing in the workplace in the USA, especially in textiles and agribusiness. The June and November 1980 issues, for instance, give information on the strike of, mainly black women, workers at Sanderson Farms chicken processing plant in Mississippi. Subscription: US$ 8 regular; $ 14 contributing; $ 20 institutions; sample copy $ 1.50; $ 15 overseas sea mail.

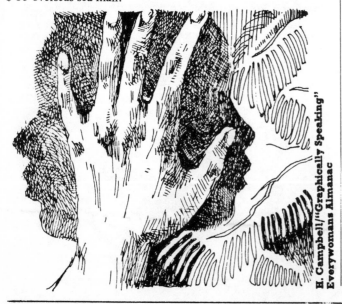

H. Campbell, "Graphically Speaking"
Everywomans Almanac

Praxis
World Student Christian Federation Asia, Kiu Kin Mansion 12F, 568 Nathan Road, Kowloon, Hong Kong.
Tel: 3-852 550.

This newsletter of the World Student Christian Federation deals occasionally with the situation of women workers in Asia. The May — August 1980 issue contains several articles on women. Of particular interest is Kumari Jayawardena's analysis of the "Participation of Women in the Social Reform, Political and Labour Movements in Sri Lanka."

Raw Materials Report
P.O. Box 5195, S-102 44 Stockholm, Sweden.

A quarterly magazine which published its first issue in October 1981, this reports on raw materials, particularly metallic minerals and the role of transnational mining corporations. It also analyzes viable alternatives to the existing exploitation of the world's resources. Subscriptions: Swedish crowns 130 per year or 150 airmail, individuals; 380 per year, institutions.

Union Women's Alliance to Gain Equality (Union WAGE)
P.O. Box 462, Berkeley, California 94701, USA.

Dedicated to achieving equal rights, equal pay and equal opportunities for women workers and to building an organization that will represent US working women, **Union WAGE** produces a bi-monthly newspaper devoted to news of women's activities in unions and union women's struggles to improve women's working conditions. It is usually limited to US issues but includes good coverage of the problems and activities of minority and migrant women within the US union movement. Subscriptions: US$ 3.50 for individuals and $ 7.50 for institutions.

books and pamphlets

Other books and pamphlets are listed under the organizations which produce them.

The Baby Killer Scandal
Andy Chetley, War on Want, 467 Caledonian Road, London N7 9BE, England. 1979.

Published in 1979, this is an update on the original **Baby Killer** written by Mike Muller in 1974. It gives considerable detail of the role of industry and its activities, and the recent action by boycott and other groups, with the responses of companies. Probably the best complete work on all aspects of the issue with the exception of the situation of women. Price £ 1.50.

Bebés de Biberón
Colmena, Apartado 470, San Pedro, Montes de Oca, San Jose, Costa Rica. 1981.

This is the Spanish-language version of the ISIS publication **Bottle Babies: A Guide to the Baby Foods Issue**, translated and adapted by a group of Latin American women. It contains a special section on the activities of baby foods companies in Latin America, Latin American resources and an updated section on current action. Price: US$ 3. Also available from ISIS.

Cigars and Support Hose: Women and the Multinationals
Joyce N. Chinen, American Friends Service Committee, Hawaii Area Program Office, 2426 Oahu Avenue, Honolulu, Hawaii 96822, USA. 1977.

A short, clear paper on why women and multinationals is an important issue, this also discusses the importance of a feminist analysis of multinationals.

The Debt Trap: The International Monetary Fund and the Third World
Cheryl Payer, Monthly Review Press, New York. 1974.

This book is an exposé of the use of international loans to pressure borrowing countries, influence policies, and undermine social change movements.

Decoding Corporate Camouflage: U.S. Business Support for Apartheid
Elizabeth Schmidt, Institute for Policy Studies, 1901 Q Street NW, Washington, DC 20009, USA. 1980.

This 127 page book examines US multinational involvement in South Africa and how it supports the racist regime of that country. Price: US$ 4.95.

Exportinteressen gegen Muttermilch
Arbeitsgruppe Dritte Welt, Rowohlt Taschenbuch Verlag, Hamburgerstrasse 17, Reinbek/Hamburg 2057, Federal Republic of Germany. 1976.

Documents the problems of bottle feeding in the third world; the advertizing methods of multinational corporations, especially Nestle; chronology of events in the Nestle trial against the Third World Action Group Bern (Switzerland) in 1974-5.

Export Processing and Female Employment: The Search for Cheap Labor
Helen I. Safa, Wenner-Gren Foundation, 1865 Broadway, New York, New York 10023, USA.

A 23 page paper, this examines women's employment in export industries as a strategy for integrating women into development and concludes that this enhances the possibilities of exploiting women as cheap labor. It gives an overview of the rise and spread of export oriented industries and their impact on women.

Feeding the Few: Corporate Control of Food
Susan George, Institute for Policy Studies, 1901 Q Street NW, Washington, DC 20009, USA. 1979.

In this 79 page book, Susan George elaborates her argument that "the battle for control of the world food system is now being waged, and its chief combatants are agribusiness and the State."

Femmes et Multinationales
Andrée Michel, Agnès Fatoumata-Diarra, Hélène Agbessi-Bos Santos, Editions Karthala, 22-24 Boulevard Aragon, 73013 Paris, France.

This is an anthology of essays from a meeting in May 1980 of thirty women, including twelve African specialists, on "Women, the International Division of Labour and Development." It is entirely devoted to Africa, and deals with the impact of patterns of trade set up by multinational companies and banks on women in Africa, both in production and consumption. There is careful examination of the way in which "development" is carried out through multinationals and how, for instance, new technologies introduced into rural areas do little to help women. It also looks at food production and agribusiness in Africa, the role of women in agriculture in France, and the textile industry.

In her introduction, Andrée Michel sums up by saying: "Multinational banks and companies are able to use a panoply of techniques: publicity, mass media, development planning, expertise in science and technology, to extend and reinforce all over the world western values, needs and models of development which are indispensable to their continuing economic domination."

Fight Back Says a Woman
Clotil Walcott, Institute of Social Studies, 251 Badhuisweg, The Hague, Netherlands.
Tel. (070) 572201. 1980.

This is a compilation of the writings of a militant woman trade unionist in the Caribbean. In them she recounts her struggles against the injustices and the exploitation of workers, especially women, in the factory where she worked. The writings span the period 1963-1980. Her wish is that her experiences may be a lesson and a guide for other workers.

D. Paabo/"Graphically Speaking" Everywomans Almanac

Finding a Voice: Asian Women in Britain
Amrit Wilson, Virago Publishing Co. Ltd., 5 Wardour Street, London WIV 3HE, England. 1978.

This book is about Asian women in Britain. The third chapter particularly speaks about the plight of Indian, Bangladeshi and Pakistani women who work in factories and sweat shops. Asian women are extensively quoted as they recount their experiences with discriminatory employers and wages, atrocious working conditions, and unionizing and strike attempts at a number of plants.

The Halfway House – Mncs, Industries and Asian Factory Girls
Soon Young Yoon, United Nations Asian and Pacific Development Institute (UNAPDI), Bangkok, Thailand. 1979.

Based on studies of young women workers in multinational export industries in South Korea, Hong Kong, Singapore and Thailand, this 45 page paper concludes that the problems of female workers stem not only from their exploitation by the corporations but also from institutional barriers, sex-segregation, a large reserve of labor, unequal education and cultural biases and myths. The paper makes some recommendations for institutional reform, including integrating women into development planning, higher investments in social development, unions which belong to the workers, and some restrictions on the private sector.

How the Other Half Dies: The Real Reasons for World Hunger
Susan George, Allenheld, Osmun and Co., New Jersey, USA. 1977.

This 308 page book is an excellent analysis of the interrelations of government elites, banks and corporations whose programs perpetuate hunger instead of ending it. The author clearly explains why technology and the "Green Revolution" are artificial non-solutions to problems of hunger and malnutrition in the third world. Price: US$ 5.95.

Microelectronics at Work: Productivity and Jobs in the World Economy
Colin Norman, Worldwatch Paper no. 39, Worldwatch Institute, 1776 Massachusetts Avenue NW, Washington, DC 20036 USA. October 1980.

The first part of this 63 page pamphlet describes the development of the microelectronics industry and the innovations this is bringing to the factory and the office. The second part explores the implications this has for workers, productivity, employment and the world economy. Accepting the microelectronic revolution as inevitable and essentially beneficial, the author points out a number of issues which must be dealt with if "the benefits ... are to be equitably shared."

Microelectronics: Capitalist Technology and the Working Class
Conference of Socialist Economics Microelectronics Group, CSE Books, 25 Horsell Road, London N5, England. 1980.

This 152 page book examines the impact of microelectronics on work and workers and especially the control of electronics by capitalist management and the implications of this on labor organizing. Price: £ 2.95.

Mujeres Dominicanas
Distributed by Centro Dominicano de Estudios de la Educación (CEDEE), Juan Sánchez Ramírez No. 41, Santo Domingo, Dominican Republic.

This is a series of nine brief pamphlets produced by the Proyecto de Investigación–Educación para Mujeres, coordinated by Magaly Pineda and Moema Viezzer, about and for women workers in agriculture, industry, free trade zones and in the home as domestic workers and housewives. Brief, simple and clear with many illustrations, they are excellent materials for women to discuss their problems, rights, and possibilities to organize.

The New Gnomes: Multinational Banks in the Third World
Howard M. Wachtel, Transnational Institute, 1901 Q Street NW, Washington, DC 20009, USA. 1977.

This 60 page pamphlet documents and analyzes the growth of third world debt by private US-based multinational banks and the impact of this new form of indebtedness on the politics and economic policies of third world countries. Price: US$ 3.

No Time for Crying: Stories of Philippine Women who Care for their Country and its People
Alison Wynne, Resource Center for Philippine Concerns, C.P.O. Box 2784, Kowloon, Hong Kong. 1979.

This book recounts, through interviews, the lives and struggles of women in the Philippines. In doing so, it gives a small voice to those who would otherwise remain unheard beyond their own place of life and work. One section of the book has interviews with several women working for multinational corporations in agribusiness and textiles. They give a real feeling of the working conditions and the attempts to organize in oppressive situations. This is an excellent resource for consciousness raising. Price: US$ 3 (add $ 2.50 for airmail). It is also available in Dutch, German and Italian.

In Dutch, available from: Filippijnengroep Nederland, van Lidth de Jeudestraat 26, 3581 GJ Utrecht, Netherlands.

In German, available from: Aktionsgruppe Philippinen, Uhland-strasse 9, 5444 Polch, Federal Republic of Germany.

In Italian available from: Kasama, c/o Lega Internazionale dei Popoli, Via L. il Magnifico 68, Florence, Italy. Price: Lire 5000.

SEWA Marches Ahead
Self-Employed Women's Association (SEWA), c/o Gandhi Majoor Sewalaya, Bhadra, Ahemdabad, Gujarat, India.

SEWA is a trade union of economically active women engaged in producing goods or rendering various services. Among the major groups of women organized in SEWA are the garment dealers and garment workers. The services provided to members include banking and loans, legal aid, child care, health and social security schemes, training and literacy classes. SEWA is an attempt to help organize some of the poorest and most exploited women workers in India.

Sexual Shakedown: The Sexual Harassment of Women on the Job
Lin Farley, McGraw Hill, New York, USA. 1978.

A feminist analysis of the sexual harassment of women in waged work, this is a good introduction to a complex subject.

Technological Change and Women Workers: The Development of Microelectronics
Marit Hult, Background paper A/Conf. 94/26, World Conference of the United Nations Decade for Women, United Nations, New York, New York 10017, USA, 1981.

This paper reviews the current debate in industrialized countries on the impact of microelectronics technology on employment, especially of women, and recommends that governments and decision-making bodies establish policies to prevent adverse effects on women.

Who Really Starves? Women and World Hunger
Lisa Leghorn and Mary Roodkowsky, Friendship Press, New York, USA. 1977.

This 40 page booklet shows how women are particularly vulnerable to the economic and social forces which bring about hunger and malnutrition. Price: US$ 1.25.

Women and Men in Asia
World Student Christian Federation, Asia Regional Office, Kiu Kin Mansion 12/F, 568 Nathan Road, Kowloon, Hong Kong. 1979.

This book is a compilation of reports and studies made by groups in several Asian countries. Of special interest are the studies on women garment workers in the Philippines and women in the plantation sector in Sri Lanka. These contain both statistical data on wages, working conditions and corporations, and statements from women workers themselves.

New Hogtown Press/Canada

Upstream/Canada

Women at Farah — An Unfinished Story
Reforma, El Paso Chapter, P.O. Box 2064, El Paso, Texas 79951, USA. 1980.

This pamphlet tells the story of what happened after Farah textile/garment workers were able to organize a union in the USA after a nationwide boycott of Farah Pants in support of their strike. Available in English and Spanish. Price: US$ 2. Postage and handling $ 1.25 for one to three copies, 20 cents for each additional copy.

Women, Men and the Division of Labor
Kathleen Newland, Worldwatch Paper no. 37, Worldwatch Institute, 1776 Massachusetts Avenue NW, Washington, DC 20036, USA. May 1980.

This 43 page pamphlet by the author of **The Sisterhood of Man,** describes the worldwide trend toward greater participation of women in the labor force and shows that their newly won access to the formal labor market has not been matched by an increased involvement of men in unpaid work in the home. The result is an unequal division of labor, a pronounced imbalance between male and female work loads, with unhappy consequences for women, men and children. Price: US$ 2.

Women, Production and Reproduction in Industrial Capitalism
Helen Safa, Women's International Resource Exchange Service (WIRE), 2700 Broadway, Room 7, New York, New York 10025, USA.

Draft paper prepared for presentation at the Conference on the Continuing Subordination of Women and the Development Process, Institute of Development Studies, University of Sussex, Brighton, England. September 16 – 22, 1978.

This 31 page paper examines the way in which larger economic forces impinge upon women's productive and reproductive roles, in two societies at very different levels of capitalist development: Brazil and the United States. The study focuses on women factory workers in these two societies and on their conditions of employment and work as well as the impact of these conditions on the roles of women in the home. Price: US$ 1.80.

Women Workers in Multinational Corporations: The Case of the Electronics Industry in Malaysia and Singapore
Linda Y.C. Lim, Occasional Paper IX, Women's Studies Program, University of Michigan, Ann Arbor, Michigan 48109, USA. 1978.

This 60 page study examines female-intensive manufacturing for export by multinational firms, effects of multinational corporate employment on women workers, and its impact on women's position in developing countries. It concludes that this type of female industrial employment benefits neither the women themselves nor the host countries.

"Women's Work Is..." – Resources on Working Women
Bobbi Wells Hargleroad, Editor, Institute on the Church in Urban-Industrial Society (ICUIS), 5700 S. Woodlawn Avenue, Chicago, Illinois 60637, USA. ICUIS Bibliography Series no. 4, 1978.

An extensive bibliography dealing with many aspects of women and work (hours, pay, health and safety, day care, history etc.) interspersed with graphics, quotes, poems, and graphs. Each book, periodical, article or film is abstracted. There is a section on women's work as an international concern, with many resources on Asia and Latin America in particular, while the rest of the book is primarily concerned with women and work as they pertain to the United States. There is also an extensive section on organizing, including names of US organizations of and for working women. In all, an excellent and well-organized resource for working women in the US, interesting reading as well as a useful sourcebook.

Working Class Women View Their Own Lives
Meera Savara, Institute of Social Research and Education (I.S.R.E.), Carol Mansion, 35 Sitladevi Temple Road, Mahim, Bombay 400 016, India.

A 43 page monograph, this highly interesting study examines "how women working in the textile industry in Bombay themselves experience their world of work and home and what their desires and aspirations regarding their own lives are." It includes case studies and reports on the discussions with women about their work in the factory and in their families, about domestic violence, about housework and about their relationships with other women.

articles

Other articles are listed under the periodicals in which they appear and under the organizations which produce them.

"Cheaper than Machines"
Diana Roose, **The New Internationalist**, April 1980. 62a High Street, Wallingford, Oxfordshire 0X10 OEE, England.

A short, succinct description of the working conditions and problems of women in the electronics factories in Southeast Asia.

Carillon/LNS

"Farming Out the Home: Women and Agribusiness"
Sally Hacker, **Science for the People**, March – April 1978. 897 Main Street, Cambridge, Massachusetts, 02139, USA.

Originally published in **The Second Wave**, this 12 page article examines the role of women in agribusiness in the United States, using first-hand accounts of women farmers and migrant women farmworkers. It also looks at agribusiness ideology and what this means for women not only as workers but as consumers and transmitters of culture. An interesting study of how agribusiness works.

"Imperialism in the Silicon Age"
A. Sivanandan, **Race and Class**, vol. 21 no. 2, Autumn 1979. Institute of Race Relations, 247/249 Pentonville Road, London N1, England.

Also available in pamphlet form (price 40 pence), this 19 page article traces the new industrial revolution caused by the silicon chip and its impact on work in both the industrialized and developing countries. The Autumn 1980 issue, vol. 22 no. 2, of this journal contains a short but very clear article on "Free Trade Zones: A Capitalist Dream," describing what a free trade zone is, how it operates and what it means for a country and its workers. Price: £ 1.50 plus 30 pence postage per copy.

"Life on the Global Assembly Line"
Barbara Ehrenreich and Annette Fuentes, **Ms. Magazine**, January 1981. 370 Lexington Avenue, New York, New York 10017, USA.

Examining electronics and textile multinationals in particular, this 7 page article gives an excellent overview of the operations of these industries both in the USA and in the third world and what it means to be a woman worker in these factories. It also looks at how United Nations agencies, the World Bank and the United States government promote the multinational corporations in the third world and, thus, the exploitative conditions for women workers. In conclusion, the authors look at how women are beginning to organize and fight back and some attempts at linking first world feminists and women struggling against multinationals in other parts of the world.

"Microelectronics and Employment"
European File, 16/80, October 1980. Commission of the European Communities, Information Department, Rue de la Loi 200, B-1049 Brussels, Belgium.

This 7 page brochure describes the impact of microelectronics on employment and the problems which will arise from this. The main concern seems to be markets and productivity rather than jobs and people's welfare.

"Multinationals and Female Labour in Latin America" Ofelia Gomez and Rhoda Reddock, **Scholas Journal**, no. 1, 1979. Institute of Social Studies, 251 Badhuisweg, The Hague, Netherlands.

In this 29 page paper, the authors examine the phenomena of multinational corporations and manufactures for export in Latin America and the use of female labor by these corporations. They argue that the present use of unskilled female labor in these enterprises does not represent an integration of women into the industrial labor force but rather a temporary exploitation or "super-exploitation" of the very fact that women are not fully integrated. The paper also reviews the main theories used to explain the position of women in the labor market.

"Politics and Technology — Microprocessors and the Prospect of a New Industrial Revolution" Michael Goldhaber, **Socialist Review**, no. 52, July — August 1980. New Fronts Publishing Co., 4228 Telegraph Avenue, Oakland, California 94609, USA.

Exploring the rapid changes being brought about by the new technology of the microprocessor, this 29 page article examines the possible responses of workers and the significance of these responses for socialism.

"Women and Chips" **Spare Rib**, no. 83, June 1979. 27 Clerkenwell Close, London EC1 OAT, England.

A basic article describing what microtechnology is and how it is affecting women's lives in Britain, this concentrates on the development of word processors, minicomputers using silicon chips. It concludes that their use will create more alienating work conditions and health problems for office workers, who are mainly women.

"Women and the U.N. Code of Conduct on Multinationals — A Development Concern" Anita Anand and Ann Fraker. United Methodist Board of Church and Society, 100 Maryland Avenue NE, Washington, DC 20002, USA.

This working paper summarizes the history and the draft resolutions of the UN Code of Conduct on Multinationals and examines the possible impact it could have on women workers. It criticizes the lack of women's participation in the formulation of the Code and the consequent failure of the Code to deal with issues of first importance to women workers.

audio-visuals

Other audio-visuals are listed under the organizations which produce or distribute them. See especially: Asian Social Institute, Earthwork, INFACT, the National Action/Research on the Military Industrial Complex (NARMIC), the Nationwide Women's Program, and the Pacific-Asia Resources Center (PARC).

Bottle Babies NCC Audio-Visual, Room 860, 475 Riverside Drive, New York, New York 10115, USA.

Filmed in Kenya in 1975, this 30 minute color film in 16mm provides an excellent introduction to the issue of the promotion and use of infant formula in third world countries. Price: US$ 270.

Controlling Interest: The World of the Multinational Corporation California Newsreel, 630 Natoma Street, San Francisco, California 94103, USA.

This 45 minute color film gives an excellent, hardhitting look at the operations and effects of multinational corporations, focusing on Brazil, Chile and the Dominican Republic. Price: US$ 550; rental $ 60.

Formula for Malnutrition Service Center, UMBGM, 7820 Reading Road, Cincinnati, Ohio 45237, USA.

A 16 minute color filmstrip with audio-cassette on the issue of infant formula and its promotion by multinationals.

Into the Mouths of Babes CBS. Available from NCC Audio-Visual Room 860, 475 Riverside Drive, New York, New York 10115, USA.

This 30 minute documentary in 16mm was made in 1978 for Bill Moyers' CBS Reports. It gives a good picture of the methods multinationals use in promoting the sale of baby foods in the third world. Price: US$ 270; rental $ 40.

Managing the Global Plantation American Friends Service Committee, 2426 Oahu Avenue, Honolulu, Hawaii 06822, USA.

This 35 minute slideshow gives the profile of one of the USA's largest agribusiness corporations, Castle & Cooke. It looks critically at the process of diversification which transformed Castle & Cooke into a global corporation, and at its impact on its workers and their communities. Rental: US$ 10.

The Shirt Off Our Back WBGH, Box 1000, Boston, Massachusetts 02118, USA.

A one-hour video program produced by David Fanning, this examines the impact of the shifting textile industry from the western to the southern hemisphere and the adverse impact this has had on workers in both parts of the world. Well documented with interviews with workers, labor organizers, and business representatives. Transcripts are available at US$ 3.

CASA Newsletter/Canada

rural development

This chapter gives an overview of the main policies and trends of the past Development Decades and strategies for the future, and especially their impact on women. Focusing on food production, income generating projects and appropriate technology, it examines these in the light of feminist perspectives and critically questions the concept of «integrating women in development». Emphasis is on how women are developing theory and action in organizing and mobilizing around these issues. The overview is followed by a review of the resources on women and rural development.

This chapter was written by Marilee Karl with help from Anita Anand.

Facing page: F. Botts/FAO

women and rural development: an overview

Marilee Karl

Poverty is most widespread in the rural areas of both developing and developed countries. Since the situation of rural areas has continued to decline over the past few decades, it is not surprising that a great deal of development thought and literature focuses on these areas. Before looking at the situation of rural women in particular, a brief survey of the main policies and trends of the Development Decades is in order.

The goal of the first Development Decade in the 1960s, according to the United Nations General Assembly, was "to accelerate progress towards self-sustaining growth of the economy of the individual nations and their social advancement so as to obtain in each under-developed country a substantial increase in the rate of growth, with each country setting its own target, taking as the objective a minimum rate of growth of aggregate national income of five per cent at the end of the Decade..."[1] During the second Development Decade, emphasis was put on aid or "development assistance" from richer countries to developing ones: "The International Development Strategy for the 1970s was designed to provide developing countries with a larger share of benefits from the economic growth of the developed countries."[2]

What is meant by "economic growth" becomes clear as country after country develops cash crop production for export and export-oriented industry in rapidly growing urban areas and becomes more dependent on western investment and technology and on the international economy. This "economic growth" has disrupted rural cultures, driving massive numbers of farmers from the land to the cities, where some are absorbed in the export-oriented industries and the tourist industry, while others are reduced to poverty, unemployment or prostitution.

Cash cropping for export and the growing investment of giant agricultural multinational corporations, or agribusiness, in developing countries has also led to a decline in food production for local needs. Countries which, before the declaration of the first Development Decade, were able to feed their own populations, are now forced to import food to meet their domestic needs.

Twenty years ago, the developing countries were self-sufficient in food. Now they import 80 million tons of food grains each year; 10% of total consumption. According to the FAO, this could well reach 145 million tons by the end of the eighties.

Lured by the need for foreign exchange earnings and with multinational companies influencing much of their investment policies, many developing countries have neglected domestic food production in favour of cash crop production. The rate of growth of domestic food production in the Third World declined throughout the seventies, particularly in Africa. Such policies have had an economic cost. Twenty years ago Zaire was a net food exporter. Today she spends $ 300 million each year, or one-third of her total export earnings, on food imports.[3]

trickle-down

The World Food Conference in 1974 called for increasing food production through the modernization of agriculture and the use of "inputs" including farm machinery, high yielding varieties of seeds (HYVs), chemical fertilizers, pesticides, herbicides, sophisticated irrigation systems and other technology. The green revolution is the best known of these attempts. It is also widely acknowledged to have failed because inputs, sold mostly by multinational corporations, exceeded outputs.

The majority of farmers in the third world are poor and often landless. The better off farmers are able to strengthen their position through the use of high input agriculture while the poorer ones, who cannot afford these inputs, become further impoverished. The hope of development planners that economic growth benefitting a few in society would "trickle down"

Facing page: ILO

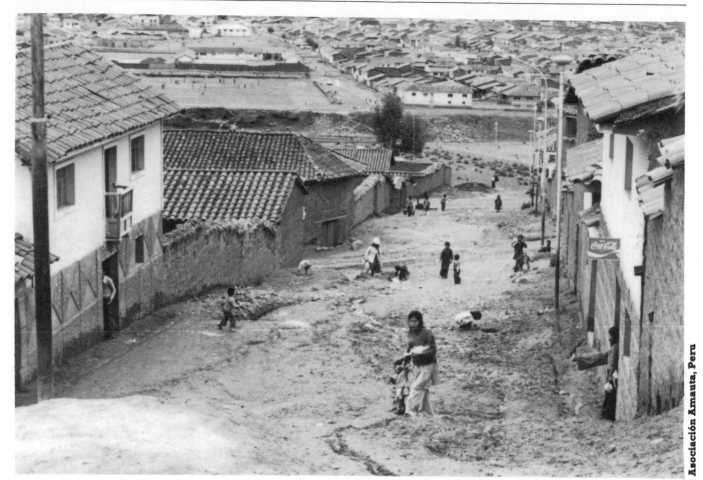

Peruvian peasants waiting for development to trickle down.

to the masses, has proven an illusion:

> The growth that has occurred has done next to nothing to remove world poverty. More people are now living in a condition of utter destitution and starvation than at the beginning of the seventies.
>
> The increase in the number of the poor is not because economic growth has failed to keep pace with the growth in population (only nine countries have shown a persistent, negative per capita growth during the last twenty years). Nor is it simply that economic growth has missed certain sections of the population; though that is a large and important factor.

It is that, in many countries, the poor now constitute a larger proportion of the total population than they did at the start of the sixties. A process of empoverishment has occurred in the Third World which economic growth, in the context of acute inequality — in incomes, in land, in access to work — has accelerated.

The process of growth seems to be forcing more and more people into a position of economic vulnerability. Economic prosperity has not simply missed these people; they have been systematically marginalised or proletarianised. Their ability to supply their own basic needs has been gradually but unrelentingly reduced.[4]

approaches to the food issue

Following the World Food Conference, three main approaches to the food problem emerged, according to a document from the United Nations Research Institute for Social Development (UNRISD). These are identified as the "neo-malthusian," the "enlightened official wisdom" and the "radical" approaches.

"The 'neo-malthusian' approach views the fundamental problem as a race between population growth and increased agricultural production." The basic solution is population control and the improvement of agricultural technologies.

Distribution of food is viewed as a separate problem to be dealt with later.[5]

The "enlightened official wisdom" approach allows for a number of variables in addition to population growth and technology. Some of these are: prices and markets for agricultural commodities, inputs, income levels, investment in food-related activities and facilities, consumption and distribution patterns of food supplies among and within countries, economic growth rates, rural poverty and cooperation among nations. While this approach emphasizes technology, it does not ignore political and economic forces at the national level.

It recommends stabilizing agricultural commodity and input prices; increased credit; investment in agriculture; improvement of inputs, food processing, distribution, storage and marketing; education, training and nutrition programs. This approach also appeals for a new international economic order, agrarian reform, more rapid development, people's participation, less extravagant food consumption in rich countries and the satisfaction of people's basic needs.[6]

The third approach is the "radical" one which maintains that the real problem is poverty caused by the exploitation of the poor by both rich industrialized countries and the elites in the developing countries. This approach argues that "not much can be done about feeding the hungry until existing economic, social and political relationships have been fundamentally reformed." The radicals see "profit-hungry" multinationals as playing a leading role in exploiting the poor. They see food aid and trade "primarily as political weapons of the powerful to maintain their power." They criticize "enlightened official wisdom" for not really altering existing power relationships among nations and classes.[7]

The UNRISD document maintains that *Food security now and during the foreseeable future, for all social groups everywhere, is the issue.*[8] Global analyses and approaches are insufficient. Solutions to the world food problem can only be found through more careful study of food systems in their social contexts.

basic human needs approach

At the World Employment Conference in 1976, the International Labour Organisation (ILO) initiated the Basic Human Needs (BHN) approach to development. The needs identified were:

- minimum requirements of a family for private consumption: adequate food, shelter and clothing, certain household equipment and furniture;
- essential services provided by and for the community at large, such as safe drinking water, sanitation, public transport, and health and educational facilities.

The strategy for attaining these basic needs would include:

- increased employment for the poorest groups in society;
- capital intensive investment in socially appropriate technology;
- more social services financed through progressive taxation;
- attempts to decrease differences in consumption patterns between social groups;

Maggie Murray

Many basic human needs are supplied by women. Women collecting water in an Ujamaa village in Tanzania.

- the creation and support of institutions which promote people's participation.[9]

The World Bank also promoted the Basic Human Needs Approach, but with more emphasis on the economic aspects and less on people's participation. "In the World Bank's model, the emphasis is given to increasing the share of the poor in new income, rather than in an initial redistribution of assets followed by high growth rates. Basic Human Needs in this model become more a guide for distributing income than a fully fledged strategy for development."[10]

Many third world countries see the emphasis on basic human needs of peoples within countries as an attempt by development agencies and industrialized nations to divert attention from the inequities within the world economic system and between rich and poor countries. Their efforts to deal with the inequities in distribution of income, food, goods and services nationally are hindered by an unbalanced distribution of resources on the international level. The focus on basic needs is a way to avoid dealing with demands for a New International Economic Order, according to this point of view.

the new international economic order

The Declaration and Action Program on the Establishment of a New International Economic Order (NIEO) was adopted by the United Nations General Assembly in 1974. Proposed

Planting rice seedlings in Sri Lanka. Women make up the majority of the world's food producers...

by the Group of 77, it came as the result of the growing realization that the enormous gap in wealth between rich and poor nations is due in large part to an international economic system which fosters these imbalances.[11]

The NIEO would encompass many elements: an increased share of world industrial and agricultural production for developing countries; negotiations and agreements on raw material and commodity prices; cooperation among developing countries to include greater flow of technology, trade and communications among themselves, balancing off dependency on the present North-South flow; fairer trade regulations; reform of the International Monetary System; development assistance, including finance and transfer of technology from developed to developing countries; regulation of multinational corporations; and third world control of its own natural resources. Since 1974, there has been much debate and negotiation, but little progress in achieving the demands of the NIEO. The North is reluctant to make concessions, although supporters of the NIEO stress that it is a mutually beneficial system, that the peace and security of the world will be threatened as long as the international economic system favors rich nations over poor.

An official from the United Nations Institute of Training and Research (UNITAR) states:

While the NIEO focusses largely on inequities between countries, the basic needs approach focusses on inequities within countries. To meet basic needs on a sustained basis in developing countries would require considerable investment and the expansion of production. It is interesting, therefore, that the pressure for the basic needs-oriented development has come from UN special agencies, and development research and donor agencies of the industrialized countries. It is a reaction to the pressure from the developing countries for a NIEO whose purpose is to remove the so-called "assymetry" in international economic relations between developed (consumer) and developing (producer) countries.[12]

strategies for the 1980s

Not until the end of the 1970s was in-depth international attention given to two essential elements of rural development: land and agrarian reform. The World Conference on Agrarian Reform and Rural Development (WCARRD) in 1979 recommended that governments take steps to ensure more equitable access of farmers to land, rural services and inputs. This was also the first intergovernmental conference since International Women's Year to give serious consideration to the special needs and situations of rural women and to call for their "integration into development."[13]

The approaches to development in the 1980s do not differ

radically from those proposed in the 1970s: they stress the importance of making the NIEO a reality, of improving economic growth and of continuing to modernize agriculture.

The seventies demonstrated how "growth-alone" strategies can worsen poverty. Nevertheless substantial levels of economic growth are a necessary precondition for the abolition of poverty in the Third World. To this end, and in order to strengthen their economies and move away from the precarious dependence on agriculture and the export of raw materials, developing countries need annual growth rates well in excess of the dismal 5% or so currently predicted for the immediate future. The world's poorest countries in particular, need a substantial injection of resources to climb out of the economic stagnation they suffered throughout the seventies.[14]

The Brandt Report, entitled *North-South: A Programme for Survival*, recommends increasing food production through more modernization, mechanization and the use of high yield seeds, pesticides, chemical fertilizers and other high technological inputs. It also calls for massive aid and transfer of resources from the developed to the developing world.[15]

Agriculture: Toward 2000, a report of the Food and Agricultural Organization of the United Nations, "proposes a strategy for development of world agriculture to the end of the century, with particular reference to developing countries."[16] According to this report, it will be necessary to increase food production if hunger and malnutrition are to be eliminated in the world. Food production can be increased only through increased modernization, mechanization and the use of more inputs. It will require more investment in agriculture and incentives, including higher prices for produce, for farmers. At the same time, attention should be given to the distribution of income and access to resources among the rural populations.

AT 2000, as the report is often called, stresses the importance of increasing crop production for export by developing countries. It discusses the issues of international trade policies and commodity prices and the importance of these. It also maintains that continued financial and technical aid must be given by developed countries to developing ones and that food aid will also remain necessary.

The report touches on the issues of population growth and its relationship to hunger, asserting that lower birth rates in developing countries would relieve some of the problems relating to hunger, but would not basically change the problems of world agriculture or the policies needed. On the controversial issue of feeding cereals to animals in a world where millions of people go hungry, the report feels that the facts and solutions put forward by people who argue that less cereal should be given to animals and more to people are too simple.[17]

women's basic needs and the NIEO

Will the Basic Needs Approach and the NIEO benefit women? There is some doubt about this. Devaki Jain of the Institute of Social Studies, New Delhi, questions the usefulness of either the NIEO or the Basic Needs Approach for women,

J. van Acker/WFP

... and almost all the world's food preparers. Upper Volta.

as these "gloss over the institutional, legal and political aspects of inequality" and do not deal with necessary attitudinal changes.[18]

Since the Basic Needs Approach is supposed to help the poorest and neediest among the rural population, why does it not improve the lot of overworked, neglected and impoverished women?

One of the general criticisms of the BNA is that it does not stress the need for the redistribution of land and other forms of wealth. This criticism can be made in even stronger terms as it applies to women. There is not even a mention of a redistribution of resources between the sexes.... But until women's direct access to resources is specified, there can be no real realignment of economic opportunities...between the sexes. This leads directly to a second criticism: women, especially rural women, traditionally produce a wide range of goods and services. The ILO document distinguishes requirements for the satisfaction of basic needs provided by the family from those provided by the community. But some of the latter, such as water, power, health and sanitation, are met entirely by women, and as such are viewed as exacting no economic or human cost. At what stage, then, or under what social impetus, are these demands on women's time and energy to be transferred to the community?[19]

A meeting of the Asian and Pacific Centre for Women and Development criticized the Basic Needs Approach because:

In the examination of the basic needs of a community, the household or family cannot be taken as the basic unit of analysis. For just as *between* households there is an inequality in the distribution of goods and services, so too *within* households there is an imbalance in distribution.... (The Basic Needs Approach) offers nothing towards raising of the community's consciousness about the myths and beliefs which stifle the lives of women; it does not encourage the growth in women of individual attributes other than motherhood or femininity; it does not lead as such to self-confidence and self-esteem nor to an increased consciousness of their strengths and abilities; it does not recognise their need for economic and psychological independence."[20]

The meeting identified some of women's "critical needs": lightening their workload; increasing their access to income; recognizing their already considerable contribution to economic and social life; education as a liberating force, and health. Women must identify for themselves their critical economic, cultural and psychological needs and for this they must have opportunities for consciousness raising among themselves and for organizing and mobilizing.[21]

Similar criticism can be leveled at the NIEO. Increasing use of technology and capital intensive investment may result, if present patterns continue, in the elimination of women from the wage labor force. The danger exists "that in taking advantage of better export returns, productivity improvements in rural areas will concentrate on export crops, and since their production is usually under the control of men—using family labour — rural women will not share equitably. The custodial role of male heads of household could also be strengthened and the backstop gardening status of women confirmed."[22]

integrating women in development

Because women's needs were largely neglected by development planners and policy makers during the first and second Development Decades, and because their situations have deteriorated, attempts have been made to integrate women in development. These range from recommendations in development documents, to directing special projects and programs to women, adding women's components to existing programs, allocating resources to such projects and components, and recruiting women in development agencies.

The question — Is integrating women into development the answer? — must be raised. Elise Boulding says that "in one sense, what has already been accomplished in the first world is precisely 'development' and the integration of women into it." Yet first world women have a subordinate position in this development, with unequal wages, the full burden of household and child care, and a lack of social services.

This is not a model of development, or of the integration of women into development, that one would care to commend to other countries... What are women to do? To cooperate with those who wish to integrate them into the present international order is to destroy all their hope for a different future. But even the much-heralded "new" international economic order, to the extent that its third-world authors have revealed their intentions, does not promise to be very different from the old — not for the poor,

least of all for women. It only offers the opportunity for more third-world women to become marginalized labor in the modern sectors of their national economies, or continue as rural landless laborers (which most of them already are) at slightly higher wages.[23]

Many women around the world are coming to this realization. This dawning can even be traced at the level of intergovernmental conferences during the International Women's Decade.

The declaration of International Women's Year and the International Women's Year Conference in 1975, the declaration of a Women's Decade and the Mid-Decade Conference on Women in 1980 all focused attention on women and development.

The World Plan of Action for the UN Decade for Women called for:

- the involvement of women in the strengthening of international security and peace through participation at all relevant levels in national, intergovernmental and UN bodies;
- furthering the political participation of women in national societies at every level;
- strengthening educational and training programs for women;
- integrating women workers into the labor force of every country at every level, according to accepted international standards;
- more equitably distributing health and nutrition services to take account of the responsibilities of women everywhere for the health and feeding of their families;
- increasing governmental assistance for the family unit;
- directly involving women, as the primary producers of population, in the development of population programs and other programs affecting the quality of life of indi-

ILO

Potters' village, Dahomey.

In both developed and developing nations, women bear the burden of the household tasks. Washing clothes, Ecuador.

viduals of all ages, in family groups and outside them, including housing and social services of every kind.[24]

The Report of the World Conference of the United Nations Decade for Women: Equality, Development and Peace, held in 1980 reviews the progress (or lack of it) in achieving these goals and sets forth a plan of action for the second half of the Women's Decade. The report shows a significant advance in recognizing that legislation and equal rights alone are not enough; that employment for women, for instance, can result in greater exploitation rather than independence; that sexist attitudes and prejudices play an important role in discrimination against women. It sets forth a considerable number of recommendations, particularly in regard to employment, health and education.[25]

The Decade for Women produced not only paper but a Voluntary Fund for small projects in developing countries and the establishment of an International Research and Training Institute for the Advancement of Women (INSTRAW). The derisory amounts alloted to these programs, however, indicate a lack of real commitment on the part of governments and international development agencies towards improving the lives of over one-half of the world's population.

Women have put in an enormous amount of effort in bringing about the Women's Decade conferences and plans of action and in getting WCARRD to focus on the needs of rural women. Their work is commendable. How much concrete improvement this sort of effort can bring is always debatable. Women can use the recommendations to urge governments

and development agencies to implement them, but governments can, and have, used such forums and recommendations to ease their consciences, to make a display of supposed concern for the well-being of women, and to absolve themselves from taking any serious steps to stop the oppression of women. Nonetheless, as Mallica Vajrathon of Thailand points out, "we should not ignore the fact that in global terms and especially in developing countries, there are many feminists who are working in the governments and many at high policy levels ....It is now up to us to see to it that the programme of action is in operation by different countries, different development groups, networks of women's organizations and individuals."[26]

Some feminists have serious doubts about the possibility of achieving very much through international intergovernmental conferences and recommendations, plans of action, and work at the governmental level. Their priority is organizing and mobilizing women on the local level. This need not be an either/or proposition. Feminists working on all levels could profit from increased communication, linking and supporting each other.

feminism and development

The feminist movement in the first world has, on the whole, taken little part in the debate about women and development.

Banking earth, Kenya.

ILO

Feminists in industrialized countries tend to look at development as an issue concerning only the third world. Preoccupied with particular issues which have been ignored and neglected in their own countries — child care, reproductive rights, violence against women— they often fail to make the connections between these issues and the political, economic and patriarchal structures which dominate the whole world. Thus they run the risk of remaining in a ghetto of so-called "women's issues."

This is unfortunate. The feminist movement has an important contribution to make· on both the theoretical and the practical levels by demonstrating the interrelatedness of oppressive political, economic and sexist institutions and by working for the transformation of all of these at the same time. At an international workshop on Feminist Ideology and Structures in the First Half of the Decade for Women, feminists from both developing and developed countries asserted that "the oppression of women is rooted in both inequities and discrimination based on sex and in poverty and the injustices of the political and economic systems based on race and class." They identified two long term feminist goals of the women's movement:

> First the freedom from oppression for women involves not only equity, but also the right of women to freedom of choice, and the power to control their own lives within and outside of the home. Having control over our lives and bodies is essential to ensure a sense of dignity and autonomy for every woman.

The second goal of feminism is... the removal of all forms

of inequity and oppression through the creation of a more just social and economic order, nationally and internationally. This means the involvement of women in national liberation struggles, in plans for national development, and in local and global strategies for change.[27]

At the Mid-Decade Conference on Women and at the nongovernmental Forum held parallel to this, a lack of communication between the "women and development" community and feminists was evident. Summing up the experience there, Anita Anand from India writes: "The feminists who have worked on the theory and praxis of feminism and the roots of oppression of women have been isolated for too long from the mainstream women's movement. Meanwhile, groups working on issues overtly affecting women have failed to interject a feminist perspective in their work."[28] There was lively and often heated discussion among women from different parts of the world as they grappled with this problem.

Some women from industrialized countries felt that the conference was too "politicized." Feminists from the third world argued that it is impossible to separate women's issues from political issues. Mallica Vajrathon writes:

> Many of the women from the developing countries were puzzled when they were accused of "politicizing the conference." They asked, "Why is the politicization of the conference such a bad thing? Aren't we supposed to participate in politics; and who said that the issues that are of concern to women are not political; and that political issues should not be discussed at the Conference on the Decade of Women?"... Why is the issue of transformation of society not of any concern to women when they compose half of the citizens of the society? It is dangerous indeed for the feminists to limit the issue which women should be concerned with only to the issue of discrimination on the ground of biological differences and leave the issue of

Returning from work in the orchards, Congo (Brazzaville).

ILO

Building anti-erosion terraces, Honduras. So why do development planners still believe the myth that women don't do heavy work?

national formation and international politics only for men to talk about. The male establishment would be just delighted to keep women busy with issues of their bodies and psychology.[29]

Feminists also made the point that "the problem with the UN official conference in Copenhagen was not that it was 'politicized,' but that it failed to consider issues from a feminist political perspective or even in terms of how they were specifically viewed or affected by women."[30]

Misunderstandings about feminism were also rampant at the conference and could be summed up in the statement which appeared as the quote of the day in the daily Forum paper: "To talk feminism to a woman who has no water, no food and no home, is to talk nonsense." About this, Anita Anand writes:

This phrase... was typical of how not only the media, but ardent proponents of integrating women into development of societies have viewed feminism. While it is true that certain basic needs — food, clothing, shelter — are essential and must be met before people can critically analyse their situations, it is not true that feminism is an "ism" or that it is a luxury for women. It is a basic approach to life. Feminism is an ideology that offers a holistic concept of how a society should be shaped in order to help all

people realize their full potential. As such, it does not separate the political, social and economic elements of a society (and as they pertain to the struggle of women) or put any one of these elements first....

In any struggle, historically, women have been made to believe that struggles against racism, imperialism and colonialism are more important and the struggle against patriarchy has been relegated to the lowest status, if recognized at all. Simply, women have been asked to choose between working on women's issues... or the "real issues." This artifically created priority has been a source of tension in and among women who want to work for a better society, as well as against the oppression of women....

Women from developing countries are forced to defend the oppression of poverty as a major agenda item to be worked on. Women from developed countries, learning from their experiences, make a case of having to work against the oppression of sexism and of challenging the patriarchal system.... With conscious attempts to bring women from different economies together, to work on building feminist theory and praxis based on their experiences, much progress has been made, and there is a mutual respect and understanding of each other's agenda. From this process has emerged a consciousness that the struggle must be waged on both fronts, simultaneously, against poverty and sexism.

Naïr Benedicto/Agência F4

Peasants resisting eviction from the land they have worked for years. Brazil, 1979.

Concentrating on one without work on the other is meaningless.[31]

A consciousness is also emerging of the need for women to join together globally to overcome their exploitation and oppression. This is not to say that there is any one approach or strategy to be followed everywhere. Women in any given place will decide themselves how best to mobilize and liberate themselves. Since so many of the elements they must deal with are global – international economic and political systems, multinational corporations, development and population control policies – women will also have to tackle these issues on a global level. Women are profiting from the exchange of experiences and ideas and by giving each other support and solidarity. As Mallica Vajrathon says:

> The strength of the Women's Movement lies *in* the variety of strategies and actions aimed at the existing structure that needs to be changed at both local and international levels. The feminist network around the world will be able to bring richness of experiences of liberation struggles from one part of the world to the other throughout this coming decade, to achieve the ultimate aim of development – which is the constant improvement of the well-being of the entire population on this planet.[32]

The following sections of this article focus on development policies in rural areas and how these affect women food producers in particular, and on some attempts to improve women's situations through the use of appropriate technology and income generating projects. These issues are examined in the light of feminist questions and insights. This article also looks at some of the actions and directions women are taking in organizing and mobilizing around these issues.

Chris Pennarts, Holland

International solidarity. Dutch women march in support of the mothers of disappeared persons in Argentina.

Footnotes

1   Cited in Debesh Bhattacharya, "Development: State of the World at Beginning of Third Development Decade," *ACFOA Development Dossier*, no. 6 (August 1981), p. 4.

2   *Towards a World Economy that Works* (New York: United Nations, 1980), p. 26.

3   Ken Laidlaw and Roy Laishley, *Crisis Decade* (London: International Coalition for Development Action, 1980), p. 24.

4   Ibid., p. 2.

5   *Food Systems and Society* (Geneva: United Nations Research Institute for Social Development, 1978), p. 5. This document lists a number of studies which represent this approach such as Lester Brown, *By Bread Alone* (New York: Praeger, 1974) and Meadows et al., *The Limits to Growth* (Club of Rome, 1970).

6   Ibid., pp. 2-9.

7   Ibid., pp. 7-8. UNRISD identifies major proponents of this approach as Susan George, *How the Other Half Dies: The Real Reasons for World Hunger* (London: Penguin Books, 1976); Frances Moore-Lappé and Joseph Collins, *Food First* (Boston: Houghton Mifflin Co., 1977).

8   Ibid., p. 4.

9   For a concise overview of the Basic Needs Approach, see David Pollard, "Basic Human Needs as a Strategy for Development," *ACFOA Development Dossier*, no. 6. For a review of the literature and a bibliography, see M. Rutjes, *Basic-Needs Approach; A Survey of its Literature*, Bibliography no. 4 (The Hague: Centre for the Study of Education in Developing Countries, 1979).

10   Pollard, "Basic Human Needs," p. 15.

11   Formed in the 1960s, the Group of 77 was originally comprised of 77 countries demanding a restructuring of the world economy. It is now comprised of 118 countries in various stages of development.

12   Robert Jordan, UNITAR, cited in Dieter Brauer, "Basic Needs Strategy – A Controversial Approach to International Development Efforts," *Development and Cooperation*, no. 5 (1979), p. 28.

13   See *World Conference on Agrarian Reform and Rural Development Report* (Rome: Food and Agricultural Organization, 1979), especially pp. 10-11.

14   *Crisis Decade*, p. 39.

15   Willy Brandt et al., *North-South: A Programme for Survival*, Report of the Independent Commission on International Development Issues (London and Sydney: Pan Books, 1980). A good summary of the Brandt report is given in John Langmore, "The Brandt Report," *ACFOA Development Dossier*, no. 6, pp. 18-21.

16   *Agriculture: Toward 2000* (Rome: Food and Agricultural Organization, 1981), p. v. This report is a revised and considerably shortened version of a report on the provisional results of a study presented to the 1979 Conference of FAO. The provisional report, which was produced in a limited number of copies, contained much more detail in regard to how the suggested strategies could be carried out.

17   The "food-feed controversy" is discussed on p. 36 of *Agriculture: Toward 2000*.

18   Devaki Jain, "Women are Separate," *Development Forum* (August 1978).

19   Ingrid Palmer, "New Official Ideas on Women and Development," *IDS Bulletin*, vol. 10, no. 3 (April 1979), p. 51.

20   *The Critical Needs of Women* (Kuala Lumpur: Asian and Pacific Centre for Women and Development, 1977), pp. 5 and 6.

21   See *Critical Needs* for the discussion of these needs.

22   Palmer, "New Official Ideas," p. 52.

23   Elise Boulding, *Women: The Fifth World*, Foreign Policy Association, Headline Series (New York, 1980), pp. 48 and 52.

24   Ibid., p. 30. This booklet contains a good summary of the events around International Women's Year and of the World Plan of Action for the UN Decade for Women.

25   See the *Report of the World Conference of the United Nations Decade for Women: Equality, Development and Peace* (New York: United Nations, 1980).

26   Mallica Vajrathon, "Discussing the Differences," *Broadsheet*, no. 93 (October 1981), p. 39.

27   *Report of the International Workshop on Feminist Ideology and Structures in the First Half of the Decade for Women* (Kuala Lumpur: Asian and Pacific Centre for Women and Development, 1979), p. 1.

28   Anita Anand, "Copenhagen 1980: Taking Women Seriously," mimeographed (Washington, DC: United Methodist Church, 1980), p. 2.

29   Vajrathon, "Discussing the Differences," p. 37.

30   Charlotte Bunch, "Copenhagen and Beyond: Prospects for Global Feminism," *Quest: A Feminist Quarterly*, vol. 5, no. 4 (1982).

31   Anand, "Copenhagen 1980," p. 2 and p. 4.

32   Vajrathon, "Discussing the Differences," p. 39.

BEFORE AID: Agricultural life was much simpler...

NOW WE'VE GOT AID... that's all changed....

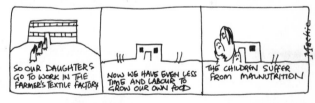

So THEY'RE GIVING US MORE AID...!

Liz Mackie/ISIS

women, land and food production

Marilee Karl

Women are the majority of the world's food producers. They make up 60 to 80 percent of agricultural workers in Africa and Asia and more than 40 percent in Latin America.[1] Women all over the world have always worked in agriculture and in food preserving, preparing and cooking. They plant, weed, supply water for irrigation, harvest, thresh, winnow, tend poultry and animals, store foods, grind flour and meal, preserve foods as sauces, syrups, juices and in many other ways.

The work they do depends not only on where they live but on their place within the rural economy: are they landless or landowning, tenant farmers or sharecroppers, members of a cooperative or communal farm; what is the size of their landholdings; do they have their own plots, their own income from the cooperative, or are these reserved for a male "head of the family"? These are some of the factors which determine women's work.

A characteristic common to most of these women is a long, hard day. The African Training and Research Centre for Women (ATRCW) describes a farmer's day like this:

She rises before dawn and walks to the fields. In the busy seasons, she spends some nine to ten hours hoeing, planting, weeding or harvesting. She brings food and fuel home from the farm, walks long distances for water carrying a pot which may weigh 20 kilogrammes or more, grinds and pounds grains, cleans the house, cooks while nursing her infant, washes the dishes and the clothes, minds the children, and generally cares for the household. She processes and stores food and markets excess produce, often walking long distances with heavy loads in difficult terrain. She must also attend to the family's social obligations such as weddings and funerals. She may have to provide fully for herself and her children. During much of the year she may labour for 15 to 16 hours each day and she works this way until the day she delivers her baby, frequently resuming work within a day or two of delivery.[2]

The Bambara women of Mali, in the villages around Segou, share all the tasks on the family worked fields, spreading organic fertilizers, weeding, banking, securing the fields against predators, harvesting and transporting crops. In addition, they work individual plots, to provide food for their families, "early in the morning when they are not cooking; before beginning to work on the collective field, or when the sun is high and when they have ceased working on the collective field in order to rest." They gather leaves and fruit and make beverages, cakes, sauces, butter and soap; raise poultry and small grazing animals; market surplus foods, drinks and cotton goods. They practice the crafts traditional to their family: pottery, dyeing or basketweaving. Cloth weaving, tool making, sewing and embroidery are done by men.[3]

Landless Harijan women in a Punjabi village of India told an interviewer:

We are up at daybreak and we don't get to see our beds until late in the night. We are on our feet all day... We have not only to harvest the crop but also tie it into bundles. If a bundle gets scattered or you take an extra minute over it, the men shower you with filthy abuses... Cooking the food, tending the cattle, fetching firewood on the way home from the fields, cooking again at night and managing the whole house, the children — it's all on our shoulders — and it's twice as much work as a man does. The pace of work is almost bewildering — there's not a moment's respite all day.[4]

In spite of these long hours, women have very little control, very little say in decisions about food production. They produce the world's food, cook it and serve it, yet they are mal-

Agricultural extension worker demonstrating the use of fertilizer, Malawi.

F. Botts/FAO

nourished. Food is distributed unequally, not only among countries and social classes, but within the family. Men eat first; women and children get the leftovers, in many places. Women's nutritional needs are greatest because of their work, childbearing and breastfeeding, but they get less food, fewer calories, less of the best available than men.[5]

development and women

Given women's essential role in food production and the great amount of work they do, it would appear to make sense that development programs would be directed to women to help them improve their farming methods, reduce their work load, and give them access to rural services such as water and fuel supplies, credit, training, land and markets. But no, rural development projects for the improvement of agriculture are directed almost exclusively to men.

Ever since Ester Boserup clearly pointed this out in 1970 in her now classic book *Women's Role in Economic Development,* many others have tried to discover the causes of this and to propose solutions. The call to integrate women into development is an attempt to rectify previous neglect of women by development planners and to fit women into plans where they have been left out. Boserup and many after her appear to assume that the benefits of modernization can be extended to women. But has modernization really been so beneficial to the majority of men? How can women fit into

development models which by their very nature marginalize women and do not promote the well-being of all people?

Researchers from many disciplines have contributed to understanding why women have been left out of the development process. Historians, sociologists and economists point out the roots of this in colonialism and the economic system. Feminists have made a valuable contribution by showing how sexist attitudes and male prejudices about women have af-

Drying cow dung for fuel, Bangladesh.

F. Mattioli/FAO

74

fected the policies of both colonial administrators and development planners. Feminists have also shown the importance of analyzing women's role in reproduction and the family, as well as in production. Socialist feminists in particular stress the intertwining of gender relations and class relations, of reproduction and production. Both must be examined to discover the causes of women's subordination and both must be addressed to overcome the oppression of women. Feminist anthropologists and ethnographers have given insights into the division of labor, families, and roles of men and women. Finally, the people who are the objects of all this research and analysis have voiced their own needs and desires, have sought their own solutions, in struggling against sexist discrimination and structures, in resisting oppressive economic systems and working conditions, and in organizing themselves.

Some of these issues and contributions, as they relate to food production, are briefly surveyed here. The resource section reviews many more.

are women invisible?

Recent development literature talks about "invisible" women, but women are not invisible. It is the development planners who are blind to them. Women are there to be seen at work in the fields, gardens, yards, courtyards and homes for anyone who will take the trouble to look. Part of the problem is that development planners often only look at work in the modern, cash sector of the economy, ignoring the unwaged but essential work of women. Thus, it is men who make up the statistics of agricultural wage labor, and it is their production which figures in the Gross National Product (GNP).

colonial roots

The roots of this situation go back a long way. Some of them can be traced to 19th century colonialism when westerners introduced a money economy, wage labor and cash crops in some parts of Africa and Asia. They absorbed only men into the economy as wage earners in mines and plantations growing crops for export. These men were grossly exploited and women suffered as much or even more. With men no longer available to help in some of the tasks, such as clearing the land, women were left with all the work involved in food production, with little or no opportunity for an independent source of income.

In Africa,

the colonialists brought with them their own beliefs that women should stay at home with the children. They primarily sought male wage labor to do the heavy work on their mines and farms. The Europeans' preconceived perceptions fit nicely with the emerging colonial pattern in which women stayed home in the rural areas, using pre-existing technologies to grow the necessary food and raise the children. This provided a convenient rationale for paying the men wages barely adequate to support themselves alone.[6]

Maggie Murray

Men and women cooperate in building a storehouse for grain, Upper Volta.

Family sugar cane processing, Bolivia.

the pattern continues

This pattern continues today. Development planners and governments promote commercial farming and cash crops for export, drawing mainly men into agricultural wage labor. They neglect the women engaged in subsistence farming, growing the food for their families. The work these women do is essential to society. "Why then have their needs not been recognized by the chief architects of development?" two women officers of UNICEF ask.

Why have women, especially poor women, not been considered seriously in the formulation of action programmes? And why has legal discrimination persisted? A number of explanations can be proposed.

First, planners, administrators, legislators, and jurists have tended, for their image of women, to rely upon an elite-derived model reinforced by Western middle-class stereotypes. Colonizers and later the mass media further strengthened these perspectives. In this view, women perform strictly domestic functions geared to family nurturance, while men undertake all the economic and political roles within both the family and the community. Moreover, those areas of customary or religious law most frequently incorporated into modern civil law have been marriage and inheritance customs, the most discriminatory areas in so far as women and property are concerned...

A second explanation for the failure to include women in development on equal terms stems from the monopoly by males of development planning, administrative, legislative, and juridical posts...

The problem is not strictly a sex-linked one, however; class positions also affect it — a third explanation. Because national leaders have almost universally come from the ranks of the educated elites, they have grown up alienated from the reality of poverty.... The heavy burden of women outside the home falls beyond their range of experience... A fourth explanation regarding the weak position allocated to poor women affirms the general failure of the development process to provide all poor people, women or men, with power...[7]

In her book, *The Domestication of Women: Discrimination in Developing Societies*, Barbara Rogers identifies the prejudices that male development planners have about women as a cause of the discrimination against women in development programs. She examines how these prejudices distort research and data collection.

worse off than before

The modernization of agriculture often leaves women food producers worse off than before. With the best land under cultivation for commercial crops, women must work harder on poorer and smaller plots of land. Not only does cash cropping deprive them of men's help, it brings them additional tasks and burdens. Once they could produce a surplus to barter or sell locally, but now they cannot compete with multinationals, commercial agriculture or cooperatives. If they cannot find the time or means to earn money or goods in other ways, they must go without.

A few of the many available examples illustrate how "development" has detrimental effects on women:

> With less time to spend on crops, travelling longer distances to reach the fields and working with poorer soil, women in Ghana began to substitute cassava for yams. Cassava may be planted any time of the year and needs little weeding. Although this crop change resulted in less work, it brought other negative results. Cassava is less nutritious and also depletes the soil to such a degree that it cannot be inter-cropped with vegetables and legumes as was the practice with yams. The vegetables and legumes no longer grown are another valuable vitamin and protein source lost to the family. As a result of such dietary changes, kwashiokor, a severe nutritional disease affecting children, has begun to appear where it was unknown before.[8]

In Upper Volta, where development agencies have been promoting animal traction, weeding, hoeing and harvesting is still done by hand.

> Whereas, previously a family would cultivate an average of 1.5 hectares, with animal traction it may cultivate at least three times as much. It follows that women's work in the fields has increased very considerably, and it goes without saying that it is men who use the plough... In a country where there are no agricultural labourers, the natural consequences of such a scheme are to maintain or increase polygamy and large families so that they can help with the

Workers on a rubber plantation, Malaysia.

agricultural work... Agricultural schemes have imposed other burdens on women. It is they who have to carry larger quantities of produce from the fields to the village or market, and to process the crop by hand when no manual or power operated machinery exists in the area.[9]

The "White Revolution" in India illustrates the manner in which an inherently good development — the introduction of dairies to improve the production and distribution of pasteurized whole milk to urban areas — can sometimes have seriously detrimental effects on rural women. In Gujarat State, women of the poorer castes used to graze the buffalo, milk them, market the butter in nearby towns and retain the skimmed butter milk for their families' diet. Now their marketing activity has largely been displaced and the dairies run by men. The meagre independent earnings they used to receive have in some cases nearly disappeared (there are very few women employed by the dairies), the family no longer has the nutritional benefits of butter milk, cash is needed to buy the milk (or is foregone if whole milk is retained), and no alternative employment or income is available... In Kaira district, where the milk producers are women, they only form 10 per cent of the co-operatives' membership and thereby do not receive a fair share of the payments.[10]

Using standard economic indicators, the Maya lowlands of Belize appeared to be developing rapidly in the early 1970s, after the expansion of the sugarcane industry. A closer study shows that men working in the industry control most of the money which rapidly flows out for the purchase of trucks, liquor and other imported goods. With men no longer helping to clear the land, the women farmers produce less food for the table and less fodder for the poultry and small animals. Pres-

Sorting coffee beans in Ethiopia.

Road building in Chile.

tige and status now lie in the purchase of western goods, with the consequent devaluation of women's role. The nutritional level of women and children has dropped.[11]

The solution cannot lie in simply "extending the benefits of modernization" to women. Modernization does not benefit the majority of men either, when it is tied to an economic system in which certain countries of the world exploit others, and certain classes within a country profit from the exploitation of other men and women. To be of benefit to women, modernization would have to be adapted to the needs of women for both production and reproduction, not women to the needs of modernization, as is usually the case.

modernization and agribusiness

Agriculture has been modernized mainly in the cash crop sector. Governments, development agencies and international financial institutions, such as the World Bank and the International Monetary Fund, encourage export cash crops as a way for third world countries to earn foreign exchange. Multinational agribusiness buys up land from rich absentee landlords and governments, as well as from marginal and small holders, converting it for production of a single crop such as coffee, bananas, coconut or sugar, to export to richer countries. With limited and poor quality land left for local crops and subsistence farming, developing countries must import basic food for local consumption.[12]

Commercial agriculture draws mostly men into the workforce, training them in the use of new techniques, inputs and machines. With women continuing to feed their families through their subsistence agriculture, agribusiness can pay low wages to men. When agribusiness hires women, it is for the most tedious and lowest paid jobs, precarious seasonal work, and food processing and packaging. Agribusiness also keeps wages low by bringing in migrant workers from other states or countries, especially when local farmers begin to organize for their rights and for better wages.

Agribusiness has created new jobs for some people, but it has put many more out of work. Mechanization decreases the need for labor. Small farmers, driven off their land or out of business by big commercial farming, become impoverished or migrate to the cities in search of work, often in multinational industries such as textiles, electronics and tourism.

This process causes abrupt and enormous disruption of families and communities. Traditional culture and ways of life are torn apart as new values and goods are introduced and new divisions of labor are created. Women are deprived of sources of income and livelihood and are burdened with additional work. People of differing castes, colors, races, ages and sexes are pitted against each other as they try to eke out a living.

Agribusiness, governments and development agencies have introduced measures which lead to increased malnutrition, poverty and greater inequality in the distribution of income and food. High technology and inputs are usually available only to the better-off farmers. The increased yields and profits of the richer farmers enable them to strengthen their positions and to squeeze out the poorer farmers, thereby sharpening class distinctions. Pursued in this manner, modernization of agriculture enables an international elite, the multinational corporations, to join hands with local and national elites to make still further inroads into the economy, at the expense of the poor.

women's lost knowledge

High technology agriculture depends heavily on imports from industrialized countries and on the multinational cor-

Rubber worker, Malaysia.

Spraying high-yield coconut seedlings with fungicide, Philippines.

porations which manufacture and market high yielding varieties of seeds (HYVs), pesticides, chemical fertilizers, tractors and other farm machinery. Since they monopolize and virtually control the production of these things, multinationals are making huge profits from high input agriculture. Genetic diversity — the number and varieties of plants and seeds — is decreasing rapidly as high yielding varieties push the others off the market. Since multinationals control the seed market, governments and farmers have no choice but to buy the HYVs. This has serious consequences when epidemics of plant diseases and pests sweep through areas where HYVs have replaced domestic seed varieties. While not as high yielding as the hybrids, traditional seed varieties have adapted to their habitat and have developed resistance to disease, pests, and climatic and geographical conditions. They usually do not require all the expensive inputs.[13]

Non-governmental organizations are compaigning for the preservation of traditional seed varieties in seed banks, set up by agencies such as the Food and Agricultural Organization. It is also necessary to preserve the traditional knowledge of how to cultivate these seeds, however. This resides with peasants and in oral tradition, not with the agricultural experts and technicians trained in high input agriculture. Women have been the traditional farmers and it is they who possess this knowledge. As Elise Boulding says: "Much valuable food-related technology is lost because it is in the hands of women and is not treated as a subject worthy of study by development specialists."[14]

To be concerned with the negative effects of modernization and with the loss of traditional agricultural knowledge does not imply a desire to return to some imagined golden age of traditional agriculture. Agriculture can and should be improved, modernized and made more productive. This,

however, can be done while using and building on the expertise and knowledge farmers already possess. The effects of modernization depend to a great extent upon the economic system and the development perspective within which it is used.

agrarian and land reform

Land is the essential resource for agriculture. The ownership, use and control of land determines who benefits from agricultural production. It is important for access to water, fuel, markets, credit and training as well as to membership and participation in cooperatives, community organizations and decision-making bodies.

Land reform, or changes in the land tenure system, must be a priority if the lot of the poorest rural food producers is to be improved. Whether these changes involve redistribution or collectivization of land, they touch issues of land ownership, power and control. Carried out within a larger program of agrarian reform, they also bring changes in access to energy, credit, markets, training and technology.

The interweaving of political, economic and patriarchal structures becomes evident in programs of agrarian and land reform. Even programs designed to alter radically the relations among rural classes may bring about or perpetuate the subordination of women.

The history of land policies, from those of colonial administrators through those of development planners and land reform programs, is the history of women losing their rights and access to land and the concomitant benefits.[15] Only

Peasants engaged in land struggle, Peru.

recently have development agencies begun to give attention to women's need for land. The World Conference on Agrarian Reform and Rural Development (WCARRD) in 1979, recommended that governments consider action to:

Repeal those laws which discriminate against women in respect of rights of inheritance, ownership and control of property, and to promote understanding of the need for such measures.

Promote ownership rights for women, including joint ownership and co-ownership of land in entirety, to give women producers with absentee husbands effective legal rights to take decisions on the land they manage.

Adopt measures to ensure women equitable access to land, livestock and other productive assets.[16]

A follow up workshop to WCARRD on the Integration of Women in Agricultural and Rural Development held in Hyderabad, India in 1980 reiterated:

The WACCRD Programme of Action, as related to rural women, requires the formulation of specific government policies, which would ensure equal access for rural women to land, water, energy, credit and cooperatives, inputs and marketing, training and social infrastructure.[17]

radical or cosmetic change?

Much of what passes for land reform is simply superficial change. An Oxfam report concludes:

Land tenure systems are bound up with national power structures and nothing will really change for the poor until these power structures are altered in their favour. To be successful a land reform needs continuing support after it has been implemented. This support has to be political, as well as technical and financial, for the reform to remain successful...

Nearly every developing country has introduced a programme which it has described as land reform. However, most of them have produced negligible results because they have not been designed to change the power structure. Only a very few countries have achieved this.[18]

There is some skepticism as to whether intergovernmental conferences such as WCARRD, and the statements they issue, are of much use. A critical group of researchers and non-governmental organizations from both third world and industrialized countries issued the Rome Declaration at the time of WCARRD, in which they stated:

Through WCARRD, many governments hope to divert attention from themselves as causes of rural suffering. They hope to lay the blame elsewhere on obstinate local rural elites, on the scarcity of funds, on unavoidable conflicts in priorities, and on unfair international terms of trade. Moreover, many governments hope to legitimate their promotion of modernization, trade, foreign aid and transnational corporate investment even though such activities are already contributing to increased landlessness and hunger...

Many so called land reforms have been inspired and carried out by dominant groups to serve their own interests, not those of the rural poor. Such reforms have ignored those most in need — the many poor workers totally deprived of land. They have exempted those who put land into production for export. At best they have allowed tenants — often a pitifully small number — to buy land from their landlords, often under onerous terms. The net effect has been to strengthen the existing rural power structure, not dislodge

Milking a buffalo, India.

In addition to all their other work, women may spend hours each day carrying water for their families' needs.

it. Such pseudo reforms must never be confused with the redistribution of economic and political power carried out with the active participation of the rural dispossessed.

Genuine agrarian reform and rural development commence only once people struggle to create their own institutions, responsive to their needs. While recognizing the critical role to be played by leadership accountable to the people, it must be understood that agrarian reform cannot be done *to* people. Nor can it be done *for* people. The process of reform is as important as the reform itself.[19]

Researchers point out cases of superficial or pseudo land reform as in Venezuela where this "involved the widespread purchase of land for distribution. The price paid to landowners was extremely favourable and the 'reform' has been seen as little more than a bonus for the landowning class and a means of payment to the peasant clients of the two main political parties."[20] An Oxfam America report contends that El Salvador's land reform program is intended to encourage landlords, who will be generously compensated for their land, to move into the modern commercial and industrial sectors. The real beneficiaries of improved crop production will not be poor peasants but middlemen and export companies.[21] In the Philippines, the land reform program has intensified the conversion of land to export crops, as such land is exempt from redistribution. After seven years, only 2,000 peasants had obtained clear title to their land, due to

the difficult terms. There was not a single poor peasant among them.[22]

Nevertheless, it can be claimed that official statements and recommendations from intergovernmental conferences and agencies can be used as ammunition and backing by those who do wish to institute real agrarian reform. While agreeing with the assertion that the majority of ruling elites have little interest in promoting radical change in rural power structures, it can also be argued that international terms of trade and the power of multinationals and the richer countries in the world economy, make it extremely difficult for those who would like to promote more equitable development in their countries. These factors also help keep progressive forces or opposition to the ruling elites powerless.

and women?

If patriarchal structures and attitudes are not dealt with at the same time, even radical reforms redistributing power and control along with land rights may discriminate against women. An FAO report on *The Legal Status of Rural Women* states: "In many countries where land has been nationalized and landownership is no longer a factor, membership in cooperatives and collective organizations is often limited to heads of families, thereby eliminating the participation of the majority of rural women."[23]

In Ethiopia, where a radical land reform program has been

الجزائر الاشتراكية شهداء) (ابن لامهات ابن الشهداء

LA VEUVE ET ORPHELIN... VAN GARDE
U COMBAT LUTTE ES AGENTS DU NEO
ONIALISME et les Contre REVOLUTIONNAIRES

LES VEUVES ET ORPHELINS DE CHOUHADA POURSUIVRONT LA LUTTE POUR STICE SOCIALE

Women have a long history of organization and mobilization. Here Algerian women demonstrate against neo-colonialism, 1965.

implemented, Zene Tadesse writes:

> Although land reform has brought significant socio-eco-
> nomic changes to the peasantry as a whole, its impact on
> women has been very limited and indirect. Due to the eco-
> nomic benefits emanating from land reform, peasant
> women now do not have to worry about where the next
> meal is coming from and are less restrained when *asking*
> their husbands to buy them new clothes or items for the
> house, etc. However, rural women are still dependent on
> their husbands economically and therefore their social and
> political position in society is still subordinate to men.
> Agrarian reform in Ethiopia cannot have a direct and
> meaningful impact on women until there is an all-out
> struggle against patriarchal authority.[24]

A study of a village in Viet Nam with a cooperative system
shows how women are still at a disadvantage in comparison to
men:

> Women have been greatly affected by the economic changes,
> it is true. The mere fact of the multiplication of harvests —
> two yearly harvests of rice and one of vegetables — has
> meant that the women are occupied all the year round in
> production tasks. A considerable amount of the work in
> the garden is carried out by women. Finally all the work in
> the home is always left to the women. They are therefore
> occupied from 10 to 14 hours and, at least in this village,
> have little time to do other things.
>
> This has several consequences. First, there is little partici-
> pation by women in cultural and political activities...
> Meetings of the women's mass movement are not very
> frequent. This is not surprising, as women are now more

heavily engaged in economic tasks without, however, having
been relieved of their duties.[25]

The importance and the difficulties of overcoming patriarchal authority are illustrated by the Chipko movement, known
for the courageousness of the hill women of India in saving
their land from "development" that would have destroyed
their sources of fuel, water and livelihood. Through nonviolent
action in which the women would block the way to the forest
and chipko, or embrace, the trees, they succeeded in keeping
the forests from being felled. For this, they had to face harassment not only from those in power, but from men of their
own class in the village who feared and resented the women's
success. Gopa Joshi, after speaking with the women involved,
reports:

> The women feel an acute need for full-time women activists
> who can travel from village to village, counter rumours,
> erode fear and spread awareness among women about the
> harassment faced by women activists, so that resistance can
> be organized. Only united and organized women will be
> able to relish the fruits of their victory. If not united, they
> will continue to be harassed for hurting the ego of village
> men.[26]

integrating women?

Women, then, are not some "vast untapped resource" to
be integrated into, or maximized for, rural development. They
are already participating in essential ways in agriculture and in
the necessary work of reproduction and caring for people's
basic needs. This work, and the knowledge women possess,

must be recognized and valued.

Women working within development agencies and institutions can pressure these organizations to overcome the sexist attitudes and prejudices which distort data collection and statistics about women and women's work. More important, women are collecting their own data and statistics. They are documenting their own lives and sharing their knowledge and experiences with each other. On the basis of this, they will be able to decide, each in her own particular situation, how to work and struggle for self-determination. If women are to have access to land, improved farming methods, rural services, training, credit and markets in a way that will lead to their greater self-determination, they need to recognize and, at the same time, organize against the economic and patriarchal structures that would exploit them. Organizing and mobilizing are essential for this. This was recognized at a meeting of the Asia and Pacific Centre for Women and Development on the Critical Needs of Women:

> The organisation and mobilisation of groups in society is a highly political and sensitive issue, yet it is only through strong organisations that oppressed groups can hope to improve their situation. The traditional women's organisations, which had had a purely welfare approach to women's problems have, by-and-large, failed to improve the situation of the majority of women. These organisations need to be revitalised or replaced by more dynamic women's organisations...
> The structural, financial and attitudinal change which must occur to satisfy women's needs and to enable them to contribute their extensive skills and talents will only come about as the result of strong and effective pressure groups. Thus women must be mobilised and organised.[27]

Organization and mobilization on the local level is crucial, but women must also develop networks and communication channels with each other in order to share their experiences and problems, break out of their isolation, and strengthen themselves: the forces they are faced with are so powerful that "only united and organized women will be able to relish the fruits of their victory," as the struggle of the Chipko movement women shows.

Footnotes

1 *WCARRD: A Turning Point for Rural Women* (Rome: Food and Agricultural Organization, 1980), p. 6.

2 Quoted in "Women and the New International Economic Order," *Development Issue Paper for the 1980s*, no. 12 (New York: United Nations Development Programme), p. 2.

3 Mariam Thiam, *Case Study: The Role of Women in Rural Development in the Segou Region, Mali* (Philadelphia: American Friends Service Committee, 1979), pp. 5-6.

4 "What is the Difference Between One Human Being and Another?" *Manushi*, no. 4 (1980), p. 18. This five page interview with landless Harijan women gives a good description of how these women see their daily lives, work, relationships with men, the community and development projects.

5 Alice Stewart Carloni, "Sex Disparities in the Distribution of Food Within Rural Households," *Food and Nutrition*, vol. 7, no. 1 (1981).

6 Ann Seidman, "Women and the Development of 'Underdevelopment': The African Experience," *Women and Technological Change in Developing Countries*, eds. Roslyn Dauber and Melinda L. Cain (Boulder, Colorado: Westview Press, 1981), p. 112.

7 Mary Racelis Hollnsteiner and Hoda Badran, "Structures of Inequality," *Assignment Children*, nos. 49/50 (Spring 1980), pp. 101-103.

8 Bette Shertzer, "The Third World of Women," *Food Monitor* (January-February 1979), p. 13.

9 David A. Mitchnik, *The Role of Women in Rural Zaire and Upper Volta* (Oxford: Oxfam, 1977), p. 20.

10 Martha F. Loutfi, *Rural Women: Unequal Partners in Development* (Geneva: International Labour Organisation, 1980), p. 34.

11 See Olga Stavrakis and Marion Louise Marshall, "Women, Agriculture and Development in the Maya Lowlands: Profit or Progress," *Proceedings and Papers of the International Conference on Women and Food*, ed. Ann Bunzel Cowan (Washington: Consortium for International Development, 1978), pp. 157-174.

12 For a concise, but more detailed, description of development policies with regard to agriculture, rural needs, cash crops and the green revolution, see especially "Land – Food," *ACFOA Development Dossier*, no. 7 (October 1981), and *Crisis Decade* (London: International Coalition for Development Action, 1980).

13 See especially: Pat Roy Mooney, *Seeds of the Earth* (Ottawa: International Coalition for Development Action and Canadian Council for International Cooperation, 1980); Alternative News and Features and International Coalition for Development Action Press Packet for the International Symposium on World Food Security and Plant Genetic Erosion (November 1981); "Agribusiness," *IDOC International Bulletin*, nos. 3-4 (1982) and "Transnational Poisoning," *IDOC International Bulletin*, no. 7 (July 1981).

14 Elise Boulding, "Women, Peripheries and Food Production," *International Conference on Women and Food*, p. 30.

15 See especially: Barbara Rogers, "Women and Land Rights," *ISIS International Bulletin*, no. 11 (Spring 1979), pp. 5-8.

16 *World Conference on Agrarian Reform and Rural Development Report* (Rome: Food and Agricultural Organization, 1979), p. 10.

17 *Report of the FAO/SIDA Workshop on the Integration of Women in Agriculture and Rural Development* (Rome: Food and Agricultural Organization, 1981), p. 11.

18 Claire Whittemore, *Land for People: Land Tenure and the Very Poor* (Oxford: Oxfam, 1981), pp. 19 and 21.

19 International Peace Research Association Food Policy Study Group, *Circular Letter*, no. 6 (1979), pp. 3 and 5.

20 Whittemore, *Land for People*, p. 22.

21 Laurence Simon and J. Stephens, *El Salvador Land Reform: Impact Audit* (Boston: Oxfam America, 1981).

22 Charles-Henri Foubert, *Les Philippines: le réveil d'un archipel* (Paris: L'Harmattan, 1980), p. 71.

23 *The Legal Status of Rural Women* (Rome: Food and Agricultural Organization, 1979), p. 60.

24 Zene Tadesse, *The Impact of Land Reform on Women: The Case of Ethiopia*, paper presented at the Informal Consultants' Meeting on Women and Development, International Labour Organisation, Geneva, May 1978.

25 François Houtart, "Problems of Social Transition: An Example from Viet Nam," *Ideas and Action*, no. 137 (1980), p. 10.

26 Gopa Joshi, "Protecting the Sources of Community Life," *Manushi*, no. 7 (1981), p. 24.

27 *The Critical Needs of Women* (Kuala Lumpur: Asian and Pacific Centre for Women and Development, 1977), p. 37.

appropriate technology

Marilee Karl

Appropriate technology has swept through the world of development policy making and planning and gained momentum in the wake of the failure of the green revolution and other strategies depending on the use of high technology. It is being advocated in both developing and industrialized countries. In the materials of organizations from the United Nations to grassroot environmentalist groups, women are often ignored and bypassed.

As the negative impact of introducing technology without considering the lives and needs of women becomes apparent, appropriate technology is being advocated for women, especially as a means of lightening their daily tasks in food production and supplying the family's fuel and water needs. Appropriate technology, however, is no magic formula, for women, men or communities. Appropriate technology should be precisely that: the technology most appropriate for a given place at a given time. Technology is not neutral, although many development planners and technocrats seem to think it is. To introduce it without a knowledge, understanding and analysis of the political, economic, social and patriarchal structures of a given situation and of the impact and implications of this technology for these structures, is to run a good risk of having a highly inappropriate technology, with all sorts of negative consequences for the community.

what is appropriate technology?

There is no single definition for the concept of appropriate technology (commonly abbreviated AT), sometimes also referred to as alternative, adapted, intermediate, soft-core, self-reliant or people's technology. These terms are most often used to describe technologies which are small scale, simple, low cost and which use local materials and labor.

Using the term "intermediate technology," E.F. Schumacher, author of *Small is Beautiful,* calls it "technology with a human face." His book is an introduction to the theory and need for appropriate technology, emphasizing that it is production by the masses, not mass production. He writes:

> The technology of *production by the masses,* making use of the best modern knowledge and experience is conducive to decentralization, compatible with the laws of ecology, gentle in its use of scarce resources, and designed to serve the human person instead of making him the servant of machines. I have named it *intermediate technology* to signify that it is vastly superior to the primitive technology of bygone ages but at the same time much simpler, cheaper, and freer than the supertechnology of the rich. One can also call it self-help technology, or democratic or people's technology – a technology to which everybody can gain admittance and which is not reserved to those already rich and powerful.[1]

In her study *Appropriate Technology for African Women,* Marilyn Carr sums up the concept thus:

> The solution to many of the problems being faced in Africa will rest largely on the development and dissemination of new types of technologies which are appropriate to existing conditions. Such technologies will not be as complex as those which have so far been transferred from the West. Nor will they be as unsophisticated as the traditional techniques which are currently employed by millions of people in Africa. The latter, although having a high labour requirement, are usually characterized by low capital and labour productivities and do not generate the surplus needed for rapid growth in capital stock... In essence, the technologies we are talking about are small, simple and cheap enough to harmonize with local human and material resources and lend themselves to widespread reproduction with the minimum of outside help.[2]

Others in the appropriate technology field stress its aspects of self-reliance, people's participation and innovation from the bottom up:

> Part of the appropriate technology strategy has been to start with and build on locally available skills and materials,

based on the initiative and full participation of local people. This should mean that local needs will be met more effectively, that mistakes will be on a scale that is understandable and correctable, and that technological and social changes that follow are more likely to harmonize with evolving local traditions and culture.[3]

appropriate technology is not new

Appropriate technology is not new. It has been used in developing implements and methods needed for survival and daily life. People in many parts of the third world, for instance, build their houses with local labor and with local materials eminently suited to their climate and needs. Some of these technologies, however, have been made obsolete by the introduction of a money economy.

While there have long been advocates of appropriate technology such as Mahatma Gandhi, who envisioned self-reliant and decentralized village technologies, AT as a movement has become widespread only in the last two decades. It has grown up simultaneously from many different sources in both the developing and industrialized world, partly from the growing realization that the model of development which includes transfer of advanced technologies from the North

to the third world is not increasing the economic well-being of third world countries. The introduction of advanced technologies has often had negative effects on the populations, increasing unemployment and impoverishment so that most of the people have been denied the benefits of modernization.

At the same time, groups and individuals, particularly in industrialized or "over-developed" countries, have become concerned about the waste and pollution caused by advanced technologies, the depletion of natural resources, the environmental and ecological imbalances, and the health hazards resulting from their use. There is a growing concern for the quality of work and life in societies where mass production, dehumanization of the workplace, high levels of consumption of luxury goods, and the use of more and more artificial foods and goods alienate people from work, nature, each other and themselves. There is a worldwide concern that a small percentage of the world's population is consuming a large percentage of the world's goods and natural resources.

From these diverse beginnings, links were forged:

By the mid-1970s there was a convergence of the various strains of alternative technology ideology, and a call for environmentally responsible techniques to produce smaller, less capital-intensive workplaces. Energy and agriculture became the primary areas in which the alternative technologies were identified and developed, reflecting the belief that the high technological forms of agriculture and energy were not viable in the long run for developed

F. Botts/FAO

Young woman showing her traditional stove which now burns biogas. She produces her own biogas in the yard of her home. China, 1980.

To build the Volta River dam, 85,000 self-sufficient farmers were moved to resettlement villages.

countries and were already wreaking havoc in many of the developing nations.[4]

While there are differences in emphasis in the appropriate technology movement in the developing and industrialized countries, there is a growing awareness that these are linked together with basic underlying concerns and needs. Environmentalist groups in developed countries, in particular those concerned with nuclear hazards, industrial pollution and wastes, and the depletion of nonrenewable energy resources, are beginning to see the need for global perspectives and strategies for these problems which are global in dimension. They must take into account the power of multinational corporations that control so much of technology and determine how and where these are used.

appropriate vs. inappropriate technology

The AT movement questions the appropriateness of sophisticated technology especially in rural areas of developing countries where the basic needs of people for adequate food, water, clothing, housing and health services have yet to be met. Introduction of modern technologies often benefits cities over rural areas and a small elite over the majority of the population. Modern, well-equipped hospitals and cardiological centers can be found in the capitals of third world countries where the majority of the population, living in rural areas, lack basic health services and personnel and where malnutrition is still one of the leading causes of death. Tractors and mechanized irrigation systems are available for cash crops in the same area that women have to try to grow enough food for their families using hoes and hauling water great distances. Farmers who can afford the pesticides and high yielding seed varieties called for in the green revolution have a great advantage over most of the farmers who cannot.

Classic examples of the inappropriateness of some uses of advanced technology can be found in the literature. In the introduction to Schumacher's *Small is Beautiful*, Theodore Roszak writes:

Today in poor nations everywhere we find far too many Western and Soviet financed projects like the African textile factory Schumacher describes: industries demanding such advanced expertise and such refined materials to finish their luxurious products that they cannot employ local labor or use local resources, but must import skills and goods from Europe and America. In Ghana the vast Volta River power project, built with American money at high interest, provides Kaiser Aluminum with stupendously cheap electricity contracted at a long-term low price. But no Ghanaian bauxite has been used by Kaiser, and no aluminum plants have been built in the country.

Instead, Kaiser imports its aluminum for processing and sends it to Germany for finishing. Elsewhere we find prestigious megaprojects like Egypt's Aswan high dam, built by Russian money and brains to produce a level of power far beyond the needs of the nation's economy, that meanwhile blights the environment and the local agriculture in a dozen unforeseen and possibly insoluble ways.[5]

Another instance is described by Marilyn Carr in *Appropriate Technology for African Women:*

Undeniably a major cause of the most pressing problems of the Third World has been the *transfer and use of technologies* which are totally inappropriate to prevailing conditions. A famous case study from one African country illustrated this point perfectly. Two plastic-injection moulding machines costing US$ 100,000 each were imported to produce plastic shoes and sandals. Working three shifts and with a total labour force of only 40 workers, the machines produced 1.5 million pairs of shoes and sandals a year. At US$ 2 per pair, they were better value and had a longer life than cheap leather footwear at the same price. Thus, 5,000 artisan shoemakers lost their livelihood which, in turn, reduced the markets for the suppliers and makers of leather, hand tools, cotton thread, tacks, glues, wax and polish, fabric linings, laces, wooden lasts and carton boxes, none of which was required for plastic footwear. As all the machinery and the material (PVC) for the plastic footwear had to be imported, while the leather footwear was based largely on indigenous materials and industries, the net result was a decline in both employment and real income within the country.[6]

When small technologies are planned and introduced from outside, they can also turn out to be absurdly inappropriate. An example is this:

In Africa where sunshine is abundant but oil, coal and wood are scarce and expensive, a solar stove should really mean utmost happiness to women – or so some eager development theoreticians thought. Field tests then showed what every experienced expert (or local woman, ed. note) could have predicted: In the African bush, meals are prepared in the morning or in the evening when the sun has not yet risen or has already set. Furthermore: which cook wants to stand in the scorching sun? Finally: the nightly fire also has a group and therefore social function.[7]

One of the third world leaders advocating a Basic Human Needs Approach to appropriate technology is Dr. Julius Nyerere, President of Tanzania. A characteristic statement of his is:

I've been telling my own people, "We've got to change, we must mechanise, we must have better tools. But what are better tools? Not the combine harvester. If I were given enough combine harvesters for every family in Tanzania, what would I do with them? No mechanics, no spare parts..." But we still have to give the people better tools, tools which they can handle, and can pay for. We are using hoes. If two million farmers in Tanzania could jump from the hoe to the oxen plough, it would be a revolution. It would double our living standard, triple our product![8]

Some third world countries, however, oppose AT because they see it as a move on the part of rich nations to keep the

Maggie Murray

Sweating over a European-designed solar stove in the scorching sun.

benefits of high technology to themselves, and to keep the third world in a state of underdevelopment by offering it less advanced technologies. This opposition is intensified by the fact that developing countries have, for years, been pressing for the transfer of technology from the industrialized countries, with few results.[9]

capitalizing on AT

While there are many appropriate technology advocates and organizations in the third world, the majority are located in the industrialized countries. From the United Nations to governments of developing, developed market and centrally planned economies; multinationals and small business enterprises; non-governmental organizations; alternative and environmentalist groups; and development agencies – all are busy capitalizing on AT. Although the movement is young, it has generated thousands of resources – books, pamphlets, bibliographies, equipment catalogues and information centers.

What are the motivations for promoting appropriate technology? These range from a concern for the environment to stimulating growth and profit. As AT has become more popular and acceptable, it has tended to become more western-dominated and controlled. For many groups the elements of self-reliance and people's participation have been forgotten. Groups and organizations and businesses carry out research and development mainly in the developed world, experiments in the developing world. Local materials, local talent and skills have been displaced by centralization and control by big business. For example, the initiatives taken by small groups around solar energy have been increasingly monopolized by large oil companies that have bought out the smaller enterprises and which now control the research and development of solar energy technology.[10] Businesses continue to see AT as a good opportunity for profit making through manufacture of "AT equipment" for sale and export to developing countries.

One AT organization speaks of this as the "erosion of the integrity of the term 'appropriate technology' " and gives this example:

A representative from a major international organization visited us recently and had this to say: His organization intends to get technically sophisticated engineers and social scientists to visit the rural areas of developing countries and design technology to fit these circumstances. Stainless-steel small-scale machines would then be produced in American factories and exported to these countries. It is rather unnerving to hear this described as "appropriate technology." It is just a formula for continued dependency.[11]

A major problem is that:

AT is a difficult approach to incorporate into large agency planning efforts. The concept of "local self-reliance," for example, is difficult to define or quantify and will vary from place to place. Furthermore, it is a quality that can either be nurtured or destroyed from outside, but never created. "Self-reliance" also sounds vaguely utopian or

Spinning mill, Korea. New technology increases productivity, reduces employment.

ideologically-tainted. To many planners it looks unnecessary, and out it goes. Equally difficult is the concept of "people's participation." "Participation" is probably the most invoked and least often attempted aspect of rural development programs. "Participation" is often interpreted to mean carrying out instructions. This kind of interpretation makes "participation" simply a measure of the degree of local acceptance of a project, not a strategy for success and human development.[12]

AT has also become part of development aid programs of the North and this has perhaps created more problems than it has solved. As Nicolas Jequier writes in *Appropriate Technology: Problems and Premises*:

This interest of aid-giving countries and organisations, important as it may be for the future of the movement, is in fact at the root of a very wide-spread misconception, namely that appropriate technology is primarily an aspect of development aid. It certainly has a part to play in development aid, but the philosophy which underlies it is precisely the opposite: appropriate technology should first and foremost be an indigenous creation of the developing countries themselves and the central problem they have to face is that of building up an indigenous innovative capability and not that of importing more foreign technology.[13]

and microelectronics?

At the same time, newer high technologies like microelectronics are creating their own revolution. With research pouring into this, microelectronics will soon come to dominate manufacturing and assembly in a major way. This has and will continue to change radically the discussion about technologies. As with other forms of high technology, it brings with it problems such as increasing joblessness, alienation and health hazards. However, there is little if any dialogue between the proponents of AT and those of microelectronics technology. Would it not be in the interest of AT supporters to pay serious attention to this question, instead of proceeding in the expectation that AT will be a major technology of the future while there is serious and growing competition in the field by the richer, more resourceful and more powerful businesses promoting microelectronics?

a male-dominated movement

In addition to being a predominantly western-dominated movement, AT is also very much male-dominated and male-oriented. The male researchers and policy makers from industrialized countries bring with them all the prejudices about women and technology found in their societies. Most of the material on appropriate technology hardly deals with women at all, still less considers the impact of this on women's lives. Just as the social, economic and political reality is ignored on the pretext that technology is "neutral," so are the patriarchal structures and sexist attitudes.

Most technological advances and improvements, whether considered to be "advanced" or "appropriate," are introduced almost exclusively to men. In the field of agriculture, men are the recipients of training and access to machines, tractors, harvesters, improved ploughs and irrigation systems in spite of the fact that women are the major food producers. In water supply, men are trained to construct and use pumps, wells, filtering systems, pipes and faucets, in spite of the fact that women have traditionally been in charge of supplying water needs. Planners then express surprise when men are reluctant to maintain and repair systems. Women lose power when charge over the water supply is transferred to men. Does lightening women's load in fetching water necessarily entail stripping them of control and status?

While some development planners now recognize the importance of women's role in water supply, they still seem to have difficulty in breaking down prejudices about women and technology. In the materials prepared by the United Nations Development Programme for the International Drinking Water Supply and Sanitation Decade 1981-1990, nearly all the illustrations of traditional means of water supply show women carrying water. The material clearly points out that "women and children bear the biggest burden" in fetching water for the household needs. It includes a good article about how village women's groups in Kenya have taken steps to improve their own water supply. Yet the great majority of illustrations of improved water systems show men building and running them. In an article entitled "Maintaining the System: Barefoot Engineers," the engineers shown are men and are referred to throughout as "he"; e.g., "he is given two days training" or "his job is to ensure."[14] To avoid sex-role stereotyping, non-sexist language and stick figures could have been used. For role reversal and consciousness raising, images of women in traditionally male roles could have been portrayed.

In areas in which men have no stake or desire to take over (routine household tasks of cleaning, cooking and child care), the experts have introduced singularly inappropriate technologies, demonstrating their complete lack of understanding and experience of women's lives and work. In addition to designing solar stoves for women who cook before dawn and after dusk, they have invented maize shellers which take longer to do the job than the women themselves and have introduced pedal-driven grinding mills in areas where women are forbidden to sit astride.[15]

Small technologies, if they were really appropriate, could do much to relieve overworked women. In her study on *Appropriate Technology for African Women*, Marilyn Carr points out several areas where appropriate technology could help women. Male planners tend to overlook these because they do not even consider them "work," or because they undervalue the enormous contributions women make to the household, community and nation. These tasks include: fetching fuel and water; food production for local consumption, including planting, weeding, harvesting, hauling, storing and processing of foods; cooking and housework. In many places, women have to do this work under extremely arduous conditions, in addition to bearing and raising children and often working in cash cropping or industry as well. They may have to walk as much as 10 to 20 kilometers a day to haul fuel and water on their heads and backs. Women's work is so time-consuming and there is so much of it, that it leaves women without sufficient time to rest and sleep. "Free time" for relaxation, socialization or other activities is unknown. This takes its toll on women's health and that of their children.[16]

Questions about the division of labor between men and women and about sexist attitudes toward this division which

In a joint venture by the FAO and the multi-national Massey-Ferguson, men are trained as technicians in farm mechanization. Colombia, 1969.

Sierra Leone: Girls being trained in domestic skills. Machines from another multinational.

automatically assign lower value and status to the jobs women do are seldom raised or addressed.

reinforcing stereotypes or liberating women?

In the developed market and centrally planned economies, women have had an increasing number of labor-saving devices to help them in their household tasks of cleaning, preparing food and cooking. They are also wage earners outside the home, yet all these women continue to bear the double shift of all child rearing and household activities. Men occasionally help out but women bear the responsibility. From their experiences, it is clear that the introduction of labor-saving devices and employment in wage labor by themselves do not address the basic questions of women's oppression.

While women's lives are very different in different parts of the world, and while political, economic and social systems vary, sexism is universal, and is a factor that links women and gives them a common battle to fight.

In industrialized countries, the appropriate technology movement demonstrates its prejudices about women's capabilities and roles, neglects women's needs and desires, and excludes women from power, decision making and control. In the booklet *Something Old, Something New, Something Borrowed, Something Due: Women and Appropriate Technology*, Judy Smith writes:

Few women are involved in appropriate technology for the same reasons that so few women are involved in traditional science and technology. (Women make up 6 percent of all U.S. scientists with college degrees in natural sciences and engineering.) Science and technology are considered men's work in this culture. Women are not supposed to understand or even be interested in these areas...

The AT movement appears to be a sex-role stereotyped movement relying on male expertise. Men do men's work and women do women's work. Men do the construction and invention. Women do clerical tasks and make the coffee.

Most of the attention on appropriate technology focuses on the traditionally male technologies of energy and transportation, rather than on traditional female technologies of food preservation and clothing production. Although women have a long history of involvement with survival technologies, their contributions are overlooked

T.S. Satyan/FAO

When women's traditional work is upgraded and professionalized, men begin to take over the field. Institute of Catering Technology, India.

in a society which values external success-linked technologies of engineering and science...

Who's in the movement anyway? Who are the experts? The founding fathers? Who's deciding what is appropriate? Who talks at meetings, gets the grants and does the inventing? Who's on the tech staff and who's on clerical?...

Visit an AT project. Who works on the solar collector? Who cans food in the kitchen? Which technology is pointed out with pride? How much time is spent encouraging and training women to do men's work and vice versa?[17]

The focus of AT in industrialized countries is on simpler, less energy-intensive technologies. What does this mean for women? It usually means fewer labor-saving devices for household tasks, less use of prepared and processed foods and synthetic fibers. Women are asked to give up their gas, electric and microwave ovens for wood stoves, to bake their own bread and preserve their own food instead of buying it from the shops. They are urged to buy or, even better, make clothes of natural fibers rather than synthetic ones, even though natural fibers require considerably more care, especially ironing. They are asked to save energy by giving up the use of cars, which have meant freedom of movement and from confinement to the home.

It is not surprising that few women in industrialized countries are willing to give up labor-saving devices and products, given that the main burden of household work and child care falls on them, and that, for most of them, wage employment is a necessity not an option.

As one of the reasons for introducing appropriate technol-

ogy to third world women, development planners argue that it will "alleviate women's burdens" in the household and enable them to participate in wage labor or "income generating" activities. There is an important lesson to be learned, however, from the lives and experiences of women in developed countries. Labor-saving devices alone cannot lighten women's work load. They only rearrange it somewhat, enabling women to take on waged work in addition to their unpaid work in the household.

Moreover, women's access to wage labor means more and more things must be bought. More money must be earned to pay for the things which women can no longer provide for themselves or which can no longer be produced locally, leading to less self-sufficiency. As Elise Boulding says:

Packaged appropriate technologies containing all the recommended small incremental improvements of food storage facilities, wheel-barrows, food dryers, flour mills and high-protein multivitamin food supplements will be sold to women, usually by multinational corporations. Whatever cash surpluses their wage increases might have generated will thus be quickly absorbed in the national or even the world economy.[18]

what would appropriate technology be like if...?

What would appropriate technology for women be like if women were setting the priorities and making the decisions?

S. Bunnag/FAO

A woman in a highly industrialized country writes:

> We don't even know what technology could possibly do for women, because women have no control over it... We don't know how different that would be, but we do know what happens to women when they don't control technology. A perfect example is what has happened with birth control technology... When birth control technology first appeared, it had very negative effects for women. The kind of technology that was made available was effective, but it did a lot of damage to women's bodies, and we have evidence that there was no adequate risk assessment of that damage. This technology was not controlled by women, women did not do the research, women did not do the marketing. What kind of birth control would be available to us now if women were the ones making the decisions...[19]

What would appropriate technology for women be like if it were not simply a matter of providing labor-saving devices; if it were placed in the context of the question of the division of labor between men and women, in the context of the social and patriarchal structures; if it included access to knowledge of technology?

what women are doing

For women to begin to define what they need for coping with present times and what skills and knowledge they already have that need to be transferred to other women and future generations, they need to come together to reflect and plan. Some of this has begun.

During the Workshop on Technical Cooperation Among Developing Countries (TCDC) and Women, held by the Asian and Pacific Centre for Women and Development in April 1978, participants analyzed the impact and implications of new technologies and of TCDC on women. According to Devaki Jain of the Institute of Social Studies, New Delhi,

Must we choose between this and that?

ILO

they concluded that "women's needs were different from men's even if they were both poor, and even if they belonged to the same ideology; that this had not been taken notice of in the design of institutions or in development strategies." The participants affirmed the importance of TCDC, but also the importance of changes that would make this beneficial, not detrimental, to women. Among the needs they identified are: to document, analyze and disseminate experiences in addition to providing directories of experts, institutions and training facilities; to create and support existing pressure groups for women's concerns and interests.[20]

Asian and Pacific women also met together in November 1980 at the second Appropriate Technology Workshop for YWCAs of the region. Ruth Lechte reports that the participants had the opportunity not only to learn about practical matters and equipment such as solar dryers and water pumps, but to discuss the whole idea of appropriate technology and to try to see it in a political context. The participants gave importance to consciousness raising and awareness building on many levels and to overcoming stereotypes of what is women's work and what is men's.[21]

Women from both third world and industrialized countries met together in June 1981 to share experiences and information about their work in the area of health and medical technologies. Organized by ISIS and the Women's Health Clinic in Geneva, this third International Women and Health Meeting brought together women working in the self-help movement, local women's clinics, community health projects and research. What is unique about these meetings is that the participants do not come to hear panels of experts but to exchange information and experiences about their own work and findings, in areas such as contraception, abortion, childbirth, and infections, and to discuss the politics of established medicine and how it affects women. The meetings are opportunities to analyze, reflect, share knowledge of new and traditional health technologies, and to begin to devise health care systems and technologies more responsive to the needs of all people.[22]

Perhaps we should speak not only about TCDC (Technical Cooperation Among Developing Countries) but TCW (Technical Cooperation Among Women): a new kind of information sharing and cooperation among women from different parts of the world who are developing and using technologies which help them gain more control over their lives and their communities. This is a very different thing from the "traditional technical cooperation for women" described by the African Training and Research Centre for Women which "meant assistance in patron-client fashion from women of industrialized countries and elite African women's organizations that had internalized their ideals giving instruction in embroidering pillows, baking scones, urging the acquisition of more electrical appliances."[23] A new kind of technical cooperation among women is not a one-way flow of information from North to South: it is South to South and South to North as well. It builds on the great store of knowledge and expertise women already have and which, in many cases, is in danger of being lost, and it opens the way for new knowledge and new technologies to develop, based on women's real needs.

Footnotes

1   E.F. Schumacher, *Small is Beautiful* (New York: Harper and Row, 1973), p. 154.

2   Marilyn Carr, *Appropriate Technology for African Women* (Addis Ababa: United Nations Economic Commission for Africa, 1978), pp. 7-8.

3   Ken Darrow, Kent Keller and Rick Pam, *Appropriate Technology Sourcebook*, vol. 2 (Stanford, California: Volunteers in Asia, Inc., 1981), p. 328.

4   David E. Wright and Robert E. Snow, "Which Technology Will Shape the Future?" *World Education Reports*, no. 19 (May 1979), p. 11.

5   Schumacher, *Small is Beautiful*, p. 7.

6   Carr, *Appropriate Technology*, p. 6.

7   Helmut Mylenbusch, "Appropriate Technology – Fashionable Term, Practical Necessity, or New Social Philosophy?" *Development and Cooperation*, no. 3 (1979), p. 18.

8   Cited in Carr, *Appropriate Technology*, p. iv.

9   At the United Nations Conference on Science and Technology (UNCSTD), held in Vienna in 1979, guidelines were set for increasing the third world share of technical research and development. The United Nations Commission on Trade and Development (UNCTAD) has been negotiating terms for the transfer of technology from multinational corporations for a number of years. The industrialized world, however, has been reluctant to make the necessary commitments or give adequate financial aid for this. In recent years, developing countries have been examining more ways to increase the transfer of technology among themselves. One such initiative was the conference on Technical Cooperation among Developing Countries (TCDC), held in Buenos Aires in 1978, under the sponsorship of the United Nations Development Programme (UNDP).

10   "The Solar Game Stakes," *Development Forum*, vol. 7, no. 6 (August-September 1979), pp. 8-9. This compilation is based on an article by Earthscan (Press Briefing Document, no. 19).

11   Darrow, *Appropriate Technology Sourcebook*, vol. 1, p. 15.

12   Ibid., vol. 2, p. 330.

13   Nicolas Jequier, *Appropriate Technology: Problems and Premises* (Stanford, California: Volunteers in Asia and OECD, 1976), pp. 13-14.

14   *International Drinking Water Supply and Sanitation Decade* (New York: United Nations Development Programme, 1981).

15   Carr, *Appropriate Technology*, p. 28.

16   Ibid., pp. 26-31.

17   Judy Smith, *Something Old, Something New, Something Borrowed, Something Due: Women and Appropriate Technology* (Missoula, Montana: Women and Technology Project, 1980), p. 7 and pp. 18-19.

18   Elise Boulding, *Women: The Fifth World*, Foreign Policy Association, Headline Series (New York, 1980), p. 52.

19   Smith, "Feminism/Environmentalism: Point-Counterpoint," *Conference Proceedings, Women and Technology: Deciding What's Appropriate* (Missoula, Montana: Women's Resource Center, 1979), p. 7.

20   *Report: TCDC and Women* (Kuala Lumpur, Malaysia: United Nations Asian and Pacific Centre for Women and Development, 1978), and "Women and Technical Co-operation Among Developing Countries," *Development Issue Paper for the 1980s*, no. 13, United Nations Development Programme (New York, 1980), p. 3.

21   Ruth Lechte, "Appropriate Technology Workshop," *Common Concern*, no. 29 (March 1981), pp. 7-8.

22   See the report of the International Women and Health Meeting in *ISIS International Bulletin*, no. 20 (October 1981). For the report in Spanish, see *ISIS Boletín Internacional*, no. 8 (December 1981).

23   Cited in "Women and Technical Co-operation," *Development Issue Paper*, no. 13, p. 4.

income generation for women

Marilee Karl

One of the approaches to "integrating women into development" is "income generating projects." These projects are an attempt to repair some of the damage of past and current development policies on women. They are based on the assumption that it is both necessary and desirable for women to earn money.

what is an income generating project?

While handicrafts remain a widespread form of income generating activity for women, the concept has taken on broader connotations. Some development researchers are even reconsidering the use of this term. One North American researcher writes: "They feel the term, itself, connotes small activities irrelevant to the mainstream of national economic development. They point out the term is seldom if ever used for men's projects of increasing agricultural production, etc." A definition of the term, income generating activity, which seems representative of the current trend in thinking includes "any self-supporting project where benefits accrue to women participants from sale of items for money, from employment for wages, or increased produce." This encompasses projects which increase the food supply or pay women in food, for instance, but excludes those which require continual support and subsidy from outside sources. The latter are classified as cultural or welfare projects.[1]

why income generating projects?

Development policies and projects have resulted in the loss of women's traditional sources of income and other means of subsistence, such as self-sufficiency in family food production and other daily needs. Economic need is thus the most pressing motivation for income generating projects.

Although there are few reliable figures, it is estimated that as many as one-third of the families in the world are headed by women who are the sole or main support of their families.[2] When husbands and/or other adult men are present in the family, women have responsibilities for supplying certain basic necessities. Many policy makers, however, still assume that men are the breadwinners in the family and that employment schemes are more important for men, especially where there is poverty and unemployment. They assume that the money men earn will benefit their wives and families and raise the standard of living of the whole household: the trickle down theory at the level of the family.

Devaki Jain of the Institute of Social Studies, New Delhi, disposes of some of these misconceptions:

> Such arguments are based on ignorance of not only the income needs, but the income-uses of a household. Studies of household income-allocation conducted by social-anthropologists... reveal that it is predominantly the women's income that goes to family food and basic needs. The man's income goes for assets, relative luxuries and liquor. The loss of a woman's income (cash or kind) results in a lowering of the nutritional level of the family, especially the children. This is especially true of poor families.[3]

The trickle down or trickle over theory within the family simply does not work. In her paper *Income Generating Activities with Women's Participation*, Marilyn Hoskins explains:

> In places such as West Africa duties and responsibilities of men and women are separate and clearly defined in such a way that there is no trickle-over. For instance, in a rice project in Upper Volta, land was parcelled out to family heads on the basis of the number of family members who could work in the rice field. Men and women traditionally worked together in the grain fields, the surplus of which belongs to the men. It is customary for women to provide the vegetables, served in a sauce for the staple grains, and to trade or sell items in order to obtain personal articles for

Women's work so often must be organized around caring for children and home.

themselves or their children. The project provided no separate land for women's gardens nor allowed women the time for trade or other income generating activities. Men earn more than ever; the income per family is higher, despite the fact that women no longer have separate incomes. Men give some, but apparently insufficient money to their wives to buy vegetables and other sauce ingredients. As a result, social worker studies report increased incidence of malnutrition in the project area. Reports show a decrease in social contact for women who no longer have the personal funds to buy the gifts expected if they return to the home village to attend weddings, funerals, etc. On the other hand, the social activities of the men have increased with growing numbers of men owning motor bikes and dress clothes. The project, now a locally run cooperative, is frequently cited as a success because of the increased per family income. But here is a case where the women participate in the labor, the men receive the cash, and the trickle-over theory does not work.[4]

Economic need, however, is not the only reason development planners are now advocating income generating activities for women. Population agencies see the employment of women as a means to reduce the birth rate. In his foreword to a study carried out by Ruth Dixon for Resources for the Future, Ronald G. Ridker asks:

If good jobs at decent wages were offered to women, particularly those living in rural areas, would such employment have an effect on family size? Would their jobs compete for the women's time as mothers and housewives, offer them an alternative route to acquiring status and a sense of purpose, and perhaps also provide the women with an independent source of income which would enable them to achieve more control over their lives?[5]

In answer to these questions, Dixon carried out research in Bangladesh, India, Nepal and Pakistan. According to Ridker:

Her findings suggest that jobs for women, while useful for

many other reasons, may have little impact on fertility unless they are combined with other changes. For maximum effectiveness, Dixon recommends that efforts be concentrated on young preferably unmarried women and that, for best results, the new employment opportunities should move the women out of their traditional home and agricultural settings and into central work places located in villages or small towns. She also recommends that women be provided with a financial stake and a voice in the operation of the business venture. Supporting services such as job training and functional literacy classes, along with family-planning, health, and child-care facilities, should be made available. In some circumstances it may be important to provide living quarters for female workers and incentives to encourage delayed marriage and birth control.[6]

For the feminist movement in both developing and industrialized countries, supporting services, economic independence of women and greater control over their own lives are primary goals. Feminists make them some of their main campaigning issues because they are so often neglected or seen as a means to some other end, such as population control. Their criticism of income generating projects which ignore these concerns or relegate them to second place is that this leads simply to a greater work load and even less freedom for women to determine their own lives.

what kind of project?

The type of project depends on the local situation and women involved: the economic level of the community and of women; the class, caste or social position of the women; the urban or rural nature of the community; and the place where it stands on the continuum from subsistence agriculture to cash economy. It depends on the available skills, materials and markets, and the other work women are already doing. Planners, however, sometimes introduce projects where the raw materials have to be imported and where there is no ready market, or where the work conflicts with other seasonal work. Women cannot take part in fruit preserving, for instance, if it comes just at the time when they harvest the basic food crop.

A project also depends on the motivations of its planners: whether it is population control or economic independence; whether it arises out of the needs of the women themselves or is imposed from outside; whether it intends to reinforce a given situation or change it. If greater control over one's own life is a primary aim, some changes in the political, economic, social and patriarchal structures may have to accompany income generation.

When basic needs must be urgently fulfilled, it is not possible to wait for structural change — a slow and difficult process. Keeping long-range goals in mind, however, can help bring these changes rather than hinder them. In the World Food Programme's food-for-work project in Bangladesh, for instance, women were earning a smaller quantity of food than the men because of the difference in the amount of physical work they could do. Men were able to work longer hours than the women, who had to cook and prepare food for the men and children and attend to other household tasks. Should this project reinforce a situation that discriminates against women and ignore women's unpaid contribution to the well-being of their families? Some mechanisms could be introduced either to relieve women of the extra tasks they must perform or compensate them in some way for this socially necessary labor. A report on this project in fact suggests a number of simple ways that this could be done. It recommends an adjusted work norm for women which would be consistent with the policy of concessions for extraordinary working conditions already in force for men; special provisions for all-women gangs and all-women projects; reserving certain activities for women, including the less physically taxing jobs at the end of the season; supplying the earth-moving spade and basket at nominal cost, to be paid in installments, to women who cannot afford to rent or buy this equipment; providing day-care facilities; adding women to the membership of all project committees; training women to be gang leaders and informing them of the rights of women in the project.[7]

Other basic questions and issues must be raised about any kind of project. How will it affect the distribution of income? Will it enable participants to become more self-reliant? Will it enable women to gain more control over their lives? Should it be based on the traditional handicraft sector or on the modern sector? Should jobs be home-based or located in central workplaces? Related issues include: the division of labor between men and women, sexual harassment in public and in the place of work, discrimination against women in wages and jobs, and the exploitation of women as a cheap source of labor.

traditional or modern sector?

Traditional handicrafts have been one of the most popular forms of income generating projects for women because they are based on skills known in the community or that women already have; no costly machines or training are necessary; local materials usually can be used; women can do them at home in odd moments, interspersed with their other work. There are also cultural and sociological reasons:

In many countries women are already the custodians of crafts, which are part of the cultural life of the people and have been passed down from mother to daughter. Such crafts may be closely linked with folk rituals and festivities, and have thus been preserved over the centuries without loss of intrinsic quality...

Rapid industrialisation without any attention to traditional employment sectors would tear society from its moorings, bringing in its train the usual evils of juvenile delinquency, broken homes and a life lived under constant pressure. It may prove fruitful for the Third World countries to remember Mahatma Gandhi's message of self-reliance, of the need to develop village industry, to preserve national culture, and to avoid imitating consumer-oriented societies.[8]

Using local raw materials for the production of handicrafts counterbalances a common trade pattern whereby third world countries export raw materials to industrialized nations and import finished products. However, many handicraft projects fail to find the necessary markets in either the industrialized world or in the local community or country, and do not become economically viable.

The market for handcrafted goods in developed countries is unreliable: fashions and fads change rapidly. Marketing and distribution are the most difficult aspects of a project to control and they often receive the least attention. A small village project seldom has the resources needed to deal with the complexities of export, promotion and foreign exchange. It cannot hope to compete with larger businesses in the field of promotion and advertizing.

Handicrafts cannot compete at home with modern manufactured goods, imported from abroad or made by large factories and businesses in the same country. Manufactured goods are often more convenient or regarded as more prestigious, cost less and are more easily marketable. Locally made clay pots may be beautiful, but aluminium pans and plastic pails are lighter and more durable. It is unrealistic to expect villages to base their production on principles of self-reliance on local materials, unless this is part of an overall development perspective and planning.

While some planners are now emphasizing the need to deal with marketing of handicrafts in a more efficient way, others are turning to the modern sector. Women are to be given

ILO

Preparing wool for traditional weaving, Ecuador.

access to modern machines, skills and training, and they are to be adaptable to the changes in their lives and communities brought about by modernization. Handicrafts, these planners argue, confine women to the traditional sector while men are moving ahead with modern tools, technology and training.

Women's traditional work varies from place to place and from culture to culture. It may not be embroidering or knitting or hairdressing at all, but commerce, farming or construction. Some planners, realizing this, advocate the upgrading and modernization of these traditional women's jobs.

Modernization in itself is no guarantee that people's lives will be improved. With the modernization of the woollen handloom weaving industry in Jammu and Kashmir in India, thousands of women who handspun the yarn and prepared the warp and the weft lost their jobs. Even the weavers using the high-productivity modern looms reported a loss of income. The project changed the nature of the weaving industry from one using local raw materials and producing for local markets to one using imported materials and exporting the finished goods.[9]

Whether it is upgrading women's traditional work or

Anita Anand

Is anyone asking women what kind of work they need?

introducing them to jobs usually reserved for men, women face discrimination on the job. Is it worth training women for jobs when they may not be accepted for such employment? When a traditional job is upgraded and modern machines are introduced, men begin to take over the field. Jobs and training alone are not enough. Women must also fight prejudice and discrimination.

at home or in a central workplace?

Should an income generating project be home-based or employ women in a central workplace?

Experience shows that many women are already overworked, growing food, fetching fuel and water, cooking, cleaning and taking care of the children. They have no time to take on income generating activities. Planners therefore often design these activities so that women can do them in their homes or nearby, in between their other work, thus enabling women to earn money while still attending to their domestic responsibilities.

In places like northern India and Pakistan where women are in purdah, secluded in their homes, any money earning activity must be home-based. Only the very poorest women, who have no choice, go out to work in the fields and public places. Usually they aspire to the social status represented by purdah. Even where women are not secluded, staying at home may be the privilege of more affluent women and the status of "housewife" something to be aspired to.

Working at home is also a protection against the sexual harassment women face in public places. A recent UNICEF study points out that "in Afghanistan and northern India, the practice of seclusion is so strong that women fear their reputation will be tarnished if they appear unaccompanied by a man on a bus or even in the local village bazaar. Women who do so are subjected to unpleasant experiences of all kinds because society defines this behaviour as an open invitation for advances by men."[10] Harassment of women, however, is not confined to these areas. It occurs in both third world and industrialized countries. A hidden issue for a long time, the feminist movement is now bringing into the open this widespread obstacle to women's freedom of movement and employment.[11]

Home-based income generating projects carry the danger of exploiting women as cheap labor, by establishing and reinforcing a pattern of isolated and unorganized women. "The entrepreneurs use this 'bottomless pool of cheap labour' for decentralized production, thereby avoiding the regulations of factory legislation and corporate taxation. The process does nothing to reduce the poverty and misery of the mainly female and child labour and acts as an obstacle to the growth of the organised or modern high-wage industrial sector."[12]

This is illustrated in a World Employment Programme study, *Rural Women: Unequal Partners in Development:*

Some illustrations may clarify the manner in which secluded women in poor households are especially disadvantaged. The lace makers of Narsapur (Andhra Pradesh, India) are an example of such workers. They take pride in being only "housewives" and not "workers." Their work is in a sense invisible even to themselves, and they are not counted in official statistics of the labour force. Yet they work 6-8 hour days for an average payment equal to only 19 per cent of the minimum wage for women (which is lower than that for men), and the real value of their earnings has even been declining in the 1970s. When foreign demand for lace drops, even these earnings are reduced. Since they are not "workers" they cannot be "unemployed." Individual women, isolated in their homes, bend and strain to make small items of lace — separate components of a lace product whose form and eventual use and user are unknown to them. Their labour is the source of the bulk of handicraft export earnings (officially estimated to be 95 per cent of Andhra Pradesh export earnings from all handicrafts), and many (male) traders and exporters have become very rich from the lace business in the past decade. Surplus obtained by richer farmers as a result of the Green Revolution has been invested in this profitable industry which is based on invisible workers. The workers' ignorance of the nature of their product and its market is essential to the profitability of this substantial industry.[13]

Home-based work is also common in industrialized countries. The textile industry in particular uses this "putting out" system, as it is sometimes called, to cut labor costs. Recent events indicate that this practice may be increasing. In October 1981, for instance, the Labor Department of the USA revoked a ban on work at home in the knitted outerwear industry, a ban which had been enacted in the early 1940s as part of the Fair Labor Standards Act setting up the federal minimum wage and standards for hours.[14]

Women who work at home in industrialized countries generally have no labor protection, no job security, insurance, sick leave, pension and so on. Just as their counterparts in developing countries, they are forced by economic need and domestic responsibilities to take work that can be combined with housework and child care.

Development planners are now calling for regulations and control of home-based work, but these will not overcome women's isolation and the limitations on their acquisition of new skills, knowledge, organizing ability and control over their own lives. As Vina Mazumdar writes in *Towards Self-Reliance*:

The desire to provide women with employment opportunities within the household sector, so as not to conflict with their family roles, tends to clash with other social objectives, e.g.:

(a) to diversify women's employment opportunities, access to new skills, knowledge and the wider society, with a view to increasing their self-reliance, bargaining power and participatory opportunities and rescuing them from their present status of unpaid family workers;

(b) to eliminate the present tendency to relegate women to

A rare picture of a woman receiving training in the use and maintenance of a modern plough, Upper Volta.

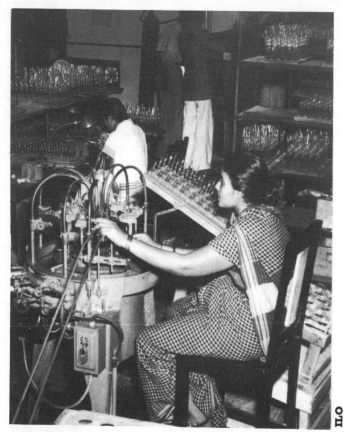

Indian lightbulb factory.

low-paid, low-skilled and low-status occupations which reinforce discriminatory attitudes and practices;

(c) to promote voluntary acceptance of the small family norm, as studies have shown that household industries tend to encourage growth of large families, and the exploitation of women's health and labour (Mitra, 1978);

(d) even a policy to promote women's self-employment in the small scale sector sometimes provides only a thin guise for men's monopoly over resources, and control over such enterprises, with the woman not even able to control her income (Planning Commission, 1978).[15]

central workplace and birth control

Population control studies show that employing women outside the home can lower birth rates, in addition to eliminating the dangers of exploitation inherent in home-based work. "Locating economic production in a central workplace," writes Ruth Dixon, "carries a number of economic and social advantages." It facilitates regulation of working conditions and wages, supervision of workers and quality control of goods, training in skills, literacy, nutrition and family planning and "it encourages delayed marriage and fertility control by posing, among other contradictions, a degree of incompatibility between worker and family roles."[16]

The powerless, physically isolated woman, entirely dependent on her husband and children for social status and economic survival, is an unlikely candidate for family planning. Home-based industries tend to encourage childbearing because they so frequently employ young children to weave rugs or saris, wrap bidis, shell prawns, make baskets, or help in other tasks. Locating production in a central workplace should devalue the economic contribution of young children and deter their exploitation as a cheap labor force.[17]

The main goal, however, is a reduction of the birth rate. For best results, employment opportunities outside the home are to be restricted to young women of childbearing age:

The proposition that jobs in these modern, small industries be reserved for women in their early reproductive years derives from the simple argument that little demographic impact will result from employing women who already have large numbers of children or who are beyond menopause or widowed. Yet, frequently it is the destitute widows and women abandoned by their husbands who are the first to come forth. These women would be good candidates for income-generating activities based in or around the home; such as growing vegetables or raising poultry or fish for the market, spinning and weaving, and other traditional tasks. But the new employment in central workplaces could more effectively be secured for girls of marriageable age and married women in the early stages of their childbearing years.[18]

Feminists see population policies as a poor basis on which to build employment opportunities for women. Moreover, incentives for a lower birth rate can be withdrawn when population policies change. In countries such as the Soviet Union and some European countries with low birth rates, governments are using a variety of ways to encourage women to bear children, including disincentives to work outside the home and restrictions in abortion and contraception services.[19]

income generation and self-reliance

Most women do work outside the home and their experience shows that this can be just as oppressive as home-based work. Last hired, first fired, women in factories, fields, shops, construction sites, offices and workshops are poorly paid, receive few benefits and are exposed to health hazards. We can learn from the women already employed in industrialized countries and from those now being exploited in multinational industries in the free trade zones and other areas of the third world.

Even income generating projects designed to be economically viable and to create a measure of economic independence may not bring self-determination. In *Towards Self-Reliance*, Vina Mazumdar presents some case studies which show that "income alone does not bring self-reliance and dignity":

Lijjat Papad claims to be a success as a worker-owned cooperative with sales of Rs. 6 crores annually (25% is in exports), 10,000 women employees and social aims of uplifting women. But do the women workers really share in these profits? Do they manage the industry? Have they

Traditional Jamaican handicrafts, now produced in a centralized setting for the tourist industry.

gained any new skills, dignity or self-reliance? No, because they are only silent workers in a vast industry, which is managed by others, mostly men. I call this sweated labour... A study of the Amul Dairy Cooperative uncovered the fact that while women do 100% of the animal care work and have increased their daily work-load by four hours, they do not participate in the meetings where the major decisions are made like how the cooperative will be managed and where the profits will go.[20]

It is possible for women to build up organizations which not only promote employment for women, but also self-reliance, consciousness raising, work and organizational skills and supporting services, and a greater degree of self-determination for women and communities. Vina Mazumdar gives an example of how this is being done by an organization of women in India:

SEWA (Self-Employed Women's Association), an off-shoot of the Textile Labour Association (TLA), Ahmedabad, has become a very important symbol. TLA's initial programmes for women were welfare-oriented to help the families of textile workers. While women workers were being forced out of the textile industry by mechanisation and modernisation of the mills, the union was establishing welfare centres, literacy classes and other activities for them.

In 1973, some self-employed women labourers (head loaders, vegetable vendors and others) approached Ela Bhatt of TLA with their problems: exploitation by money lenders and harassment by the police and municipal authorities. The women knew their problem and wanted protection.

So SEWA was born, now numbering 10,600 self-employed women in Ahmedabad.

They have their own cooperative bank which extends credit, does wholesale bulk purchasing, pays their tax and utility bills and provides many other services determined by the bank's management who are the women themselves. SEWA also runs child-care centres, a maternity and health insurance scheme and a housing scheme.

This is what I call women's development. SEWA has given these women the confidence, strength and skills to manage problems which were overpowering them earlier. Yet it has not made them dependent on anyone's charity which is so often a characteristic feature of welfare work. Collective strength, conscious decision-making and dealing with powerful agencies of modern development like banks, insurance companies, municipalities and the police on equal terms has transformed the self-perception of these women. Such organisations of under-privileged women which protect and generate employment, provide access to skills and other types of knowledge, health and child-care services, and above all function as pressure groups to increase their participation in development decisions are powerful instruments. Yet in the present setting, it is nearly impossible for an individual, self-employed woman or even organisations smaller than SEWA to succeed to the same extent, the economic and political structures that control the market being too complex and powerful.[21]

When women are successful in organizing and begin to achieve the degree of success that the women in SEWA have had, they also meet opposition from powerful sources on all sides. In 1981 the TLA expelled SEWA and Ela Bhatt from its organization and premises and requested its unions to withdraw their money from the SEWA bank. An account of this break, given in the Indian feminist journal *Manushi*, identifies the underlying causes as the male-dominated leadership of the TLA and the way this caste non-worker leadership collaborates with the upper strata of society rather than with the lower and non-caste workers: "TLA leaders felt increasingly threatened by the women's advance towards self-independence, and methods of struggle which were not only opposed to TLA policy of compromise and collaboration, but also provided a dangerous role model to the male workers! They also resented the press publicity and widespread recognition given to Ela Bhatt's work..."[22]

Ela Bhatt writes: "SEWA owes its existence to TLA, but when SEWA women slightly show their little bit of independence and self-dignity, it is being destroyed. With so much effort, we had been able to bring urban and rural self-employed women into the fold of a trade union, and now their effort is to totally throw us out of the trade union world!... With the strength of our members, dedication of my colleagues, support of many, many friends known and unknown, and god's blessings SEWA will go ahead, SEWA will not die..."[23]

lessons we have learned

Women are being offered undesirable choices by men, profit hungry corporations, insensitive governments and development agencies. Women should not have to choose between exploitation in home-based industry or in outside employment.

One of the reasons women are confronted with these undesirable choices is that they are burdened with the full responsibility of all the household work and child rearing. To help them cope with both domestic responsibilities and waged work, a number of aids are being proposed: appropriate technologies or labor-saving devices, child care facilities, social services, legislation for the provision of maternity benefits and leave, flexible hours and part-time work.

Demands for child care facilities and social services are important issues for the women's movement in most parts of the world. Even when these demands are fulfilled, however, the responsibility for housework and child care remains with women. In times of economic difficulty, when governments and business want to reduce the labor force and spending on social services, it is the women who are expected to return to full-time household responsibilities. As Elise Boulding says: "Since no socialist state could afford to duplicate the individualized breeder/feeder role of women as a public service, and no capitalist state wanted to, it was easy to turn this task back to women in the end."[24]

While social services and child care facilities remain high priorities with the women's movement, feminists are also addressing the question of the division of labor between men and women in the household and calling for more equitable sharing of housework and child rearing. The need for this is now recognized by some intergovernmental agencies.

Notes on Enhancing Women's Participation in Development of the Asian and Pacific Centre for Women and Develop-

Bangladesh.

ment states that "co-sharing of tasks on the home front is also to be sought. Breaking down the traditional division of labour within the household is a prerequisite for the success of wider attempts at economic and social transformation."[25] A document of the World Conference on Agrarian Reform and Rural Development (WCARRD), held in Rome in 1979, stresses the need to "promote understanding of men's responsibilities to share household duties."[26]

The *Report on the World Conference of the United Nations Decade for Women,* held in 1980, states that it is "essential that household chores and family care should be shared by men, and special emphasis should be placed on the obligation of couples to share household tasks with a view to facilitating the access of women to gainful employment."[27]

How is this to be done? One concrete suggestion is given by a World Employment Programme study in a chapter entitled "A New International Order Begins at Home":

An equitable sharing of domestic responsibilities is facilitated where discrimination against workers with family responsibilities is eliminated. The ILO has taken the initiative in drafting a Recommendation to that end which is currently under consideration. It would add to or supersede the 1965 Recommendation (No. 123) which considers only female workers. Advancing the idea of supporting men as well as women undertaking domestic work by, for example, allowing more flexibility in working schedules, and job security in spite of that flexibility, is a means of moving towards greater equality.[28]

Women at election rally, Kenya, 1974.

Childbearing and breastfeeding cannot be shared by men, but women should not have to choose between being mothers or paid workers, or be penalized for their ability to bear children. Jobs for women do not have to create "incompatibility between worker and family roles" or be dependent on the policies of population control. Participation in paid work, as well as knowledge and use of contraceptive means, should be liberating not repressive.

Provisions for maternity leave and benefits enable women to be mothers without loss of jobs or income. Legislation for this sometimes backfires, however. Employers do not like to hire women because of the cost of providing benefits. A UNICEF regional report for Asia states:

> Perhaps the only answer to this dilemma is to devise strategies which do not tax the industries employing women directly, but which spread responsibility for compensation over a much broader base. This amounts to indirect redistribution of income, and is justified because, after all, it is society as a whole which benefits from the special biological and nurturance roles of women.[29]

Paternity leave can help if it is made worth men's while to take it. In Sweden, where this option has been available for many years, only a relatively small percentage of men take advantage of it. Likewise, flexibility in work hours and part-time work can be beneficial to women if this does not simply reinforce their complete responsibility for housework and child care, as Italian feminists contend that such legislation in Italy is likely to do.[30]

double oppression - double struggle

Employment alone cannot emancipate women. Income generating activities and jobs can contribute to promoting women's self-determination and dignity, or they can hinder it. To promote it, the jobs offered will have to be non-exploitative: offer decent wages, equal to those of others doing similar work; be accompanied by access to training and job opportunities; and provide child care, social services and benefits. They must offer women the possibility to organize and to share fairly in decision making and control in the workplace.

Legislation for and provision of all these things are essential, but not sufficient. Here again, the economic and patriarchal structures of oppression are intertwined. Women must fight for recognition of the value of their work, whether it is in the field of production or reproduction: childbearing and caring for the needs of their families and households. They must battle the sexist stereotypes, attitudes and institutions which portray and maintain women as subordinate and passive, capable of certain activities only; place responsibility for child care and domestic work with women exclusively and then assign a low value to it; make women into sex objects and then subject them to harassment, restricting their freedom of movement; and exclude them from participation, decision making and self-determination in public and community life.

Development planners can try to ensure, as far as possible, that their projects and programs do not reinforce or create oppressive situations. Much will depend, however, on women's own ability to raise their consciousness and organize themselves effectively. This need is no less great in industrialized countries than it is in the third world. Sensitive change agents can help this process.

Women are, of course, already organizing. They are working within labor unions and they are forming their own. Women in central workplaces are creating their own organizations, as well as women who have greater difficulties in coming together because they are isolated in their homes: women in the "putting out" system, domestics, migrant women, welfare mothers, unemployed and self-employed women. Since there are so many who benefit from the double oppression of women — both the economic elite and men of whatever class — this is no easy task. When women do come together to define their own needs, goals and strategies, and to work for these, they must be prepared, as the history of SEWA shows, to face opposition from all those in power. It is a long and difficult struggle.

Footnotes

1   Marilyn W. Hoskins, *Income Generating Activities with Women's Participation* (Washington, DC: USAID, 1980), pp. 3-4.

2   *Field Directors' Handbook* (Oxford: Oxfam, 1980), p. 34-4, and Mayra Buvinic and Nadia H. Youssef, *Women Headed Households: The Ignored Factor in Development Planning* (Washington, DC: International Center for Research on Women, 1978).

3   Devaki Jain, "Women's Employment," in *Notes on Enhancing Women's Participation in Development Planning* (Kuala Lumpur: Asian and Pacific Centre for Women and Development, 1980), p. 30.

4   Hoskins, *Income Generating Activities*, pp. 20-21.

5   Ruth B. Dixon, *Rural Women at Work* (Baltimore and London: John Hopkins University Press, 1978), p. xi.

6   Ibid., p. xii.

7   *Women in Food-for-Work* (Rome: World Food Programme, 1979), pp. 27-32.

8   Jasleen Dhamija, "Handicrafts: a Source of Employment for Women in Developing Rural Economies," *Women Workers* (Geneva: International Labour Organisation, 1976), p. 178 and p. 181.

9   *A Case Study of the Modernisation of the Traditional Handloom Weaving Industry in the Kashmir Valley*, Asian and Pacific Centre for Women and Development Occasional Paper, no. 1 (Kuala Lumpur, 1978).

10   Andrea Menefee Singh, *The Integration of Women in the Development Process and its Impact on the Well-Being of Children* (New Delhi: UNICEF, 1979), p. 49.

11   See especially: *Aegis,* a North American feminist "Magazine on Ending Violence Against Women" and *Manushi*, an Indian feminist journal. Feminist publications from all parts of the world are bringing the issue to the fore.

12   Vina Mazumdar, "The Status of Women: Economic Aspects" in *Towards Self-Reliance,* Jessie Tellis-Nayak and Selena Costa-Pinto, eds. (New Delhi: Indian Social Institute, 1979), p. 17.

13   Martha F. Loutfi, *Rural Women: Unequal Partners in Development* (Geneva: International Labour Organisation, 1980), p. 18.

14   *International Herald Tribune,* 10-11 October 1981.

15   Mazumdar, *Towards Self-Reliance,* pp. 19-20.

16   Dixon, *Rural Women at Work,* p. 26.

17   Ibid., p. 27.

18   Ibid., p. 29.

19   See especially: "Birth Rate Politics in Eastern Europe and the USSR," *Labour Focus on Eastern Europe* in *ISIS International Bulletin,* no. 7 (Spring 1978), pp. 26-28; "Soviet Women: Less Choice – The New Employment Restrictions," *Women in Eastern Europe,* no. 4 (March 1981), p. 16; and Gail Warshofsky Lapidus, *Women in Soviet Society* (Berkeley: University of California Press, 1978), pp. 292-309.

20   Mazumdar, *Towards Self-Reliance,* pp. 17-18.

21   Ibid., pp. 18-19.

22   *Manushi,* no. 8 (1981), p. 13.

23   Ibid., p. 15.

24   Cited in Loutfi, *Rural Women,* p. 57.

25   Padma Ramachandran and Geeta R. Bharadwaj, *Notes on Enhancing Women's Participation in Development Planning,* p. 10.

26   *World Conference on Agrarian Reform and Rural Development Report* (Rome: Food and Agricultural Organization, 1979), p. 11.

27   *Report of the World Conference of the United Nations Decade for Women* (New York: United Nations, 1980), p. 30.

28   Loutfi, *Rural Women,* p. 57.

29   Singh, *The Integration of Women in the Development Process,* p. 56.

30   See especially: Birgitta Wistrand, *Swedish Women on the Move* (Stockholm: The Swedish Institute, 1981), pp. 32-34 and Lelia Di Paola and Roberta Tatafiore, "Tempo di Lei," *Noi Donne,* vol. 27, no. 19 (May 1982), pp. 59-71.

S.O.S. Mulher, set up by the womens groups of Sao Paolo, takes effective action against violence against women. Brazil, 1980.

Nair Benedicto/Agencia F4

resources for research & organizing

An enormous amount of material has been produced on women and development and most of it deals in some way with rural development. What follows is not a complete listing, but a selection based on usefulness for research and organizing from a critical and feminist perspective. Some lesser-known resources have been highlighted, and we have tried to indicate the perspective and assess the usefulness of governmental, intergovernmental and better-known development sources.

The listings are arranged first by United Nations bodies, a major source of material; then resource centers (organizations, institutions and groups producing regular material on this issue); then by periodicals, bibliographies, pamphlets and articles. There is a great deal of material specifically on appropriate technology, so this is listed separately.

United Nations

The United Nations is a major source of information on women and development. The almost overwhelming amount of material its agencies produce varies considerably in quality and perspective. Since UN agencies are intergovernmental, their materials seldom criticize governments or specific policies directly, but tend to be descriptive and statistical. Some UN documents are acritical and non-committal to the point of being bland and completely useless. In spite of these general limitations, there are a number of very useful resources, and a few excellent ones. First and foremost, the UN is a very good source of background material, factual information, project descriptions and statistical and technical studies. It is also an excellent source of information on governmental and intergovernmental development policies and about the negotiations going on around development issues such as the New International Economic Order, the Basic Human Needs Approach and so forth. Some UN material does take a critical and analytical approach to the issues. In recent years it has focused more attention on development policies in relationship to women. A feminist perspective and an awareness of the need to analyze patriarchal structures are not generally to be found in UN documents, yet occasionally these do appear.

What follows is a brief guide to UN materials relating to women and development. We are listing many of the UN bodies with an indication of the scope and range of the fields they cover and a number of specific materials which we feel are representative of their work on women and development. We have tried to point out those which we find most valuable, and especially any which bring a feminist perspective to the issues.

African Training and Research Centre for Women (ATRCW) P.O. Box 3001, Addis Ababa, Ethiopia.

ATRCW grew out of the women's program of the United Nations Economic Commission for Africa (UNECA). Founded in 1975, its purpose is to encourage and assist the member states to improve opportunities and skills for women, especially in rural areas, with a view to enabling them to participate more effectively in the development of their countries. ATRCW organizes conferences and seminars, undertakes research and development projects, and serves as a resource centre and clearinghouse for materials on women and development in Africa.

An **Information Kit for Women in Africa** (1981) produced by the International Women's Tribune Centre, Inc., New York in collaboration with ATRCW contains detailed information on ATRCW's activities and publications as well as projects in various parts of Africa. This kit also describes selected projects run and funded by governmental and non-governmental organizations. The first 80 pages of the kit are devoted to information on funding and technical assistance, including how to write a project proposal and where to apply for funds. It is available in English and French.

The ATRCW has produced a great many useful descriptive and background documents including bibliographies, conference and workshop reports, and case studies. Examples of the kinds of materials available are: **Women and Development: An Annotated Bibliography** (1978) with several hundred entries of United Nations publications, documents and other studies and articles; **Progress and Obstacles in Achieving the Minimum Objectives of the World and Africa Plans of Action: A Critical Review** by Margaret Max-Forson, a report of the Second Regional Conference on the Integration of Women in Development, held in Lusaka, Zambia in December 1979; **Law and the Status of Women in Nigeria** by Dr. (Mrs.) J.O. Debo Akande (1979); **Women and the Fishing Industry in Liberia** by Ms. Olubanke Akerle (1979); **Women and the Mass Media in Africa** by Elma Letitia Anani et al. (1981); and **Manual on Child Development, Family Life, Nutrition** by Jean A.S. Ritchie (1979).

The directory of **National, Subregional and Regional Machineries for Women in Development** is a useful source of addresses and information on governmental organizations dealing with women's issues, although it does not give any assessment of the perspective or effectiveness of these.

A particularly valuable publication is **Appropriate Technology for African Women** by Marilyn Carr (1978), a critical and insightful examination of technology and its effects on women and their work in Africa. Another especially well-done and useful publication is **Women and Development in Tanzania: An Annotated Bibliography** by Ophelia Mascarenhas and Marjorie Mbilinyi (1980). In the introduction, the authors explain the conceptual framework of the bibliography and their selection of materials. It is a good overview of some of the burning concerns of women and an excellent explanation of the concepts of sexual division of labor and patriarchal relations. The entries are selected in this framework and are annotated at sufficient length to give the reader a good idea of the content and the strengths and weaknesses of each document. It is an extremely useful critical guide to the material and contains a section of general materials as well as those specific to Tanzania. This is the kind of bibliography we need. Highly recommended. Most publications are available in English and French. A complete publications list is available from ATRCW.

Asian and Pacific Centre for Women and Development (APCWD)

Asian and Pacific Development Centre, Pesiaran Duta, P.O. Box 2224, Kuala Lumpur, Malaysia.

The APCWD is a training and research institution of the United Nations Economic and Social Commission for Asia and the Pacific (ESCAP). Established in 1977, it aims to ensure the full participation of women in the economic and social development of their communities. It was located first in Teheran, Iran, then in Bangkok, Thailand and now in Kuala Lumpur, Malaysia. The **APCWD Women's Resource Book 1979**, produced in collaboration with the International Women's Tribune Centre, Inc., New York, provides a detailed description of APCWD activities and publications up to 1979.

It also lists United Nations agencies, governmental and some of the more well-established non-governmental organizations involved in women and development issues in the various countries of Asia and the Pacific, without, however, indicating their perspective or evaluating their work.

Among the materials available from the Centre are studies and reports from various workshops and meetings, including: **Notes on Data Collection with Special Reference to Women** (1980); **Women's Employment–Possibilities of Relevant Research** by Devaki Jain (1980); **The Critical Needs of Women** (1977), a report of the Expert Group Meeting on the Identification of the Basic Needs of Women of Asia and the Pacific. The latter in an excellent examination of the basic needs approach and its inadequacies. Analyzing the basic needs of women from a feminist perspective, the report identifies both the critical material needs and other types of basic needs as well, such as freedom from violence and debilitating work hours. It points out that imbalances in the distribution of goods and services exist not only between households but within households and stresses the need for changing the structures which lie behind and create unequal social and economic relations. Another excellent publication is the report of a workshop organized by the APCWD in Bangkok in June 1979 on **Feminist Structures and Ideology in the First Half of the Decade for Women**, which raises many questions about development and how women's goals can be translated into real structural and social change. Interesting too is the **Declaration on Technical Co-operation Among Developing Countries and Women** (1978). A bibliography of all the materials available at the Centre has also been produced along with a **Directory of Fellows and Consultants 1977-1980**.

The Economic Commission for Latin America (ECLA)
Casilla 179 D, Santiago, Chile.

In 1975, ECLA published a study entitled **Mujeres en América Latina: Aportes para una Discusión** which examines the position of women in Latin American countries and makes some hypotheses about the participation of women in the development of Latin America. This book also contains the report of the first regional seminar on the integration of women in development held in Caracas in 1975 in preparation for the Mexico Conference. It is still useful, mainly for the wealth of statistical data on the position of women in society in Latin America. In 1977, ECLA created a Special Unit to deal with issues related to the integration of women in economic and social development. One of the main activities of this unit is to develop a Reference Service on women, i.e. to collect and process adequately relevant data on women. This is done in collaboration with the Centro Latinoamericano de Documentación Económica y Social (CLADES) of ECLA and with the Information Communication System (DOCPAL) established by the Latin American Demographic Centre (CELADE).

In 1979, ECLA published **Inventario de Proyectos sobre Integración de la Mujer al Desarrollo en América Latina**, with information on the most significant projects in the region, being implemented with the cooperation of UN agencies and which promote the participation of women in development. ECLA also prepared a Directory in 1979 with information on human resources, activities and/or projects relating to women. Other publications include bibliographical listings of ECLA materials and a number of more recent reports and papers on the integration of women in development in Latin America.

The Food and Agricultural Organization (FAO)
Via delle Terme di Caracalla, 00100 Rome, Italy.

The specialized agency of the United Nations dealing with agriculture, food issues and rural development, the FAO has a great impact on the development of rural areas through its policies and programs. Although women are the majority of the world's food producers, it is only since International Women's Year in 1975 that the FAO has given significant attention to the needs and situations of rural women. Most programs and research on women have been, and continue to be, channeled through the nutrition division, which has made considerable effort to direct programs to women and to improve their access to food. The Freedom from Hunger Campaign/Action for Development is another FAO program which has given attention to women and produced useful material on this issue.

For International Women's Year, the FAO Information Division produced a booklet, richly illustrated with photographs, entitled **The Missing Half – Woman 1975**. An introduction to the situation of rural women, this booklet emphasizes how women's situations have deteriorated due to neglect by development agencies and policies and it calls for integrating women into development. In 1977, the FAO Documentation Centre, in cooperation with the Population Documentation Centre, published an annotated bibliography of FAO publications and documents from 1966 to mid-1976 on **Women and Family in Rural Development**. A computer print out, it is unfortunately very difficult to read. The FAO Review on Development, **Ceres**, has done some special issues on women, in 1975 and 1980 on the occasion of the UN conferences on women, but otherwise has not focused very much on women.

The FAO World Conference on Agrarian Reform and Rural Development (WCARRD) in 1979 was one of the few international intergovernmental conferences to give serious attention to rural women. A number of preparatory and follow-up materials deal with women. In an article "The Role of Women in Agrarian Reform and Rural Development" in the FAO Review **Land Reform, Land Settlement and Cooperatives**, no. 1, 1979, Ingrid Palmer draws up a "checklist of demands that can properly be made on agrarian reform on behalf of women." Another 1979 publication, **The Legal Status of Rural Women**, reviews the laws in a number of countries affecting women's access to land, credit, membership in cooperatives and collectives, as well as laws affecting women agricultural workers. Another preparatory document is the survey of **Rural Women's Working Conditions: An Extreme Case of Unequal Exchange**, prepared in April 1978. In January 1979, the WCARRD secretariat published a **Review and Analysis of Agrarian Reform and Rural Development in the Developing Countries since the Mid-1960s** which includes a point on the "Integration of Women in Development." This looks at the roles of women in agricultural production and at women's access to resources and their control, employment and income-producing opportunities, health and nutrition, and policy making and programming for rural services. The document describes the processes of marginalization of the rural poor and of women in particular. The **Report of the World Conference on Agrarian Reform and Rural Development** gives the conference decisions about the "Integration of Women in Rural Development," under the headings of Equality of Legal Status, Women's Access to Rural Services, Women's Organization and Participation, and Educational and Employment Opportunities. In 1980, the FAO issued a 16 page illustrated booklet entitled **WCARRD – A Turning Point for Rural Women**, which comments and expands on quotations from the conference decisions, with examples and illustrations from various parts of the world. Another follow-up document to WCARRD is the **Report of the FAO/SIDA Workshop on the Integration of Women in Agriculture and Rural Development**, held in Hyderabad, India in 1980. Concentrating on several Asian countries, the workshop developed some project proposals and action ideas for integrating women in development.

The **Freedom From Hunger Campaign/Action for Development (FFHC/AD)** is an FAO program which aims to stimulate critical awareness of development issues and promote people's participation in development. It works with non-governmental organizations (NGOs). FFHC/AD has produced some very good material on development issues. Although its selected bibliography on development in 1974 contained very little about women, materials produced since have improved. Two regular publications are particularly useful. One is the **Development Education Exchange Papers** (DEEP), a bi-monthly publication which reviews recent materials on development and gives information on activities of groups and organizations. The reviews are thorough enough to be useful, and DEEP does not neglect women. The other valuable publication

is the bi-monthly magazine **Ideas and Action Bulletin**, issued in English, French and Spanish, with reports on development initiatives and reflections on strategies. Attractively illustrated, this Bulletin covers the issue of women and development regularly. Some articles of particular interest are: "Women and Development – The Need for a Really Innovative Approach," no. 112, 1976/5, by Monica Fong; "Women in Development: A Caribbean Perspective," by Peggy Antrobus, no. 130, 1979/4; "Where are all the Women Now? An Evaluation of a Project List," by Sue Tuckwell, no. 131, 1979/5; "Integration of Women into Development – What Does it Really Mean?," by Mary Roodkowsky, no. 137, 1980/5; "Training Change Agents in Asia," no. 140, 1981/2; and "The Role and Training of Development Activists," by Kamla Bhasin, Vasant Palshikar and Lakshmi Rao, no. 142, 1981/4.

The FFHC/AD regional office in New Delhi has produced some excellent materials on training and on change agents in Asia which show a clear understanding and perspective on women's needs for self-determination, organization and mobilization. These include the booklets **Participatory Training for Development** and **Breaking Barriers** by Kamla Bhasin and the book **Readings on Poverty, Politics and Development** edited by Kamla Bhasin and Vimala R. This collection examines the roots of people's problems in Asia through relating experiences and through analysis by people working directly in the field. It is a highly readable and very valuable book.

Liz Mackie/ISIS

The International Drinking Water Supply and Sanitation Decade
c/o UNDP Division of Information, 1 United Nations Plaza, New York, New York 10017, USA.

In 1977 the **United Nations Water Conference** in Mar del Plata, Argentina, designated the period 1981-1990 as the International Drinking Water Supply and Sanitation Decade. Several organizations of the United Nations development system have formed a "Steering Committee for Co-operative Action," chaired by the United Nations Development Programme (UNDP), to coordinate the Decade work. It is estimated that US$ 30,000 million will be spent annually for water supply and sanitation related development projects.

The UNDP's information kit on the decade contains the **Decade Dossier** outlining the dimensions of the need and the Decade strategies for action, four case histories on water/sanitation activities, a **Decade Action Guide** with suggestions and examples of specific activities for various Decade participants, a listing of further information materials available. Despite an article on women and a clear awareness of water supply as women's work, most examples of training and the use of appropriate technology refer to men. The material could have been improved by more emphasis and illustration of women's need for this training as well as for decision making power in the management of water supplies.

One of the best analyses of this problem is a paper presented by Noracy de Souza at the Mar del Plata Conference on Water, **Water, Women and Development — Women as Water Carriers: a Case for Evaluating Technology Transfer to Rural Areas.** After pointing out that, in rural areas, water supply could become the focal point of integrated rural development projects since it supports multisectoral developments in health, food production, land use, employment and education, the author shows that discussion on rural water supply and water technology oftentimes overlooks the needs of the peasant women and their relationship to the problems involved, even though women are traditionally the water carriers in their community. The lack of appropriate technology to alleviate women's burden directly affects the overall agricultural development. There is a case for water technology appropriate to women's needs.

The International Research and Training Institute for the Advancement of Women (INSTRAW)
United Nations, New York, New York, 10017, USA and Santo Domingo, Dominican Republic.

First proposed at the 1975 Mexico Conference, INSTRAW is intended to become a clearinghouse for the collection, processing and dissemination of information on research, training and action programs regarding women all over the world, as well as a place where research and training related to societal problems involving women can be conducted at an international level, particularly as regards the planning and implementation of programs for the advancement of women. INSTRAW became operational at the beginning of 1980. Its headquarters were temporarily housed in New York and moved to Santo Domingo in the course of 1982. As one of its first tasks INSTRAW prepared a survey of existing data and activities related to research on and training of women carried out within the United Nations system and in international, regional and national institutions on women. As a result of the first phase of the survey, two directories were published in 1980, on **Research on Women** and on **Training for Women**, both bearing the subtitle: **An Inventory of United Nations Sponsored Activities**. The documents focus on on-going projects on women, conducted or funded by organizations of the United Nations system in the developing countries in the spheres of employment, health and education. The directory on research records 232 projects and the one on training 400.

Joint United Nations Information Committee (JUNIC) and United Nations Non-governmental Liaison Service (UNNGLS)
United Nations, CH-1211 Geneva 10, Switzerland.

With a number of UN and non-governmental organizations the JUNIC and the NGLS are producing a series of kits on the theme of Women and Development. The first kit, published in September 1981 on **Women and Disability** was prepared by Eva Zabolai-Csekme. It examines a very neglected aspect of women and development: the situation and needs of disabled women. Inspired by the "firm conviction that a real change must be brought about on behalf of disabled women," this well-prepared and highly useful kit contains a series of papers on many aspects of the lives of disabled women, on causes of disabilities, on prevention and rehabilitation with suggestions for discussion and action. The kit also contains a listing of resources, both written and audio-visual and of organizations working on this issue. Other kits in the same format are **Women, Health and Development; Women and Food;** and **Women and the North-South Dialogue.**

The NGLS also provides a number of services and materials for non-governmental organizations. One useful publication is the **United Nations Development Education Directory** (1981) which lists all the United Nations system agencies, sources of development information and services with addresses, contact persons and a brief listing of services available and subject areas covered.

Liz Mackie

UNICEF produces two excellent and recommended publications: **UNICEF News**, a quarterly magazine and **Assignment Children**, "a multidisciplinary journal concerned with major social development issues, with particular reference to children, women and youth." Both regularly contain articles related to women and development. **UNICEF News** contains short, interesting articles dealing with particular problems in various countries of the world. These are well-illustrated overviews and introductions to the issues. **Assignment Children** gives more in-depth and analytical studies. Both are usually incisive and represent some of the more progressive thinking on women and development within the United Nations.

Both the headquarters and the regional and country offices of UNICEF are sources of reports, studies and background papers. Just two examples are: **The Situation and Problems of Women and Children in South Central Asia** by Andrea Menefee Singh (1979) with both description and statistics on demography, health, socio-economic factors, urbanization, employment, child labor and political participation. The author brings out issues of violence against women and why maternity laws oftentimes work against women. **Mid-Decade Conference on Women - Bangladesh Perspective** edited by Shamima Islam and Jowshan A. Rahman for the Women's Development Unit of UNICEF, Dacca, reports on the sharing of experiences about the conference in a post-conference seminar.

United Nations Decade for Women
United Nations Plaza, New York, New York 10017, USA. Advancement for Women Branch, Vienna International Centre, P.O. Box 500, A-1400 Vienna, Austria.

As preparation for and as a result of the UN Decade for Women and the two international conferences on women in 1975 and 1980, the UN has produced a number of reports. These include the following: **Meeting in Mexico** is a booklet giving the background of the International Women's Year Conference in Mexico and reprinting the Declaration of Mexico on the Equality of Women and their Contribution to Development and Peace, as well as the World Plan of Action for the Implementation of the Objectives of the International Women's Year. In addition, the booklet also has the Plan of Action for the Integration of Women in Development adopted in 1974 by the Economic and Social Commission for Asia and the Pacific and the Plan of Action adopted for the Region of the Economic Commission for Africa.

The World Plan and the regional plans of action – including the June 1978 plan adopted for the region of the Economic Commission for Western Africa and the plan adopted in 1977 for the region of the Economic Commission for Latin America – are all reprinted in 1980 in a special booklet produced by the United Nations on the occasion of the Copenhagen Conference.

The **Report of the World Conference of the United Nations Decade for Women: Equality, Development and Peace**, Copenhagen, 14 to 30 July 1980, contains the text of the Program of Action for the Second Half of the United Nations Decade for Women, the resolutions and decisions adopted by the conference, as well as background information about the conference itself: its origins, attendance and organization of work, summary of the general debate, the reports of subsidiary

United Nations Children's Fund (UNICEF)
United Nations, New York, New York 10017, USA and United Nations, Geneva, Switzerland.

UNICEF gives particular attention to the needs of infants and children in both development programs and in worldwide emergency measures. Over the years UNICEF has given increasing attention to women, particularly to mothers of children. It supports projects in the fields of health, education, agriculture, communications, information, public administration, water supply and community development, stressing the basic needs of rural areas and urban slums. It also actively undertakes development education in industrialized countries.

bodies and action taken on these reports by the Conference, a list of official documents, national reports, background papers, and submissions by non-governmental organizations.

The background papers and documents are far too numerous to list, but are well worth looking at. They range from evaluations of the situation of women in various countries and regions of the world to the examination of the role of women in liberation struggles, the effects of apartheid on women, women and the media and reports from the various UN agencies. The document on **Recommendations Relating to Women and Development Emerging from Conferences Held Under the Auspices of the United Nations or the Specialized Agencies** is a good summary of UN conferences from 1974 to 1979 and how they have dealt with or failed to deal with women and issues of particular concern to women.

A brief but interesting publication is **Women Helping Women** (1980), a booklet which describes a number of projects for women throughout the world, designed to help achieve the goals of the Decade.

In January 1982, the General Assembly of the United Nations adopted a resolution to carry out a world survey on the Role of Women in Development. It was also decided that the coordination and preparation for the 1985 UN Conference to mark the end of the Women's Decade would be carried out in Vienna at the Advancement for Women Branch of the Centre for Social Development and Humanitarian Affairs. This Centre should also coordinate the implementation of Decade plans and activities.

United Nations Development Programme (UNDP)
1 United Nations Plaza, New York, New York 10017, USA.

The UNDP Background Brief **Global-1**, entitled "The United Nations Development Programme and Women in Development," gives an overview of this agency's programs, activities and publications in the area of women and development. The UNDP has produced a number of useful resources on women. The report on **Rural Women's Participation in Development** is the result of a study carried out with other UN agencies to assess past development programs. It was published in 1980. Other studies include **Building New Knowledge Through Technical Co-operation Among Developing Countries**, the experience of the Association of African Women for Research and Development (AAWORD), 1980 and **Promoting and Accelerating Women's Participation in the Caribbean Through TCDC**, the experience of the Women and Development Unit (WAND) of the University of the West Indies, 1981. An early booklet **Integration of Women in Development: Why, When, How** by Ester Boserup and Christina Liljencrantz was published in 1975, while the 1981 **National Household Survey Capability Programme** explains UNDP's activities to improve the data base about households and women's contributions to them.

The 1977 **Programme Guidelines on the Integration of Women in Development** are intended to advise UNDP staff on the participation of women in development programs. Informational publications include the **Development Issue Papers**, nos. 12, 13 and 16 on "Women and the New International Economic Order," 1980, "Women and Technical Co-operation Among Developing Countries," 1980 and "Northern Women and the New International Economic Order," 1981.

The UNDP has also produced a number of audio-visuals under the title of **Women in Development — Courses for Action in 1975**, consisting of slide tape programs with discussion guides on "Overview: Development and Women," "Small Technology: New Tools for Women," and a number of case studies. Two 16 mm color films are also available: **Outside GNP** (9 minutes) and **Into the Mainstream** (26 minutes). These cost US$ 60 and $150 respectively; the slide tape programs cost $ 40, while the publications are free.

United Nations Educational, Scientific and Cultural Organization (UNESCO)
7 Place de Fontenoy, 75700 Paris, France.

UNESCO aims to promote cooperation among nations in the fields of education, science and culture. Its main activities are in the fields of literacy programs, education levels and human rights education. Subjects related to UNESCO's work range from communication and informatics to earth sciences, environment, the new international economic order, the new world information and communication order and population. Women are also listed as a priority item in UNESCO's work. UNESCO's programs are implemented through its national commissions. There are also regional and specialized offices.

Like all UN bodies, the quality and usefulness of its resources vary greatly. On the negative side, one example is a film entitled **More Than Fair** which is supposed to show the increasing opportunities opening up for women and to promote the advancement of women. Unfortunately, it gives a very superficial and often stereotyped view of women, is patronizing in tone, and fails to deal adequately with the issues. Much more useful are UNESCO's numerous surveys and statistical studies about women and education in the various countries of the world.

UNESCO has also done a great deal of useful work in the area of women, media and communication. It has produced a number of very valuable surveys of women's image and participation in the media, some of which are reviewed in the Education and Communication section of this Guide. It has also supported efforts to improve the image and coverage of women in the mass media through such things as the **Women's Feature Service** in Latin America and several conferences.

United Nations Environment Programme (UNEP)
P.O. Box 30552, Nairobi, Kenya.

UNEP was established because of the growing concern about the environment and the growing awareness of the relationship of the environment and development. It deals with issues which are of vital concern to everyone and which have a direct impact on women food producers in rural areas. It spells out these issues in a very brief **Environmental Brief 4/80**. It has also produced several other small pamphlets on women and water, environment, work and health.

United Nations Fund for Population Activities (UNFPA)
485 Lexington Avenue, New York, New York 10017, USA.

UNFPA started operations in 1969 as a service of the UN for population activities. It publishes a monthly newsletter **Population**, a quarterly journal **Populi** and a yearly **Report**. The Health chapter of this Guide points out the complexity of the issues of population and the criticism which feminists especially direct at some of the population policies promoted by the UN and other development agencies. In recent years the UNFPA has placed more emphasis on the need to place population programs within overall development plans of a country and to relate these to areas such as health, education, rural development, income generation, the status of women and communication.

United Nations Research Institute for Social Development (UNRISD)
United Nations, CH-1211 Geneva 10, Switzerland.

UNRISD is the only organization within the UN system with an explicit mandate to conduct research on social development, with a view to identifying the causes of poverty and the mechanisms that perpetuate it and to helping the poor and powerless participate in the development process and benefit from its results.

UNRISD has a program on people's participation which has resulted in a number of debates on the theory and practice of participation, published in a series of occasional papers. These papers also include a number of case studies. Most of the debaters are male and only a small amount of attention has been focused on the specific issues which affect women's participation in development. One article about this was included in **Dialogue about Participation 2** (April 1982): "Women and Popular Participation: Ideas for Research and Debate" by Elizabeth Jelin. It is to be hoped that this will receive more attention in the future.

The Voluntary Fund for the United Nations Decade for Women
1 United Nations Plaza, New York, New York 10017, USA.

The Voluntary Fund for the United Nations Decade for Women was created by the UN General Assembly, following the International Women's Year, 1975. It is intended to provide supplementary financial and technical support, particularly to the least developed, land-locked and island countries which have limited financial resources for carrying out their national plans and programs for the advancement of women and the World and Regional Plans of Action concerning women and development. Unfortunately, only relatively small amounts of money have been given to this fund, indicating a general low priority given to women by many members of the United Nations.

Resource materials from other United Nations agencies such as the **World Health Organization (WHO)**, the **United Nations Commission on Transnational Corporations**, and the **United Nations Industrial Development Organization (UNIDO)** are listed in the resources of other sections of this Guide.

resource centers

LNS/cpf

American Council of Voluntary Agencies for Foreign Service, Inc. (ACVAFS)
200 Park Avenue South, New York, New York 10003, USA.

The ACVAFS is a confederation of 44 member agencies established to assure the maximum effectiveness of the overseas programs of American Voluntary Agencies. During International Women's Year in 1975, a Subcommittee on Women and Development was established. One of its tasks was to produce **Criteria for Evaluation of Development Projects Involving Women** which has been published in booklet form. This checklist points out the importance of women being involved in planning and decision making throughout the various phases of a project. It is a very good beginning, but could be improved. It does not, for instance, raise any basic questions about the goals or models of development.

The ACVAFS has a very useful information service which provides directories, bibliographies, publications lists and data, mainly for US organizations involved in development work. These represent a very wide range of perspectives on development policies and action. This is carried out through **The Technical Assistance Information Clearing House (TAICH)**, a "center of information on the socio-economic development programs abroad of US non-profit organizations, including voluntary agencies, church missions and foundations. Through publications and the maintenance of an inquiry service, TAICH responds to the need for current information about development assistance with particular reference to the resources and concerns of the private, non-profit sector." TAICH operates with support from the US government.

TAICH publications include: **US Non-Profit Organizations in Development Assistance Abroad**. This directory provides profiles of 456 US non-profit organizations which operate or support development assistance programs in Africa, Asia, Latin America, the Middle East and the Pacific. The 525 page directory includes voluntary agencies, church missions, foundations, professional associations, membership organizations, and affiliates and branches of the business, labor and cooperative sectors. Profile entries give agency history and structure, executive staff, objectives, a brief description of agency programs, countries of assistance, financial and personnel data and publications. Price: US$ 6.

TAICH prepares a series of **Country Reports** which provide information on the development programs of US non-profit organizations; **TAICH News**, a newsletter issued four times a year, with short news on development projects and new resources; **TAICH Acquisitions List**, a bi-weekly annotated list of publications received at the clearing house; **TAICH Serials Holding List**, a listing of serial titles received by TAICH, publishers, addresses, frequency, price and subject index included; **Women — A Bibliography**, an annotated listing of materials on women in the TAICH library.

Except for the directory, all of the TAICH materials are free of charge.

American Friends Service Committee (AFSC) International Division
1501 Cherry Street, Philadelphia, Pennsylvania 19102, USA.

The International Division of the AFSC carries out a large number of programs and development projects in several regions of the world, many of which are particularly concerned with women. Its **Women and Development Program** in Africa has developed several economically successful income generating projects for women in the area of soap making, cloth dyeing and rug weaving. It gives particular attention to developing cooperatives and local women managers as well as to training women in improved techniques. Soap making, for instance, has been a traditionally women's occupation but it has often been men who are trained in new techniques. The AFSC **Women and Development Program** gives this training to women so that they can keep control over a trade and a product which is in great demand on the local market. The **Women and Development Program** in based in Mali and Guinea Bissau, but the AFSC also has women's projects in Zambia and Zimbabwe as well as in Asia, Latin America and the Middle East. Further information may be obtained from the International Division. The American Friends Service Committee also has a **Nationwide Women's Program** and coordinates the **Women and Global Corporations Network**, both of which are extremely useful resource centers and communications networks. They are described in the resource listing of the Multinational section of this Guide.

LNS/cpf

Asian Students Association (ASA)
511 Nathan Road, 1/F, Kowloon, Hong Kong.

Established in 1969 with membership from 17 countries, the ASA sees itself as part of the people's movement in Asia and takes a strong anti-imperialist, anti-colonialist and anti-racist stand. Its Women's Commission, set up in 1975, is currently chaired by the League of Filipino Students (LFS). It promotes the emancipation of women and encourages the formation of national women's groups. The Commission grew out of the ASA-organized workshop on "The Role of Women in the Third World" held in Thailand. The Report of the workshop, reprinted in 1982, affirms that the liberation of women is part of the general struggle for national liberation, while acknowledging the special oppression of women. It calls for a united struggle of men and women for both national and women's liberation. A second workshop was held in the Philippines in 1982 on the "Role and Rights of Young Women in Developing Asia," focusing especially on students, workers in manufacturing industries, and prostitution tourism. The Women's Commission is engaged in an ongoing study of these areas and expects to publish the results in 1983. ASA publishes a bi-monthly **Asian Students News** with regular information about women's struggles in Asia. Subscription: US$ 10 per year.

Asian Women's Institute
International Office, c/o Association of Kinnaird College for Women, Lahore-3, Pakistan.

In addition to its activities in the field of education and women's studies mentioned in the Education section of this Guide, the Asian Women's Institute is engaged in rural development projects for women. These projects generally emphasize the importance of consciousness raising and the achievement of dignity as well as economic growth and show an understanding of the real felt needs of rural women. More information may be obtained from the Institute.

Associated Country Women of the World (ACWW)
50 Warwick Square, Victoria, London SW1V 2AJ, England.

Established in the 1930s, ACWW has a membership of 8.5 million country women and homemakers in 70 countries in the world. With consultative status with several United Nations agencies, ACWW participates in many UN activities and speaks for rural women at the UN. Its international, national and local structures are involved in a wide variety of development projects. While much emphasis is given to improving traditional homemaking skills, attention is also given to agricultural training and income generation. The quarterly newsletter **The Countrywoman** reports on members' activities and UN activities of particular interest to women. It stresses the need for equality, but does not have a pronounced feminist perspective.

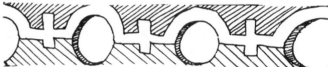

Association of African Women for Research and Development (AAWORD)
B.P. 11007, CD Annexe, Dakar, Senegal.

AAWORD was created by a group of African women researchers who felt the need to organize themselves in order to meet, share experiences and discuss priorities and methods of research. AAWORD sees the need for research carried out by Africans themselves, which is not solely theoretical, but related to women's practical needs and problems. The Association also emphasizes the importance of communication and networking. It calls for the recognition of the large amount of work women are already doing in rural areas and for the development of policies and programs which will work for the elimination of all types of exploitation and oppression of women. This requires the direct participation of the local women themselves. The guidelines and priorities for research were drawn up in a meeting held in Dakar in 1977 entitled "African Women and the Decolonization of Research." Since then, AAWORD has organized or assisted in the organization of many conferences, workshops and seminars. These include a seminar on "Women and Rural Development in Africa" organized by the International Labour Organisation in 1981 in collaboration with AAWORD which prepared most of the papers. Another seminar was on the theme "Another Development with Women" and was held in June 1982.

AAWORD is making an extremely valuable contribution to analyzing and understanding the basic issues of women in the process of development. It brings a feminist perspective to its work and stresses the need to relate theory and practice.

Associazione Italiana Donne per lo Sviluppo (AIDoS)
Piazza Capranica 95, interno 4, 00186 Rome, Italy.

Founded in late 1981, AIDoS, or the Italian Association for Women in Development, is a non-governmental organization which aims to raise the consciousness of the Italian public on the role of women in the development process through meetings, seminars and conferences with the participation of third world women's groups. It also attempts to influence the aid policies of the Italian government to channel funds to projects initiated and implemented by women. It has a documentation and resource center.

Bangladesh Rural Advancement Committee (BRAC)
66, Mohakhali Commercial Area, Dacca 12, Bangladesh.

A non-profit, private organization of Bengalis engaged in development work, BRAC initiated the Jamalpur Women's Program in 1976 on the request of a group of women who would plan, manage and implement the program. The program reaches hundreds of some of the poorest women in the area. The program centers around functional education of women; i.e. education which is immediately useful to them, including literacy, cultural awareness, health and skills training. The program has established a number of cooperatives in the areas of food production, silkworm farming, weaving and fishing. Emphasis is on training the women to manage the cooperatives themselves. BRAC regularly reports on the Women's Program in its mimeographed newsletter. Information and slides of the program are also available from Oxfam America, 302 Columbus Avenue, Boston, Massachusetts 02116, USA, which funds the program and considers it as a potential model for projects aiming to promote both economic independence and self-determination for women.

Centre for Development Research
9 Ny Kongensgade, 1472 Copenhagen K, Denmark.

A number of women researchers in this centre have been carrying out studies on development projects and policies in the third world from a feminist perspective. Their research covers areas and aspects which have usually been neglected by development agencies and policy makers, including the impact of projects on women, women's roles and unpaid work, women's organizations and differences within households between men and women. One of the purposes of the research is to influence Danish development policy makers and funders.

ADAB News/Bangladesh

Centre for Women's Development Studies
B-43, Panchsheel Enclave, New Delhi 110017, India.

Established in 1980, the Centre undertakes research on women and development; provides training and consultancy services in this area; assists action programs for women's development, particularly among disadvantaged women; is developing a clearinghouse of information and ideas; promotes publication and communication activities. It was founded by women active in women and development issues who felt a need for a new perspective in this area, which takes into consideration the factors within the development process itself that have led to the deterioration of women's situation and which recognizes the already considerable contribution women are making. It is making a highly valuable contribution to analyzing the root causes of women's oppression and to understanding women's real needs for self-determination and development.

Centro de Estudios de la Mujer
Olleros 2554 –P.B., Buenos Aires 1426, Argentina.

This women's studies center conducts research, collects documentation, teaches courses and organizes meetings on women. It promotes interdisciplinary exchange on women's issues.

Mujer y Sociedad /Lima, Peru

Centro de la Mujer Peruana "Flora Tristan"
Jirón Quilca 431, Lima 100, Peru.

Founded in 1973, this women's center carries out research and action, from a feminist perspective, on concerns of rural and urban poor women. It has a number of publications for use in this work. The center also organizes meetings and is a source of information and contact with feminist groups and organizations in Peru.

CIDHAL (Comunicación, Intercambio y Desarrollo Humano en América Latina)
Apartado Postal 579, Cuernavaca, Morelos, Mexico.

A documentation and action center for Latin American women, CIDHAL has a large collection of materials. In addition to providing information and producing publications, the center organizes meetings and study groups. It focuses especially on rural and working class women. The center brings a feminist perspective to its work.

Clearinghouse on Development Communication
1414 22nd Street NW, Washington, DC 20037, USA.

An information center on the application of communications technology to development problems, the Centre publishes a quarterly **Development Communications Report** with articles, book reviews and news. The **Report** covers everything from the use of simple technologies and techniques to telecommunications. It also gives information about the development and use of computerized data bases. It is a very good source of information on an important area of development issues. Subscriptions are free to readers in the developing world.

I am a woman and if I live and I fight and if I fight I contribute to the Liberation of all women and so victory is born even in the darkest hours

cpf/Women: A Journal of Liberation

Consultants in Development,
2130 P Street NW, Suite 803, Washington DC 20037, USA.

An agency dedicated to promoting the distribution of ideas and techniques in the development field, Consultants in Development offers assistance to small industry development. They also offer a wide range of publications. Among these is "Can Technology Help Women Feed Their Families?" by Maryanne Dulansey, revised in June 1979, an article presented at the American Association for the Advancement of Science Workshops on Women and Development. Giving different examples taken from field observation, the author stresses the need to recover many indigenous technologies. A publications list is available.

Co-operative College
P.O. Box 474, Moshi, Tanzania.

Members of the Co-operative College in Moshi have been involved in studying and carrying out development projects with women, especially cooperative activities. The experiences gained here could well be useful for others interested in co-operatives for women. An interesting example is the Kilimanjaro Quick Service Cooperative Society, Ltd. set up by women to provide a number of services and products. Apart from lack of capital for investment, the cooperative ran into marketing problems which led the members to undertake more thorough investigation of the market and to select products which would not have great competition from others in the local market.

Council for the Development of Economic and Social Research in Africa (CODESRIA)
B.P. 3304, Dakar, Senegal.

Created in 1973, CODESRIA's "main objective is to activate concerned African social scientists and research institutes to undertake fundamental as well as problem oriented research from a perspective which is more relevant to the needs of the African people and thus challenging the existing orthodox development theories which have often led many African countries to stagnation and under-development." Its activities include the building of networks among African researchers and institutes, the dissemination of information through the journal **Africa Development**, books and papers, directories and the bi-monthly newsletter **Africana**, and through conferences and seminars. One of the 22 priority research themes identified is Women and Development in Africa. Up until now, not a great deal has been done on this area.

Development Education Centre (DEC)
121 Avenue Road, Toronto, Canada M5R 2G3.

An independent resource center offering alternative educational perspectives on Canada, the third world and contemporary issues, DEC maintains a library and distribution service. Its annual **Literature List** covers women.

Development Studies and Research Centre
University of Khartoum, P.O. Box 321, Khartoum, Sudan.

Patterns of Family Living: A Case Study of Two Villages on the Rahad River by Ellen Gruenbaum (1979) looks at women's work and the division of labor in the family in these two Sudanese villages. While it is mainly descriptive, it attempts to correct the bias of most studies of women's work which neglect to calculate the subsistence and domestic labor activities of women.

The University's Institute of Environmental Studies has published a collection of research papers on **Women and the Environment,** edited by Diane Baxter, which were presented at a workshop in April 1981. These contributions from both Sudanese and expatriates cover the issues of Women and the Social Environment, Water and the Environment, Women and the Living Environment, and Women and Food. They range from a practical study on the use of charcoal stoves to criticism of development policies in relation to women and appropriate technology. A review of this collection in the February 1982 issue of **Sudanow** points out a weakness of the conclusions: "Grandiose schemes for the enhancement of the environment, the improvement of women's lot and the rescue of the economy are suggested and inevitably followed by the passive 'should be done, noticed, changed'." But who should be doing the noticing and changing? Nevertheless, the papers make many important points and are a very important contribution to the discussion.

Join Hands/LNS

Environment Liaison Centre (ELC)
P.O. Box 72461, Nairobi, Kenya.

Established in 1974, the ELC is composed of non-governmental organizations (NGOs) concerned about the environment and human settlements. It maintains communications links with the United Nations Environment Programme (UNEP) and the United Nations Centre for Human Settlements (HABITAT). Its quarterly publication **ECOFORUM** provides a place for groups working on environmental issues to share views and experiences, on subjects such as pesticides and high-yielding varieties of seeds, dumping of hazardous products in the third world, multinational promotion of infant formula, use of hazardous contraceptives in population control programs, water sources, and appropriate technology.

The ELC has a very useful information system containing data on organizations with environmental activities. From this information, the ELC compiles directories and answers information requests. It has a manual file of 4,000 NGOs around the world and a computer file summarizing the information of 3,000 of these. In addition, it has smaller files on research and educational institutes and on government and UN organizations. An example of one of ELC's directories is the **Report and Directory on Organizations in Developing Countries Working on Renewable Energy**, produced in May 1981. After clearly setting out and summarizing the main areas and the issues involved, the directory provides an annotated listing of almost 300 groups and organizations in 75 third world countries. The ELC is a very useful source of information on action-oriented NGOs, of which at least some seem to be aware that "people" includes women.

European Association of Development Research and Training Institutes (EADI)

c/o Development Research Institute, Postbus 90153, 5037 GC Tilburg, Netherlands.

Created in 1975, EADI aims to promote exchange among European scholars concerned with development issues and exchange between European development research and its counterparts in Africa, Asia, Latin America and the Middle East. Among its working groups is that on Women and Development which promotes exchange of ideas among its members and debate on policy issues through meetings and publications. The group has been working on two major themes: 1) The implications of development processes which neglect the actual input as well as the potential of women and which maintain discriminatory situations. 2) The role of social scientists in researching those aspects of development processes which are unfavorable to women. The group has also been working on a collective publication in French, "Femmes et développement ou les métamorphoses d'un développement masculin" (Women and Development or the Metamorphoses of a Male-centered Development).

Feminist Resource Centre (FRD)

13 Carol Mansion, 35 Sitladevi Temple Road, Mahim, Bombay 400016, India.

This Feminist Resource Centre carries out action-oriented research from a feminist perspective on many issues, including health and contraception, population policies, violence against women, women's paid and unpaid work. The Centre has a collection of documentation and organizes and participates in workshops and conferences. It emphasizes many of the issues which have been ignored by mainstream development research groups and makes clear links between development and the issues which affect women in particular. An excellent resource.

Fundaçao Carlos Chagas

Avenida Prof. Francisco Morato 1565, 05513 São Paulo SP, Brazil.

This foundation's women's program carries out a wide range of research on women. Many of the researchers bring a feminist perspective and analysis to their work.

Indian Council of Social Science Research (ICSSR)

IIPA Hostel, Indraprastha Estate, Ring Road, New Delhi 110002, India.

The Women's Studies Programme of the ICSSR, begun in 1976, carries out research on a wide range of subjects, including women's employment in urban and rural areas, wage structures, migration, the division of labor, the impact of the green revolution and the links between clase inequality and sexual inequality. The ICSSR's unit on Women's Studies has also organized workshops and symposia on women and development. In addition it assists other organizations, both governmental and non-governmental, in preparing research and seminars.

Indian Social Institute (ISI)

Programme for Women's Development, Lodi Road, New Delhi 110003, India.

The Programme for Women's Development of the ISI aims to increase the participation of women at different levels in the development process through training courses for women community organizers, on-the-spot consultation, promoting programs for women, studies of disadvantaged women and the publication of articles and books. Among its useful publications are **Non-Formal Education for Women – The Grihini Training Programme**, reviewed in the Communication and Education section of this Guide and **Towards Self-Reliance**, edited by Jessie Tellis-Nayak and Selena Costa-Pinto, in 1979. The result of materials gathered for a workshop for Organisers of Income Generating Programmes for Women, this 101 page book raises a number of critical questions about the theory and policies behind income generating projects. Examining these in the larger context of women's economic situation and lives, it suggests that income generation alone will not bring about dignity and self-reliance. This must be accompanied by other political, economic and social changes. A large part of the book is devoted to case studies which evaluate the achievements and problems of various projects from the economic, management and social development point of view. The ISI has also produced a paper by Jessie Tellis-Nayak on **Innovative Strategies for Motivating and Organizing Rural Women for Development** (1979).

Institut Africain Pour Le Développement Economique et Social — Centre Africain de Formation (INADES — FORMATION)
08 B.P. 8, Abidjan 08, Ivory Coast.

INADES-Formation is an African information and training center on development working in 17 countries of Africa. Headquartered in the Ivory Coast, it has national offices in Burundi, Cameroun, Ethiopia, Upper Volta, Rwanda, Togo and Zaire and representatives in Kenya and Chad. INADES-Formation offers a number of services and publications, including a correspondence course for farmers and trainers, written in simple French; an introductory correspondence course on development, particularly in Africa, for those who have completed secondary education; and training courses for farmers and rural development workers. **Agripromo** is a quarterly journal for farmers and rural development workers, written in simple French and presented in a very readable and attractive format with photographs, drawings and comics. Each issue deals with a particular area such as rural co-operatives, water use, nutrition, finance, commerce of agricultural products, literacy, soil conservation, handicrafts and credit unions. Recognition and attention is given to the work of rural women and a special issue deals with women's work (no. 27, 1979). Each theme is dealt with on both the theoretical and practical level. The issue on women's work points out that a great amount of the work that women do is not considered "work."

Other publications include two booklets on **L'Eau et La Santé** which give practical advice on how to protect the family from water borne diseases and on how to protect water sources. INADES-Formation has also produced a series entitled **Femmes des Villages, Aujourd'hui** comprising nine booklets covering a range of subjects from water to meal preparation, child birth, family life, children, and farming. As with the other publications, these are written in simple French, with many illustrations. They also include questions for reflection and discussion.

The INADES-Documentation department produces a bibliographic bulletin on cards as well as various bibliographies of materials in its documentation system. Photocopies of these documents may be ordered. The documentation department will also answer written requests for information about agriculture, economy, sociology, appropriate technology, adult education and so forth. A complete list of publications with prices and ordering information is available.

The Bread is Rising/USA

Institute of Development Studies (IDS)
University of Sussex, Brighton BN1 9RE, England.

Since 1975 IDS has focused attention on women and development through an ongoing program of study, research, workshops, seminars and publications. These have been carried out from a feminist perspective with particular attention to the subordination of women in the development process, the double oppression of women in production and reproduction and the division of labour between classes and sexes. The women who have participated in this program come from all over the world and have produced a great deal of extremely valuable material on both the theoretical and practical levels.

Two issues of the **IDS Bulletin** report the results of some of this work: the "Special Issue on the Continuing Subordination of Women in the Development Process" in vol. 10 no. 3, April 1979 and "Women and the Informal Sector" in vol. 12 no. 3, July 1981 are particularly interesting and useful. In addition to the bibliographies **Women in Social Production** and **Women Workers in Export-Oriented Industries** in Southeast Asia listed under the resources in the Multinational section of the Guide, the program has also produced a bibliography on **Women Workers in Tourism in Southeast Asia** by Shireen Samarasuriya. Like the others it is well-annotated. Another recommended publication is a pamphlet on **Women's Emancipation Under Socialism: A Model for the Third World?** by Maxine D. Molyneux (January 1981), which documents some of the policies of socialist states that are responsible for the continuing inequalities between the sexes. An extremely valuable contribution towards developing a feminist perspective on development is the book **Of Marriage and the Market** (1981), based on work done at the Institute. It is reviewed under books.

Institute of Development Studies, Jaipur (IDS (J))
C-13, Moti Marg, Bapu Nagar, Jaipur 302004, India.

Established in 1981, this institute intends to develop library and documentation services on development studies. It has produced **Development: A Select Bibliography** with 750 entries and has a quarterly **Library Bulletin** listing materials, especially non-books, added to the library. Many of these are by Indian authors and there are some entries specifically on women.

Institute of Social Studies (ISS)
5 Deen Dayal Upadhyaya Marg, New Delhi 2, India.

The ISS in India, founded in 1964, is a voluntary, non-profit research organization. Since 1975 it has concentrated on the areas of women's employment, women's integration in development and the strengthening of women's organizations. The ISS disseminates its findings through participation in national and international forums and through the publication of books, papers, and articles in journals and newspapers. Many of its papers have been published by other organizations such as the ILO and United Nations agencies. The ISS studies are particularly useful and valuable because they incorporate an acute awareness of the importance of the differences within households (division of labor, income, benefits, etc.) as well as between households. They also point out the role played by attitudes towards women and the importance of women organizing themselves. Some interesting studies include: **Women's Quest for Power — 5 Case Studies**, which examines some attempts at organizing women workers in India (1979); **A Case Study on the Modernization of the Traditional Handloom Weaving Industry in the Kashmir Valley** (1979); **The Importance of Age and Sex Specific Data Collection in Household Surveys** (1980). The latter is a study of four projects involving the employment of women in rural areas of India. It emphasizes the impact and implications of these projects on women's lives and suggests changes which should be made in order to avoid detrimental effects. It also attempts to show how and where research can have an impact on decision makers and development planners and thus enhance the quality of women's lives. The paper includes a list of research papers on women and work in India and other Asian countries. A complete publications list is available from the ISS.

VOW/Zambia

Institute of Social Studies (ISS) Women's Studies Programme
Badhuisweg 251, 2597 JR The Hague, Netherlands.

A feminist perspective and a concern for not separating theory and practice, academic study and activism, characterizes the Women's Studies Programme on Women and Development of the ISS. The program grew out of a Workshop on Women and Development held at the Institute in 1977. Its participants include women from every continent. The program is making a very valuable contribution not only to breaking down the contradictions between women's studies and women's struggles but also between feminism and development issues. It has also contributed to the understanding of the inter-twining of oppression based on sex, class and race. Among the program's very useful publications are **Women and Development: A Bibliography** (1980) by Ettie Baas, a partially annotated listing of materials available at the ISS, published since 1970. Earlier editions include pre-1970 publications. The ISS Occasional Series Papers, include **Towards a Methodology of Women's Studies** (1979) by Maria Mies, a very important analysis of the need for a feminist methodology and approach to research. After examining the theoretical and methodological shortcomings of established "scientific" research, the author gives some methodological guidelines for women's studies.

Feminism in Europe: Liberal and Socialist Strategies 1789-1919 (1981) by Maria Mies and Kumari Jayawardena with a bibliography by Ettie Baas is a 208 page book of lectures given for the purpose of making the history of the feminist movement in Europe more widely known and placing the contemporary movement in an historical perspective.

As the result of a 1980 seminar on Women's Struggles and Research, the Women's Programme has produced two collections of theoretical papers and testimonies of struggle, edited by Maria Mies and Rhoda Reddock, on the themes of **National Liberation and Women's Liberation** and **Fighting on Two Fronts: Women's Struggles and Research**. The seminar examined and attempted to overcome the separation between the women's movement and struggles and women's studies programs, the gap between North American and European women and third world women researchers and activists, the contradictions between the aims of women's emancipation and research methodologies. The seminar also contributed to building a theory of human oppression which deals adequately with the oppression of women on an international basis. Not meant to be the final answer, these books offer important insights and are invaluable contributions towards making the connections between feminism and development.

International Center for Public Enterprises in Developing Countries (ICPE)
Titova 104, 61109 Ljubljana, Yugoslavia.

An inter-governmental organization of developing countries concerned with the management of public enterprises, the ICPE concentrates on issues of training, workers' participation in management, and related areas. It also undertakes studies on women and public enterprises. Among its publications is **Women and Development: A Selected Annotated Bibliography** (1980) which is primarily a listing of United Nations documents and resolutions about women. **Women as a Factor of Development and the Responsibilities of Public Enterprises in This Regard** is a report of an International Expert Group Meeting held in Yugoslavia in 1980. While the participants' views vary, much emphasis is given to increasing women's employment and to education and training for women. Some mention is made of the need to socialize certain household and family duties and some criticism is leveled at the "feminist-activist" approach to women's problems. In general more weight is given to unjust social and economic structures at the national and international level as the cause of women's oppression than to sexist discrimination.

International Center for Research on Women (ICRW)
1010 16th Street NW Washington, DC 20036, USA.

Sponsored by the Federation of Organizations for Professional Women, the ICRW was established in 1976 "to institutionalize the growing interest in research on the impact of development on women." It aims to collect and disseminate current research on women, especially as related to development and to encourage improved research on the impact of development on women. It has organized a number of workshops, conferences and meetings and maintains a library of research on women and development.

International Coalition for Development Action (ICDA)
22 rue Bollandistes, B-1040, Brussels, Belgium.

Founded in 1975, ICDA is a network of development-oriented groups in 18 industrialized countries which campaigns for a "more socially equitable and efficient international economic system" through development education and lobbying for changes in the government policies of the North. ICDA monitors United Nations conferences and negotiations on the New International Economic Order (NIEO) and has carried out a variety of campaigns around the issues of transnationals, seeds and genetic diversity, and others affecting North/South relationships. It produces resource materials for use by non-governmental organizations in these campaigns. A particularly useful publication is **Crisis Decade: The World in the Eighties** (1980), a 52 page booklet with a clear overview of the major development issues of the first two Development Decades and strategies for the future. Price: US$ 1.25. As a whole, ICDA has not made women and development issues a priority, although some members have brought feminist perspectives to some of the campaigns.

International Foundation for Development Alternatives (IFDA)
2, Place du Marché, CH-1260 Nyon, Switzerland.

Established in 1976, IFDA is an organization committed to promoting "another development and to genuine international cooperation." It promotes dialogue among policy makers, action-oriented researchers and communicators on how to attain these goals. Emphasis is on the need for basic restructuring of international relationships, on self-reliant, indigenous and ecologically sustainable development which is people-centered and involves the whole political, economic and cultural process. One of its main vehicles for this dialogue is the bi-monthly **IFDA Dossier** with contributions from progressive researchers from all over the world. This has included some good contributions from and about women such as a series of articles reflecting on the Copenhagen conference of the UN Decade for Women (January/February 1981); and "L'Emploi des femmes dans une perspective de changements sociaux et de libération des femmes: le cas de l'Afrique" by Marie-Angélique Savané (September/October 1981). Taking the situation of women in Africa, the author examines how women's employment is conditioned by roles assigned them and concludes that their liberation depends on changing both structures of production and patriarchal structures.

International Labour Organisation (ILO)
CH-1211 Geneva 22, Switzerland.

The ILO has a number of excellent and highly useful programs, publications and studies on women workers, and is a valuable source of data and information on the work women do around the world. Many of the studies take a critical look at attempts to integrate women into development and a number bring a feminist analysis and perspective to the issues. The ILO produces a journal **Women Workers** twice a year, with articles, statistics and news about women's employment and labor legislation affecting women both internationally and in various countries. It contains good bibliographies about women and work. In 1980, the ILO submitted a report to the World Conference of the United Nations Decade for Women

on the **Measures Taken to Implement the Programme of the UN Decade for Women** reviewing ILO's activities for women workers in the fields of international standard-setting; research and studies; information and communication; and meetings and seminars. After evaluating the impact of these, the report outlines ILO policies for the second half of the Decade.

The ILO also focuses specifically on rural women. In 1978 the World Employment Programme of the ILO organized a meeting of consultants to define the most pressing areas of research, policy and action on the issue of women and rural development. The participants looked at modes of production, agrarian structures and women's work; sex roles and the division of labor in rural economies; and the effects of the penetration of the market on rural women. Abstracts of the papers presented at this meeting are contained in the booklet **Women in Rural Development: Critical Issues** (1981).

The Programme on Rural Women was established after recommendations to the ILO in 1979. This Programme carries out studies, workshops and seminars and gives technical assistance to women's projects. The booklet **Women Workers in Rural Development** by Zubeida M. Ahmad and Martha F. Loutfi (May 1982) describes the program and the studies which have been completed and which are currently being carried out. It also lists the books, articles, papers and reports of workshops and seminars which are available from the ILO. Among the many very interesting publications are: **Rural Women: Unequal Partners in Development** by Martha F. Loutfi (1980), an 81 page review of women's paid and unpaid work in rural areas of developing countries. It shows why it is important to pay attention to rural women in particular and not just the rural poor in formulating development plans and policies. **Rural Development and Women in Asia** (1982) reports on the presentations and discussions of a 1981 seminar held in India on this subject. Similarly **Rural Development and Women in Africa** (1982) reports on a seminar held in Senegal in 1981 and **Desarrollo Rural y La Mujer** (1982) is the report of a Latin American seminar held in Peru in 1981. All of these raise and discuss the relationship of the exploitation of women as workers and as women. Other important issues discussed are the effects of development policies on women, the "putting out" system, and the participation and organization of women.

Housewives Produce for the World Market: The Lace Makers of Narsapur by Maria Mies is an ILO study published by Zed Press (1982). This detailed and excellent study shows how the green revolution has exacerbated the exploitation of secluded women who produce lace at home. The mechanisms at work here apply to other situations as well. **Women and Development: The Sexual Division of Labour in Rural Societies** edited by Lourdes Benería (1982) is another extremely valuable contribution to understanding the oppression of women and the steps which must be taken to overcome this.

International Women's Tribune Centre, Inc.
305 East 46th Street, New York, New York 10017, USA.

The International Women's Tribune Centre began in 1976 as a follow-up to the International Women's Year Tribune held in Mexico City, 1975. Its purpose was to respond to the requests for information generated by the Tribune on development projects, United Nations activities and future plans. It has since developed a resource centre, a number of publications and audiovisual materials, and other services, aimed especially at women involved in development projects. The resource centre has a collection of materials on women and development, women's projects, United Nations materials and women's magazines, newsletters and reports. From this documentation the Centre can respond to requests for information and assist projects being undertaken in the regions with their project activities and with information in regard to fund raising. Close contact is maintained with UN activities and an effort is made to disseminate this information.

The Centre publishes a quarterly **IWTC Newsletter** in English and Spanish. Highly illustrated and simply written, this is not meant to give in-depth analyses of the issues, but to highlight some of the main issues affecting women and development as well as resources, projects and groups on issues such as food, credit, water and appropriate technology. The Centre has also produced a number of information kits, aimed mainly at women in developing countries. These kits contain a wealth of information on funding, how to write proposals, where to go for grants and technical assistance. They also contain listings of development and women's organizations.

IWTC Newsletter

APCWD Women's Resource Book 1979, produced in collaboration with the Asian and Pacific Centre for Women and Development (APCWD) of the United Nations. This contains a description of APCWD activities and materials; a directory of United Nations agencies, and governmental and non-governmental organizations involved in women and development issues in the region and various countries; information on fund raising with an annotated listing of funding agencies. Hard cover, three ring binder. Price: US$ 6; free to groups in Asia/Pacific. **Movilizando La Mujer** is a project development manual for women in Latin America with sections on identifying needs; project design; and resources, each with theoretical background and participatory group activities. Three ring binder, 300 pages,1980. Price: US$ 8; free to individuals and groups in Latin America.

Information Kit for Women in Africa, produced in collaboration with the African Training and Research Centre for Women (ATRCW) of the United Nations, this contains sections on funding assistance, with information on agencies and how to write a proposal; women's projects in Africa, with emphasis on income generation; ATRCW publications; and ATRCW activities. 288 pages, 1981. Available in English and French. Price: three ring binder, US$ 8; paperback stapled, US$ 6; free to individuals and groups in Africa from UNECA/ATRCW, P.O. Box 3001, Addis Ababa, Ethiopia.

The Caribbean Resource Kit for Women is a 304 page ring binder of information on the English-speaking countries of the Caribbean, on development projects for women, and sources of funding. It lists organizations, literature and audiovisuals on agriculture, appropriate technology, education, health and small businesses. This kit was prepared with the Women and Development Unit of the University of the West Indies (WAND), and published in March 1982.

Women of the World Meet Together, a kit of materials describing some of the major activities and issues at the Non-governmental Organizations (NGO) Mid-Decade Forum and the World Conference of the UN Decade for Women in Copenhagen, July 1980. It includes 80 color slides, a 15-minute tape, 2 IWTC newsletters and the Newsletter of the World Conference Secretariat. Price: US$ 50.

JR/ISIS

ISIS — Women's International Information and Communication Service
Via Santa Maria dell'Anima 30, 00186 Rome, Italy. Tel: (06) 656 5842. P.O. Box 50 (Cornavin), 1211 Geneva 2, Switzerland. Tel: (022) 33 67 46.

An international information and communication service by and for women, ISIS was created in 1974 in response to the need of women in many countries for an organization to facilitate global communication among women and to gather and distribute internationally materials and information by women and women's groups. ISIS promotes direct contact, networking and solidarity among women in both industrialized and third world countries. From the beginning, ISIS has focused especially on exchanging ideas and experiences from a holistic feminist perspective which examines the patriarchal as well as political, economic and social aspects of issues with which women are concerned. ISIS emphasizes the importance of women organizing and mobilizing ourselves in our local situations. Our contacts with women's groups extend to over 130 countries.

ISIS has a resource center with a wealth of materials — periodicals, books, pamphlets, papers, information about films, projects, and more — covering a wide range of areas, including health, media, work, education, technology, violence against women, women's organizations, feminist theory, food production. From this material, ISIS can respond to requests for information and provides a number of resource materials. These include:

Resource Guides: **Bottle Babies: a guide to the baby food issue,** in English and German (1976); The Spanish edition was updated and adapted for Latin America in 1981. Price: US$ 5 surface; US$ 8 airmail.

International Women and Health Resource Guide (1980), a joint project of ISIS and the Boston Women's Health Book Collective. This multi-lingual guide provides overviews and annotated resource listings of materials and groups working on health issues from a community and women-oriented perspective, from both developing and developed countries. Price: US$ 5 surface; US$ 8 airmail.

The present **Resource Guide on Women in Development** brings together overviews of the material and resource listings, critiqued from a feminist perspective.

The **ISIS Women's International Bulletin** appears quarterly in English and Spanish and brings together documentation on themes of particular concern to women, reflecting action and resources around the world. Among the issues covered are: health, migration, tourism and prostitution, mass media and communications, multinationals and technology, land and food production.

ISIS coordinates the **International Feminist Network (IFN)** which mobilizes rapid support and solidarity among women on an international scale when needed. ISIS also provides training and technical assistance in communication and information skills, and produces documentation packets and bibliographies. More information is available on request.

Kahayag: The Foundation for Development Support Communication
121 University Avenue, Juna Subdivision, Matina, Davao City, Philippines.

Kahayag carries out a number of consciousness raising and action programs for people in its area on issues of health, consumer rights, energy and the environment, community organization and development. It has a special program aiming at consciousness raising among Muslim women about their own attitudes and those of the community which help or hinder their participation in development. The Foundation has produced and makes available written and audio-visual resources which raise critical questions about issues relating to development, such as the use of western medical systems, the removal of squatters, the imposition of imported consumer goods, nuclear power and so on. Resources are available in English, Tagalog and other languages of the Philippines. Kahayag's publication **Musharwarah**, in Tagalog and English, presents information in simple, well-illustrated, often comic-strip style about health, consumer issues, food production, improved simple technologies and methods as well as about women's struggles. A short article in the July 1982 issue raises questions which must be asked before introducing income generation projects if these are to be "a means of bettering the women's lives and not just one more drudgery for the already overburdened to bear."

Kvindernes U-landsudvalg (KULU) Women and Development
Købmagergade 67 1 tv., DK 1150 K Copenhagen, Denmark.

KULU, the Women's Committee on Developing Countries, formed in 1976, is an umbrella organization of women's groups and organizations in Denmark who are concerned with the issues of women and development. With an explicit feminist perspective, KULU is engaged in informational and educational activities and is attempting to influence national policy on development assistance. It also gives direct support to women in developing countries. KULU is doing an excellent job in building solidarity between women in developing countries and Denmark and is contributing to building a feminist analysis of the root causes of women's oppression. It could well serve as a model for groups in other countries. Materials available from KULU include several slide tape shows, a bi-annual journal **K.U.L.U. Bladet** on women in developing countries, several papers and materials for study groups as well as posters showing women workers in various countries. A publications list is available.

Match
401-171 Nepean, Ottawa, Ontario, Canada K2P OB5.

Match was founded by women who attended the non-governmental Tribune in Mexico during the International Women's Year Conference in 1975. It aims to assist projects planned by third world women themselves, helps find co-financing of projects and matches skills, needs and resources in Canada and the third world.

Maendeleo Ya Wanawake Organisation
P.O. Box 44412, Nairobi, Kenya.

A member of the National Council of Women of Kenya, this organization is involved in a great many development projects with rural women in the areas of water and fuel, income generation, vocational training in both homemaking and agricultural skills, and literacy. It produces a magazine **The Voice of Women**.

Minority Rights Group
36 Craven Street, London WC2N 5NG, England.

An information and research organization working to secure justice for minority or majority groups suffering discrimination, the Minority Rights Group has published a number of reports specifically on women. These include: **Arab Women** (1976) in English and French; **Female Circumcision, Excision and Infibulation: Facts and Proposals for Change** (1980) in English, French, Arabic and Italian; and **Women in Asia** (1982) in English. Subscription: £ 5 for 5 issues. Price per issue: £ 1.20 plus postage.

Meg Winter

National Council on Women and Development Ghana
P.O. Box M. 53, Accra, Ghana.

A governmental organization, this council is an example of many which have been set up or revitalized in Africa since International Women's Year and which have a growing concern for women and development. It promotes the participation of women in national development and is directly involved in a wide range of projects for women. The Council has material available describing its work. A Report and Directory of **National, Subregional and Regional Machineries for Women in Development** in Africa, available from the African Training and Research Centre for Women of the United Nations (ATRCW), gives information and addresses of other governmental organizations for women in Africa. See entry for ATRCW.

❧

Organisation for Economic Co-operation and Development (OECD) Development Centre
94, rue Chardon Lagache, 75016 Paris, France. Publications office: 2, rue Andre-Pascal, 75775 Paris Cedex 16, France.

The OECD is an organization of industrialized countries, set up in 1960, to promote policies designed to "achieve the highest sustainable economic growth and employment and a rising standard of living in Member countries, while maintaining financial stability, and thus to contribute to the development of the world economy..." The purpose of the Development Centre is to bring together knowledge and information from member countries in regard to policies of economic aid. It has a large number of publications available, many of them specialized and technical studies and journals on finance, economics, trade, oil and related subjects. It also has publications of more general interest and use, including a number of directories which can be very useful for those wishing to locate organizations located or working in various countries and regions. These directories include: **Appropriate Technology Directory** (see listing under appropriate technology resources); **Directory of Food Policy Institutes**; and **Directory of Non-Governmental Organisations in OECD Member Countries Active in Development Co-operation**, listing 1702 NGOs with a description of the nature, scope and geographic location of their activities. Published in 1981, this is a two volume, 1500 page work which costs US$ 64. The **Newsletter of the OECD Development Centre**, published twice a year, brings information about its research programs, seminars, publications and information services. A catalogue of publications is available.

Women and development has not been a strong issue in the OECD, nor is the OECD noted for a feminist perspective. It has produced a book on **Women in Development: At the Right Time for the Right Reasons** by Winifred Weekes-Vagliani (1980), a statistical study of women in Malaysia, Fiji, Sri Lanka and the Dominican Republic, which examines factors affecting and the implications of the marriage age of women. In the introduction to the book, the author states that "If women are to contribute to the development process, they must be encouraged to marry at the 'right' age for the 'right reasons'. Identifying the 'right' age and the 'right reasons' will be the major purposes of this study." Price: US$ 13.50. Most publications are available in both English and French.

Oxfam
274 Banbury Road, Oxford OX2 7DZ, England.

Oxfam is an aid and development agency providing both emergency relief and funds for long term projects. It has shown great sensitivity to the complexity of political situations and human rights, including those of women. Project guidelines point out how projects may be detrimental to women if they do not take into consideration things such as women's present workload, the unequal distribution of income within families, the effects of cash crops on family food production and so on. The information office of Oxfam provides well-written project descriptions which are useful in that they usually point out mistakes and problems as well as successes. Some of Oxfam's publications include: **The Role of Women in Rural Zaire and Upper Volta** (1978) by David Mitchnik, which examines the implications of directing agricultural development schemes and training at men when women are the major food producers.

Oxfam Field Director's Handbook (1980). Cased in a strong ring binder, this 460 page handbook summarizes the objectives and strategies utilized by Oxfam field staff in assessing projects and provides advice based on project experience for the information of field staff, project holders and others. Throughout the handbook, there is a sensitivity to the needs of women and to the necessity to avoid detrimental effects on women in planning and implementing projects in agriculture, land reform, technology and health. There is also a special section on women's projects which explicitly spells out the particular problems of women and how these have often been worsened by development policies. A good bibliography of materials on women and development is included. The handbook also displays an awareness of social inequalities among groups and within communities and families and the danger of exacerbating these. Because of this, it is recommended as a positive example and resource. Price £ 10 plus 15% postage.

Land for People: Land Tenure and the Very Poor by Claire Whittemore (1981). An excellent, clear and concise look at the political and economic structures and interests surrounding the issues of land and land reform, this booklet critically questions many of the theories about land and food put forward by development agencies. It argues for the need for basic structural change if agrarian reform is really to benefit those who work the land. This booklet would be still more useful if it had gone further and examined the patriarchal structure and its effects on women.

Women's News Service/Australia

The Population Council
One Dag Hammarskjold Plaza, New York, New York 10017, USA.

The Population Council is a private US-based organization focusing on population issues. Its pamphlet **Including Women in Development Efforts** is based on a speech by George Zeidenstein in January 1978 and is a plea to developers to look at and understand "what is acceptable and accessible within women's cultures — those world views that are distinct from those of men and that are particularly intense with regard to the nurturing of families." One of the publications of the Population Council is **Population and Development Review**, a quarterly on the interrelationships between population and socioeconomic development and a forum for discussion of related public policy issues,which occasionally publishes articles on women. Another publication in **Studies in Family Planning,** a monthly journal with occasional special issues dealing with one particular subject, such as the November/December 1979 issue entitled **Learning About Rural Women** edited by Sondra Zeidenstein. This deals with methods of collecting and analyzing data on rural women, including studies on women's self-perception of their roles in rural society.

Particularly interesting is **International Programs Working Papers** No. 7 "The Nemow Case — Case Studies of the Impact of Large Scale Development Projects on Women," September 1979, by Ingrid Palmer. This insightful study of the impact of development projects on women was carried out to demonstrate "how a concern with women's roles is intrinsic to a concern with development" and to show that such studies are feasible. In all its studies and work on women's issues, the Population Council's underlying concern is the impact on demography: how development projects will affect family size and population.

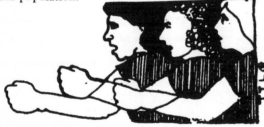

Regional Pan African Institute for Development — West Africa (R-PAID/WA)
Box 133, Buea, Cameroon.

A number of publications are available from this Institute on development including bibliographies on **Integrated Rural Development**, and the **Role and Problems of Self-Help Organizations/Institutions in Rural Development**. Of particular interest is the 63 page annotated bibliography on **Women and Rural Development**, compiled by Eugene O. Nwanosike which is drawn up on the basis of materials available for consultation in the library/documentary service of the Institute. It covers a wide range of topics from general studies to food production, population, health and women's participation in development projects. It also lists ongoing research projects, mainly but not exclusively in Africa. Another study from the Institute is an **Evaluation of Community Development Women's Work in the South West and North West Provinces** (of Cameroon). This attempts to discover why these programs were not as successful as hoped.

Research Unit on Women's Studies S.N.D.T. Women's University
1 Nathibai Thackersey Road, Bombay 400 020, India.

The quarterly **Newsletter** of the Research Unit on Women's Studies is a useful resource for information about organizations and institutions in India involved in research and projects on women and development. It makes connections between feminism, women's studies and development issues.

Secretariat for Women in Development
New TransCentury Foundation, 1789 Columbia Road NW, Washington, DC 20009, USA.

The Secretariat for Women in Development was created in 1977 with a grant of the US Agency for International Development. Its mandate is "to assist private and voluntary agencies improve the impact of their programming on Third World Women" and "to foster and facilitate integration of women's needs into the development process." The first task of the Secretariat was to collect studies, documents and publications on women in development. A first collection of 287 documents can be found in May Rihani's book, **Development as if Women Mattered: an Annotated Bibliography with a Third World Focus**, published in April 1978 by the Overseas Development Council in Washington, as ODC Paper no. 10. A second bibliography — unfortunately not annotated — of about 700 entries was published in 1979 and revised in March 1980 under the title **Women in Development: a Resource List**. It is available directly from the Secretariat.

In July 1978, the Secretariat published a 96 page Bulletin on **Funding Resources for Women in Development Projects**, offering descriptions of 26 US–based foundations, UN agencies, private voluntary organizations and US government agencies which make grants for projects involving women in the third world. The bulletin provides information about potential funding sources, types of women's projects funded and grantsmanship tips. In 1980, the Secretariat published **European Funding Resources for Women in Development Projects**, a 120 page directory that includes a description of about 32 international organizations, government agencies, non-governmental organizations and private foundations based in Europe which give grants for development projects. It is written for the use of organizations working in the third world, giving information about funding sources, items to be included in a project and grantsmanship tips. Both these directories are valuable guides to funding sources.

The **Directory of Projects Involving Women** is an ongoing series of project profiles describing women's involvement as staff and beneficiaries in the planning and implementation of projects. Volume III of the Directory was published in April 1980.

The secretariat works with the US Peace Corps to examine programs in six Peace Corps countries, with a concern for programming in basic human needs and the involvement of women. The Secretariat is also involved in organizing and attending a variety of workshops on the role of women in development.

United Methodist Church (UMC)
Women's Division, 475 Riverside Drive, New York, New York 10115, USA.

The Women's Division of the UMC has a special program on the issue of women in development. It also focuses on women food producers. Among the material it has available on these issues is an audio-visual entitled **As Strong as the Land**. A 19 minute, 96 frame color filmstrip with cassette, this is an excellent resource about rural women food producers and development policies. It clearly sets out the facts about women's involvement in agriculture in Asia, Africa, Latin America as well as in the USA and shows how development programs have affected women in both negative and positive ways. It also shows the global nature of policies and problems and brings up issues of control and power. A highly useful aid for education and consciousness raising about women, development and food production. A study guide accompanies the filmstrip.

United States Government Office of Women in Development (WID), Agency for International Development (AID)
US Department of State, Room 3243 NS, Washington, DC 20523, USA.

The WID office of USAID produces and/or distributes a very large amount of material on women and development. In 1973, the Percy Amendment to the US Foreign Assistance Act mandated that Foreign Assistance "shall be administered so as to give particular attention to those programs, projects, and activities which tend to integrate women into the national economies of developing countries, thus improving their status and assisting the total development effort." In response to this Congressional mandate, the Agency for International Development created an Office of Women in Development. WID promotes the collection, analysis and distribution of data; organizes studies, research and conferences; helps train development experts and researchers and sponsors projects.

WID has a resource center which distributes a wide variety of publications on women and their role in the development process with an emphasis on agriculture and food production, energy and technology, employment and income generation, education, the status of women in developing countries and women's organizations. As a government organization, WID naturally accepts US development policies on the whole. The material does represent a wide range of opinion, however, and there is some critical examination of the effects of policies on women. The material is useful especially for its wealth of background information. The center issues regular **Bibliographies of Available Material**. This material includes:

Women-Headed Households: the Ignored Factor in Development Planning by Mayra Buvinić and Nadia H. Youssef with Barbara Von Elm of the International Center for Research on Women, Washington DC, March 1978. This study shows the importance of women as heads of household in developing societies, and underlines the socioeconomic factors contributing to the rise of women-headed households. **Women in Forestry for Local Community Development — A Programming Guide** by Marilyn W. Hoskins, September 1979. **Evaluating Small Grants for Women in Development** by Judith F. Helzner, January 1980. **Assessing the Impact of Development Projects on Women** by Ruth B. Dixon, May 1980. **Women and Energy: Program Implications** by Irene Tinker, June 1980.

Successful Rural Water Supply Projects and the Concerns of Women by Paula Roark, September 1980, stresses the role of women in rural water supply projects: women as the traditional water carriers and managers and as the controllers and purveyors of the local learning systems of the society are the ones deciding whether to use the water source and whether it is worth the expenditure of effort to maintain it or have it maintained. **Women's Organizations: Resources for Development** by Katherine Blakeslee Piepmeir, October 1980, discusses the vital role of local women's groups in instigating change directed at reorienting governmental development policies and programs to incorporate women's concerns. It recommends directing development assistance to poor women through women's groups or non-governmental organizations with women's programs.

Illustrative Statistics on Women in Selected Developing Countries, prepared for WID/AID by the Bureau of the Census of the US Department of Commerce, revised September 1980. This chartbook presents comparative statistics on women in 27 selected developing countries. It is planned to extend the existing data base to include all countries, both the more developed and the less developed, with a population of five million or more. **Women, Migration and the Decline of Smallholder Agriculture** by Elsa M. Chaney and Martha W. Lewis, October 1980. This paper "suggests that any policy designed to increase food for the poor will not succeed unless they take into account women's role as food producer..."

Various Perspectives of Using Women's Organizations in Development Programming by Marilyn W. Hoskins, July 1980. This paper summarizes information that came out of a series of conferences and meetings which WID held with "representatives from less developed countries, women's organizations, private voluntary organizations and donor groups... These representatives discussed current activities and the future potential of women's organizations to implement projects, deliver services and cooperate with poor women in identifying, developing and carrying out WID programs." The appendix describes six different organizational frameworks and strategies among selected non-indigenous, mainly US-based intermediaries. **1980 Report to the Committee on Foreign Relations of the United States Senate and the Committee on Foreign Affairs United States House of Representatives**. This gives information on AID's activities in the support of and cooperation with the activities and goals of the UN Decade for Women. **Income Generating Activities with Women's Participation** by Marilyn W. Hoskins, December 1980. This paper gives an overview of policies about income generating activities. It looks at some of the political, economic and social elements that affect or can be affected by income generation and shows why some projects have failed to improve women's lives. It also considers the concept of participation and how this has evolved in development planning. Finally, it presents several brief case studies in the light of the foregoing aspects. A publications list is available.

ADAB News/Bangladesh

Women and Development Network of Australia
P.O. Box 151, Collingwood 3066, Victoria, Australia.

Formed in 1981, this network is made up of several groups of women throughout Australia concerned with the low priority accorded women in the programs and projects of Australian aid and development agencies as well as with the generally low status of the positions held by women within these agencies. The Network aims to change this situation and to lobby for a feminist perspective in aid and development through various means including the collection and dissemination of information on relevant issues. The network **Women in Development Newsletter** is produced in turn by the various member groups and contains information about activities, meetings and resources as well as articles such as "The Lowanna Group Declaration," with specific recommendations to various Australian aid agencies concerning women. Another interesting article on "Sexual Harassment — Women Must Act" makes the point that violence against women is very definitely a development issue although development literature is almost totally silent about this. This network is one of a growing number of women's networks working to promote a feminist perspective in development.

Women and Development Unit (WAND)
University of the West Indies, Extra-Mural Department, Pinelands, St. Michael, Barbados.

WAND was established as the result of a seminar on the Integration of Women in National Development in the Caribbean, held in Jamaica in June 1977 and attended by women representing the governments of the English-speaking countries of the Caribbean. The purpose of WAND is to monitor the Plan of Action developed at the seminar and to: provide training of trainers and resource persons; promote technical assistance programs; publish and distribute materials; and develop research programs and programs for legislative change. WAND produces a quarterly newsletter entitled **Woman Speak!** which provides interesting and useful information on women and development projects, seminars, conferences and news, ranging from governmental to non-governmental ones. WAND also produces **Concerning Women and Development**, a continuing series of articles to stimulate discussion and debate in the Caribbean region, such as "Women in Development: A Caribbean Perspective" by Peggy Antrobus. WAND has a number of other studies, papers and audio-visuals available which focus on and are especially useful for women in the region.

Women in Development, Inc. (WID, Inc.)
6 Bartletts, Christ Church, Barbados.

Founded in 1978, WID, Inc. is a private organization funded by and working with a number of private and public agencies to promote employment and business opportunities for women. It provides training and a revolving loan fund for women in small businesses and carries out research such as **A Study of Low-Income Women in Barbados**, published in August 1980.

Women for Women
Road no. 4, House no. 67, Dhanmondi R.A., Dacca, Bangladesh.

A research and study group in Bangladesh, Women for Women has produced several publications listing research activities on women in Bangladesh as well as case studies. A particularly interesting book is **Inside Seclusion: The Avarodhbasini of Rokeya Sakhawat Hossain** edited and translated by Roushan Jahan, 1981. Rokeya, a Bengali Muslim woman, was born in 1880 and her writings are among the rare documentations of purdah written by a woman who experienced it herself. The introduction to the book describes Rokeya's life and times while the second part of the book is a translation of her book "Avarodhbasini" which describes actual cases of many women who lived in purdah or seclusion, from a critical point of view. Another publication is the book **Women and Education**, reviewed in the Communication and Education section of this Guide. **Indigenous Abortion Practitioners in Rural Bangladesh** (1981) by Shamima Islam is particularly useful especially in that it is one of the few studies which is based on speaking with the practitioners themselves. Price: US$ 3 plus postage.

Women's Action for Development (WAFD)
D-139 Anand Niketan, New Delhi 110021, India.

"A secular Indian organisation of Christian inspiration working for the development of women and children belonging to the weaker sections" of the community, WAFD carries out projects such as home economics training for girls, literacy classes, creches and income generation through cooperatives. Its mimeographed newsletter **WAFD Links** reports on activities and gives information on simple technologies, improved nutrition and health.

World Education
1414 Sixth Avenue, New York, New York 10019, USA.

A private agency founded in 1951, World Education provides professional assistance primarily for non-formal education projects in developing countries, working with both government and private agencies. It has a great deal of resource material available on women's projects, including audio-visuals about projects and training techniques, training kits, and monographs. It also has a quarterly magazine **Reports**. The July 1980 issue is devoted to women's projects and contains an interesting interview by Noreen Clark of African anthropologist Achola Pala Okeyo, who explains her views on the necessity of reestablishing complementary work patterns between men and women in Kenya. A literature list is available.

World Hunger Education Service

2000 P Street NW, Washington, DC 20036, USA.

Founded in 1976, this organization works with the hunger programs of major religious bodies and other anti-hunger organizations in the USA. In addition to providing resources, consultations, and organizing meetings, the service publishes a monthly newsletter **Hunger Notes** with articles, news and resource listings. Issues on women include that of August 1978 on women and development and March 1980 on **Agrarian Reform: A Women's Issue at Mid-Decade.**

World YWCA

37, Quai Wilson, Geneva, Switzerland.

Common Concern, the quarterly magazine of the World YWCA, is a very interesting source of information about what the national YWCAs and their international office are doing. Reading these pages, it is evident that many of the YWCAs are actively involved in women and development work with a wide range of health, income generating, appropriate technology and food production projects as well as training workshops in all these areas, plus leadership, communications skills and much more. While these vary widely from country to country, it is also evident that generally they are not welfare-oriented activities but are promoting the self-determination of women as well as social justice. Common themes are human rights, apartheid, refugees, energy and the environment, health and peace. The quarterly also lists useful resources. The **World YWCA Directory** lists the addresses of all the national YWCAs around the world.

periodicals

Other periodicals are listed under the resource centers or organizations which produce them.

Al-Raida

P.O.B. 13-5053, Beirut University College, Beirut, Lebanon.

An excellent source of information on women in the Arab world, this quarterly magazine produced by the Institute for Women's Studies in the Arab world contains news and articles on research, meetings and publications from the Middle East and Arab authors. The materials come from a wide range of sources: governmental, academic, institutional and feminist and thus represent a range of opinions and views. It covers issues of health, education, rural women, rights, families, and feminism. Subscription: US$ 10 per year.

Change International Reports

Parnell House, 25 Wilton Road, London SW1V 1JS, England.

Change is a series of reports on the condition and status of women all over the world which aims to inform public opinion about inequalities imposed on women through law, practice and custom. Among these reports are "Economic Development and Women's Place: Women in Singapore" by Aline K. Wong (June 1980), and "Providence and Prostitution: Image and Reality for Women in Buddhist Thailand" by Khin Thitsa.

Development Dossier

Australian Council for Overseas Aid (ACFOA), P.O. Box 1562, Canberra City, ACT 2601, Australia.

This quarterly dossier provides in-depth treatment of a particular theme relating to development in each issue. This is a very good source of background materials on key issues such as land, food and the north-south dialogue. These very useful and clear overviews of the issues would be still more valuable, if they gave the same thorough examination to the effects of the sexual division of labor, the differences within households as well as between households and the importance of women's role in food production.

Famille et Développement

BP 11007 CD Annexe, Dakar, Senegal.

A quarterly African magazine in French, **Famille et Développement** is an excellent forum on a whole range of development issues, from solar energy, to polygamy to clitoridectomy, drugs, drought and economics. Written in clear, simple language, its approach is critical and direct. The emphasis is on self-reliance and solutions to problems. A feminist perspective is evident throughout, not only in the articles dealing with problems particular to women but in the fact that women are central to all issues raised. Written by Africans for Africans, it is one of the best magazines approaching development from the perspective of people's needs and well-being. The format, design and graphics are of high quality.

Kenya Women

National Council of Women of Kenya, P.O. Box 43741, Nairobi, Kenya.

Published quarterly in English and Swahili, this is the magazine of the National Council of Women of Kenya which groups over forty women's organizations ranging from professional associations to religious organizations to consumers unions and self-help groups. The magazine provides information on the activities of member organizations as well as articles on issues such as legislation affecting women, agriculture, health and work. The Council also carries out projects for women.

Manushi

C1/202 Lajpat Nagar, New Delhi 110024, India.

"A Journal About Women and Society," **Manushi** is an excellent source of information, news and analysis about women's situations and struggles in India. Published in English and Hindi, it brings a feminist perspective and analysis to the issues and breaks down the barrier between so-called "women's issues" and "development issues" in the narrow sense. It clearly shows, for example, that violence against women has a great deal to do with development and that feminism has important things to say about women's access to food, shelter, and dignity. In each issue, women share their analyses and experiences of organizing and taking action. The articles cover areas such as women's health and bodies, violence against women, dowry marriages and burnings, agricultural and factory workers' situations and actions and much more. In addition, there are book and film reviews, news from women's groups, international news from the women's movement, and exchange of ideas and experiences through letters. One of many valuable contributions to understanding what women's lives in rural areas are really like is "Family Life — The Unequal Deal" by B. Horowitz and Madhu Kishwar in **Manushi**, no. 11, 1982. This study examines the distribution of labor contributions and benefits within the households of agricultural workers in a Punjab village, a different approach than taken by most studies, which tend to look at households as a whole and thus ignore the inequalities between males and females within families. This journal is highly useful, readable and stimulating. Subscription rates cover six issues and vary according to country: India, Bangladesh, Nepal, Rs 26; USA and Canada, US$ 18; Europe, Japan, Australia, US$ 17; Asian countries, US$ 9; African countries US$ 11; Libraries and institutions in all foreign countries US$ 24. Bankers cheques and international money orders (no personal cheques, please) should be made out to Manushi Trust.

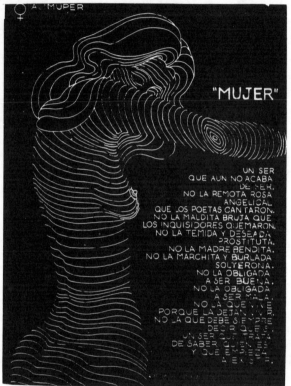

Allmuper/Peru

Mujer y Desarrollo
Apartado 325, Santo Domingo, Dominican Republic.

A mimeographed quarterly newsletter, this presents news and information in popular form on issues such as health care in the home, nutrition, breastfeeding, kitchen gardens, how to raise income for women's groups, and how to form co-operatives. Using simple drawings, cartoon strips and stories, the newsletter is also a vehicle for consciousness raising among women about their oppression and how they can overcome it. It is produced by Mujeres en Desarrollo Dominicana, Inc. (MUDE), a non-profit organization aimed at helping women participate in economically productive activities by developing systems of credit and technical assistance and preparing communities to secure social services.

Network
Belize Committee for Women and Development, 28 Dean Street, Belize City, Belize.

A quarterly newsletter with information about the activities of the Committee on Women and Development.

New Internationalist
62a High Street, Wallingford, Oxon. OX10 OEE, England.

This monthly magazine reports on world poverty, the unjust relationships between rich and poor worlds, the radical changes needed if basic needs are to be met, and ideas and action in the fight for world development. It regularly carries articles focusing on women. A special issue entitled **Women Hold Up Half the Sky** (October 1977) gives a good introduction to the plight of third world women and the negative effects modernization and development schemes have had on women.

For the World Conference of the United Nations Decade for Women in 1980, the **New Internationalist** prepared a press packet which could serve as a good introduction to many issues: brief articles describe women workers in multinational industries, how economic development has brought malnutrition and loss of prestige to women, as well as give an overview of the huge amount of work women do around the world. Other issues of interest include **Stop the Babymilk Pushers...** (February 1982). In almost all its articles, on whatever subject, this magazine shows an awareness of women. Thus articles on farming or water speak of both men and women and not just of the "farmer, he..." as we unfortunately still find in some development journals.

Prisma: The Indonesian Indicator
c/o LP3ES, P.O. Box 493 JKT, J1. S. Parman 81, Slipi, Jakarta Barat, Indonesia.

This quarterly journal of the Institute for Economic and Social Research, Education and Information has produced a special issue on women in Indonesia (no. 24, March 1982). This is a collection of very interesting and well-written articles covering women's image in Indonesian films and books, women in myth and reality, women's emancipation, and the self-image of Indonesian women. It also contains an interesting book review of an Indonesian study on the sexual division of labor. Published in English and Indonesian. Price per copy: US$ 2.25, Asia and Australia; $ 3.25, Europe and America.

Resources for Feminist Research (RFR)
Department of Sociology, Ontario Institute for Studies in Education (OISE) 252 Bloor Street West, Toronto, Canada M5S 1V6.

A very important resource for women, **RFR** is a substantial quarterly journal which brings well-written and clearly presented abstracts and reviews of books, research, periodicals and organizations dealing with issues of concern to women. It has a feminist and international perspective and makes the links between feminism and development issues, as well as between women's action and research, between women's struggles in industrialized countries and the third world. Recent issues of special interest are on **Women and Trade Unions** vol. 10 no. 2, July 1981, and on rural **Women and Agricultural Production** (1982). With its wealth of material in each issue, this journal is definitely among the most useful and valuable resources for both researchers and activists.

Signs: Journal of Women in Culture and Society
University of Chicago Press, 11030 S. Langley Avenue, Chicago, Illinois 60628, USA.

A feminist scholarly journal, **Signs** is published quarterly and each issue brings about 250 pages of study and research, usually on a specific theme. The journal has dedicated several issues to development, feminist theory, and to the relationship between the two. Issues of particular interest include. **Women and National Development: The Complexities of Change**, vol. 3 no. 1, 1977, the report of a conference on women and development, held in 1976 at Wellesley College, Massachusetts, USA. This report was later published as a separate volume by the University of Chicago Press. The conference brought together women scholars from all parts of the world and this volume reproduces the papers of about 30 of them, covering a wide range of topics and disciplines such as the participation of women in the labor force in various countries, the effects of migration on women in Africa, and theories of development. As such, this volume is representative of much of the thinking on women and development in the first half of the 1970s. The book also lists the other papers presented and contains five short reflections and criticisms of the conference. The discussion provoked by the conference is perhaps as important as the papers presented: this revolved around who should be doing research on third world women and how such research should be done. The gap and the relationship between theory and practice was debated.

A more recent issue of **Signs** deals with **Development and the Sexual Division of Labor**, vol. 7 no. 2, 1981. The contributions, again from women researchers from several different countries, reveal a great development in the thinking about women and development in the five years since the Wellesley Conference. There is much more questioning of the concept of "integrating women into development" and a much stronger feminist perspective. In the article "Accumulation, Reproduction, and Women's Role in Economic Development: Boserup Revisited," Lourdes Benería and Gita Sen emphasize the necessity to analyze both the spheres of production and reproduction in order to reach an understanding of why development has bypassed women, to analyze both class and gender to get at the root causes of women's oppression. Several other excellent articles in the same issue point in the same direction or elaborate similar points. Since there are so many stimulating ideas in these articles, it is unfortunate that some of them are written in a very dry, academic style. These could be made much more interesting and readable. This would also make them more accessible to a wider range of people, and help overcome the gap between academics and activists. The highly interesting issue on **Feminist Theory**, vol. 7 no. 3, 1982 could have been enriched if it had contained contributions from third world feminists.

Onlywomen Press/England

bibliographies

Other bibliographies are listed under the resource centers or organizations which produce them.

Why Has Development Neglected Rural Women?
Nici Nelson, Pergamon Press Ltd., Headington Hill Hall, Oxford 0X3 OBW, England. 1979.

Sub-titled "A Review of the South Asian Literature," this 108 page book raises the question of why so little research has been done on rural women and development. It gives an overview of literature available and assesses how much knowledge we have about rural women in South Asia. It then raises questions about women's situations which have yet to be adequately answered by research and recommends areas which should be studied, including women's paid and unpaid work, the sexual division of labor, household management, women and new technology and assessment of women's projects. The author also makes some suggestions for methodological approaches to this research. The bibliography contains some 300 entries. This review of the literature raises many important questions and issues about women's lives and roles in rural areas and is thus much more valuable than a simple bibliographic listing of materials would be.

Claudius

Women and World Development: An Annotated Bibliography
Mayra Buvinić, Overseas Development Council, 1717 Massachusetts Avenue NW, Washington, DC 20036, USA. 1976.

A companion volume to the report of the 1975 Seminar on Women in Development, **Women and World Development**, this well-annotated bibliography of almost 400 published and unpublished studies and articles is a good source book for much of the literature on women and development written prior to 1976. The emphasis is on academic studies and articles published in scholarly journals. It also contains a list of bibliographies.

Women in the Caribbean: A Bibliography
Bertie A. Cohen Stuart, Department of Caribbean Studies, Royal Institute of Linguistics and Anthropology, Stationsplein 10, Leiden, Netherlands. 1979.

This well-annotated bibliography lists 651 books and articles and bibliographies, grouped together by subject. It covers works in seven different languages about women in all countries of the Caribbean. A very useful book for research.

Women in Development

Eastern and Southern African Management Institute (ESAMI), Njiro Hill, Arusha, Tanzania.

A recent bibliography of materials available in the library of ESAMI, this lists over 300 books and publications on all aspects of women and development. Most of them are from Africa and in English.

Women in Development: A Selected Annotated Bibliography and Resource Guide

Linda Gire Vavrus with Ron Cadieux, Non-Formal Education Information Center, Institute for International Studies Michigan State University, East Lansing, Michigan 48824, USA.

This annotated bibliography deals with the changing role of women and women's education and how this is affected by development studies.

Women of South Asia: A Guide to Resources

Carol Sakala, Kraus International Publications, Millwood, New York, USA. 1980.

This large volume contains 4629 annotated entries of both historical and contemporary materials, from and about India, Pakistan, Bangladesh, Sri Lanka and Nepal, ranging from primary source materials to scholarly interpretation and analyses. The introduction explains the scope and organization of the materials. The final section gives information about libraries, archives and other sources of materials on women of South Asia, located in the various countries of the region and in the United Kingdom. This is a valuable resource for researchers and those needing background information on a vast range of issues relating particularly to women.

books & pamphlets

Other books and pamphlets are listed under the resource centers or organizations which produce them.

African Women: Their Struggle for Economic Independence

Christine Obbo, Zed Press, 57 Caledonian Road, London N1 9DN, England. 1980.

An African anthropologist, the author describes the conditions of women and their jobs as well as their strategies to improve their lives. A valuable contribution to understanding the situation of many women in Africa. Price: US$ 9.95.

Building Feminist Theory: Essays from Quest

Longman Inc., 19 West 44th Street, New York, New York 10036, USA. 1981.

This volume brings together 24 articles on feminist theory and practice from the North American **Quest: A Feminist Quarterly**. Grouped under the headings: Power and Practice; The Politics of Everyday Life; Feminist Perspectives on Class; and Organizations and Strategies, these articles reflect the range and development of thinking on feminist theory in North America in the 1970s. Highly stimulating and readable, this book is an excellent basis for understanding the recent developments of feminism in North America. It is an important contribution to the ongoing discussion of developing feminist theory and practice. It does not make the relationship between feminism and development, however.

Chipko Movement

Anupam Mishra and Satyendra Tripathi, Gandhi Book House, 1 Rajghat Colony New Delhi 110002, India. December 1978.

This 37 page booklet explains the background and the efforts of the hill people in India, especially the women, to save their forests, through non-violent action, from "developers" who would destroy their sources of fuel, water and livelihood as well as unbalance the eco-system of the whole region in the name of progress.

Debate Sobre la Mujer en América Latina y el Cáribe: Discusiones acerca de la Unidad Reproducción - Producción

Magdalena León de Leal, ed., Asociación Colombiana para el Estudio de la Población (ACEP), Carrera 23, no. 39-82, Bogota, D.E. Colombia. 1982.

This important and highly valuable collection of 45 articles, published in a series of three books, aims to stimulate analyses and theoretical debate on issues concerning women and development in Latin America in particular; to alert policy makers and planners about the inadequacies and detrimental effects of their programs on women; and to relate to women who are actively involved in struggling for liberation. It is intended to bridge the gap between academics and activist feminists. The first volume, entitled **La Realidad Colombiana**, examines the effects of agribusiness on women workers in rural areas, women workers in urban areas, sexuality, mass media and women organizing in feminist and political organizations. Volume 2 focuses on **Las Trabajadoras del Agro** and goes more deeply into the situation of rural women, particularly as they are affected by agribusiness. **Sociedad, Subordinación y Feminismo** discusses patriarchal structures in particular and how these affect women as both producers and reproducers. It also looks at both the theory and practice of feminism. While most of the contributors are Latin American women, the book also reproduces articles from women from other parts of the world. These three books bring together a wealth of significant and stimulating articles. It is an important contribution to carrying forward the discussion of women and development from a feminist perspective. Price for the collection: US$ 25 plus $ 15 airmail or $ 2 surface mail.

The Domestication of Women

Barbara Rogers, Kogan Page Ltd., 120 Pentonville Road, London N1 9JN, England. 1980.

Sub-titled "Discrimination in Developing Societies," this extremely interesting book points out and illustrates how the prejudices and biases about women held by policy makers, who are mostly male and western, have led to discrimination against women in development plans and projects and to the distortion of data collection on which development planning is based. The author discusses the structural sexism of development agencies and the impact of discriminatory policies on women food producers in particular. This is a hard hitting critique of the development planning process. One wishes that Rogers would have gone even further to question the whole concept of "development" itself. Nevertheless, the book is an important contribution to understanding how and why development agencies and policies are worsening the situation of women. Price: £ 8.95.

The Exchange Report: Women in the Third World

The Exchange, 26 East 22nd Street, New York, New York 10010, USA. 1981.

At the non-governmental Forum which met in Copenhagen in July 1980 during the Conference on the United Nations Decade for Women, a new organization called the Exchange set up a series of workshops and discussions on women and development which drew women from all over the world. This is a 48 page report of those workshops done in a lively style which reflects the varied points of view of the women participants. These women speak about appropriate technology, the advantages and disadvantages of income generating projects, the problems with funding, about politics, education, health, culture, female circumcision, research and policy making, all in a very forthright way. They discuss the relationship of feminism and development, of third world women and women in western countries. Representing a very wide range of opinion from that of grassroots organizers to staff of the World Bank, these reports are a good look at the complexity of the issues. The report also contains interviews with a number of women including Peggy Antrobus, Rounaq Jahan and Marie-Angélique Savané.

Frogs in a Well: Indian Women in Purdah

Patricia Jeffery, Zed Press, 57 Caledonian Road, London N1 9DN, England. 1979.

A very interesting study of women in purdah or seclusion in India, this book places these women's lives in an analysis of the total social framework. Price: US$ 10.50.

Off Our Backs/USA

Up the Slope/LNS

Handbook of International Data on Women

Elise Boulding et al., Sage Publications, Inc., distributed by Halsted Press, New York, New York, USA. 1976.

This substantial handbook contains data on women and economic activity, literacy and education, life, death and reproduction, and political and civic participation, gathered during International Women's Year in 1975. The authors feel that too little is known about how women function in society and that it is necessary to provide this information to policy makers. This handbook is a good start. It has become a standard reference work, but it would be very useful to have this updated and expanded, especially in view of new insights into women's work and contributions which are usually neglected in the collection of statistics.

The International Conference on Women and Food: Proceedings and Papers

Consortium for International Development, available from USAID, Washington, DC 20523, USA. 1978.

Volume 1 of these papers gives a summary report on the conference on Women and Food held in 1978 at the University of Arizona. It also includes the background papers which represent a range of perspectives on the issue. One particularly valuable article is "Women, Agriculture and Development in the Maya Lowlands: Profit or Progress" by Olga Stavrakis and Marion Louise Marshall which shows how "successful" development based on cash crops has meant greater malnutrition and loss of economic independence and prestige for women. The authors give concrete examples of this. "Sex Roles in Food Production and Food Distribution in the Sahel" by Kathleen Cloud examines the effects of development aid and projects on women. Volume 2 gives an overview of the conference sessions. The article "Women and Development Literature: A Survey," in this Guide gives a critical review of this conference.

Jhagrapur: Poor Peasants and Women in a Village in Bangladesh

Jenneke Arens and Jos van Beurden, P.O. Box 11742, Amsterdam, Netherlands. 1977.

This is a highly interesting study written by a Dutch couple who spent several years in Bangladesh and one in the village they describe. It is a vivid report of daily life which gives insights into the political and economic realities and the effects of development policies. It clearly brings out the double exploitation of women and links class struggle with the struggle for women's liberation.

Message from the Village
Perdita Huston, The Epoch B Foundation, P.O. Box 1972, Grand Central Station, New York, New York 10017, USA. 1978.

This book is an attempt to convey what poor women in developing countries feel about birth control. The author interviewed women in Kenya, Egypt, Sudan, Sri Lanka, Tunisia and Mexico about their lives, education, choices, roles in the family and how this relates to the size of their families. She also sought direct information about their attitudes and use of traditional and modern means of birth control. These "messages from the village" are recorded with only a minimum of interpretation. However, the author describes the villages and how she conducted the interviews. A highly interesting and readable book. A longer version with an analysis of the data is published in **Third World Women Speak Out** (listed below).

Mujer y Capitalismo Agrario
Magdalena León de Leal et al,, Asociación Colombiana para el Estudio de la Población (ACEP), Carrera 23 no. 39-82, Bogota, D.E. 1 Colombia. 1980.

A study of four regions in Colombia, this volume is a follow-up to the 1977 study **La Mujer y el Desarrollo en Colombia**. It is an analysis of the sexual division of labor in agriculture and examines the economic, political and ideological changes in the process of the development of capitalism in agriculture. The study shows the great amount of work women do in agriculture and the importance of women's contribution which, however, is not reflected in most studies and statistics.

La Mujer y el Desarrollo en Colombia
Magdalena León de Leal et al., Asociación Colombiana para el Estudio de la Población (ACEP), Carrera 23 no. 39-82, Bogota, D.E. 1 Colombia. 1977.

This volume is the result of a research project covering a range of issues in regard to women: political participation, education, health, work, legislation, family law and status within the family. It is a contribution to filling the gap of data and information about women.

Mujeres Dominicanas
Distributed by Centro Dominicano de Estudios de la Educación (CEDEE), Juan Sánchez Ramírez no. 41, Santo Domingo, Dominican Republic.

Already mentioned under the resource listing in the Multinational section of the Guide, the series **Mujeres Dominicanas** is an extremely useful set of booklets for rural and urban women. Written in simple language, these deal with women's lives and problems. They are meant to promote consciousness raising and organization. The series is complemented by booklets in comic book style about **Mujer y Sociedad** (Women and Society) as well as by audio-visual material and a play. This material has been found very useful as a model for developing consciousness raising material in other countries of the region as well as other parts of the world. It deals with women's oppression as workers and as women.

Of Marriage and the Market: Women's Subordination in International Perspective
Kate Young, Carol Wolkowitz and Roslyn McCullagh, eds., CSE Books, 25 Horsell Road, London N5, England. 1981.

An excellent and extensive examination of women's subordination, this 222 page book is an important contribution towards a theory of social relations of gender. While the authors bring different theoretical perspectives to their analyses, they challenge the traditional political, economic and development theories about women's position in society. They find much of the literature on women and development highly unsatisfactory from a feminist perspective because it has "tended to isolate women as a separate category. In our view the theoretical object of analyses can not be women, but rather the relations between men and women in society." The articles stress that women's subordinate position in society cannot be explained solely by economics. The authors examine women's position in the market, but also give great importance to the social relations between men and women, the sexual division of labor inside and outside the home, and the concept of the domestic sphere. This is a very valuable contribution of a feminist perspective on development issues. Price: £ 4.95.

Our Own Freedom
Maggie Murray, Sheba Feminist Publishers, 488, Kingsland Road, London E8 4AE, England. 1981.

In the introduction to this book of photographs, Buchi Emecheta writes: "These photographs of women in Africa show that the basic things of life — obtaining water, fire, shelter, the care of the young and the sick, the growing of food — are almost entirely done by women. These are the basic necessities of life and yet there is little or no compensation to the women who do them. Because they are unpaid, such tiring and boring chores are called women's work." Maggie Murray has kindly given us permission to reproduce some of her photographs in this Guide. These give an idea of how moving and powerful her book is. Price: £ 3.75.

Proceedings of the Workshop on Women's Studies and Development
Deborah Fahy Bryceson and Najma Sachak, eds., Bureau of Resource Assessment and Land Use Planning (BRALUP), University of Dar Es Salaam, P.O. Box 35097, Dar Es Salaam, Tanzania. 1979.

This summary of the papers and discussions at the September 1979 workshop examines and discusses many aspects of women's lives and roles as well as aspects of production and reproduction. It looks at patriarchal relations in rural areas, the involvement of peasant women in research on their own problems and possible solutions to these. It also covers the sexual division of labor in the home, education, mass media and more. It contains a complete list of the papers presented, most of them by Tanzanian women. An excellent resource. Price: US$ 5; air mail postage $ 2.50 extra.

Suni Paz

Suni Paz

Recognizing the "Invisible" Woman in Development: The World Bank's Experience
Gloria Scott, World Bank, 1818 H Street NW, Washington, DC 20433, USA. 1979.

This 33 page pamphlet, available in English, French and Spanish, describes how development projects have many times bypassed, ignored or displaced women. It shows an awareness of women's double workload, the lack of recognition of women's economic contributions and their lack of power. It describes some World Bank projects which attempt to overcome these problems. A World Bank publication, this pamphlet basically accepts the overall development policies of the Bank.

Rural Women at Work
Ruth B. Dixon, John Hopkins University Press, Baltimore, Maryland, USA and London, England. 1978.

This book, 227 pages long, asks the questions: "If good jobs at decent wages were offered to women, particularly those living in rural areas, would such employment have an effect on family size? Would their jobs compete for the women's time as mothers and housewives, offer them an alternative route to acquiring status and a sense of purpose, and perhaps also provide the women with an independent source of income which would enable them to achieve more control over their lives?" Based on research in South Asia, it answers that "jobs for women, while useful for many other reasons, may have little impact on fertility unless they are combined with other changes. For maximum effectiveness, Dixon recommends that efforts be concentrated on young, preferably unmarried women and that for best results, the new employment opportunities should move the women out of their traditional home and agricultural settings and into central work places located in villages or small towns. She also recommends that women be provided with a financial stake and a voice in the operation of the business venture. Supporting services such as job training and functional literacy classes, along with family-planning, health, and child-care facilities, should be made available. In some circumstances it may be important to provide living quarters for female workers and incentives to encourage delayed marriage and birth control." The book then presents a number of case studies which incorporate some of these suggestions. While many of the suggestions are commendable and would certainly help to improve women's situations, they should not depend on their usefulness in decreasing the birth rate. Feminists especially criticize the population policies of development agencies which make a reduced birth rate the main goal.

SEEDS
P.O. Box 3923 Grand Central Station, New York, New York 10017, USA.

SEEDS is a series of pamphlets jointly sponsored by the Carnegie Corporation, the Ford Foundation and the Population Council. Each pamphlet is a case-study of an innovative and practical program developed by and for low-income women in developing countries: "The projects described in SEEDS have been selected because they provide women with a cash income, involve women in decision making as well as earning, are based on sound economic criteria, and are working successfully to overcome obstacles commonly encountered." These include: **Village Women Organize: the Mraru Bus Service** by Jill Kneerim (1980), the story of the Mraru Women's Group in Kenya which in 1971 raised money, bought a bus and began a profit-making public transportation service. **Hanover Street: An Experiment to Train Women in Welding and Carpentry** by Peggy Antrobus with Barbara Rogers (1980), describes the experiment in training women for jobs usually held only by men which was begun in 1976 by the Jamaica Women's Bureau established by the Government. **Market Women's Cooperatives: Giving Women Credit** by Judith Bruce (1980). This history of the experience of FUNDE, the Nicaraguan Foundation for Development, in developing savings and loan cooperatives to meet the market women's needs for credit, begins in 1972. However, it makes no reference to the huge problems the country faced during this period — dictatorship, civil war, reconstruction. All statistics end in 1970 and, unfortunately, no information is given on if and how this project was assessed or continued in the national reconstruction program in Nicaragua.

Sex and Class in Latin America: Women's Perspectives on Politics, Economics and the Family in the Third World
June Nash and Helen I. Safa, eds., J.F. Bergin publishers. Distributed by Zed Press, 57 Caledonian Road, London N1 9DN, England. 1980.

A scholarly and interdisciplinary study of the double oppression of women in Latin America, this book is a good contribution to understanding the structures which determine women's lives. Price: US$ 12.50.

The Sisterhood of Man
Kathleen Newland, Worldwatch Institute and W.W. Norton & Company, Inc., 500 Fifth Avenue, New York, New York 10036, USA. 1979.

Sub-titled "The impact of women's changing roles on social and economic life around the world," this book gives an overview of women's situations in the areas of legal status, education, health, the mass media, politics, work and family life. The author presents data which contradict several myths about the marginality of women's economic contributions and needs. She argues that the social and economic costs of sex discrimination are a heavy burden for society. A good, documented overview. Price: US$ 3.95.

Slaves of Slaves: The Challenge of Latin American Women
Latin American and Caribbean Women's Collective, Zed Press, 57 Caledonian Road, London N1 9DN, England. 1980.

An excellent book describing the situation of women in several Latin American countries as well as their struggles to overcome oppression. Price: US$ 10.50.

A Special Caste? Tamil Women of Sri Lanka
Else Skjønsberg, Zed Press, 57 Caledonian Road, London N1 9DN, England. 1982.

An anthropological study of the sex, class and caste relationships in a fishing village in Sri Lanka, this 160 page book gives a picture of the oppression of women there. Available in hardback only. Price: US$ 25.

The Status of Women in Nepal
Centre for Economic Development and Administration (CEDA), Tribhuvan University, Kathmandu, Nepal. 1979-80.

Volume 1 of the CEDA Status of Women Project consists of a series of five monographs published in 1979, covering various aspects of women's lives in Nepal. Funded by USAID, the project's purpose is to collect information about Nepalese women to "support planning to facilitate the increased integration of women into the national development process." Part 1 by Meena Acharya deals with the "Statistical Profile of Nepalese Women: A Critical Review." A dismal picture emerges of early marriage, high infant mortality, high death rate, limited education, low pay and high displacement with the introduction of mechanized, western technology. The author points out the limitations of statistics in revealing what women's everyday lives are really like and especially the inaccuracy of statistics regarding women's work and contribution to society which fail to take into consideration much of women's unpaid work in agriculture and home-based activities.

Part 2 by Lynn Bennett examines "Tradition and Change in the Legal Status of Nepalese Women." Part 3 by Bina Pradhan on "Institutions Concerning Women in Nepal" concludes that these have not been very effective in improving the lot of women. One of the criticisms of traditional women's organizations is their conservative view of women's role and their programs which seem designed only to improve housekeeping skills. Part 4 by Indira Shrestha is an "Annotated Bibliography on Women in Nepal." Part 5 by Pushkar Raj Reejal deals with Nepal's national plans and programs and the extent these take into consideration women's participation in economic activities.

The second phase of the project involves research resulting in the publication of several case studies of village women in Volume 2. The third phase attempts to channel the findings of the project into a draft **National Plan of Action for Women**. Considering that these are government sponsored studies, they are remarkably critical and incisive. A good model for others.

Study of Income Generating Activities for Farm Women
C.M. Wijayaratne, A.M.T. Gunawardana and Samir Asmar, Agrarian Research and Training Institute, 114 Wijerama Mawatha, Colombo 7, Sri Lanka. February 1978.

This 73 page study of five villages attempts to show the role of farm women in farming and household work and in paid employment as well as examines which of their skills might be used for employment purposes. It provides much needed statistics on women but does not analyze the political, economic or social implications of income generation for women.

Third World – Second Sex: Women's Struggles and National Liberation
Miranda Davies, ed., Zed Press, 57 Caledonian Road, London N1 9DN, England. 1982.

A compilation of experiences and perspectives from women's organizations in over 20 third world countries, this 256 page book provides a wealth of material on how women are challenging male-dominated structures in the third world. Price: US$ 11.50.

Third World Women Speak Out
Perdita Huston, Praeger Publishers, 383 Madison Avenue, New York, New York 10017, USA. 1978.

Published in cooperation with the Overseas Development Council of the USA, this book is a fuller version of **Message from the Village**. The author lets the women from Kenya, Egypt, Sudan, Sri Lanka, Tunisia and Mexico relate in their own way their thoughts and feelings about their lives, education, work, roles in the family and especially about controlling the size of their families. A very interesting and readable book which illustrates how many of the economic changes in their societies have made life harder for the women. There is an analysis of the data by social scientists at the end.

The Triple Struggle: Latin American Peasant Women
Audrey Bronstein, WOW Campaigns Ltd., 467 Caledonian Road, London N7 9BE, England.

In this book, women from Bolivia, Ecuador, El Salvador, Guatemala and Peru describe their lives as peasants and their triple struggle against the oppression of underdevelopment, the poverty of the peasant class, and the position of women in a male-dominated society. Price: £ 3.

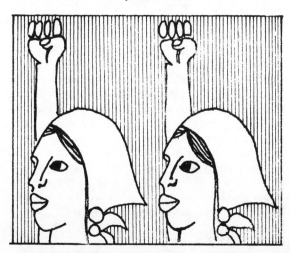

We Carry a Heavy Load – Rural Women in Zimbabwe Speak Out
Kate McCalman, Zimbabwe Women's Bureau, 152b Victoria Street, Salisbury, Zimbabwe. December 1981.

With the independence of Zimbabwe in 1980, the Women's Bureau was able to extend its activities to rural areas. One of its first tasks was a country-wide survey to collect information on how women perceive their lives and needs. Travelling on foot and by bus, the team of interviewers spoke with nearly 3000 women. This vivid and moving report is the result. It summarizes and defines the problems women face in agricultural work and food production, in access to land and control of money and land, in household work, health, education, access to communications media, legal status and in their participation in cooperatives and community decision making. Quoting extensively from the women, the report illustrates how women are already actively involved in both rural production and in maintaining their families. It concludes that this work must receive more recognition, must be made less arduous and that women must have more control over the fruits of their labor in order to enjoy its benefits. This highly valuable report is also illustrated with photographs. Price: US$ 3, plus $4 airmail postage.

We Will Smash This Prison! Indian Women in Struggle
Gail Omvedt, Zed Press, 57 Caledonian Road, London N1 9DN, England. 1980.

A compelling account of women's struggles in western India in the 1970s, this book is highly recommended. Price: US$ 10.50.

Who Really Starves? Women and World Hunger
Lisa Leghorn and Mary Roodkowsky, Friendship Press, New York, New York, USA. 1977.

This 40 page booklet is a good introduction to the role women play in agriculture and to why development is often detrimental to their lives. It is meant as a study guide.

Women and World Development
Irene Tinker and Michèle Bo Bramsen, eds., Overseas Development Council, 1717 Massachusetts Avenue NW, Washington, DC 20036, USA. 1976.

This is a collection of papers presented at a Seminar on Women in Development which was held in Mexico City in 1975 just prior to the World Conference of International Women's Year. The papers, written by authors from various parts of the world, represent some of the significant thinking on women and development at that time. By the time of the mid-decade conference in 1980 some of these same writers had carried their research and study considerably beyond what is presented here. Nevertheless, this collection remains a valuable source of basic information on the situation of women and the effects of development policies on women's lives. The book also summarizes the discussion held on these issues during the seminar.

Women in Asia for Justice and Development
Association of Christian Institutes for Social Concern in Asia (ACISCA), Kansai Seminar House, 23 Takenouchi-cho, Ichijoji, Sakyo-ku, Kyoto 606 Japan. 1980.

This booklet contains the report of a women's consultation held in 1980. It deals with the issues of the exploitation of rural women and women industrial workers as well as the sexual exploitation of women, particularly through sex tourism, and with the self-image of women. The booklet shows an understanding that development cannot be considered without considering all these interrelated areas. Price: US$ 5.

Women in Food-For-Work: The Bangladesh Experience
World Food Programme, Via delle Terme di Caracalla, 00100 Rome, Italy. 1979.

A glossy 34 page pamphlet, which contrasts greatly with the impoverished women in its photographs and descriptions, this recounts the experience of the World Food Programme's food-for-work project in Bangladesh and its impact on women. It points out the great need of many women for employment and some of the obstacles they face in the project: the obstructionism by officials implementing the program, discrimination against women because they cannot afford to rent or buy the equipment needed for the work, or because they cannot work as long hours as men since they must provide unpaid services to men and children. This report also suggests some ways to ensure equal access of women workers to employment opportunities.

Women in Food Production, Food Handling and Nutrition
Protein-Calorie Advisory Group (PAG), United Nations, New York, New York 10017, USA. 1977.

Although it is somewhat dated now, this substantial report of the PAG is an important examination of the research and literature perspectives on women, food and nutrition, especially in Africa. It raises critical questions and points to the need for much more analysis of women's role in food production. The report concludes with implications for research and action and a very helpful bibliography. This can be a valuable basis for further research and study.

Women in the Twentieth Century World
Elise Boulding, Sage Publications, Inc., distributed by Halsted Press, New York, New York. 1977.

Using the statistics in the **Handbook of International Data on Women,** a book she helped to write, Elise Boulding illustrates the situation of women in the world today, focusing especially on food producers in the third world. She also examines women's organizations and suggests how these can help bring about needed change. This is a good introduction to some of the important issues. The author carries her insights further in a later book: **Women: The Fifth World.**

Women: The Fifth World
Elise Boulding, Headline Series 248, Foreign Policy Association, 205 Lexington Avenue, New York, New York 10016, USA. February 1980.

This excellent essay, in the form of a 64 page pamphlet, questions not only the policies of development planners who have so neglected women during the past development decades, but also those who would "integrate women into development." While not giving any blueprint for the future, the author makes suggestions and illustrates the ways women's groups and networks are dreaming, dialoguing and building together a different world for themselves.

Women's Role in Economic Development
Ester Boserup, George Allen & Unwin Ltd., London, and St. Martin's Press, Inc. 175 Fifth Avenue, New York, New York 10010, USA. 1970.

A pioneering study, this book surveys women's activities in various farming systems, the impact of modernization and development, concepts of land ownership and other influences. Ester Boserup clearly shows how many development programs and policies are detrimental to the lives and needs of women. This book has become something of a classic in the literature on women and development and has been the basis for a great deal of further research and discussion. It has been used by many as a basis for calling for the integration of women into development. Others have criticized it for not going far enough and for its basic acceptance of modernization and present development policies without a more critical analysis. Pro or con, almost everyone acknowledges this book as a milestone and a catalyst for thinking on the role of women in development.

articles

"Capitalist Development and Subsistence Reproduction: Rural Women in India"
Maria Mies, **Bulletin of Concerned Asian Scholars** vol. 12 no. 1, 1980. P.O. Box W, Charlemont, Massachusetts 01339, USA.

An important contribution to understanding the roots of women's oppression, this article illustrates how capitalist penetration is leading to impoverishment and marginalization, especially of women who are engaged in subsistence production in India. It is also leading to a polarization of classes and sexes, with women losing status and power. The article draws both theoretical and practical conclusions.

"Copenhagen 1980: Taking Women Seriously"
Anita Anand, available from the United Methodist Board of Church and Society, 100 Maryland Avenue NE, Washington, DC 20002, USA. 1980.

This short but important article clearly sets out why development is a feminist issue and why feminism has a great deal to say about development, in describing the tensions around this at the United Nations Conference on the Decade for Women, held in Copenhagen in 1980.

"Peasant Movements and Women's Liberation: Some Questions on Action and Research Strategies"
Gerrit Huizer, Third World Centre, University of Nijmegen, Netherlands. 1980.

In the introduction to this 40 page paper, the author acknowledges that during 15 years of work on and with peasant movements, he neglected to take women into account. He came to this realization after contact with the women's liberation movement and feminist colleagues. In an attempt to remedy this failing, the author looks at the history of women's participation in peasant struggles, the present deterioration of peasant women's lives and some factors affecting present research strategies.

"Women in Development"
CCPD Network Letter no. 9, January 1981, Commission on Churches' Participation in Development (CCPD), 150 Route de Ferney, 1211 Geneva 20, Switzerland.

Most of this issue of the quarterly CCPD newsletter deals with the issue of women and development, reporting on proposals about women's participation in development from the 1980 CCPD Africa Regional Meeting and on some women's programs in various parts of the world. It also contains articles on "Rape: A Tool of Subjugation," showing the political and economic issues at stake; "Is Tourism Losing its Human Face?" and "The Condition of Proletarian Women" dealing with India.

"Women: Producers and Reproducers in Underdeveloped Capitalist Systems"
Marjorie Mbilinyi, University of Dar es Salaam, Tanzania. 1976.

Although somewhat old, this 38 page study remains an important contribution to the understanding of the nature of the labor process in which women are engaged, in both production and reproduction of the labor force, particularly in underdeveloped agricultural areas, in both precapitalist and capitalist systems. Written from a socialist position, the paper attempts to understand and explain the contradictions specific to women in order to ensure that women's liberation is an objective part of socialist transformation.

resources for research & organizing

The resources listed here have been sifted out of the hundreds of books, pamphlets, manuals, catalogues, articles and organizations dealing with appropriate technology. A large part of the material available is practical: manuals on how to dig a well, filter water, build a stove, store grain, etc. Rather than list all of these, we have selected materials dealing specifically with women and appropriate technology; some major resource centers which provide a wide range of theoretical and practical materials, directories, manuals and assistance; some basic books on the concept of appropriate technology, and some resource guides to organizations and materials.

Unfortunately it is impossible to list all of the many appropriate technology organizations around the world. However, the resource centers and guides listed here should provide information about national and local organizations and materials.

resource centers

Appropriate Technology Development Association
P.O. Box 311, Gandhi Bhawan, Lucknow, Uttar Pradesh 226001, India.

Affiliated with the Intermediate Technology Development Group (ITDG), this organization promotes AT and research on AT in India. It produces a quarterly newsletter, technical reports, case studies and a directory of appropriate technology centers. All publications are in English.

Centre for Science and Environment (CSE)
807 Vishal Bhawan, 95 Nehru Place, New Delhi 110019, India.

In 1981 the CSE undertook a review of its reports from a feminist perspective. This non-governmental research organization, which aims to increase public awareness of the role of science and technology in national development, discovered that its past failure to take into account the power relationships between men and women had led to mistaken conclusions in its reports on the use of appropriate technologies. This is explained in the paper "Introducing New Technologies —I: Try Asking the Women First" by Anil Agarwal (April 1982). The author concludes that treating the poor as a monolithic whole may lead to progressive policies from a socialist point of view, but that these may have a devastating effect on women if a feminist perspective is lacking. The CSE is to be commended for its efforts to review its policies and correct its mistakes. Other papers include "Greening the Countryside" by Ravi Sharma (1981) which looks at firewood as a feminist issue; and "Men Propose, Women Oppose: The Destruction of Forests" by Gopa Joshi (January 1982).

Comité de Coordinación y Promoción de Tecnología Apropiada en Latinoamérica (COCOP)

COCOP is a Latin American Appropriate Technology Network bringing together organizations in Mexico, Central America and northwestern South America to promote cooperation and exchange in this field. Some of the main contact groups are: Centro de Investigaciones Multidisciplinarias en Tecnología y Empleo (CIMTE), Apartado Aéreo 2188, Cali, Colombia, which produces **Diálogo**, an AT newsletter for the Region Andina Norte; Centro Mesoamericano de Estudios sobre Tecnología Apropiada (CEMAT), Apartado Postal 1160, Guatemala, Guatemala, which has a number of publications; CEBIAE, Casilla de Correos 10252, La Paz, Bolivia. Information on materials and organizations in these regions may be obtained from these addresses.

Intermediate Technology Development Group (ITDG)
9 King Street, London WC2E 8 HN, England.

Founded in 1965 by Dr. E.F. Schumacher, ITDG has developed small scale and low cost technologies in the areas of agriculture, building, food, cooperatives, health, transportation, power and industry. It gives technical advice to developing countries and aid agencies, and supports appropriate technology centers in Latin America, Africa and Asia. Its publications branch, Intermediate Publications Ltd., produces and distributes a wide range of materials from the theory of appropriate technology to economic policy to practical manuals. Among its many publications are: the **Appropriate Technology** quarterly journal, concerned mainly with simple technologies (Subscription: £ 5 per year); and **Economically Appropriate Technologies for Developing Countries: An Annotated Bibliography** by Marilyn Carr, a good source of reference material on the economic appropriateness of intermediate technologies for developing countries, compiled by one who has shown concern for the impact of AT on women. Still useful, although it dates from 1976. Price: £ 2.75. A catalogue of publications is available.

Rural Communication Services
17 St. James Street, South Petherton, Somerset, England.

This organization "collects and recycles information on methods of appropriate technology, relevant to rural communities around the world." It has produced a very useful **Village Technology Handbook**, with nearly 300 loose sheets listing organizations, groups, projects, books and periodicals dealing with appropriate technology. It is especially useful for contacting local or national organizations and projects in various countries around the world. Price: £ 1.75 plus postage.

South Pacific Appropriate Technology Foundation (SPATF)
P.O. Box 6937, Boroko, Papua New Guinea.

Established in 1977 as a project of the governmental Office of Village Development, SPAFT aims to promote information about and use of appropriate technologies using local materials and skills in Papua New Guinea and other countries of the South Pacific. It provides technical assistance and a series of publications and manuals as well as a quarterly newsletter **Yumi Kirapím**. SPATF gives attention to the special problems and interests of women in the area of appropriate technology and has published a report on the 1978 Papua New Guinea National Women's Workshop on Appropriate Technology entitled "Tradition-Linked Technology." A complete list of publications is available.

TOOL
Mauritskade 61a, 1092 AD, Amsterdam, Netherlands.

TOOL is a Dutch foundation promoting appropriate technology through responding to technical enquiries, research, publication of "how-to" materials, direct technical assistance, and a library of materials indexed in SATIS — Socially Appropriate Technology Information System. A publications list is available.

Transnational Network for Appropriate/Alternative Technologies (TRANET)
P.O. Box 567, Rangeley, Maine 04970, USA.

TRANET aims to promote the development, use and understanding of appropriate technology through education and networking among groups and individuals around the world involved in this field. It acts as a clearinghouse of materials and publishes a quarterly newsletter. Each issue is filled with well-annotated resource listings and a directory of groups and organizations, ranging from the theoretical to the practical, from governmental to alternative sources in all parts of the world. Addresses are always included. This is a very useful resource. TRANET's Board of Directors come from five continents and are associated with a variety of governmental, non-governmental and academic institutions. Subscription: US $ 15.

Elizabeth Eddy

Circolo de Mujeres/ Colombia

Volunteers in Asia (VIA)
Box 4543, Stanford, California 94305, USA.

An independent organization, VIA began its appropriate technology project in 1975 with the aim to gather and disseminate information on information in this field. Its major publication is the two-volume **Appropriate Technology Sourcebook**, an extensive guide to the publications on all aspects of village and small community technology. It also contains an excellent introduction to and overview of the concept of appropriate technology. It reviews the major general books on the theory and practice of AT and periodicals dealing with this subject. This is one of the most useful resource books on AT, both because of its extensive coverage and because its reviews are ample and critical enough to give a real sense of the content and orientation of the material. Written in 1976 and revised in 1981, volume 1 is 304 pages and costs US$5.50; $2.75 for individuals and local groups in developing countries plus $1 postage; the 496 page volume 2 dates from 1981, and costs $6.50; $3.25 for individuals and local groups in developing countries, plus $1.38 postage.

Volunteers in Technical Assistance (VITA)
3706 Rhode Island Avenue, Mt. Rainier, Maryland 20822, USA.

A private development organization established in 1960, VITA responds to requests about appropriate technologies, provides technical assistance and training, maintains a documentation center, publishes technical manuals and two newsletters, and provides skilled volunteers to assist developing countries. Among its publications is the **Village Technology Handbook**, in English, French and Spanish, with easy to read and use construction plans covering areas of well-digging, pumps, tools for agriculture, sanitation, food storage and more.

books & resource guides

Appropriate Technology Directory
Nicolas Jéquier, Organization for Economic Cooperation and Development (OECD), Publications Office, 2 rue Andre-Pascal, 75775 Paris Cedex 16, France.

This directory contains descriptions of almost 300 organizations in the field of appropriate technology all over the world. Produced in 1979, it is a useful source of information on national, regional and international groups, but unfortunately very expensive. Price: US$22.50.

Appropriate Technology for African Women

Marilyn Carr, United Nations Economic Commission for Africa/African Training and Research Centre for Women (UNECA/ATRCW), P.O. Box 3001, Addis Ababa, Ethiopia, 1978.

This is one of the best examinations of the impact of appropriate technology on women. The author begins with a historical perspective on appropriate technology and gives examples of the disastrous results of introducing inappropriate ones. She proceeds to a discussion of the deteriorating situation of women in many developing countries and how really appropriate technologies could help improve women's lives. Finally, she gives some examples of appropriate technology for women in Africa and includes a good selected bibliography of materials and addresses.

Appropriate Technology: Problems and Promises

Nicolas Jéquier, ed., Organization for Economic Cooperation and Development (OECD), Publications Office, 2 rue Andre-Pascal, 75775 Paris Cedex 16, France.

Written in 1976, this 344 page book presents an introduction to the theory and issues around appropriate technology as well as papers from various authors discussing problems and policy. It is a very useful overview of the concept of appropriate technology and examination of its impact and implications on most aspects of society, although it does not address the particular situation of women. Price: US$12.50. The introductory essay is available from Volunteers in Asia for the USA and developing countries only. Price: $2.50, USA; $2, developing countries.

Conference Proceedings Women and Technology: Deciding What's Appropriate

Women's Resource Center, University of Montana, Missoula, Montana 59812, USA, April 1979.

This 40 page booklet contains the major addresses of the Conference on Women and Technology: Deciding What's Appropriate. It grew out of a felt need to link up the women's movement and the ecology movement. These highly interesting papers examine the implications of technology and the move towards simpler technologies in industrialized countries on the lives of women. They also bring up the often ignored but crucial issues of whether technology has expanded or limited women's roles, whether the move to simpler technologies in the industrialized countries means "back to the kitchen" for women, and the social changes necessary if women are to have any decision-making power in the area of technology.

Guide to Convivial Tools

Valentina Borremans, **LJ Special Report** 13, R.R. Bowker Company, 1180 Avenue of the Americas, New York, New York 10036, USA.

This reference guide, dated 1979, lists 858 books and articles on alternatives to industrial society, with special emphasis on hard to find and little known materials produced by alternative groups and networks. It also lists, with addresses, alternative periodicals and small, special and unusual sources of materials Price: US$7; cash with order, $5.95.

A Handbook on Appropriate Technology

Canadian Hunger Foundation, 323 Chapel Street, Ottawa, Ontario, K1 7Z2, Canada.

Developed together with the Brace Institute, this book contains sections on: concepts, case studies, glossary, as well as many examples of agricultural equipment and lists of groups and people interested in appropriate technology. Available in English, French and Spanish.

Lightening the Load: Self-Reliance for Women

World YWCA, 37 Quai Wilson, Geneva, Switzerland, 1982.

This workbook is divided into four sections: 1) Appropriate Technology: what it is, why it is important, its use for women; 2) Introducing Appropriate Technology Activities to Women: convincing others, introducing change, activities for women; 3) Resources; 4) Selected Appropriate Technology Projects for Women. Prepared by the World YWCA South Pacific Area Office, it is produced by the International Women's Tribune Centre, New York.

Lik Lik Buk

Melanesian Council of Churches. P.O. Box 1920, Lae, Papua New Guinea.

A handbook for village self-help, this has been found a useful model in many developing countries. Contains information on many aspects of appropriate technology.

South Baltimore Voice/USA

Project Status Report on Science and Technology for Women

Centre of Science for Villages, Wardha 442001, India. 1981.

This report is a descriptive inventory of technologies available in different parts of India specifically to help women in villages. They are categorized as helping to do one of five things: a) provide employment opportunities to women; b) reduce the drudgery in the life of women; c) improve sanitation and environmental conditions; d) improve the health and nutritional status of women, and e) protect women from hazards.

Rural Women: Their Integration in Development Programmes and How Simple Technologies Can Help Them

Elizabeth O'Kelly, 3 Cumberland Gardens, Lloyd Square, London WC1X 9AF, England.

There are so few publications on women and appropriate technology or even ones that acknowledge the existence of women, that it is a pity this 84 page booklet is out of print. In addition to listing some technologies which would help women in their daily tasks in Africa and Asia, Ms. O'Kelly notes how development projects either often neglect women or affect them negatively. More important are her suggestion and examples of the creation of small women's organizations working on appropriate technology projects.

NCN

Simple Technologies for Rural Women in Bangladesh

Elizabeth O'Kelly, UNICEF, Women's Development Programme, Dacca, Bangladesh, 1977.

This 48 page illustrated manual describes a number of simple technologies ranging from stoves and coolers to post harvest activities and systems of water supply. The techniques are simply described and there is no discussion about their impact. The manual lists resources including publications, organizations and manufacturers of the equipment illustrated. Interestingly, more than half of the manufacturers listed are located in developed countries, notably Japan, France and the United Kingdom.

Small is Beautiful: Economics as if People Mattered

E.F. Schumacher, Harper and Row, 10 East 53rd Street, New York, New York 10022, USA.

This is a classic book of the philosophy of appropriate technology by one of its leading proponents and the founder of the Intermediate Technology Development Group (ITDG). In it, he puts forward the case for people-oriented economic policies in a clear and concrete way. Many later writers on the theory and practice of AT owe much to this book, written in 1973. It is also available from ITDG (see above).

Something Old, Something New, Something Borrowed, Something Due: Women and Appropriate Technology

Judy Smith, Women and Technology Project, 315 S. 4th E., Missoula, Montana 59801, USA, October 1980.

An excellent feminist critique of the male domination of the appropriate technology field, this 30 page booklet discusses the importance and implications of technology for women, and the need for women to organize around the issue of appropriate technology. It includes a resource list of publications and groups in the USA in the field of appropriate technology.

Women and Technological Change in Developing Countries

Roslyn Dauber and Melinda L. Cain, eds. Westview Press. Distributed by Bowker Publishing Company, Erasmus House, Epping, Essex, CM16 4BU, England.

In this 266 page collection of papers from the 1979 AAAS (American Association for the Advancement of Science) National Annual Meeting, a number of prominent women in the field of women and development present their research and thinking on women and technology in developing countries. The papers represent a variety of perspectives and approaches to the complexity of the issue and range from detailed case studies to broad overviews. They include: "Women and the Development of 'Underdevelopment': The African Experience" by Ann Seidman which presents clear evidence of the detrimental effects of technological change on women and argues for the necessity of institutional change; "Technologies Appropriate for Women: Theory, Practice and Policy" by Marilyn Carr, a clear, concise summary of some of the issues involved in developing technology appropriate and useful for women; "The Differential Impact of Programs and Policies on Women in Development" by Hanna Papanek; "The Plight of the Invisible Farmer: The Effect of National Agricultural Policy on Women in Africa" by Louise Fortman; and several others. Most of the authors urge planners to consider the needs of women, not only for the benefit of women alone but for the benefit of development overall. This book provides a useful overview of development thought on women and technology, a good basis for further analysis and well-documented raw materials in the form of statistics and case studies. Price: £10.

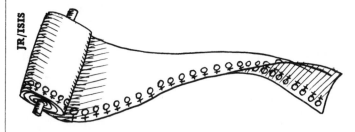

JR/ISIS

articles

"Appropriate Technology for Women"
Marilyn Carr, **Appropriate Technology**, no. 1, 1978, Intermediate Technology Publications, 9 King Street, London WC2E 8HN, England.

In this brief article, the author points out the long hours worked by African women and how modern equipment has increased rather than decreased their work. She describes some of the UN projects on technology for women.

"Appropriate Technology for Women"
Elizabeth O'Kelly, **Development Forum**, June 1976, United Nations, Geneva, Switzerland.

A short article stressing the need to alleviate women's burdens and overcome prejudices about women and technology, this also describes a number of areas where small technologies could help women.

"Rural Women, Rural Technology, Rural Development"
Marilyn N. Carr, **Populi**, vol. 3 no. 4, 1976, United Nations Fund for Population Activities (UNFPA), 485 Lexington Avenue, New York, New York 10017, USA.

An introduction to the issue, this article gives a good overview of appropriate technology, of women's work in rural areas of Africa, and of the importance of considering women's work and contributions in any program involving the application of appropriate technology.

"The Use of Appropriate Technology to Help Rural Women"
Elizabeth O'Kelly, **Appropriate Technology**, no. 2, 1977, Intermediate Technology Publications, 9 King Street, London WC2E 8HN, England.

Stressing the need for appropriate technologies in rural areas, this short article shows how these can help women increase the productivity of their work in food production. She also discusses the importance of village-level clubs or associations for women.

"What do Women Want?"
Barbara Rogers, **Appropriate Technology**, no. 4, 1979, Intermediate Technology Publications, 9 King Street, London WC2E 8HN, England.

This short article discusses how development planning has neglected women's needs and wants for appropriate technology to help them in their work, especially in food production.

"Women and Appropriate Technology"
International Women's Tribune Centre, Inc., Newsletter no. 9, April 1979, 305 East 46th Street, New York, New York 10017, USA.

This issue of the newsletter contains a brief introduction to the issue of appropriate technology for women, some examples of projects, and a very good bibliography of resource centers and materials. Also available in Spanish.

"Women Changing Technology"
Bev Eaton, **New Roots**, December/January 1981, Box 548, Greenfield, Massachusetts 01302, USA.

A short article, this deals with how "men create, define and control technology in our society and are designated as those with the know-how to keep it under control," and suggests how women can change this situation.

HOW AID HELPS YOU

Liz Mackie/ISIS

health and development

In this chapter we examine some of the major factors affecting women's health, approaches made by development agencies, and some of the ways in which women themselves are dealing with matters affecting their health. Emphasis is on women-determined health programs, research and practice. There is a descriptive list of women-oriented health groups in different parts of the world and a selected bibliography.

This chapter was written by Jane Cottingham.

women and health: an overview

Jane Cottingham

Health touches every part of our lives. It is by no means only a question of curing diseases or preventing them. The right to health means not only the right to be free from disease, it also means physical, emotional and mental well-being. Health has to do with all aspects of our lives, from the kinds of food we eat to the kind of house we live in and the kind of work we do. Health cannot be separated from the political, economic and cultural systems of our societies. It cannot be isolated from our roles as women within these societies.

In many ways women and health are synonymous. Our roles as care-givers and our potential for using any health system make us central to health. Cultural and geographic differences are, of course, enormous, yet women's centrality to health cuts right across these differences. Consider the following:

— as mothers we are responsible for the health of our children and families, for providing food for them and caring for them when they are sick;

— as potential mothers we face the problems of repeated pregnancy, of contraception and abortion;

— as workers both in production outside the home (usually concentrated in low-paying jobs) and within the home, we are over-worked, over-tired, subject to poor working conditions and exposed to a multitude of health hazards;

— as consumers for the family, we are susceptible to advertising about health, food, medicine etc.;

— as women we are subjected to laws and systems of health made by men, and not geared to our needs or those of our children;

— as objects of desire or possession, we are expected to correspond to certain ideas of beauty and "womanhood", thus being vulnerable to encouragement by industry (and others) to buy beauty products, to fight old age, or to undergo plastic surgery for "beauty" purposes; or we are mutilated to conform to certain standards of sexuality or virginity;

— as women confronted by and confined to all these roles, we are treated as mad for not adjusting to them, and given drugs or locked up as a solution.

Women are central to health. We are the majority of workers in **all** health systems of the world. Yet two startling facts have to be pointed out: first we have little or no control over the health systems or kinds of care given; second, in most societies our health is not improving. On the contrary. It has declined in many of the poorer countries of the world, while in the richer countries other, often medically or socially induced illnesses are on the increase. Why?

health systems: the medicalization of society

Over the past three decades health care and services have been increasingly defined in terms of medicine and medical care, rather than in terms of those activities and behaviours which actually produce health, or ill-health. This is true of both industrialised and developing countries. Water, food, air, and lifestyle or life stress are conceded by most public health researchers to be the major determinants of health, rather than the activities of the medical profession. Yet most countries continue to pour out increasing resources for curative, high technology medicine, which is not only extremely costly but also requires modern, western-style institutions and expensively-trained personnel to administer. This type of care usually benefits only an urban élite population (which can pay for "modern" care) while long-term investments in public health, such as eliminating pollution, providing water, sanitation, access to food and vaccination — measures which could ultimately guarantee an equitable standard of good health for the majority — are by-passed.

There are many instances of money being poured into enormous modern hospitals in areas where the majority of the population does not have access to clean water or adequate sanitation. In Lesotho, for example, a newly-built hospital

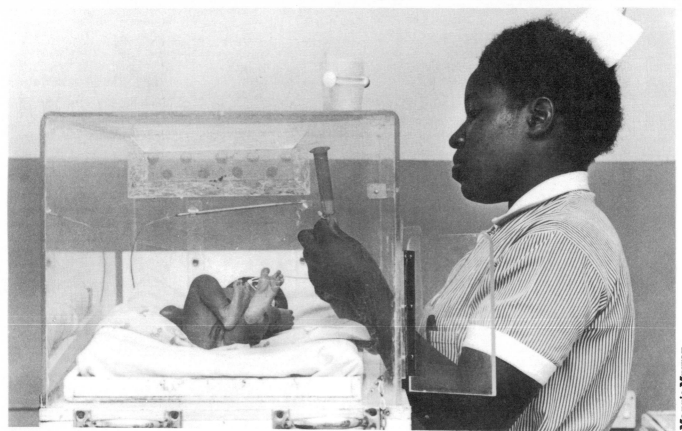

Locally-built premature baby unit. Mvumi hospital, Tanzania.

Maggie Murray

costs US$4.6 million per year to run, whereas the entire health budget is only US$3.2 million.[1] In Yemen, the hospitals in the three largest towns, catering for only seven percent of the population, contain more than one half of the doctors in the country and 60 percent of all trained nurses.[2]

Although such examples are shocking in developing countries, a similarly skewed situation appears in industrialised countries, where emphasis put on drugs and medicines far outweighs the importance given to a good balanced diet.

the pharmaceutical industry

The growth of "medical care" as opposed to "health care" is intimately connected with the development of the pharmaceutical (drug) industry. The pharmaceutical industry is one of the most profitable in the world. Studies show that since the mid-1950's it has consistently recorded profits that are substantially higher than the average for all industry in both the USA and the United Kingdom, and was often the most profitable manufacturing industry.

The development of the multinational drug companies dates from the 1940's when expansion of the petro-chemical industry on which they are based, was at its most rapid. At first many small companies mushroomed, but these have since been swallowed up to the point where, for instance, in Britain, five companies control 30 percent of the market, in the USA ten companies control over 40 percent and the three Swiss firms, Ciba Geigy, Sandoz and Hoffmann La Roche account for some 15 percent of world sales.[3]

The structure of the industry is highly complex, since, like all multinationals (with one or two exceptions), these companies have branched out from the simple manufacture of chemical-based medicines. They are now involved in producing and marketing everything from fertilisers, insecticides and special kinds of food grains, to soaps, detergents, cosmetics and perfumes. They are as much involved in making products for chemical warfare as vitamins and baby foods. The direct impact of drug companies' activities on women's daily lives especially is thus enormous. The fact that women are the biggest consumers of drugs worldwide from contraceptives to "psychoactive" drugs, and that they are most crucially affected by the dangers of pesticides, fertilisers or chemical warfare products means that the pharmaceutical industry plays a central role in the "health" of women.*

---

* One example is the explosion in July 1976 in Seveso, Northern Italy, caused by the faulty operating of the only safety valve at the ICMESA chemical plant there. A huge noxious black cloud spread over the area, and after 20 days 46 people had been hospitalized. At the end of two months, an area of nearly 350 hectares was declared contaminated and more than 2,000 people were evacuated. The poison which had escaped was dioxin, one of the most dangerous chemicals in the world, whose effects are slow and long-lasting, sometimes only becoming evident after one generation. It penetrates the skin, the blood, the liver, the kidneys, the stomach, the lungs and the central nervous system. It causes cancer and genetic mutations (changes in the species). It also attacks pregnant women and their unborn babies. Several women managed to get abortions, but one woman gave birth to a stillborn baby without a brain, and children born since have suffered from stomach abnormalities. The full effects of this contamination will only be known after 20 - 25 years. ICMESA is a subsidiary of Givaudan, a Swiss chemical and cosmetic manufacturer owned by Hoffmann-La Roche, the biggest pharmaceutical company in the world, best known for its top-selling tranquillizers, Librium and Valium[4].

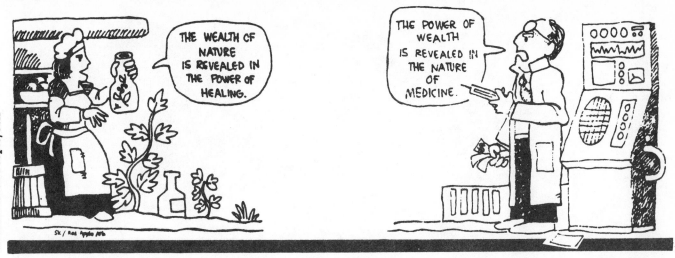

Whereas it is true that some research on drugs has undoubtedly grown out of very specific health needs, such as vaccines against dire diseases like small pox, yellow fever and tetanus, it is also true that currently 50 times more money is spent on researching cancer than on all the tropical diseases put together.[5] A tremendous amount of research is done into drugs which will be profitable. Pharmaceutical companies compete for markets with their own "brand name" products which are one particular company's version of, say, a pain killer. The generic name, e.g. aspirin, will become "Kenalgesic", "Majoral", "Aspro" etc.[6] Companies may produce any number of slightly differing formulae for a drug in order to gain increased access to the market. They will also spend valuable research money on producing their own, patentable version of a drug already in existence. Brand names cost more because the company has to spend money developing and promoting the product. What is more, they are able to charge whatever prices the market will bear, and this is often vastly different from one country to another. Tricks like "transfer pricing" — "selling" the active ingredients of a drug to a subsidiary for production in a developing country — enable the company to increase profits even more.

In effect, the pharmaceutical companies will influence health care by investing in drugs which they think will sell. This involves developing ever more sophisticated versions of drugs which may not necessarily be a solution to a health problem and indeed may provoke additional problems. The development of "psychoactive drugs" is one such area. Psychoactive drugs comprise anything from tranquilisers to behaviour modifiers. In the USA, 67 percent of psychoactive drugs are given to women, and each year one-third of women over the age of 30 receives prescription tranquilisers, stimulants and/or anti-depressants.[7] Vitamin injections are another example — given frequently to people everywhere as a "solution" to fatigue. Neither of these drugs ultimately improves the health of the taker, and certainly does nothing to address the cause of the problem. "Pain killers, so-called health foods and tonics and other hope-giving pills only add to the confusion and misery of the people. Enormous amounts of money are spent on dubious medicines. Drug production and distribution has no relation to the real health needs of the country."[8]

The companies' major outlets are, of course, the health systems — doctors, nurses, hospitals, clinics, pharmacies and drug stores. In order to promote their drugs, the companies will inevitably influence the health systems, using the whole array of advertising gimmicks available, from free samples and product-stamped stationery to frequent visits by the company representative and funding for research or conferences. They thus have considerable influence on the kinds of care provided, and to some extent on the very concept of such care. One report from Bangladesh stresses:

> Medical education doesn't include instruction in the economics of drug production/marketing and its social implications. Consequently, patients are deprived of nutrition education which should be given instead of alcohol-addicting vitamin tonics. A poor man will often pay as much as one-half his weekly wage to obtain a drug that could well be harmful to him and at most, is probably useless or unnecessary. Our estimate of the ratio of drug representatives to doctors in Bangladesh would be 1:7. In Tanzania it is 1:4 while in Britain 1:20. These marketing representatives are guilty of "conning" doctors and consumers alike into identifying the healing properties of drugs with brand names (and therefore higher prices). This is made all the more easy by the fact that the only promotion material available is provided by the drug company and is usually in a language which is foreign to the person prescribing as well as to the person buying. To stop such exploitation the health profession needs continued education and consumers need access to the "restricted" information about the drugs they are prescribed to take.[9]

The World Health Organisation has recognised this problem and has developed a "model list of essential drugs" listed by generic names only and numbering around 200. The implications for governments of applying such a list in practice, though, are enormous. In a country like India at least 30,000 branded drugs are sold, and reducing these to less than one percent — the 116 generic drugs which can satisfy the basic drug needs of the country[10] — would mean a major revolution both in the country's health care system and in its trading. It is hard to imagine pharmaceutical companies willingly accepting such a situation.

the health profession

As a major dispenser of pharmaceutical products, the medical profession plays a crucial role in the medicalisation process. The profession is an old establishment which has built up its prestige over several centuries. This prestige, and the transformation of healing into a "profession" has been created by a

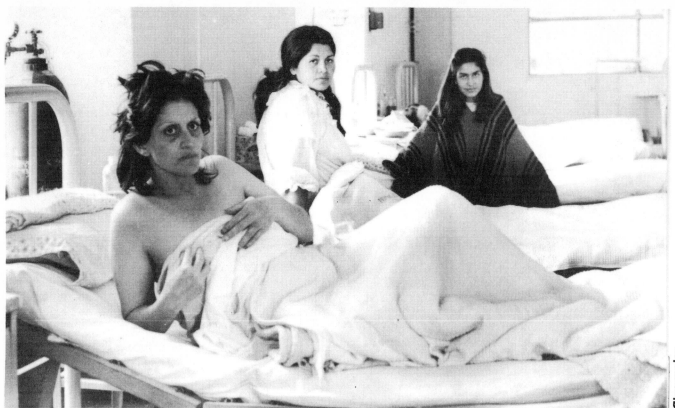

Victims of clandestine abortions in the Public Hospital. Bogota, Colombia.

long struggle from which men emerge dominant. Ehrenreich and English describe it this way:

> Women have always been healers. They were the unlicensed doctors and anatomists of western history. They were abortionists, nurses and counsellors. They were pharmacists, cultivating healing herbs, and exchanging the secrets of their uses. They were mid-wives, travelling from home to home and village to village. For centuries women were doctors without degrees, barred from books and lectures, learning from each other, and passing on experience from neighbor to neighbor and mother to daughter. They were called "wise women" by the people, witches or charlatans by the authorities. Medicine is part of our heritage as women, our history, our birthright.
>
> Today, however, health care is the property of male professionals. Ninety-nine percent of the doctors in the US are men; and almost all the top directors and administrators of health institutions. Women are still in the overall majority — 70 percent of health workers are women — but we have been incorporated as workers into an industry where the bosses are men. We are no longer independent practitioners known by our own names, for our own work. We are, for the most part, institutional fixtures filling faceless job slots: clerk, dietary aid, technician, maid...[11]

They explain how this struggle was political, linked both to the decline in the status of women generally, and to class: women healers were people's doctors, whereas male professionals served the ruling class, and their interests were advanced by universities, philanthropic foundations and the law, all of which excluded women.

The authors are, of course, describing industrialized countries and in particular the USA. There, the women's health movement is challenging this domination and "professionalism" and women are beginning to re-learn the ancient arts of healing. In other parts of the world women are still major healers and care givers, although health planners have totally ignored this.

In many third world countries, the health system has developed from the western male-dominated services brought by the colonisers for their own use. This means that large sophisticated hospitals have been built which must be run by people who receive training in the West. This has produced an absurd situation where, in West Africa, for instance, a doctor's training costs the equivalent of a peasant's income for 100–200 years. These people are, of course, nearly always men. Thus when he has finished this training, the doctor finds it totally inappropriate to the problems he has to deal with in the country, both because it is too technical and because it does not apply to the people who need health care most — malnourished women and children. He has become a member of a privileged class, removed both by his language, foreign to the indigenous population, and by the position he gets in the hierarchical health system in his own country (based on western models). Women in third world countries are the particular victims of this medical classism and sexism since (a) they are potentially greater users of the services because of their role in childbearing and caring, and (b) a high proportion of them are illiterate.

In the West, most women are not illiterate, but the prestige of the medical profession still keeps them in awe. They often do not know what is wrong with them until they have been to a doctor, and they expect the doctor to give them pills. In 1974, doctors in Britain wrote an average six prescriptions for every woman, man and child.

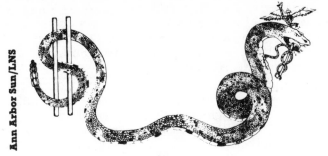

governments

Clearly governments are also implicated in this situation. The colonial legacy of many third world countries leaves them increasingly dependent on the pharmaceutical industries as employers, investors and sources of taxable revenue. They receive aid in the form of hospitals, research units and trained personnel from the rich countries. In Bangladesh, for instance, ninety percent of the Government spending on health goes to six percent of the people, and the wealthiest are found in that six percent, not the poorest. Medical students are still trained to meet the needs and stresses of the wealthy, and are taught nothing of the so-called "tropical diseases." In Tanzania, spending on drugs now accounts for 28 percent of the Tanzanian Health Ministry's allocation, compared with 11 percent in Britain.

There are exceptions, though. Studies indicate that countries which have tried consciously to take a different route have been able to develop a more far-reaching popular health system. Mozambique, for instance (population 18—19 million) has 35,000 health instructors of various grades after 10 years of independence whereas Tanzania (population 12—13 million) had only 323 health instructors after the same period.[12] The example of China is frequently cited as a model for popular health systems, and there may be lessons to be learned from that country.

health as a development concept

Unfortunately, the western model is undoubtedly the dominating one, and this has grave implications for women in both industrialized and developing countries. "Health" as one concept in the development packet was almost universally taken to mean promoting curative medicine. Until the early 1970's the World Health Organisation was uncritically promoting the system of western medicine: the massive introduction of medical technology, drugs, hospitals, surgical intervention and all the attendant expertise and equipment. As we know, this did little to reach most of the world's populations — the rural poor. Indeed, still today, three-quarters of third world doctors work in cities where three quarters of the health budget is spent. But three-quarters of the people and three-quarters of the ill-health are in the rural areas.

In 1975 WHO director Halfdan Mahler admitted, "In spite

Meeting of women who occupied the disused obstetrics unit of the Rome Polyclinic for three months, to make the new law on abortions effectively available to women. July 1978.

Nutrition and training center, Ghana.

Botswana. She goes on, "Health education has revolutionary potential if it leads to awareness, organization and action. But if people are to participate in a real and relevant way in their own health care, it means they also have to participate in the control and exercise of power."[15]

A major problem which seems to be surfacing already, though, is that PHC has to do with "self-help". In industrialized countries, the women's health movement has used the term "self-help" to denote the taking back of power over their own bodies, until now usurped by the medical profession. But in developing countries the situation is totally reversed: the vast majority of women have **no** access to any kind of health care system, and where it exists it is inadequate and probably expensive. The notion that one should "care for oneself" then is dangerous. It can come to be viewed as a means for governments to withdraw all attempts to provide health care services, with significant consequences for women. As Padma Prakash points out, "Unless sex-typing of roles in a family is rooted out, it will only mean an extra burden on the woman of the house."[16] The assigning to women of yet another unpaid, unrecognised job in the home can have nothing to do with development. In this respect, the PHC report from the Alma Ata conference gives little grounds for jubilation when it says, "women can contribute significantly to PHC especially during the **application** of preventive measures", but men can "contribute by **shaping** the community health system".[17]

population, maternal and child health

Nonetheless, PHC is a welcome advance in that it promises to address problems of women's health in all areas. Until now, when considered separately at all, women have been seen uniquely in their role as child bearers. Maternal and child health services have been the traditional "women's health" units, where on the other hand, women's malnutrition, fatigue and overwork, stress and the environment, have been barely addressed.

This approach has been complicated with the absorption of "population problems" into the area of health. In 1960 WHO was prohibited by its member states from having anything to do with family planning. It was during the 1960's that the rapid rate at which the world's population was growing became an urgent concern, and in 1969 the United Nations Fund for Population Activities (UNFPA) was set up.

UNFPA's job is to "play a leading role in the UN system in promoting population programmes on the problem of fast population growth as well as on the problem of under population, which could, among other things, hamper rapid economic development".[18]

This "concern for the world's population" has been reflected in the enormous rise in the number of non-governmental agencies dealing with the "population problem", from the International Planned Parenthood Federation and the Pathfinder Fund, to population research centres and councils. The concern, however, has frequently been translated into aggressive policies of stopping women's fertility at all costs. Indeed, it was rarely if ever seen in terms of women's health, but only of limiting the number of people. The women's movement internationally has played a crucial role in documenting the results of this approach — from forced sterilization, to the mass introduction of any form of contraceptive, however harmful. The

of tremendous strides in medicine and technology, the health status of the majority of people in disadvantaged areas of most countries of the world remains low."[13]

In the 1970's a radical rethinking took place, and the Alma Ata Conference of WHO and Unicef in 1978 launched the concept of "Primary Health Care". Primary Health Care (PHC) is defined as "essential health care that is accessible, affordable and acceptable to everyone in the country." It implies a variety of approaches including promotive, preventive, curative and rehabilitative action. It should cover: nutrition, adequate safe water, sanitation, maternal and child health including family planning, treatment of common diseases and injuries, immunization, prevention and control of locally endemic diseases, and health education. As one document says, PHC is about ditches, water, pipes, nutrition, latrines and contraceptives.[14] The approach is revolutionary in that it officially regards health as being related to a whole gammut of things, and not just lack of disease or availability of medicines.

The promotion of PHC is only just beginning, so it is too early to know what the impact is. However, although social, political and economic factors are raised in PHC, it is not clear that they can or will be dealt with. For instance, providing water to a village in, say, India, by the sinking of a tube well raises the question of whose land it shall be sunk on, and who (in a caste system) has priority access to it. Training village health workers may raise their status so much above that of the villagers that they and their ideas are no longer accepted. "There is an unresolved conflict of interest between those who have power, money and knowledge, and those who have none", says one Norwegian doctor who worked for seven years in approach has had two major effects: first, that women's health issues have tended to be relegated to and defined entirely in terms of their reproductive capacities; second, that the whole issue of family planning (often called "population and development") has become crucial in development thinking, with theories that population control can solve the "development" issue, and practices which alienate and dehumanize people. It has done little to help women take control of their own lives.

The notion that women might want to control their fertility for their own and their children's health is one that is only just beginning to surface in population thinking. The concern that women's health might be improved by limited births — that this might benefit their own and their children's situation — has not been a motivating force, by and large, in the population control establishment.

Abortion, contraception and sterilization are among the fundamental issues of concern to women and their health everywhere. Forced sterilization in some countries (e.g. Puerto Rico) is matched with the difficulty in obtaining sterilization when desired in others (e.g. France). Contraception is characterized the world over by mostly inadequate, unpleasant or harmful products. In some countries they are more available than others. Abortion laws may be liberal or highly restrictive depending on the natalist policies of the government in conjunction with religious forces; but they have little to do with concern for women and their health. Illegal abortion remains the greatest women's health problem in the world, with thousands of women dying every day and thousands more becoming sterile later from infections.

The issue for women is contraception — being able to control their fertility, with the widest range of options possible, and full information on side-effects and follow up care when necessary. Continuous pregnancy and childbirth are tiring and ultimately debilitating and dangerous; the fight for good, safe, cheap and available methods of contraception is clearly a major priority for women and their health.

nutrition

Adequate nutrition plays a major role in people's health. We know that dietary deficiencies caused by lack of food have grave effects such as blindness caused by lack of vitamin A, scurvy and lowered resistance by lack of vitamin C, rickets by lack of vitamin D, fatigue by lack of iron. Lack of food generally greatly increases susceptibility to infection and disease.

However, malnutrition is still one of the greatest causes of death in the world. "In spite of increasing per capita food production, hunger and malnutrition are increasing in both developed and developing countries. According to the latest data from FAO, the number of hungry and malnourished increased from 401 million people in 1970 to 455 million in 1974 in the developing countries alone."[19]

For many years, the causes of malnutrition were seen as ignorance or lack of motivation on the part of the individual and the failure of individuals to use the existing resources properly. Traditional nutrition education programmes were (and still are) geared to attacking this ignorance. Women have

Maggie Murray

Ghana.

Child care center worker in India discusses health, nutrition and cleanliness with village mothers and girls.

been regarded as central in this process. As one study on women in Africa describes it:

> Women are regarded as medical cases, particularly vulnerable to adverse nutritional conditions because of their reproductive functions and therefore needing specific curative and preventive care in order to improve their biological role in nutrition. Secondly, women are regarded as social actors responsible for other people's nutritional conditions, usually on the assumption that this role can be strengthened by improving their knowledge and practices by educational measures alone.[20]

In this context development programmes have been aimed at educating women in food values, food preparation and conservation, with everything encompassed in the "home economics" approach.

While not necessarily negative as such, this approach has been totally inadequate in that it ignores the whole range of factors involved in what people eat and why. In some developing countries there are food taboos — certain foods which women may not eat. There may also be customs whereby men eat first, taking the lion's share, and women last, eating whatever is left. (The study cited above warns, however, that food taboos have often been used to explain why nutrition programmes fail, and that it would be better to look at the broader issue of power structures within a society.)

Emphasis of nutrition programmes on pregnant and breastfeeding women, while useful in some ways, have been singularly lacking in perspective too. Kamala JayaRao writes, "The reason is, firstly that in such an approach the female is viewed only in the context of her motherhood and, therefore secondly, the problem is seen in isolation. The problem should be understood as fundamentally an offshoot of a deeper and more complex malady, namely the inferior status and expendable nature of the female in Indian society."[21]

What is clear is that women play a central role in food production, handling and nutrition whether or not they are pregnant or breastfeeding. In the developing world 50—90 percent of agricultural workers are women. In all countries of the world they prepare, preserve and cook food. Yet this situation in no way reflects the control which women have over food production or what is consumed. A complex web of interrelated factors affects this: access to land, policies of agricultural production affected by patterns set up under colonialism and continued in trade agreements today, migration from rural to urban settings, multinational food companies' priorities, changes in kinds of food consumed, food aid, cost of food. The earlier chapter on Rural Development — section on women and food production — deals with many of these aspects in more detail.

It is important to add here that world patterns of food production are geared to high profit-making and have little to do with healthy eating. Wheat, for instance, one of the major food staples of the world, is used in enormous quantities not for people's consumption, but as cattle feed; it is transformed into high-energy, expensive protein. Beef produced in this way costs the world 100 times as much energy, labour and money as does the equivalent amount of wheat, and is available to a small minority of the world's population. Flowers and tomatoes are grown in Colombia for direct export to the USA. Cocoa and coffee are grown in Ghana and the Ivory Coast specifically for export to Europe. Many countries now have virtually one-crop economies — based on, for instance, sugar, cotton, coffee, or groundnuts – which means they have to import quantities of staple foods to feed their populations. Prices for these staples are set by world commodity markets. Increases in these prices mean such countries have to export more and more of their own crops in order to assure the same quantity of food for their people. Imports from western countries also include expensive highly processed foods such as coca-cola, baby milk powder, canned beans and even bread. These products usually have a detrimental effect on people's nutrition both because they are less nourishing than locally-produced food, and also because they are much more expensive. In addition, local foods are often considered inferior. One good example of this is breastmilk. Imports of canned baby milk powder and the image of the "bouncy bottle-fed" child (amongst other things) have led to the belief that bottlefeeding is superior, thus denying children the most valuable (and indigenous) form of nourishment available in the crucial beginning years.

In industrialised countries, women have long since lost control over land, which is mostly farmed with a minimum of labourers and a maximum of machinery, fertilizers and pesticides. Instead they have the edifying task of going to the store to choose among the various pre-packaged, pre-prepared, industrially processed foods on the shelves. Many such processed foods have had so many of the natural nutrients taken out of them that these elements have to be put back again artificially, warranting the claim "enriched". Others have become so worthless that a vital part of one's diet consists of bottled vitamin and mineral tablets, also marketed in impressive quantities in the drug store. Finding food which has not been chemically tampered with becomes a major task, and the rise of the "health food store" as a speciality is a good comment on how most food is no longer inherently nutritious or health-giving. There is not necessarily a relationship between affluence and health. "Mal"-nutrition also exists in richer countries where overconsumption can lead to heart diseases, obesity, colon cancer etc.

Education of women **and** men about food values is only one small aspect of the question of health and nutrition. What is needed is a recognition of the total role that women play in food production, handling, processing, preparing and marketing, and of the broader socio-political issues which affect these processes.

Provision of water is another process in which women are intimately involved. In most developing countries women provide water for the household, often walking long distances and carrying heavy loads of water. This in itself has a detrimental effect of their health – fatigue and backache. "In addition, in many places women spend more time actually working in the water – washing clothes, for instance – and so may be more often exposed to the water-borne diseases."[22] (The water-borne diseases are: diarrhoea, polio, typhoid, schistosomiasis, river blindness, malaria.) Because it is women's task, the provision of water is undervalued. Thus technology to alleviate this task is lacking and insufficient efforts are made to provide communities with safe and convenient sources of water.

overwork

Perhaps one of the least considered factors affecting women's health is overwork. The back-breaking tasks of fetching water and subsistance farming done by rural women in developing countries (and examined in more detail in the chapter

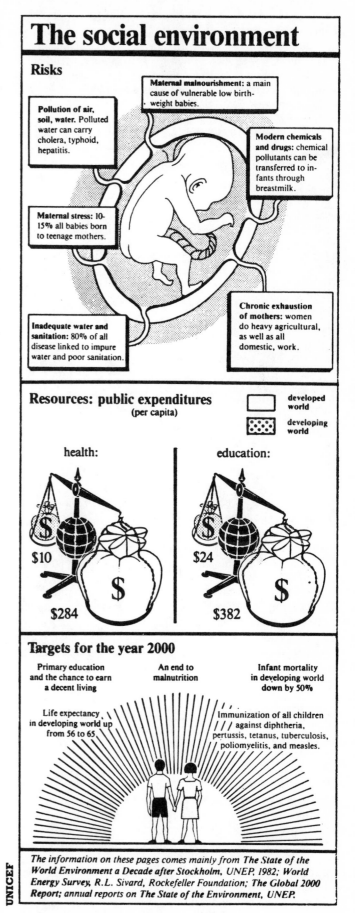

The social environment

Risks

Pollution of air, soil, water. Polluted water can carry cholera, typhoid, hepatitis.

Maternal malnourishment: a main cause of vulnerable low birth-weight babies.

Modern chemicals and drugs: chemical pollutants can be transferred to infants through breastmilk.

Maternal stress: 10-15% all babies born to teenage mothers.

Inadequate water and sanitation: 80% of all disease linked to impure water and poor sanitation.

Chronic exhaustion of mothers: women do heavy agricultural, as well as all domestic, work.

Resources: public expenditures
(per capita)

☐ developed world
▨ developing world

health:
$10
$284

education:
$24
$382

Targets for the year 2000

Primary education and the chance to earn a decent living

An end to malnutrition

Infant mortality in developing world down by 50%

Life expectancy in developing world up from 56 to 65

Immunization of all children against diphtheria, pertussis, tetanus, tuberculosis, poliomyelitis, and measles.

*The information on these pages comes mainly from **The State of the World Environment a Decade after Stockholm**, UNEP, 1982; **World Energy Survey**, R.L. Sivard, Rockefeller Foundation; **The Global 2000 Report**; annual reports on **The State of the Environment**, UNEP.*

UNICEF

on Rural Development) is only one side of the coin. Women everywhere have inferior status, so that education and employment opportunities lead them into low-paid arduous jobs such as working on an assembly line for electronics companies, as check-out counter clerks in big supermarkets, as domestic workers and as prostitutes. In all countries of the world it is women who have major responsibility for childcare and housekeeping and for most women this means a double or triple workload with outside employment too.

This can only have a long-term detrimental effect on women's health: fatigue, mental and physical stress, incurring increased susceptibility to infection.

Testing thermal environment in the workplace, Turkey.

women-oriented health/action

Issues which are fundamental to women and their health are: nutrition, sanitation, infections, stress, overwork, work hazards, drugs, contraception, pregnancy and childbirth, and sexuality. All these aspects are rooted in the fact that women are regarded as second-class citizens whose roles are diminished and downgraded in nearly all societies. Women are and have always been providers of health care, yet they have little or no control over the shaping of health services, research, the environment or the work they do.

The women's health movement, grown up over the past two decades, has now become one of the strongest elements of the women's movement internationally. In June 1981 the Third International Women and Health Meeting took place in Geneva, Switzerland, bringing together 500 women from 35 countries of the world. Organised by ISIS and the Women's Health Centre in Geneva, the meeting was remarkable for the exchange that took place: regardless of country, continent or socio-economic status, women found that they face very similar problems: everywhere they are subject to laws, customs and mental attitudes which institutionalise their supposed inferiority. Whether it is forced sterilization as in Puerto Rico, or the denial of sterilization to women who want it, as in France, whether one considers "family planning" centres in India or the increasingly restricted availability of abortion in the USA, the result is the same: women do not have the right or possibility to control their own bodies.

The Geneva meeting was important in contributing towards a feminist analysis of women and health, and in providing information about women's action. The summaries and recommendations below are based on the reports from the meeting (cf. **ISIS International Bulletin** no. 20, 1981).

health systems and services

Large, complex health services with expensive hospitals and technologies and highly qualified doctors are not only inappropriate for providing health care but do not reach most people in the world. Paramedical workers — a vast majority of whom are women — are crucial in providing basic health services. In developing countries they have a much more important role than paramedics in industrialised countries. In the latter, the hierarchy is more rigid and dominated by the medical system which limits paramedics' freedom of action even though it is they who are in continual contact with the patients and who do the work — giving medical care as well as psychological support. A report from Bangladesh sums up this situation:

When a paramedic goes to the village during the day, there are mostly women at home. All the men work in the daytime. In Bangladesh the women are often shy in front of men. They are afraid to let a strange man into their house. They are even more afraid if a male doctor must touch them. It is best, then, if paramedics are women. At Gonoshasthaya Kendra, sixty percent of the paramedics are women... The women paramedics of Savar do tubectomy surgery, go to the village on bicycles, keep statistics, cure patients, give the pill, injections and do pathology work. Everything depends upon the application of real education and simple, comprehensible training.[23]

Recognition of women's major role in this respect, plus simple, comprehensible training designed and given by women, are fundamental to improving women's — and everyone's — health.

methods of healing

Many of the drugs currently marketed all over the world are expensive, inadequate, dangerous or inappropriate to answer people's health needs. In fact a very limited number of these drugs is necessary to treat diseases (vaccines, antibiotics, anti-

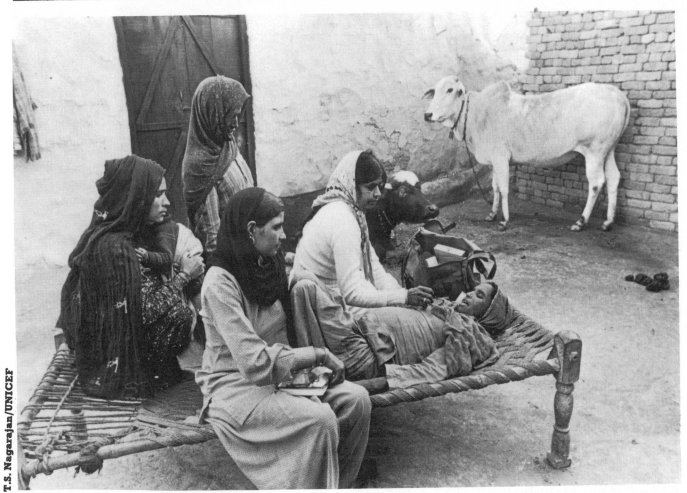

Indian local midwife examines a pregnant mother.

infectious drugs, pain-killers, disinfectants and skin prepara-
tions). The prestige of western medicine and the cult of pill-
popping as a "solution" to anything from fatigue to diarrhoea
have clouded the real reasons for ill-health, and have frequently obscured or taken over from indigenous methods of healing.
Other methods of healing have existed for centuries and are
much cheaper, more available to people than chemically-based
drugs which must be manufactured, distributed and paid for,
often in foreign currency.

In the West, the women's health movement is researching
and using these methods: homeopathy (treating likes by likes,

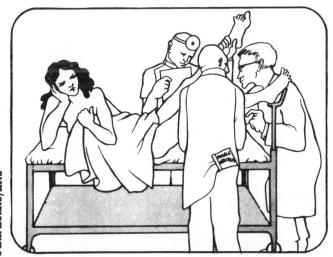

the treatment of the whole person with medicines prepared
from plants, minerals and animal tissue diluted and dynamised,
whose curative power is also the disease-producing power);
acupuncture and acupressure (on the principle of restoring the
natural balance and harmony within the human system); herbal medicine (based on plants) and nutrition. At the Geneva
meeting women from developing and industrialised countries
shared their knowledge and experience in these methods and
spoke of how this will be lost unless we can document and reinforce these methods.

There is an urgent need for women to document and share
knowledge and experiences of "soft" healing methods. This
will give more power and control to women over their own
and their families' health needs. It is particularly important
that pharmaceutical companies do not take over this domain
by expropriating plants, patenting them, then selling them as
any other drug at exorbitant prices.

reproduction and sexuality

An international network for women to share information
about all aspects of contraception already exists (ICASC – International Contraception, Abortion and Sterilization Campaign, see below). This is an important step in understanding
the issues involved and the powers which control and influence

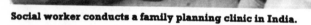

Social worker conducts a family planning clinic in India.

women. Women at the Geneva meeting had much to say on all these issues, including the following:

> We demand that abortion be made safe, legal and available in all countries of the world and that it be done in a dignified, comfortable, non-judgemental atmosphere so that women everywhere will be able to control their reproductive lives and make choices about their own bodies.

> Experimentation: there are two types, the first, women on women — using natural methods as well as barriers. The second is widespread experimentation on whole populations. We must take a stand against this widespread experimentation.

> Solutions: we must find solutions for women in all parts of the world and we can only do that through better research programmes.[24]

In this context the meeting frequently emphasized the need for **contraceptive research** to be not only women-oriented but conducted and controlled by women. Only then can solutions which do not hurt women be found.

Emphasis on women-oriented childbirth must be encouraged against the tide of technological interventions. Traditional birth attendants, village midwives, etc. must be supported and given training in infection-preventing techniques.

Information about all aspects of sexuality is vital to women everywhere, especially to eliminate taboos and practices such as genital mutilation. Again the sharing of information **prepared by women** has been a major part of the women's health movement and the fact that a book like **Our Bodies Ourselves**

(see resources) has been translated into fourteen languages selling several million copies is testimony to the need for such information.

Not all women are heterosexual and the assumption that they are must be changed. Non-discriminatory practices and information about lesbianism are equally important.

Sex education for both women and men will help them determine the use of their sexuality and reproductive rights. A document from the National Council of Women of Kenya says:

> We see it as a matter of urgency that widespread educational seminars be organised, aimed at Kenya's adult male population. The educated youth in Kenya do not need to be persuaded as to the merits or the necessity of Family Planning. We must ensure, however, that the prejudice of the fathers, based on ignorance, do not get transmitted into the children. The fathers must be educated. It is also very important for us to realise that the majority of women in this country do not make the decisions or are not in a position to do so. In many instances, they will go by what their husbands say or think. We, see it as crucial that men are educated on this subject. We should also consider the publication of Family Planning Education materials that are aimed specifically at the male population.[25]

nutrition

Since women are responsible for it, infant nutrition is always stressed. It is not difficult to realise that breastfeeding is the best way to feed infants from birth to at least six months. Breast milk has all the vital nutrients for beginning human development and for the child to grow into a healthy person. It also gives vital immunities which protect against infection.

Many factors make breast feeding difficult for women all over the world. Women at the Geneva meeting were clear in their statements:

As women we cannot simply be "in favour of" breast feeding in a vacuum. We have to fight especially on the question of material conditions everywhere in the world — adequate income, maternity leave, housing, food and the importance given to having children in optimum conditions. The idyllic description frequently given of the joys and advantages of breast feeding are not in themselves, meaningful to us without all the other conditions fulfilled.[26]

Women need appropriate technology to help them in their work of food production, processing and preparation and for water collection and treatment. This technology must be designed and developed by women for it to be "appropriate".

Since pregnancy, childbirth and breastfeeding are a drain on women nutritionally, contraception and child spacing play an important role in women's nutrition and thus their total health. But again, population control activities which employ techniques of mass introduction of (harmful) contraceptives, sterilization etc. without valid informed consent, must be stopped. **Research** in this area must be controlled and carried out by women.

work

Overwork, stress and strain, sexual harrassment, hazards at the workplace, and violence, all affect women's health adversely. They all have their source in the sexist nature of society whereby women are undervalued and discriminated against at every turn, or simply regarded as sex objects. The profound and fundamental changes which are needed to break this situa-

Nair Benedicto/Agencia F4

We want creches! Brazil.

tion encompass much more than issues of health. Probably — as with every other area — women will simply have to fight at many levels for even small changes to occur. The publication of this book is one contribution to that process.

Footnotes

1 Earthscan, "Primary Health Care," *Press Briefing Document,* no. 9, September 1978, p. 25.

2 Dianna Melrose, *The Great Health Robbery* (Oxford: Oxfam, 1981), p. 10.

3 Haslemere Group, *Who Needs the Drug Companies?* (London: 1976), p. 4.

4 Les Femmes du Groupe de Travail Seveso, *Seveso est Partout* (Geneva: 1976).

5 *Health for the Millions,* vol. 7 nos. 2 & 3, April-June 1981, p. 9.

6 Ibid, p. 14.

7 Concerned Rush Students, *A Critical Look at the Drug Industry: How Profit Distorts Medicine* (Chicago: 1977), part 6, p. 4.

8 *Health for the Millions,* vol. 7 nos. 2 & 3, April-June 1981, p. 19.

9 *Gonoshasthaya Kendra Progress Report,* no. 7, August 1980, p. 44.

10 *Health for the Millions,* vol. 7 nos. 2 & 3, April-June 1981, p. 14.

11 Barbara Ehrenreich and Deirdre English, *Witches Midwives and Nurses* (New York: The Feminist Press, 1973), p. 1.

12 Malcolm Segall, "The Politics of Health in Tanzania," *Development and Change,* vol. 4 no. 1, 1972-3.

13 Earthscan, "Primary Health Care," p. 7.

14 Ibid, p. 5.

15 Marit Kromberg, "New Music, Old Harmony," *Development Forum,* June 1978, p. 6.

16 Padma Prakash, *Women and Health: Health Issues in the Context of the Women's Movement in India* (Bombay: 1980), p. 5.

17 Quoted in Patricia Blair, *Programming for Women and Health* (Washington: Equity Policy Center, 1980), p. 40.

18 UNFPA, *What it is, What it does* (New York, no date).

19 "Rethinking Food and Nutrition Education," *Food and Nutrition Bulletin,* vol. 2 no. 2, 1980, p. 23.

20 Protein-Calorie Advisory Group of the United Nations, *Women in Food Production, Food Handling and Nutrition* (New York: 1977), section 3, p. 2.

21 Kamala JayaRao, "Who is Malnourished: Mother or the Woman?" *Medico Friend Circle Bulletin,* no. 50, 1980, p. 1.

22 Unicef Office for Europe, *Women, Health and Development* (Geneva: 1981) section 2, p. 28.

23 Gita Chakravarty, *Case Study* (Dacca: Gonoshasthaya Kendra, 1978), p. 2.

24 *ISIS International Bulletin,* no. 20, 1981, pp. 8 and 10.

25 *Kenya Woman,* vol. 1 no. 6, 1978.

26 *ISIS* no. 20, p. 13.

O toiling women
who labour in the house and out
—come on, unite!

Ganga, you've worn yourself out
Working in the mill for twenty years.
Your hair has become white
While the boss has gotten rich.
Still the axe of unemployment
Is hanging over your head
And workless women everywhere
Sell vegetables in the streets
Give us work! Come on, unite!

Where are you going, Miss Mary?
You're going to your factory?
Why is your face so pinched?
Why are you smiling just a little?
So- you've decided to marry
And your cheeks are blushing—
Then why is your face so sorrowful?
The boss will demand your resignation!
'Now the problem faces me...,'
Come on, unite!

Wearing a clean white sari
Who is walking so hurriedly?
This is our sister nurse
Who is the mother of the patient.
An eight hour shift in a day
A Twelve hour shift at night,
No hospital quarters for your family
So they tell you to live alone,
What to do, tell me? Come on, unite!

Here comes the teacher...
She lectures the whole day
But listen to the words in her mind:
'I teach one hundred children,
My children are left at home,
This is what is pinching me
Rooted deep in my mind.
What to say to anyone? Come on, unite!

Bhagubai goes out each morning,
On her head a basket, on her back her baby
For so many days she has searched for work.
If she's late the arrogant owner refuses.
Starvation work at a rupee a day,
Collecting kindling on her way home
With her hungry children before her eyes—
'Where can I borrow some grain?
So much worry?...' Come on, unite!

From the dawn, cooking grinding
Cleaning the cowshed and the courtyard,
The peasant woman goes to the fields
Weeding for the whole day,
Back in the evening for cooking,
Finally settling down to sleep
Harrassed with fear for her daughters marriage
This goes on from year to year! Come on, unite!

In the fields and in the factories,
In the offices and schools
In hospitals and in banks,
How many sisters are working!
Without a holiday, without rest
Any day off is spent in housework,
Now after centuries of slavery
More exploitation in service
Weariness is in my heart. Come on, unite!

Rise up, all you women,
Let us all unite together,
Let us go tell the government
Now we are no longer helpless!
Give in to our demands,
See our army rising up—
We will not retreat,
We vow by our children. Come on, unite!

by Suman Katve, 1975.

from: 'a woman's calendar 1981' by "Reaching Out", a feminist group in Bombay, India.

resources for research & organizing

health groups: some examples

Following are a few examples of women-oriented health groups — those who take many of the points elaborated above as a basis for their work.

international

International Contraception, Abortion and Sterilization Campaign (ICASC)
374 Grays Inn Road, London WC1, England.

"Nowhere in the world do women have the unconditional right to control their own fertility. ICASC has grown out of the many campaigns, groups and individuals who are fighting for this right in many countries. The forces against a woman's right to choose are powerful. They include governments, churches, the medical profession, drug companies, political parties, population control agencies and anti-abortion organizations, all of which operate on an international level. We need an international campaign to fight them effectively." (From an ICASC brochure).

Set up in 1978, the aims of ICASC are to create an international solidarity network; to develop links between existing campaigns and groups; to support the building of campaigns in countries where they do not yet exist. Every year they organise an international day of action in support of the struggle for reproductive rights of women.

ICASC publishes a quarterly newsletter, **ICASC Information** which brings together news of actions of different national groups, campaigns, and the status of laws in different countries.

Africa

Muvman Liberasyon Fam
5 rue St. Therese, Curepipe, Mauritius.

MLF is a feminist group set up in 1976 to deal with the many issues confronting women in Mauritius. From the beginning they thought it necessary to learn about their bodies and help other women to do the same. They organise workshops on themes such as contraceptive methods, abortion, sexually-transmitted diseases, vaginal infections, pregnancy, virginity, masturbation — taboos and myths. They work with women and high school students in different neighbourhoods, always taking a consciousness-raising approach. They also publish **Fam Lite** (in creole) on issues relating to women's health.

National Council of Women of Kenya
P.O. Box 43741, Nairobi, Kenya.

Founded in 1964, NCWK has served as the umbrella organization for Kenya's many women's organizations. Projects include: water, village sanitation, prevention of infectious diseases, maternal and child health.

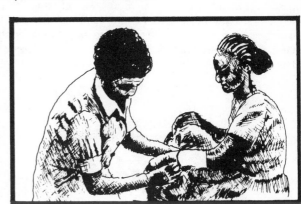

Organization of Eritrean Women/EPLF

Asia & the Pacific

Gonoshasthaya Kendra
P.O. Nayarhat, District Dacca, Bangladesh.

Gonoshasthaya Kendra (GK) — "people's health centre" — came into being with the birth of Bangladesh and its development cannot be separated from the life struggle of the country itself. It is a non-governmental voluntary organisation dedicated to the promotion of rural health and community development. GK started taking a primary health care approach to health long before the term was coined by the international aid agencies. They work at village level, training and relying greatly on paramedical workers, and concentrate on drawing villagers into active participation in various programmes — health, agriculture, vocational, educational, etc. They constantly struggle to find ways of dealing with the inequalities in the country, by, for instance, setting up a health insurance scheme for the poor, providing preventive medicine, family planning services, water and tubewell projects, farming programmes, and workshops or factories producing metal, shoes, or pharmaceuticals.

The vocational training programme was set up on the basis that "one unacceptable argument would be that which depicts women as creatures with greater limitations than men. Narikendra (the vocational centre) activities are based on a simple philosophy that includes fundamental literacy classes and other teaching in broader terms which can help them understand the causes of their own underdevelopment and what to do to bring about change. Unless this happens, they will still be tied to a male-dominated, class society." The GK family planning programme experimented with depo-provera (the injectable contraceptive), but because of questions raised about its safety, has now withdrawn it.

Gonoshasthaya Kendra Pharmaceuticals has been set up to produce quality generic drugs (the essential ones) at low cost. It employs a large number of rural women and is 100 percent owned by the GK Charitable Trust. Fifty percent of the profits will be ploughed back for factory expansion and 50 percent to help volunteer programmes in the country with emphasis on social sciences and indigenous herbal medicine research.

GK produces many publications, amongst which: **Gonoshasthaya Monthly** in Bengali designed to give information on all aspects of basic health care and to promote the use of quality, generic drugs. Also many papers in English such as: "Basic Service Delivery in Underdeveloping Countries — a view from Gonoshasthaya"; "Research: a Method of Colonization"; "The Role of Midwives and Paramedics in Voluntary Sterilization Programmes", and many others on the population control debate. Their regular **Progress Report** is a fund of information and excellent analyses.

Off Our Backs/USA

Voluntary Health Association of India (VHAI)
C-14 Community Centre, Safdarjung Development Area, New Delhi, 110 016, India.

Set up in September 1974, VHAI is a non-profit federation of state and regional voluntary health associations. Its purpose is to assist in making health a reality for all the people of India, especially the millions of neglected rural people. It encourages involvement and participation through the voluntary health sector, and provides teaching and advisory services, and a wealth of teaching materials.

VHAI publishes **Health for the Millions**, a bimonthly journal carrying articles and news on health care in India, but from a critical perspective: "We talk about the usefulness of indigenous systems of medicines, of herbs and leaves; and the comparative failure of drugs and pills as redeemers of people's health. Medical education many of us see as irrelevant to the country's needs. The list of what needs to be done in health is endless. But little seems to have been tried in practice..." Note especially vol. VII no. 2 & 3, April–June 1981, entitled "Medicines as if people mattered", which includes articles about herbal remedies, homeopathy, acupuncture and acupressure, and drugs to be avoided.

Rural Women's Health Group
Rural Development Society, 15/1, Periya Melamaiyur, Vallam Post, Chingleput-603002, South India.

"The group has been functioning since June 1980. It consists of a core group of eight women of which six are from the villages of Chingleput district of Tamilnadu, South India. These six women belong to agricultural labour or peasant families, but have had at least eight years of schooling, and began to work two years ago in their villages as adult educators for women. The remaining two in the group are young women originally from the city and college-educated, but who started work in the villages three years ago in 1978 as part of the nation's massive literacy drive. The drive came to an end in 1980 with a change in the government, but work that had started initially as a literacy campaign had evolved into discussion groups with women. These groups met regularly to discuss a wide range of issues directly affecting women — from the lack of basic amenities and what action should be taken for it, to equal wages for the same work in agriculture.

It was, however, only in June of 1980 that discussions began on a systematic basis about women's bodies and their health, and also children's health as a necessary corollary. Meetings have been held once every week in eight villages, and discussions so far have been on puberty, menstruation, conception, pregnancy, childbirth and miscarriage, and abortion. Charts and flash cards with detailed diagrams have been prepared, and a genuine attempt is made to bring into the open the fears and doubts plaguing the minds of these women. It was only after several meetings that an "open" (relatively) atmosphere began to emerge, and instead of being question and answer periods, the sessions became genuine discussions where we exchanged thoughts and feelings as "women", though from different backgrounds. The response to these meetings has been encouraging.

Discussion about lack of adequate health care facilities has also led women in some villages to organise themselves and act to demand their rights. They have made representations to the Primary Health Centres of the government and successfully led an immunization programme for pregnant mothers and children under five, and have also succeeded in some villages in seeing to it that the "Health Visitor" of the government's Health Centre pays regular visits to pregnant mothers and children under five. Broader and more important issues such as protected drinking water supply and latrine facilities have been frequently represented to the local officials, but to no avail. The women are increasingly becoming aware of the causes of ill-health that are rooted in their conditions of living — poor amenities, very low wages and so on — and we hope that alongside increasing control over their bodies and themselves they would begin to organise towards increasing control over the structures that enslave them."

bülbül©

YIS
Jl. Kenanga 163, Solo, Indonesia.

YIS, the Indonesian Welfare Foundation is a private agency whose major focus at present is a nutrition program. An important part of this program is the training of volunteers. After completing the training program, each woman becomes a local consultant on health and nutrition for about ten families in her village. Village health care is important because 65 percent of Indonesian people live in villages. Most doctors. however, being middle-class, do not want to live in the villages. They either live in the cities, or leave Indonesia for Germany, where they can make more money.

One of the workers at YIS sees two problems with the volunteer program. The first is that the education aides are usually younger than the mothers they work with since the aides are often drop-outs from regular school who haven't yet married themselves. Village women will accept nutrition and some health advice from the volunteers, but not information on birth control or child care. The mothers do not trust the aides in these areas since the younger women do not have the practical experience of the mothers themselves.

The other problem she sees is the lack of self-confidence. She hopes to make additions to the training program in order to develop organizing, communication and policy making skills in the women. She sees a need to develop self-confidence in Indonesian women. "If even one man comes to a meeting", she says, "the women will not speak up."

Another important change she feels needs to take place is in the attitudes of the people towards change itself in both economics and health — although in fact she sees the basis of health problems as economic. For example, people work the land, but neither the land nor their produce belong to them. "We say in my country that Indonesia is a second US because of the number of US multinationals. They say they are working with the Indonesian government for the Indonesian people. But in reality it is only a few Indonesians who benefit. Thus, one can not avoid the political aspect because it is basically a political issue."

Europe

Feministisches Frauen Gesundheits Zentrum e.V. (FFGZ)
Postfach 360368, 1000 Berlin 36.

Set up in November 1977, the Feminist Women's Health Centre (FFGZ) is a self-help centre run by a collective of women. "Self-help means that every woman can get to know her body, and, through conscious health preservation techniques, can avoid ailments and diseases or at least recognize them. Self-help includes breaking down external controls over our bodies. Emancipation from dependency on authority is one precondition for it." FFGZ is set up as an alternate and necessary complement to conventional health care. The collective works on a totally non-hierarchical basis. Main emphasis of their work is: cancer prevention; vaginal infections; contraception; alternative cures and nutrition; counselling on pregnancy, abortion, sexuality and lesbianism. Also offer self-help courses and have an archive of medical information open to all women during office hours.

They publish **Clio**, a quarterly journal of self-help. Each issue deals with a specific subject and gives information on other groups, on-going activities, conferences, etc. The only women's German-language journal devoted entirely to women and health.

FFGZ has also published **Hexengeflüster** (Witches' Whisperings), a book written by women about population and family policy, sexuality, self-help, alternative healing techniques and health care by women. Illustrated. 1977.

Latin America

Acción para la Liberación de la Mujer Peruana (ALIMUPER)
A.A. 2211, Lima, Peru.

ALIMUPER is an autonomous socialist-feminist group which recognizes that women are a socially oppressed sector with specific forms of oppression and that, because of this, women must develop their own line of action. ALIMUPER sees this line of action as one of converting the sphere of private life into public revolutionary and political struggle. Only in this way, they believe, will the patriarchal, capitalist system be exposed: sexuality, the relationship of couples, the nuclear family, monogamous marriage, the ideology of maternity, sexist education of children, etc.

The objectives of ALIMUPER are to investigate, discuss and expose from a feminist perspective everything to do with health, and to create the possibility for women to confront and discuss these issues: the relationship of the couple, whether or not to have children, abortion, mental and physical violence of husbands.

ALIMUPER is currently working to create an information centre for women's health because of the following:

- the total ignorance of women with respect to their bodies and their bodies' functions;
- the great importance of health education in the prevention of illness and death in women and children;
- the inadequacy of health services which cannot even provide curative medicine, much less give information;
- our meagre knowledge of the reality of women's health in the country as a whole.

The centre is an institution of popular education and fills two broad functions: research; and the preparation of films or slides and illustrated pamphlets on such themes as: the young woman, the sick woman, contraception, problems of violence against women, drugs. It is open to all women in the Lima area and especially concentrates on the needs of women in the suburbs.

The group also publishes **Acción**, a quarterly newspaper which frequently deals with women's health issues.

Coletivo das Mulheres do Rio de Janeiro
Caixa Postal 33114, Rio de Janeiro, Brazil.

Started in March 1979 with some discussion groups and some working groups, including one on women and violence. In October 1979 a group started working on sexuality and abortion and made a brochure on contraceptive methods and abortion, with all the technical information thought essential for Brazilian women. Like abortion itself, any information on abortion is forbidden. In January 1980 the Coletivo organized a demonstration and solidarity action for two women arrested for having abortions. This launched the "abortion campaign" in Brazil.

Comunicación Intercambio y Desarrollo Humano en America Latina (CIDHAL)
Apartado 579, Cuernavaca, Mexico.

A documentation centre which offers resources on a wide variety of women's issues, open for study several hours each week (write ahead for times). Also has information on a range of community education projects: liberacy, health, food, etc. Publishes simple illustrated booklets in Spanish on several women's health issues: **Menopausia**, and **Qué Comemos Los Mexicanos?** (on food and nutrition). Also available, a basic statement of the group about the condition of women in Mexico and Latin America: **Carpeta básica sobre la mujer**.

Mujeres en la Lucha
A.A. 52206, Bogota, Colombia.

This group started in 1977 to stimulate women to reflect and then to organize. They conduct workshops with women of different class backgrounds, centering on the problems of health, sexuality and the family. They also work to develop a theory on the situation of women, and to establish contact with feminist groups at both the national and international level in order to share experiences and to plan and carry out joint projects.

They have written **Self-Help for Latin American Feminists: A Reformist or a Revolutionary Alternative?** which is a 22 page manuscript giving a glimpse of what Latin America is, which elements compose health policies, and the significance of self-help programs within the Latin American context. The authors acknowledge the improvement in women's health through self-help, but point out how third world health strategies based on a self-help philosophy are in practice a means for government administrations to discharge their responsibilities towards broad segments of the population while at the same time establishing new forms of control on popular demands. (In English and Spanish).

In July 1981 they helped organize the First Latin American and Caribbean Feminist Meeting which brought together 250 women from 25 countries.

Taller Salud
Apartado 8464, Estación Fdesz. Juncos, Santurce 00910, Puerto Rico.

This group of eight women have been organised since December 1979 on a volunteer basis to work on women's health in Puerto Rico. They translate, print and reproduce information leaflets on different aspects of health, and distribute them to women in the various communities. They also give workshops on topics such as: sterilization, contraceptives, abortion, anatomy and physiology, vaginal diseases, surgery on the reproductive system, and self-help and self-examination. Their plans for the future include setting up a self-help centre and/or resource centre.

Bonnie Acker/
Women and Life on Earth

North America

Boston Women's Health Book Collective
Box 192, West Somerville, Massachusetts 02144, USA.

Begun in 1969 as an informal discussion/action group on doctors, childbirth, and abortion, the Boston Women's Health Book Collective has emerged through the decade of the seventies as a catalyst and leader on the many fronts of the US and international women's health movements. Best known for their two books — **Our Bodies, Ourselves**, a source book on women's health and sexuality, and **Ourselves and Our Children**, an examination of parents' lives and needs (see resources in this chapter) — the eleven women in the Collective also carry forward a wide variety of projects aimed at gathering and disseminating crucial women's health information. As part of a growing activist network which it has helped to create, the Collective monitors issues and policies which affect women's health in the USA and elsewhere.

The Collective has extensive files on women's health, which are used to answer hundreds of requests each month for information, referrals, and women's health group contacts. These files are also used by journalists, students of all ages, women's health activists, childbirth educators, nurses, physicians, consumer advocates and individuals with specific interests and problems. Members of the Collective often speak to groups about women's health and parenting issues, and run workshops for high schools, colleges, physician and nurse training programs, prisons, community organizations, professional conferences, and church groups.

The Collective also compiles special bimonthly packets of current women's health information and health group activities, and distributes these packets on a donations basis to more than five hundred women's health groups in the USA and other countries.

National Women's Health Network
224 Seventh Street S.E., Washington DC 20003, USA.

The only national membership organization devoted exclusively to women and health, with a focus on Federal policy, NWHN is the "umbrella" of the US women's health movement. Group and individual members receive **Network News**, "Newsalerts" about issues requiring immediate action, and access to the Network's clearinghouse. Network membership US$25, $35 for women's health or consumer group, $50 for business or institution, $100 sponsor.

resources

Please note that many publications are produced by the groups described above, and details are given in that section.

Alternativas-Salud
Creatividad y Cambio, Jr. Callao 573, Apt. 5132, Lima, Peru.

A brochure analysing the causes of ill-health and the deficiencies of the health system in Peru. Gives statistics.

Creatividad y Cambio also produces practical health guides, especially for women, such as "metodos para limitar los nacimientos" (methods of birth control) which explains birth, different methods of contraception including the "Billings" ovulation method and barrier methods. Simple language, clearly produced.

Creatividad y Cambio/ Peru

Bon Sang!
Association pour le journal **Bon Sang!**, C.P. 130, 1211 Genève 1, Switzerland.

A bulletin of counter-information on women and health, produced by a collective of users of the women's health centre in Geneva. Includes information about the medical insurance system in Switzerland, dangerous drugs, research that women are doing for effective and harmless treatment, and groups which are practising alternative healing methods. The September 1981 issue is a report from the Third International Women and Health Meeting in Geneva, June 1981.

Caring for Ourselves: An Alternative Structure for Health Care
(A report on the Vancouver Women's Health Collective), Nancy Kleiber and Linda Light, School of Nursing, University of British Columbia, 2075 Wesbrook Place, Vancouver, British Columbia, Canada V6T 1W5. 1978.

A description and analysis of an alternative women's health model, the report includes detailed information on philosophy, politics and practical arrangements integral to a non-hierarchical system. The group's varied services — educational and medical — are also discussed in detail.

"Dokumentation — Selbsthilfekongress April 1980"
Clio, no. 14/15, August 1980, Feministisches Frauen Gesundheitszentrum, Postfach 360368, 1000 Berlin 36.

The papers and reports from the second International Self-help Health Conference which took place in Hannover, West Germany, April 1980. Detailed presentations of women's self-help groups in different European countries are given, and reports on the numerous workshops from abortion to menstruation, herbal medicine, childbirth, drugs and sexuality.

For Her Own Good: 150 Years of the Experts' Advice to Women
Barbara Ehrenreich and Deirdre English, Doubleday/Anchor Books, New York, USA, and Pluto Press, Unit 10 Spencer Court, 7 Chalcot Road, London NW1 LH, UK. 1978.

Important feminist history of the rise of professional advisors to women during the period of US industrialization. Exposes the unscientific basis of "scientific" expertise used to control women. Contains important lessons for women everywhere about the function of the professions in modern societies, including medicine, childrearing, nutrition, etc.

See also by the same authors: **Complaints and Disorders: the Sexual Politics of Sickness**, 1974 (from The Feminist Press, Box 334, Old Westbury, NY 11568, USA); and **Witches, Midwives and Nurses** — a History of Women Healers, 1973 (from the Feminist Press as above), which traces the origins of the women's health movement from the Middle Ages.

Genital Mutilation: a Statement from Africa
Association of African Women for Research and Development (AAWORD), B.P. 11007 CD Annexe, Dakar, Senegal. 1979.

Firmly condemning genital mutilation, this statement by African women holds that African women must "speak out in favour of the total eradication of all these practices, and they must lead information and education campaigns to this end within their own countries and on a continental level." The women set forth how they intend to carry on the fight against genital mutilation and explain why they feel it should be done in this way. They discuss the negative reaction in Africa to actions against mutilation.

The Hosken Report: Genital and Sexual Mutilation of Females
Fran P. Hosken, WIN, 187 Grant Street, Lexington, Massachusetts 02173, USA. 1979.

A 368 page study on genital mutilation of females. It is an important and well-documented report with case histories from several different countries of Africa and Asia. The report includes the medical aspects, the history, and the effects of this mutilation on the health and lives of women. Strong recommendations for the abolition of this mutilation are also given. Included is a report of the World Health Organization Seminar held in Khartoum, Sudan, February 1979, a good part of which was devoted to this issue. Includes a lengthy bibliography.

Peg Averill/LNS

Health Needs of the World's Poor Women

Patricia W. Blair, Editor, Equity Policy Center, 1302 18th Street NW, Suite 502, Washington, DC 20036, USA. 1981.

Based on the proceedings of the International Symposium on Women and Their Health sponsored by the Equity Policy Center (EPOC) in June 1980, this 205 page collection of articles deals with strategies for improving the health of women, particularly in developing countries. Written by primarily third world health planners, practitioners and researchers, it represents a diversified range of views as it examines health in relationship to women's roles as worker, mother and citizen. Price: US$ 17.50 plus postage. Quantity discounts available.

Health Resource Guides

National Women's Health Network, 224 Seventh Street S.E., Washington DC 20003, USA.

The nine **Guides** are: **Breast Cancer, Hysterectomy, Menopause, Maternal Health and Childbirth, Birth Control, DES, Self-Help, Abortion**, and **Sterilization**. Each **Guide** offers articles which give an analytical overview of the problem and usually include some personal experience and/or practical insight on coping with it. As a supplement, each subject has its own bibliography, list of resource persons or groups to contact, and audiovisual materials as available. At the end of every **Guide** is a comprehensive listing of US women's health groups and other useful resources. Price: US$5 each, set of nine: $36.

HealthRight: a Women's Health Newsletter

41 Union Square, Room 206-9, New York, New York 10003, USA.

Published by the HealthRight Collective, this is a comprehensive quarterly on women's health, USA and internationally. Special issues on international women's health: vol. IV no. 4, 1978, and vol. V no. 1, 1979, entitled "Women and Health Care Around the World". They include reports from Australia, Bangladesh, Chile, Italy, New Zealand, Zimbabwe, and special topics such as Depo-Provera.

The Hidden Malpractice: How American Medicine Mistreats Women

Gena Corea, JOVE paperbacks, 757 Third Avenue, New York, New York 10017, USA. 1978.

Powerful, well-documented history of how male-dominated medicine took over control of women's basic reproductive functions in the USA, and the abuses of women that have resulted. One of the best explanations for the rise of the women's health movement.

Amazon/LNS

International Women and Health Guide

Boston Women's Health Book Collective and ISIS, C.P. 50, CH-1211 Geneva 2, Switzerland. Also from BWHBC, P.O. Box 91, West Somerville, Massachussetts 02144, USA.

Gathered from sources all over the world, this is a multi-lingual resource book containing overview articles followed by annotated listings on literature and groups dealing with women and health. Material is collected under nine headings: women's role in health, reproductive issues, drugs and drug companies, food and eating, having children, menopause and ageing, our health and our environment, self-help and healing ourselves, and basic international resources. Cross reference listing by country and region. Price: US$5.

"Tercer Encuentro Internacional Mujeres y Salud"
ISIS Boletín Internacional, no. 8, 1981, via Santa Maria dell'Anima 30, 00186 Rome, Italy.

A special issue dedicated to a complete report of this meeting organised jointly by ISIS and the Dispensaire des Femmes in Geneva, 6–8 June 1981, when 500 women from 35 countries came together. Workshop reports cover 15 topics including the politics of self-help, women and the medical system, contraception, breastfeeding, natural medicine, madness. Includes papers, resolutions, resources and addresses. Good feminist resource on the women's health movement internationally. Price: US$ 4 individuals, $ 6 institutions.

"Third International Women and Health Meeting"
ISIS International Bulletin, no. 20, 1981, C.P. 50, CH-1211 Geneva 2, Switzerland.

This is the English version of the report of this meeting described above. Price: US$ 4.50 individuals, $ 6.50 institutions.

ISIS Boletín Internacional no. 2, 1980
ISIS, Via S. Maria dell'Anima 30, Rome, Italy.

This issue of the quarterly ISIS bulletin in Spanish analyses the control of women's health and reproduction and contains articles on health from Latin America and Africa. It includes an overview of the self-help movement in Europe and North America and resource listings. Price: US$ 4 individuals, $ 6 institutions.

ISIS International Bulletin no. 8, 1978
ISIS, C.P. 50, CH-1211 Geneva 2, Switzerland.

Presents a selection of articles about specific projects and action being taken on women's health around the world. Countries covered are: Philippines, Bangladesh, Indonesia, Switzerland, Italy, and broader articles on Africa, USA and Europe: Price: US$ 4.50 individuals, $ 6.50 institutions.

Manushi ("Woman")
C1/202 Lajpat Nagar 1, New Delhi 110024, India.

A collectively produced magazine, first appearing in January 1979. Provides a medium for women to "speak out", to analyse their situations and to "move towards a shared understanding". **Manushi** regularly carries articles about women's health and issues which affect it. Also published in Hindi.

Mujer y Desarrollo
Mujeres en Desarrollo Inc., Apartado 325, Santo Domingo, Dominican Republic.

Well-illustrated and written in simple language, this newsletter is intended for women in rural areas, and deals with basic health issues such as nutrition, growing food, breast feeding and infant feeding, how to prevent and care for illnesses. It emphasises women taking control of their lives.

Mujeres en Desarrollo/ Dominican Republic

Our Bodies, Ourselves
Boston Women's Health Book Collective, Simon and Schuster, 1230 Avenue of the Americas, New York, New York 10020, USA. 1979 (revised edition).

Our Bodies Ourselves was the first major guide to health issues of concern to women, written from a women's viewpoint by Americans. Medicine's control over contraception, abortion, childbirth, gynecological surgery, menopause, breast cancer, sexuality, nutrition and basic health care is challenged and demystified through personal experiences, factual information and some political analysis. Charts, drawings, photos, and bibliographies accompany the text. The first newsprint edition, in 1970, has been succeeded by two commercial edition, 1973 and 1976, followed by a 1979 update, selling over two million copies altogether. The Collective is currently undertaking a third major revision. There are Chinese, Dutch, French, German, Italian, Spanish and Swedish editions and other language editions are in preparation in various parts of the world. Write to the Collective directly for more information: BWHBC, Box 192, West Somerville, Massachusetts 02144, USA. Price: US$ 6.95.

Spare Rib
27 Clerkenwell Close, London EC1R OAT, UK.

British women's liberation monthly magazine with excellent regular coverage of women's health, internationally. "We carry articles on the practice and politics of birth control, abortion, pregnancy and childbirth. Our concern extends to all aspects of health and disease and this has been reflected in our coverage of women and work hazards, anorexia, and depression. We look at conventional and alternative treatment." See also the **Spare Rib Diary** 1982 which contains extensive information on health.

"Women and Health"
Voice of Women, no. 3, March 1981, 529 Bauddhaloka Mawatha, Colombo 8, Sri Lanka.

A ten page section of this feminist quarterly covering contraceptives and the "dumping" of pills and the use of Depo-Provera (injectable contraceptive) in Sri Lanka. Stresses the importance of women's decisions in contraception. Also deals with nutrition and the issue of breast feeding and how this is not really a choice for many women as long as working and living conditions remain unfavorable to women.

WIN News
Women's International Network, 187 Grant Street, Lexington, Massachusetts 02173, USA.

A quarterly covering a wide range of topics of concern to women including: United Nations actions and conferences, health, violence, development, media, clearinghouse (career opportunities internationally), and reports from around the world. Detailed coverage on genital mutilation.

The Women's Health Movement: Feminist Alternatives to Medical Control
Sheryl Ruzek, Praeger Special Studies, USA. 1978.

The most complete and up-to-date feminist history of the US women's health movement, from an academic perspective. Well referenced.

"Occupational safety and health"
Women and Global Corporations: Work Roles and Resistance, Directory of Resources, Nationwide Women's Program, American Friends Service Committee, 1501 Cherry Street, Philadelphia, Pennsylvania 19102, USA. 1980.

A bibliography of books, articles and films on occupational health and safety.

Women's Occupational Health Resource Center
School of Public Health, Columbia University, 60 Haven Ave., B-1, New York, New York 10032, USA.

This center is a resource for literature on many aspects of women and occupational health including the hazards of housework. Publications list available.

Connexions

Women and Work Hazards Group
c/o British Society for Social Responsibility in Science (BSSRS), 9 Poland Street, London W1, UK. 1981.

This group has published a series of pamphlets, packs and books on different aspects of women and health hazards at work. Particularly worthwhile is: **The Office Workers' Survival Handbook** which deals in detail with stress, noise, lighting, dangerous substances, temperature and ventilation, welfare facilities and hygiene, physical hazards, the new technology and a whole section on how to use the law and how to organise for better working conditions. This is an extensive and important women's tool.

Everywomen's Almanac 1980

BSSRS also has a Politics of Health Group which exists to develop a better understanding of how health and disease are produced in our society. They believe that the fundamental causes of ill-health lie in the social and economic structure of society, and that they are matters for public debate and political action. Their pamphlet, **Food and Profit — it makes you sick**, examines the food industry as an example of the way in which ill-health is produced in our society.

Working for Your Life
Andrea Hricko and Ken Light, Labor Occupational Health Program, University of California Center for Labor Research and Education, Institute of Industrial Relations, 2521 Channing Way, Berkeley, California 94720, USA.

Colour film, 60 minutes 16 mm. showing scenes from over 35 different US workplaces featuring interviews with women workers, and focusing on the hazards they face — both the risk of injury and potential reproductive effects. Illustrates the response of employers to eliminate women rather than improve the workplace for everyone. Purchase: US$475; Rental: $65 from LOHP Films, Transit Media, 779 Susquehanna Avenue, Franklin Lakes, New Jersey 07417, USA.

nutrition

(See also chapter on Rural Development for references on women and food production.)

Women in Food Production, Food Handling and Nutrition, with Special Emphasis on Africa
Protein Advisory Group of the United Nations, New York, USA. June 1977. Available from ISIS, C.P. 50, CH-1211 Geneva 2, Switzerland.

This report of the now-defunct Protein Advisory Group (PAG) of the UN presents a thorough examination of the literature and research perspectives concerning women, food and nutrition. Its intent is to raise questions about current nutrition research, with a demand for much wider analysis to include women's role in food production, processing and handling. Emphasis is on Africa because of women's key position in production systems. Describes how women are dealt with in the current debate on food and nutrition strategies, looking at UN policy papers. A final section deals with implications for research and action, and suggestions for follow-up studies. An extremely important resource, and helpful bibliography.

The Feeding Web: Issues in Nutritional Ecology
Joan Dye Gussow, Bull Publishing, Box 208, Palo Alto, California 94302, USA. 1978.

Excellent resource by a prominent food activist. Chapters include: population growth, world food supply, energy and food, food technology, and food advertising. Addresses important food and agricultural policy issues at both national and international levels. Price: US$9.95.

"Who is malnourished: mother or the woman?"
Kamala JayaRao, **Medico Friend Circle Bulletin**, no. 50, February 1980, c/o National Institute of Nutrition, P.O. Jamai Osmania, Hyderabad 500 007, India.

An examination of the inferior status of Indian women in Indian society, showing that this has a specific impact on the nutrition of women. Welfare and nutrition programmes are seen as useless: "neither nutritionists who formulate and recommend the programmes nor the administrators who are responsible for their implementation appear to view the female first as a woman and an individual, but seem to view her only in her role as a mother. Implied therein is the view that the woman is important only because she is the bearer and nurturer of children"... "All along we have devised welfare programmes for women and directed all developmental activity towards men."

Women, Food and Health in Tanzania: The Political Economy of Disease
Meredith Turshen, Onyx Press Ltd., 27 Clerkenwell Close, London EC1R OAT, UK. 1980.

Explores capitalist underdevelopment of Tanzania and how twentieth century colonial exploitation affected women in particular — their social and political status, their function as food producers, and the health of their families. Price: £3.50.

Liz Mackie/Sourcream

—AND, AS YOU CAN SEE, WOMEN WILL PLAY A CENTRAL PART IN OUR PLAN!

pharmaceuticals

A Critical Look at the Drug Industry: How Profit Distorts Medicine
Concerned Rush Students, c/o Bob Schiff, Box 160, 1743 W. Harrison Street, Chicago, Illinois 60612, USA. n.d.

A collection of papers raising a series of issues related to drug companies' activities in the USA and their attempts to corner markets by influencing medical practice. They examine the winning over of medical students during college, advertising, gifts, the use of brand names over generic terms for drugs, and the entering into everyday lives by medicalising normal social behaviour such as worry, frustration, over work, etc. An excellent exposé of drug company practices.

"The Politics of Health in Tanzania"
Malcolm Segall, **Development and Change**, vol. IV no. 1, 1972–3, Institute of Social Studies, Badhuisweg 251, The Hague, Netherlands.

Analyses the economic reality of Tanzania and the need for preventive medicine rather than curative services which currently take the lion's share of the health budget. Looks at the influences involved in this western-style medicine on a poor country (neo-colonialism, overseas investment, working relations in health system, urban élite) and shows the disastrous effects.

The Great Health Robbery
Dianna Melrose, OXFAM Public Affairs Unit, 274 Banbury Road, Oxford OX2 7DZ, UK. 1981.

Subtitled "baby milk and medicines in Yemen", this well-written and presented study describes the health situation in Yemen, and shows how efforts to improve health are aggravated by the promotion of artificial baby milk and medicines in conditions that make their safe use impossible. An excellent case-study of the health/sickness situation in developing countries, with suggestions for action that can be taken at various levels.

Health Action International
c/o International Organisation of Consumers' Unions, P.O. Box 1045, Penang, Malaysia.

An international "antibody" set up in May 1981 to resist ill-treatment of consumers by multinational drug companies. It comprises a broad-based network of consumer, professional, development action and other groups, one of whose concerns is to look into contraceptive drugs and pharmaceutical companies' activities in this field. Produces **HAI News**, a bimonthly newsletter on current actions, publications and meetings on pharmaceuticals.

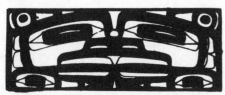

John Mack/LNS

Insult or Injury? An Enquiry into the Marketing and Advertising of British Food and Drug Products in the Third World
Charles Medawar, Social Audit Ltd., 9 Poland Street, London W1V 3DG, UK. 1979.

Excellent discussion of how misleading advertising and marketing to poor people affects nutritional status, health, and ultimately development. Detailed examples of strategies and activities of multinationals are given. They operate in a business climate where low or no controls and standards are enforced, and where bribery is easy. Excellent bibliography.

Social Audit is an action-research unit, concerned with improving government and corporate responsiveness to the public generally. It has published several books and leaflets on multinational drug companies. Important source of information in this domain.

International Organisation of Consumers' Unions
P.O. Box 1045, Penang, Malaysia.

An independent, non-profit and non-political foundation. It promotes world-wide cooperation in the comparative testing of consumer goods and services and in all other aspects of consumer information, education and protection. Includes 115 consumer associations in 47 countries. IOCU produces (amongst others) a medical newsletter which gives details of research and publications especially on drugs and baby foods.

Major Issues in Transfer of Technology in Developing Countries: a Case Study of the Pharmaceutical Industry
S. Lall, UNCTAD/TD/B/C.6/4, United Nations, 1211 Geneva 10, Switzerland. 1975. French and English.

An analysis of (1) the structure of production and marketing of pharmaceutical products in the world — 80 percent of which takes place in developed market economy countries; (2) principal characteristics of the industry — the role of the multinationals, their power over the market and the direct and indirect consequences of this for developing countries; and (3) proposals for ways in which developing countries may acquire necessary techniques to establish their own pharmaceutical industries.

Les Médicaments et le Tiers Monde
Andras November, Editions Favre/Centre Europe Tiers-Monde, 37 Quai Wilson, CH-1201 Geneva, Switzerland. 1981.

A study of the pharmaceutical industry, with emphasis on the Swiss companies, and the relationship of this industry to health in the third world. Looks at production, market research, over-consumption of drugs and the total dependence of third world countries in this domain. Suggests solutions such as development of indigenous pharmaceutical industries, and a profound change in medical practice both in developing and industrialised societies. Includes statistics on the industry.

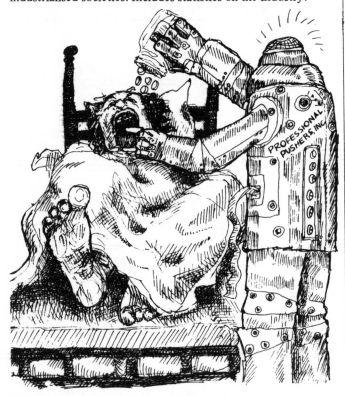

"The Charge: Gynocide, the accused: the U.S. Government", Barbara Ehrenreich, Mark Dowie and Stephen Minkin, **Mother Jones**, November 1979.

An extensive exposé of the way in which the US Government has actively followed a policy of "dumping" unsafe contraceptives on third world countries. Deals with the Dalkon Shield IUD, high-estrogen birth control pills and Depo-Provera, the injectable contraceptive. All of these have been ruled unsafe by the Federal Drug Administration, and the article elaborates on some of the nocive effects of these drugs. This whole issue of **Mother Jones** is entitled "The Corporate Crime of the Century", and looks at other products involved in this kind of dumping process.

"Medical Industry Thrives, Health Care Fails"
Charles Dougherty, **Science for the People**, vol. 13 no. 2, March–April 1981, 897 Main Street, Cambridge, Massachusetts 02139, USA.

An examination of the health situation in the Philippines, showing how foreign drug companies are flourishing there, while the health of the majority of the population is bad and declining. Demonstrates how difficult and costly it is to become a health worker, and how the Government is using "health care" to stem opposition movements. Briefly examines some of the alternatives being set up in different areas.

Science for the People is a bimonthly magazine which frequently carries articles on health, especially on drug companies and health care systems. Subscription: US$10 USA, $14 overseas, $24 institutions.

Seveso Est Partout
Les femmes du Groupe de travail Seveso, C.P. 111, 1227 Carouge, Switzerland. 1976.

A collection of documents concerning the escape of the highly poisonous chemical dioxine at Seveso, Italy in July 1976. Gives chronology of events, including public statements by La Roche-Givaudan, the company responsible, interviews with women from the Seveso area, and a detailed look at the Swiss companies involved, including their activities in Switzerland. Particularly analyses the effects of these on women — pollution, drugs and cosmetics, with specific examples. A feminist analysis.

Who Needs the Drug Companies?
Haslemere Group, 467 Caledonian Road, London N.7, UK. n.d.

Clear, illustrated pamphlet on how the drug industry works. Gives examples of malpractices in both industrialised and third world countries. The role of drugs in relation to the real health needs of developed and developing countries is questioned, and a final section suggests possibilities for change both in the way the drug industry operates and in consumer and doctor attitudes towards drugs. A good basic study with extensive references.

population control & birth control

Abortion Internationally
National Abortion Campaign, 374 Gray's Inn Road, London WC1, UK. 1978.

A collection of articles on abortion conditions and laws in different countries: Chile, Australia, Eastern Europe, and the USSR, China, Bangladesh, India, Japan, USA and Italy. Also includes aims and structure of the National Abortion Campaign in Britain.

Contraceptives and Common Sense: Conventional Methods Reconsidered
Judith Bruce and S. Bruce Schearer, The Population Council, 1 Dag Hammarskjold Plaza, New York, New York 10017, USA. 1979.

Examines with good data, the use and effectiveness of barrier methods (condom, diaphragm, cap), those groups for whom these methods have an appeal and discusses how current pharmaceutical research could help overcome drawbacks of existing barrier methods. Stresses the importance of women's health groups in such research, and the work that has already been done by these groups. An important feature of the book is the chapter on barrier methods in developing countries — how they can be made more widely available and what culture-specific adaptations could be made. Stresses the importance of information and counselling, and the fact that, the world over, these methods can be women-controlled and used without the intervention of health "professionals". Ends with recommendations for policy and action.

Depo-Provera: A Report by the Campaign Against Depo-Provera
Campaign Against Depo-Provera, 374 Gray's Inn Road, London WC1, UK. 1981.

Depo-Provera is a contraceptive injection. It is given to thousands of women all over the third world. Yet it is not considered safe enough for general use in Britain or the United States. Why are there such double standards? **Depo-Provera: A Report** gives detailed evidence of the drug's abuse by governments, drug companies, and the international family planning agencies. The booklet sets out the grim health hazards of the injection — risks of cancer, dangers to the children of women taking the drug, and alarming side-effects.

The Campaign Against Depo-Provera argues for a world-wide ban on this contraceptive and accuses the international family planning agencies of racist double standards in encouraging the use of the hazardous injection. Price: £1.50.

En Defensa del Aborto en Venezuela
Giovanna Machada. 1980.

Describes the situation of illegal abortion in Venezuela — 65 out of every 100 pregnancies ending in abortions in women aged between 35 and 40. The book has been instrumental in launching a campaign in favour of the legalization of abortion in Venezuela.

"Manifestaciones en torno al aborto"
Fem, vol. III no. 9, October—December 1979, Nueva Cultura Feminista, A.C. Universidad 1855, Desp. 401, México 20 D.F.

This short article recounts the actions of the Mexican feminist movement during 1979 in their struggle for free abortion on demand and includes a statement of their position on abortion and voluntary motherhood. **Fem** is a Mexican feminist journal which frequently carries articles on women's health.

"Contraceptive Research"
Judy Norsigian. **ISIS International Bulletin no**. 7, 1978, C.P. 50, CH-1211 Geneva 2, Switzerland.

Testimony given on behalf of the National Women's Health Network, USA, by one of the co-authors of **Our Bodies, Ourselves**, analyses how contraceptive research decisions are made by the US Government — what kind of research receives priority, who carries out that research, and who makes policy decisions in this area. Increased emphasis on more invasive, irreversible and dangerous methods was noted, as was lack of informed consent for third world women in the USA and other countries who are using these methods. The dominance of males in this research, as well as the failure to meet clinical investigatory standards, is also documented.

Off Our Backs/Women's Survival Manual/LNS

People
International Planned Parenthood Federation, 18—20 Lower Regent Street, London SW1 4PW, UK. English, French and Spanish.

Quarterly magazine of a major population control organization, self-described as "a development magazine, reporting worldwide on the effort to balance resources and population, to promote planned parenthood and to improve the human condition." Specific themes each time, e.g. ageing in Europe, the Muslim world, population and employment. Good articles, news and updates and book reviews. Since it is dealing broadly with population, always carries information of interest to women on abortion, abortion laws, contraception, breastfeeding, etc. Also produces charts from time to time on e.g. availability of contraception, abortion laws, etc.

Population Target: The Political Economy of Population Control in Latin America
Bonnie Mass, Women's Press, Toronto, Canada. 1976.

Marxist analysis of population control policies and their application in different countries, specifically on the abuses of women. Good documentation with references.

Report of Workshop on "Women Health and Reproduction"
Feminist Resource Centre, 13 Carol Mansion, 35 Sitladevi Temple Road, Mahim, Bombay 400016, India.

From a feminist workshop held in Bombay, April 1981, this report places health in the context of inequalities in society: industrialized/developing countries, urban/rural, rich/poor, men/women; and women's health in the context of their status in society and the family, stating that the women's health movement can only be part of the broader movement for women's emancipation. Stresses the importance of women understanding their own bodies, and states that many family planning programmes in India only create greater dependency of women. Even endogenous research is male-dominated, and generally dangerous to women. It is seen essential to develop an independent organisation of feminists which would investigate the contraceptives being tested and to take action against contraceptives which are harmful to women. An action programme is outlined, covering safe abortion, traditional medicine, contraceptives, information and communication.

Sex Education and Population Policies in Brazil
Carmen Barroso, Fundaçao Carlos Chagas, Av. Prof. Francisco Morato 1565, Sao Paulo, Brazil. 1980.

A six-page paper which outlines pro- and anti-natalist policies in Brazil, and goes on to speak of women's rights: "To block women's access to contraception is a form of coercion that forces a woman to have a child she does not want. On the other hand, not to provide women with basic means to feed and raise children, is equivalent, in practice, to prohibit women even to desire children." Supports fundamental economic and social changes, sex education, and availability of contraception and abortion.

Third World Women Speak Out
Perdita Huston, Praeger Publishers, USA. 1979.

A very human and unstatistical book presenting women's views of change, development and basic needs in their own words, from interviews with women of diverse economic and social backgrounds in Egypt, Sudan, Mexico, Tunisia, Sri Lanka and Kenya. They echo the need to change social attitudes that stand in the way of their development, particularly the taboos against contraception. They express an overwhelming need to be able to earn money; they speak universally of the exhaustion of working such long hours without help or adequate food. The majority of rural women work day and night to squeeze out enough money for their children's school books in the hope of saving them from the imprisonment of illiteracy.

Woman's Body, Woman's Right – A Social History of Birth Control in America
Linda Gordon, Penguin Books, 625 Madison Avenue, New York, New York 10022, USA. Or Penguin, Middlesex, UK. 1977.

Traces the history and development of the birth control movement in the USA, covering political, social and economic aspects. Excellent feminist analysis.

Women's Health/LNS

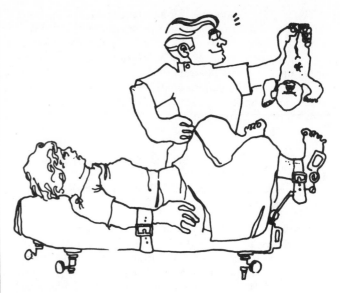

Chevron/LNS

Women Under Attack: Abortion, Sterilization Abuse and Reproductive Freedom
Committee for Abortion Rights and Against Sterilization Abuse (CARASA), 386 Park Avenue South, Rm 1502, New York, New York 10016, USA. 1979.

Excellent presentation of the current issues surrounding abortion and reproductive rights in the USA, includes history, politics of right-wing opposition, the law, victims of funding cutbacks, etc. Particularly good linking the issues of sterilization abuse and abortion cutbacks. Good bibliography. Price: US$ 2.50.

CARASA also produces **Carasa News**, which includes reports and updates on abortion rights, population control and sterilization abuse.

More than Numbers
United Methodist Communications, 1525 McGavock Street, Nashville, Tennessee 37202, USA.

A 12 minute colour film which looks at all aspects of the population/hunger question, focusing on women's rights, infant mortality, overconsumption, old-age security, social status, family planning and national and international policies. Price: US$50; rental US$10.

La Operación
Ana Maria Garcia, Sterilization Abuse Project, 80 East 11th Street, New York, New York 10003, USA.

A 30 minute colour documentary film on widespread sterilization among Puerto Rican women. Puerto Rico, where over one-third of all women of childbearing age have been sterilized, has the highest sterilization rate in the world. The film analyses this social phenomenon in the context of a population control policy carried out by the Puerto Rican and United States governments. Shows the role of the medical profession and the objective conditions in women's lives which motivate them to submit to an irreversible method of "birth control" at an early age.

primary health care

ACHAN – Asian Community Health Action Network
Flat 2A, 144 Prince Edward Road, Kowloon, Hong Kong.

Set up in June 1980, Achan has two basic objectives: firstly to propagate, popularize and pursue a philosophy of community health, and secondly, to facilitate the exchange of information among its members and help initiate, support and sustain community health work among non-governmental organisations in Asia. Achan's philosophy sees health as the physical, mental, social and spiritual wholeness of the individual and the community, not the mere delivery of a medical service. This means making health understandable and accessible to all, using tools such as auxiliary care, indigenous remedies, appropriate technology and the involvement of the community in planning, implementing and evaluating health care programmes. Achan is developing a data bank of people, programmes, technologies and provides documentation of Asian experiences in community health done by Asians themselves. It also assists members in developing training techniques and programmes.

"Social and economic factors affecting women's health"
Maaza Bekele, **Assignment Children**, no 49/50, Spring 1980, Unicef, Villa Le Bocage, Palais des Nations, 1211 Geneva 10, Switzerland.

Arguing that women's ill-health in developing countries is to a large degree the result of discrimination, inequitable social and economic policies and the low levels of development prevailing in most countries of the third world, the author highlights some of the major issues: the exhaustion of unrelieved drudgery and multiple pregnancy, high fertility and maternal mortality, infection from abortion, debilitating working conditions in industry, increasing stress of new and conflicting roles, and the limited care provided for women. She goes on to stress the importance of primary health care, and of providing health-related services for women, such as day-care for working mothers, safe water and environment, health education, and shared responsibility for family planning.

Assignment Children is an excellent quarterly publication frequently carrying case studies and practical documentation relating to all aspects of women, children and youth. Issue 49/50 is devoted to the condition of women and children's well-being. It is published in English and French.

"New Music – Old Harmony"
Marit Kromberg, **Development Forum**, vol. VI no. 5, June 1978, Office of Public Information, United Nations, 1211 Geneva 10, Switzerland.

A critique of the concept of primary health care, showing that unless radical steps are taken to have people participate in the control and exercise of power in the area of health and their lives, nothing will fundamentally change. Gives concrete example of a project in Botswana where Family Welfare Educators were trained, given salaries, and became unacceptable and alienated from the village people they were supposed to help.

Donde No Hay Doctor (Where There Is No Doctor)
David Werner, The Hesperian Foundation, P.O. Box 1692, Palo Alto, California 94302, USA. Spanish, English, Portuguese and Swahili.

Over 400 pages long, this manual of medical and health care is intended for use especially in rural areas where professional help is not readily available. Written in simple language, it deals with diseases, injuries, nutrition, birth control, childbirth and hygiene. Wherever possible, this manual gives information about home and herbal remedies and discusses which traditional medicines and practices are useful and which are not. It also draws the links between health and political-economic-social structures.

What is primary health care?

Priority should be given to mass primary health care because most cases could be prevented by relatively cheap methods:

adequate water supply

adequate nutrition

safe sanitation

immunization against major diseases

community participation in deciding on and supporting preventive health plans

back-up referral service for training of primary health care workers

treatment for cuts and common ailments

parental education

UNICEF News 108

"Primary Health Care"
Earthscan Press Briefing Document no. 9, 1978, Earthscan, 10 Percy Street, London W1P ODR, UK.

A 68 page briefing on the issues involved in primary health care, as a contribution to the Alma Ata Conference on Primary Health Care in September 1978. Describes the world health situation, and deals extensively with the philosophy of PHC and what it implies – appropriate health technology, self-reliance, paramedics, traditional medical practitioners. Includes an examination of the World Health Organisation's policies and documents pertaining to PHC. Earthscan is a media information unit on global environment issues.

Famille et Développement
B.P. 11007 CD Annexe, Dakar, Senegal.

Quarterly French language African review of education (revue trimestrielle africaine d'éducation). Covers areas of food, agriculture, medicine, health, nutrition, sexuality, polygamy, abortion, contraception, environment, tourism. All these issues are dealt with from a (West) African perspective, setting them firmly within the socio-political context of the continent. It is one of the rare "development" magazines where the importance of women in all these areas is taken for granted and their particular oppression stressed.

Health and the Status of Women

World Health Organization, Division of Family Health, 1211 Geneva 27, Switzerland. 1980.

This 27 page background paper to the World Conference of the UN Decade for Women (July 1980) deals with a whole range of issues related to the health of women, and emphasizing the connection between women's health and their status. Lists selected WHO publications on women and health. A useful overview document.

"Women and Health Service in Morocco"
Fatima Mernissi, **ISIS International Bulletin**, no. 7, 1978, C.P. 50, CH-1211 Geneva 2, Switzerland.

This extract from a longer study (in French) of the relationship between the users and the health system in Morocco looks at how and why women (who are mostly illiterate) are by far the greatest users and describes what this implies for them in terms of their role in society.

Salubritas

International Health Programs, American Public Health Association, 1015 15th Street NW, Washington DC 20005, USA. English, Spanish and French.

A quarterly information exchange among health workers in developing countries. Covers a wide range of topics. (Funded by US Agency for International Development).

"Health for some or health for all?"
Unicef News 108/1981/2, United Nations Children's Fund, New York, New York 10017, USA.

An issue of this quarterly UN publication devoted entirely to health, covering bare-foot doctors in China, traditional birth attendants in Somalia, village health workers in Pakistan and Ivory Coast, and health care programmes in Kenya, Indonesia and India. Also gives ideas for health and nutrition education.

Prevention is better than cure

According to some estimates, three-quarters of health budgets in the developing world are spent on expensively curing the ailments of the few rather than on cheaply preventing the ill-health of the many.

Nutrition

At least 1 child in 3 in the poorest countries is unhealthy because of inadequate nutrition.

Water and sanitation

Four children out of every 5 in the rural areas of the developing world do not have adequate water supply or safe sanitation.

Health care

Seven children out of every 10 born in the less privileged parts of the world are never seen by health workers.

Women and Water-Related Disease

Dr. Letitia E. Obeng, paper prepared for the International Symposium on women and their health, Washington DC, USA. June 1980.

Demonstrates the relationship between women and water, showing how women are the carriers of water in many parts of the world. This means that they particularly are vulnerable to infection by some water-related diseases, and that therefore strategies concentrating on providing safe household drinking and domestic water supply, effective waste disposal systems and realistic health education programmes would greatly improve women's health.

Women, Health and Development

Development Education Centre, Unicef Office for Europe, Palais des Nations, CH-1211 Geneva 10, Switzerland. 1981.

"Recognizing that ill-health is often the result of poor socio-economic conditions, this kit emphasizes that health is a prerequisite as well as a result of human development. It points to the unmet health needs of women, their role in the community, as providers of water and food and as agents of primary health care, and to the fact that their health condition is related to their status as women." This kit is a series of brief papers covering the above subjects — as a kind of "inventory" on women and health and how this relates to development. It is constructed for educational use for local, national and international organisations. Gives suggestions for discussion and action, and contains resource papers and a bibliography. It is the second in a series of development education kits, the first being "Women and Disability" and the third, "Women and the North-South Dialogue". Price: SFr10.

Medico Friend Circle Bulletin
c/o National Institute of Nutrition, Po. Jamai Osmania;
Hyderabad, 500007 India.

A monthly news journal providing radical critiques of health
services and health policies in India, always recognizing the importance of socio-economic factors. Readers use the Bulletin
as a forum, engaging in dialogues about such issues as community health workers, alternative models of primary health care
services, and alternative models of medical education. Excellent.

Message from the Village
Perdita Huston, Epoch B. Foundation, P.O. Box 1972, Grand
Central Station, New York, New York 10017, USA. 1978.

A report, using extensively reproduced conversations with
women from Kenya, Sudan, Egypt, Sri Lanka, Mexico and
Tunisia. The author made prolonged visits in all these countries, conducting informal discussions with groups of women,
exchanging stories on anything from housing, food and politics, to relationships, children, love and family planning. An
invaluable source of original comment from women in these
countries.

The New Internationalist
62a High Street, Wallingford, Oxon OX10 OEE, UK.

A magazine reporting on the issue of world poverty, focussing
attention on the unjust relationship between rich and poor
world, and debating the campaign for the radical changes necessary within and between nations if the basic needs of all are
to be met. It frequently covers issues like food, health, multinationals, population, environment. Although not specifically
from a women's perspective, gives useful information and analysis. Frequently carries articles on population and health, plus
many aspects involving people's health.

Programming for Women and Health
Patricia Blair, Equity Policy Center, 1302 18th Street NW,
Washington, DC, 20036, USA. 1980. Prepared for the Office
of Women in Development of the US Agency for International
Development.

Describes the health problems of third world women falling
roughly into three inter-related categories — personal health,
reproductive health and occupational health. Argues that the
low status and health of women must be combatted by three
major efforts: expanding the number of women in decision-
making positions, making better use of women's organizations,
and recognizing women's need for time and money. The basic
contention of the paper is "that women's health needs will not
be met if programming continues to focus narrowly on the
health sector alone. Such problems as malnutrition, fatigue,
excessive fertility, to say nothing of various forms of violence
against women, are intimately bound up with women's generally low status and lack of opportunity for education and employment."

Upstream/Canada

education and communication

In this chapter, we examine the part played by the education system and the communication media in reinforcing traditional sex roles, often having a negative influence on women's social and economic development. We also look at how women are beginning to shape these to serve their own needs.

This chapter has been written by Ximena Charnes, Teresa Chadwick and Valsa Verghese with the help and support of the other members of ISIS.

Facing page: Pietro Gigli/FAO

education and communication: an overview

Valsa Verghese, Maria Teresa Chadwick & Ximena Charnes

Developing countries as well as western development planners look upon education as one of the most important instruments for social and economic development and modernization. Desired changes in literacy levels, attitudes, values and skills are to be implemented with the help of education: a) by changing and revising the formal education system, b) through various non-formal education programmes, such as adult literacy courses, education in modern agricultural techniques, health and family planning education, and c) bringing about changes in attitudes and values or reinforcing already existing ones informally through the media — radio, television, the press, literature, films and other means of cultural expression.

Education is the means through which a society perpetuates and spreads its own culture. From the point of view of the individual, education is the process of "bringing out" or "developing" an individual's natural abilities and interests. It is thus a basic right of every human being.

In both the developed and developing countries, the education system as well as the media help to reinforce the patriarchal values and attitudes existing in society. In the lower classes, women and girls have been, and still are, discriminated against: there is no equal access to educational opportunities or to the media. The contents of both reflect the narrow traditional male images of women as housewives and mothers, or as occupying subordinate positions in society.

Development education programmes, which are usually based on the western (male) patterns of growth, discriminate against women and girls. These programmes, though well-meaning, often overlook the specific situation and needs of women in developing countries, with the result that (economic) "development" of a community more often than not adversely affects the status of women in that community.

The Report of the International Workshop on Feminist Ideology and Structure, held in Bangkok in 1979, states:

"Most development efforts aim at restructuring the economic basis of society and changes in class relationships. Though occasionally these attempts may have some impact on the family form, family and social structures such as patriarchy are remarkably persistent and unaffected by intervention. The control of the female role and its definition by the males in the circle of a woman's relationships is such that economic changes in family status may actually worsen women's oppression. In many developing countries, improvement in the economic status of a class has led to more unequal treatment of women."[1]

Women in the women's movement are working to expose the nature and extent of this discrimination against women, to show that it is a world-wide phenomenon and stems from the patriarchal nature of world culture which assumes that women are by nature inferior to men and so should occupy a subordinate social position.

Both in the west and in developing countries, women are increasingly questioning the very basis of these assumptions. Women are beginning to create their own knowledge and culture, based on their own experiences. We are no longer willing to accept male definitions of us and the world because we know today that they are biased and one-sided and come from a culture which has crippled and enslaved us for centuries.

As a result of women's actions internationally in this direction, society is slowly beginning to recognise the need to improve the social status of women. The re-evaluation of the education system in order to introduce changes benefitting women is one of the tasks which various national governments and development agencies have set themselves. Such views are reflected in the call — often seen in United Nations literature on development — to educate women in order "to integrate women in the development process." It is a fact that many third world governments are beginning to sponsor women's studies' courses in their own universities. But what is clearly lacking is the understanding that the root of the problem of women's low social status is patriarchal relations, which are still all-pervasive.

We have a long way to go before we can hope to achieve social conditions which allow for the full development of every individual regardless of sex, class or colour. It is absolutely necessary that development planners take note of, and learn from, the women's movement, if they want to create pro-

Facing page: Noi Donne

Mauritania. One of the rare boarding schools for girls.

ly cover or even reach remote agrarian regions or the marginal populations of large cities. It is, above all, tailored for the urban middle classes who use it to achieve status and power, and as a mechanism for upward social mobility. The education system is unsuited to meet the needs of a dynamic modern society. Instead, it seems more suited to maintaining the status quo, catering to the interests of the upper and middle classes of society. In terms of accessibility and content, formal education in most developing countries discriminates against many sections of society, such as the rural masses, the lower classes and above all, women and girls.

Studies of school text books in a number of developing countries have revealed that women are most often portrayed playing stereotypical roles as wives and mothers, or occupying subordinate positions in employment. This discrimination is evident at various levels of the education system.

The following is an excerpt from an analysis made by Vivian Lowery Derryck on education in developing countries. She describes how formal education discriminates against women and girls.

grammes which are oriented towards the real development of women.

In Part I of this chapter, we examine the role of education and communication vis-à-vis women and development. In Part II, we have elaborated on how women have responded to the discrimination that exists in the education and communications media by creating their own alternatives. Part III of this chapter consists of annotated resources on education and the media. They include information on groups and organizations, as well as useful readings and bibliographies.

1. education and communication

In this section, we examine how the education systems and the media help to reinforce traditional social attitudes towards women. They help to keep women in subordinate social positions — deprived of their basic rights to full personal development and an equal social status with men.

formal education

(education through institutions such as schools, universities and vocational training institutes).

The type of normal education which is predominant in developing countries generally has a hierarchical teaching structure, like a pyramid with a base which is as diffused as possible. It is a schooling system based on massive free primary education, but with university as the final point of achievement and a lack of openings for other sorts of work at the intermediate level. In most cases, it is a continuation of the system established during the colonial period to serve the requirements of the colonizers. Very rarely does the system adequate-

women and education: the current assessment

"Recent studies by the World Bank and other international institutions have found that formal education is often discriminatory, inefficient and ineffective. The basic assumptions underlying educational priorities and policies should be reexamined, for analysis has proved these very assumptions questionable at best, untrue at worst.

Thus, many of our assumptions about the synergistic relationship of education and employment, the potency of education as a means of upward mobility and the importance of education as a democratizing agent have been severely challenged.

In addition to educational assumptions being challenged, the performance of formal education has also come under close scrutiny and been found wanting. Retention of literacy, numeracy and basic education cognitive skills, is depressingly low; in a follow-up study one to two years after completion of a two-to-three-year adult basic education course in Tunisia, 80 percent of the participants had returned to illiteracy. In a 1968 study in India, formal school leavers with 6 years of schooling had lost 20 percent of their skills, while participants in 6 years of literacy classes had a literacy lapse rate of 45 percent.

In short, the formal education system, as currently constituted, is of questionable effectiveness and highly inefficient...

Having discussed current dissatisfaction with the formal education systems of developing countries, we now examine the role of women in education...

Women have not been part of the mainstream of educational activity anywhere in the developing world. An estimated 65 percent of the world's illiterates are women. Women and girls are less likely to enter school in the first place, and more likely to drop out because of social and economic pressures.

In the developing world, women do not have equal access to formal education at any level from primary school through to higher education.

Female enrolments in less developed countries (LDCs) do not come close to parity with male enrolment figures. Although the number of females in primary schools has risen significantly in all of the developing areas, girls attend school from one-half to one-tenth as frequently as males of similar

Marc van-Appelghem/WCC

In all the developing countries, girls attend school from one half to one tenth as frequently as boys and the pressures on them to drop out are far higher.

ages. In a rough division into developed and developing nations, girls in LDCs are more likely to be school dropouts than boys. For every 37 boys who dropped out of school in 1960, 49 girls left school; for every 40 male dropouts in 1970, 46 girls left school.

In access to vocational and technical education, females are again under-represented. A UNESCO report on female education and training noted: '... marked by a far-reaching numerical and sectoral imbalance, the opportunities open to girls in technical and vocational education are still far from equal to those enjoyed by boys.' Moreover, girls are usually enrolled at the non-supervisory worker training level, rather than at the managerial technician one; consequently, they are trapped in low-skilled jobs and are not candidates for advanced training for positions requiring higher levels of education and expertise.

There is other similar *de facto* discrimination against women in education. For instance, the percentage of educational expenditures allocated for higher education is invariably many times higher than that allocated to primary school. In Uganda, for example, in 1971 for every 470 shillings spent for primary education, 560 were spent for higher education. In the same year, for every 24 dinars spent on primary education in Tunisia, 986 dinars were spent on higher education.

Female enrolments are in inverse proportion to the amounts spent. Indonesia reflects the decreasing female enrolments as one moves up the education ladder. Females comprise 46 percent of primary enrolments but, by university level, females are only 29 percent of enrolments, while males move from 54 percent of primary to 71 percent of university enrolments. Not only are females under-represented in first and second levels, but they also receive a proportionately smaller share of

university monies, due to their even smaller numbers at the higher levels.

The university, however, is not only the institution on which the largest portion of the education budget is spent; it is often the place where critical development decisions are made. Institutional capacity-building is a continual thrust at most LDC universities. University students are tapped as researchers, field assistants and teaching assistants in the development and execution of in-country research projects. Females who dropped out after primary school have lost twice: first, the opportunity to acquire sophisticated cognitive skills and, second, the opportunity to expand their employment and social options.

Why and how did women's education reach this dismal state? The reasons for discrimination against females are varied and far-reaching, ranging from parents' distrust of the unknown school to vehement denial of the necessity of education for women. In many LDCs, parents are reluctant to invest in a girl's education because her major role is still viewed as nurturing children and remaining in the traditional sector of society. Moreover, in many societies, the monetary return on parents' investment in their daughter's education will be enjoyed by her spouse, not the family that sacrificed and faced the derision of friends and neighbours to send her to school.

Other reasons involve the fear of the changes in girls that education might bring. A young girl may become "sassy" or "frisky" or think that she is better than her family. Another fear, this one based on fact, is that the girl may see her options expanded by moving away from her parents and home, usually to an urban area. A related social constraint is the lack of separate residence facilities for females at boarding schools. Parents will not send their daughters to schools that cannot guarantee

Peasant girls at agrarian school in Chile.

that cultural norms of sex segregation will be maintained.

In the 1945 to 1960 period of nationalist sentiment, the number of girls and women educated did not increase dramatically. In 1960, the year of independence for many African states, girls and women comprised 37 percent of primary level, 28 percent of secondary level and 25 percent of higher education students. Since 1960, the situation has improved both in Africa and worldwide. Developing countries moved from 46 percent of school age populations in school in 1960 to 62 percent of school age populations' total enrolment in 1975. Although female enrolment rates are rising rapidly, major disparities between male and female enrolment rates still exist.

Despite the increases in enrolments, the current education outlook for girls and women is bleak. Nowhere in sub-Saharan Africa do female enrolment rates at any level of education equal male enrolment. Percentage increase may have been larger for girls, but in absolute numbers, female enrolments still lag behind those of males. Moreover, these disparities will increase in the decade from 1975 through 1985, according to UNESCO projections.

Access to school placement — "getting in" — is just part of the problem. Although she cleared the first hurdle, admission, seven-year-old Baindu, a west African schoolgirl, will find it difficult to continue her education. The difficulty will grow with each passing year. The dropout and wastage rates are usually three to four times as high for girls as for boys. Girls are the first to be asked to leave school if there is a financial squeeze in the family. Moreover, they usually achieve lower grades than boys, for a variety of reasons. First, in most cultures, they are not spared their household chores because of school attendance; they are usually physically tired. Second, the self-fulfilling prophecy is at work. Teachers expect them to achieve less than boys; they in turn internalize this subexpectation and do, indeed, perform below capacity. Since promotion is based on mastery as indicated by test scores in most African nations, girls are often asked to repeat a grade.

Even if Baindu manages to overcome problems of access, fatigue and lowered expectations, and manages to reach secondary school, she must now fight the education system in tracking. Most girls are tracked in liberal arts as opposed to the hard sciences, commercial and clerical skills courses as opposed to industrial training ones.

Vocational and technical training programmes present more obstacles to Baindu. Statistically, her chances of getting into vocational or technical programmes are one in eight. Education officers rarely encourage females to enter vocational skills training programmes. These males argue that it is useless to train women in vocational skills because no one will hire them, due to cultural considerations. Although response to this argument must be country-specific, employers, when presented with qualified women in usually tight labour markets, have invariably accepted the females in nations as diverse as Morocco and Liberia.

The vocational and technical school biases become more clear when one looks at access and enrolment figures. Until the mid 1970s, girls were actually prevented from participating in vocational and technical education programmes in several nations.

If Baindu has opted for a professional career, chances are 8 out of 10 that she will be a teacher. However, she cannot teach at just any level. Usually, she will become a primary school teacher. Although women comprise the bulk of the primary school teaching force in many nations, for example, in Brazil, Dahomey and the Philippines, women rarely become principals. Data from around the world confirms that women are discriminated against in administrative and decision-making jobs in education. In a US sample of 400 vocational school directors, males held 93 percent of the top administrative posts. In the Philippines, while 77 percent of primary school teachers are female, 22 percent of principals are women, 57 percent of secondary school teachers are female, but only 12 percent of secondary school principals are women."[2]

"IT'S A GIRL!"

Marlette/LNS

non-formal education

(including all organized efforts to educate individuals outside the formal education system, for example, most adult literacy and development education programmes).

Non-formal education arose out of the need in developing countries to compensate for the inability or failure of their formal education systems to reach the majority of the people. It is seen as particularly useful for adult populations which no longer have an option to use the formal system. The programmes are more flexible and can provide cognitive and manipulative skills directly related to the individual in his or her environment, at lesser costs and in a much shorter period than the formal system. It has become a key element in rural development projects.

Since women have been discriminated against in the formal

education system, one would have hoped that the non-formal programmes for women would help to correct this imbalance. But they have, in fact, helped to strengthen the social oppression and marginalization of women.

As a result of a rather belated realization by development planners that it was important to involve women in any process of change, they have introduced varying non-formal education programmes for women. But, being guided by patriarchal principles, they took for granted that women's nature was to play a supportive and subordinate role in social and economic development. Women would stand by to help if necessary, they would be reserve labour in case of shortages, but their main role is seen to be at home, as wives and mothers.

Therefore, women are provided education in so-called "female" occupations such as health, nutrition, sewing, handicrafts, childcare, home economics. These skills, though necessary, in no way help to integrate women into the development process. They only keep them outside the mainstream of life and underscore their marginalized position. The western model of economic development with its emphasis on cash crops and the use of western agricultural technology, taught only to men, completely overlooked women's key role in farming, food processing and production.

The contents of the education offered women are often inappropriate and ineffective. There is very little effort made by the change agents to understand the real situation and needs of women. Examples in health education are the introduction of western medical practices and techniques in conditions where the necessary basic infrastructure is lacking, and the introduction of baby foods in regions where the conditions are unsuit-

Open-air literacy class in Somalia.

UNICEF

able, leading to the death of thousands of children due to malnutrition and disease. (The section on health deals more extensively with these subjects.) Women have been robbed of their indigenous knowledge of the healing property of herbs and deprived of the degree of self-sufficiency they previously enjoyed in health matters.

The education offered in no way provides the stimulus and conditions for the real development of the inherent capacities of women, enabling the growth of mature and independent individuals, capable of contributing to social development, to the creation of a more balanced and just society.

Vivian Lowery Derryck describes the discrimination against women by non-formal education programmes as follows:

"The rationale usually states: since women have been discriminated against in access to educational opportunities, compensatory programmes should teach them much-needed skills that will facilitate their entrance into the modern, market economy and generally help to integrate women into development activities. Since they have been the victims of discrimination, they should be tracked in great numbers into compensatory and remedial programmes.

It may be that non-formal programmes offer women the best opportunities for literacy training and skills development, but discrimination exists in non-formal education as well. Females do not enjoy equal access to non-formal programmes. In many LDCs, women continue to perform the bulk of agricultural and domestic work while men attend classes to learn about labour-saving devices. Men are identified as participants to learn about new agricultural machinery, cooperatives and most important, credit and banking.

The pattern of sex-defined programmes in which women learned health and hygiene has been transformed: now women learn handicrafts and hairdressing and similar low-paying jobs. Meanwhile, men continue to acquire new skills in agricultural production, commercial and industrial expertise, new knowledge about cooperatives and credit.

The goal of non-formal education has been used to further exacerbate existing inequalities of opportunities and access for women. This discrimination has ranged from outright ignoring of women, to streaming them into male-perceived appropriate training — invariably, home economics, extension work or as assistant extension agents. Similarly, in Korea, women were included in agricultural development programmes only as spouses of male participants and provided home economics classes exclusively.

These disparities of content point up a possible danger of non-formal education programmes: a dual track system in which women are tracked into home-oriented training courses that do not offer them competitive market economy job skills, while males learn market economy skills and enjoy attendant higher incomes and earning power.

Evidence of this disparity has begun to appear. Women are entering the monetized economic sector in developing nations in record numbers. But they are the population most likely to be unemployed, underemployed and on the bottom of the wage scale.

In Brazil, women rose from 16.78 percent to 20.47 percent of the labour force between 1960 and 1970, while their percentage of national income rose from 10.94 percent in 1960 to 13.49 percent in 1970. In other words, 20.48 percent of the labour force earned only 13.49 percent of national income. Moreover, although both sexes showed average income increases of over 38 percent, in actual fact, males averaged 306

A Western nutrition expert teaches home economics class at the University of Swaziland.

F. Botts/FAO

cruzeiros per month, while women made 186 cruzeiros on average per month. These World Bank compilations corroborate a similar finding by Glaura de Miranda that Brazilian women earn one third the wages and salaries of similarly employed men, per annum. These figures demonstrate that Brazilian women experience more unemployment, work for less money and receive lower wages for similar work than do their male cohorts.

In Liberia, the dual system in which women are the economic underclass, seems to be entrenched. The major occupational group, according to the 1974 Indicative Manpower plan, is Farmers, Fishermen, Hunters, Loggers and Related Workers; the group comprised 68.2 percent of the workforce in 1972 and is projected to comprise 58.2 percent in 1982. Female participation in non-formal programmes related to this sector is less than 5 percent. The second-largest sectoral occupation in the 1982 projections is Clerical and Sales Workers, who are expected to form 12.2 percent of the workforce. One would think that this is a natural market economy entry point for females, especially with the tradition of the west African market mammies. However, the urbanized market storeowners and managers want literate sales persons, and with a female illiteracy rate of 93 percent, few Liberian women can meet the literacy criterion.

Liz Mackie/Sourcream

I REALLY WANTED TO BE A MECHANIC BUT THERE WERE NO APPRENTICESHIPS FOR WOMEN

Perhaps the most flagrant and best known dualism occurs in rural areas in agricultural training programmes in which women's meager access to training programmes in no way reflects the overwhelming percentage of time that they spend in agricultural labour. Particularly in Latin America, an abundance of evidence has revealed that women generally spend a great deal more time in agricultural pursuits than previously realized. In fact, worldwide female agricultural input has been undercounted, while conversely, their representation in non-formal programmes which teach innovative techniques, introduce credit management practices and facilitate participant contact with the modern world, has been very limited.

These non-formal programmes have tertiary spinoffs. They provide participants with exposure to new ideas and often establish initial contacts with urban officials for rural residents, even if it is only through the extension worker. These ideas and contacts often translate in inter-personal communications skills that are useful in political settings. Women's projects,

oriented towards incorporating traditional skills and cushioning the impact of social change, often do a disservice by not forcing women to interact more in the modern world."[3]

Vivian Lowery Derryck's study clearly demonstrates that formal education has provided disappointing returns and non-formal programmes have discriminated against women, most of whom have not enjoyed equal access to any kind of educational opportunity.

informal education

All of an individual's life, from the time of birth, is a process of learning which takes place mostly informally, in the course of everyday living, in relationships with members of one's family and society. Even before we enter into the formal or non-formal systems of education, even without participating in any such "organized" forms of education, we acquire the dominant (patriarchal) values, attitudes and norms of our culture and society. Little girls learn very early in life what is expected of them, and how to behave in a "socially accepted" manner.

Religion, the family and community and the media can be identified as the chief agents of informal education.

religion

Most existing world religions are patriarchal and define women as being either inferior or subordinate to men. It is considered to be the duty of women to bear children, to look after the needs of the family and to respect and obey the wishes of first her father, then her husband and, in some cultures, in old age, even her son!

Women are generally considered to be one of two extremes: either absolutely pure and good, or evil, to be guarded against. Various restrictions and taboos are imposed on women in order to keep them "pure." These conditions stifle the personal growth of women.

According to Mallica Vajrathon,

"Tradition has forced women to conform to codes that restrict their behaviour and make them subservient to men — whether fathers, husbands or brothers. These codes were enunciated long ago in religious texts and elaborated in plays, poems and stories. In China, for example, Confucius and Mencius instructed women to adorn themselves, to please, to do housework willingly and not to talk too much. In India, Hindu literature taught male supremacy and female submissiveness. Daughters were 'precious jewels lent to parents until their husbands claimed them'. In Latin America, the teachings of the Catholic Church relegated women to an inferior status and represented wives as belonging to their husbands. Buddhist literature portrays women as a cause of the craving, anxiety and unhappiness of men."[4]

In most of the Islamic world, women suffer from very severe legal as well as social restrictions. Discrimination takes the most extreme forms. Women are forbidden to participate in social, political and economic activities outside the home and, if they do appear in public, they are expected to hide themselves behind a veil or chaddor. Least priority is given to women's education; they do not have a choice; their role is clearly demarcated as wife and mother.

Christianity, with a few exceptions, denies women the right

Indian women protest against marriage dowry system, 1975.

Noi Donne

to hold religious office. A Hindu woman is expected to regard her husband as her god. A Hindu widow was, and still is, socially discriminated against and regarded as an ill omen. In the past, she was forbidden to remarry and was made to shave her hair and refrain from wearing coloured clothing and ornaments. Among some sects, she was even expected to throw herself on the funeral pyre of her husband and end her life as a "sati." A menstruating woman is still looked upon as unclean and there are innumerable taboos and restrictions on her.

Religions generally deny a woman control over her own body, which is viewed as the property of her husband who has a right to it when he pleases. Her duty is to submit and to bear and raise the resulting children. As Mallica Vajrathon says, "such oppressive 'codes' created by male-dominated societies 'kill without drawing blood' (as the Chinese saying goes). Their destructive effects have prevented women from realizing their potential for centuries."[5]

the family and community

The family and the community provide the environment within which socialization occurs. It is here that a woman in-

ternalizes social and religious values and attitudes. The nature of culture imposed on women is defined by the needs of others. Such are the 'female values' passed on by philosophers, religions, myths, literature, mass media and science. "An entire ideological apparatus, from culture, education, customs, language, dress etc., ... through to all spheres of society, has not only been imposed on her, but it has been accepted as the inevitable situation of women."[6]

In developing countries, most young girls hardly have a childhood. As soon as she is able, a girl begins to look after the younger children while her mother goes out to work. Soon, she begins to share in all the household work — cooking, cleaning, laundry, fetching water, fuel, etc. By puberty, she is married off and goes to serve in her husband's house. A girl learns very quickly that her needs are of secondary importance in relation to her male relatives and that she is more a burden to her parents, who regard the expenses and effort spent to educate her a waste, since it is not they who will enjoy the benefits of her education.

According to Mallica Vajrathon,

"Masculine and feminine stereotyping exists in almost every culture. Men are supposed to be strong, logical, analytical, systematic, fearless and assertive, whereas women are supposed to be the opposite: soft, emotional, uncertain, timid, shy, intuitive and fearful...

From one generation to another, parents mould their sons' and daughters' personalities to fit such masculine/feminine patterns. Men grow up with the 'masculine mystique' motivating all their behaviour in society; the masculine mystique supports the feminine mystique and these mystiques are mutually reinforcing. Human beings with 'masculine' qualities dominate society. Rules and social structures are set up by men to suit their own purposes, which, even if this is seldom blatantly articulated, serve to keep them in permanent power and full control of the total human society. All superior activities are male activities. Whatever women do in the society is almost always looked upon as inferior. Male supremacy is drummed into women by all educational and socialization processes from the time they are born to the time they die. Boy children are given more sophisticated toys than girl children. Parents encourage boys to play with each other in organized activities and girls to play with dolls and cooking utensils."[7]

media

The mass media as represented by the press, television, radio and films, has become one of the most powerful instruments for the transmission of culture in the west and also, increasingly, in the developing countries. Its role is crucial in the development of attitudes and values and in the perpetuation of social aspirations.

In a rapidly changing society, with the breakdown of close family and community ties, the media is perhaps the cheapest and the most accessible form of entertainment available. Moreover, it is often the only means an individual has of keeping in touch with developments around the world. Yet unlike direct communication between individuals, the media offers a "one-way only" communication, rendering its readers or audience passive participants. It is this growing centrality of the media in the lives of individuals which makes it so influential.

It is not an exaggeration to say that there is no neutral media. Most of the news and information in the world is owned and controlled by the western transnational news agencies. Television programmes and films are massively imported from the USA and other western countries by others who cannot afford to make their own programmes or develop a film industry. Right across the globe then, the media inevitably represents the interests and values of the dominant culture, which is both western and male.

But this is not the whole picture. Margaret Gallagher shows that

"although it is true that the particular sex biases expressed in the media of the United States can be detected in many countries of Western Europe, in certain Latin American output and in the media of countries such as those mentioned above (Philippines, Egypt, Yugoslavia and Finland), these account for only part of the total picture. The overall findings of at least one cross-cultural review that, from one culture to another — even in those countries which rely less, or not at all, on imports — the media present a somewhat distorted picture of reality vis-à-vis the demographic characteristics of men and women, is of sufficient significance to indicate that media bias against women starts at home, even if this becomes reinforced and perhaps transformed by other foreign influences..."[8]

the mass media and women

In the following excerpt, Marilee Karl describes the role of the mass media in reinforcing and maintaining the traditional inferior social status of women.

"Women have always had their own informal communications systems whether it be exchanging news and information around a village well, or in a sewing circle, or through 'gossip' at the market, or handing down lore from mother to daughter. With the advent of mass communications and sophisticated technology, however, women have been left out. The control of the mass media — television, radio, cinema, the daily press, periodicals and advertising — is solidly in the hands of men.

Whatever little research has been done on the participation of women in the media helps to highlight the severe underrepresentation of women on all levels of media organization except for the very lowest (i.e., clerical and secretarial). Women are almost completely excluded from key decision-making posts. This research has turned up cases of flagrant discrimination in recruitment, training and pay in both the industrialized and developing world.

Research on the image of women in the media is somewhat more extensive, although still not great. Much of this research has been initiated and carried out by feminist groups concerned with the impact of images of women in the media on attitudes towards women.

Some general findings of this research are true for almost every area of the world, both industrialized and developing, although their manifestations differ. They can be summarized as follows:

1. Women are virtually absent from the 'important' news of

Women's meeting discusses priorities for projects for the village, Senegal.

Maggie Murray

the world, whether transmitted by press, radio or television.

2. Very little media coverage is given to women's work, achievements, situations or needs.

3. The media are responsible for perpetuating and disseminating traditional stereotypes of women. While there are variations from society to society, from culture to culture, the basic images remain the same: women are portrayed as inferior, submissive, subordinate, emotional, irrational, confined to home and to roles assigned by a patriarchal society. Women are also portrayed as sex objects and commodities.

4. When women are involved in organizing and action and especially when they step out of their traditional roles, the media often distorts and ridicules. The transnational news agencies have succeeded in portraying the women's movement in the industrialized countries as a lunatic fringe of middle class 'bra-burners', and as nonexistent in other parts of the world. The more progressive, but still male-dominated, media on the other hand often describe the women's movement as 'bourgeois feminist', or as a 'diversion from the main issues'.

5. Women lack access to information they need and to which they have a right, information which would help them answer questions affecting their daily lives, problems and needs.

On the other hand, the mass media are replete with the kind of information a consumer, profit-oriented, male-dominated society wants women to have: the latest fashions, hairstyles, cosmetics, domestic appliances and household goods, cleaning tips, recipes for fancy meals. Even the poor are bombarded with the messages of the consumer society and instilled with aspirations for these things. Women's pages, magazines, radio, television and cinema all give women messages on how to behave.

The problem is compounded by the presentation of partial or falsified information. A case in point is the advertisement of infant formula to convince women that it is the best thing they can feed their babies. Another case is the selling of certain contraceptives without informing women of potentially dangerous side-effects."[9]

women and pornography: media violence against women

In the following excerpt, Roxanne Claire writes of the harmful effects on women of the increasing use of pornography by the media.

"Pornography, at the risk of oversimplifying, is the dehumanization of women, the presentation of women as objects of male 'pleasure' and male violence (the two are often indistinguishable). The message of pornography is, as Adrienne Rich puts it, 'This is what you are; this is what I can do to you.'

... to question pornography is to question male attitudes towards women. That to examine pornography is to realize that

Massive and prolonged action by women in support of a rape victim effectively focused public opinion on the sexism of the legal system. Italy, 1977.

J. Maillard/ILO

The media promote the image of women it suits them to exploit.

it both glorifies the forms that male domination over women takes (even speaking cross-culturally) — rape, wife-beating, incest, genital mutilation, enforced prostitution and enforced heterosexuality — and expresses the underlying value system of those societies in which it is found."[10]

Today, pornography is becoming more and more a feminist issue, not only in the west but also in the developing countries, because

"Pornography is no longer restricted to seedy back street movie houses, no longer to be found only in unobtrusive 'adult' bookstores. Men now make films such as 'Dressed to

« I guess it takes a few more years before they find out they're the weaker sex ! »

Kill' (in which a woman invites/seeks her graphically depicted rape/murder), intended for and indeed shown in 'serious' and even 'family' theatres. Men put it on display in corner drugstore magazine racks, where magazine covers show women going into meat grinders. Men use it in ads for slick-paged magazines, where a woman in seductive clothing and pose coos 'hit me with a club'. Men call it 'art' when the cover of a European photography magazine is a crotch shot of a woman with the muzzle of a revolver (cocked!) an inch or two into her vagina.

And there's more, no less dangerous because less blatant. Television programmes, movies and advertising use the female body for decoration, to 'attract the viewer's attention' and to sell products. This objectification of women too is violence against women."[11]

media manipulation of women

It is a little-known fact that the media is used to manipulate and influence people's attitudes and that, often, women are the prime target of propaganda in the political or economic interest of those who own and control the media. This is well illustrated in the following excerpt from a book review of *The transnational order and its feminine model — a study of women's magazines in Latin America*, by Adriana Santa Cruz and Viviana Erazo (Editorial Nueva Imagen, 1980, Mexico).

"This recently published book presents a picture of the way in which the transnational structure of communication plays on the culture of the region in order to involve and alienate Latin American women, through the message carried by women's popular magazines.

A thorough study by the authors shows how the transnational power system promotes particular images — those which benefit certain economic interests. One of these is the 'feminine model' cultivated and manipulated through communications systems. Here popular women's magazines play a fundamental role, directed specifically at the urban middle classes who are in fact the end point of all transnational processes, both ideological and consumer.

Publicity is the financial force which sustains popular women's magazines (and so many other media) and is analyzed here as one of the factors determining the formal and ideological content of these magazines.

Women's magazines promote transnational products and at the same time depict styles of consumption which become more and more imitative and dependent. The success of this economic model depends on mass consumption of an enormous quantity of products, a lifestyle and culture based on consumerism and an image of women as functional — to be used to the utmost by the system. This functionality of women with respect to the system appears on several levels:

— as consumers (responsible for 75–85 percent of private consumer decisions)
— as wife and chief sustainer of the nuclear family
— as a productive, cheap reserve labour force
— as the most susceptible receiver of cultural values put across by the mass media, advertising, etc. and at the same time, transmitter of culture (education of children etc.)
— transformed into an object, she is a powerful decoy for the promotion of consumer goods
— as a reserve political force, activated only when the established order is threatened."[12]

On 6 January 1974, the Washington Post published an article called "The Brazilian Connection." It said:

"Women are a most effective political weapon... they have time, and a great capacity, to develop emotion and mobilize themselves rapidly. For example, if you wanted to spread a rumour that 'the president has a drinking problem' or 'his health is not good,' you would use women. The following day, the rumour would be all over the country... Women are the most directly affected by left-wing economics and politics which create a lack of supplies in the shops. The women will complain at home and can poison the atmosphere. And, of course, there are the wives of military men and politicians." (Cited by Gabriela Plankey.)

"... it has been established that women's frustrations and fears, their state of being semi-childlike and dependent, can be clearly channelled *for* the system when it wants to sell: sell products, ideas, continuity or panic that some enemy force could alter this tiny world in some way.

Between November 1970 and June 1972, *El Mercurio*, the daily newspaper most representative of the Chilean bourgeoisie, dedicated 121 editorials to women. On Channel 13, the block of afternoon programmes for women, traditionally meant to entertain and advise housewives, became a potent focus for sedition, along with certain women's magazines (such as *Eva*). Radio programmes controlled by the bourgeoisie took on an exactly similar role. Together, they orchestrated a careful campaign directed towards instilling terror into housewives and later, to bring them out into the streets to defend what were depicted as their interests. The housewife was led to believe that it was her acquired power which was being affected, that her children would die of hunger or be 'robbed' by the 'Marxist State'. She was told that Marxism was sordid, and it was painted all grey; that she would have to wear a uniform, without make-up, that there would be no more hair-colouring and she would lose all her attractiveness; that the sacred in-

Women use their own media for massive mobilization around women's issues, Italy 1978. Banners read: Abortion - women's decision. An end to clandestine abortions.

Noi Donne

timacy of her home would be invaded by the necessity to share it with other families; that her children's education would amount to brainwashing; that because of scarcity she would not be able to shine as a housewife; that she would spend her life queuing up. In other words, she was being told that the imperatives of 'femininity' could not be fulfilled. The 'natural female' would be limited and find it impossible to satisfy her 'legitimate aspirations'. She would not be able to look at herself or the world around her as she had before. In short, the campaign of terror centred on the vulnerable target of women who are housewives and mothers.

The success of this operation was absolute. The women of the bourgeoisie and other sectors thus mobilized, were present at all the critical moments from the 'march of the saucepans' to the demonstration in front of General Prats' house — which led him to resign and thus opened up the way for the military coup."[12]

Liz Mackie/Womens Directory

2. feminist response to patriarchal education and communication

After centuries of subordination to male culture, women have begun to question the validity of male notions. In all areas of life, women in the women's movement are recreating knowledge based on our own experiences, and are struggling to regain control over ourselves, our bodies and our lives.

In the field of education and communication, the development of 'Women's Studies' and the feminist press are women-oriented alternatives to the existing male systems. 'Women's Studies', women's media, art, literature, music, etc. are the beginning of the creation of women's culture. With regard to religion — the influence of the women's movement can be seen in the trend towards the creation of feminist theology amongst certain sections of the Christian church.

women's studies

Women's Studies came into existence in the late 1960s when women in the west began to realize that we had been left out of knowledge. According to Dale Spender, "... men had been the knowledge makers and they had validated their own knowledge — about us — by reference to each other." Women were in no position to create our own knowledge to "counter

their false descriptions of us," thus justifying in male terms our inferiority.

"That we do not find our experience of the world affirmed in much traditional knowledge can undermine our confidence and magnify our doubts so that we have little alternative but to believe the myths men have created. However, when we engage in the task of making our own knowledge, we can appreciate that the deficiencies lie not in us but in a system that has excluded us...

It is not that women have not made contributions in the past, but that men have not recognized that which does not subscribe to their own view of the world...

We cannot accept the meanings which we have inherited, but instead must forge our own, and in the process, we are learning things which are unknown and almost undreamt of within the male frame of reference...

We are demonstrating that the male view of the world is not the only view of the world. It has its origins in male subjectivity just as ours has its origins in female subjectivity."[13]

Since it has been only men who have laid down the standards of excellence, any knowledge which women create which conflicts with the male viewpoint runs the risk of being classified as "inferior" or even dismissed. It is vital that women should create our own means for producing and validating knowledge which is consistent with our own personal experiences.

Women's studies are very different from male studies (almost all of the conventional curricula), both in their content as well as their processes. "In constructing this knowledge, we are engaging in revolutionary activity. We are discarding the forms of thought, the images, the symbols which restrict us and which men have constructed in the interest of maintaining patriarchal society."[14]

Jo Nesbitt/Sourcream

And this, Dale Spender says, is politics. She says that learning for women has been a dynamic process which has influenced even the way we live our lives. We are still resisting the pressures to have leaders, experts, "teachers" who can tell us "how it is," as in hierarchical educational models encoded by men; we define learners as autonomous beings discovering the truth of "how it is" for ourselves, based on our own experiences. These new models of education are more productive in terms of learning and more effective in terms of promoting social change.

Women's studies evolved because "Those who formed consciousness-raising groups or self-help health groups, or feminist action groups were able to define their own needs and

First Latin American and Caribbean feminist meeting. Bogota, Colombia, 1981.

share their resources, accumulating information from each other, from their experiences within the group and from material sought in books, articles and experiences outside the group..."[15]

With enthusiasm and commitment, western women started to organize 'women's studies' courses in the institutions of which they were members. Initially, they faced great resistance and also difficulties, but today, women's studies courses are springing up all over — in universities, at women's resource and research centres, women's groups and adult education courses. Many developing countries have also begun to promote the introduction of women's studies into their universities. Feminists feel that one of the few sources for generating meanings that oppose patriarchy is with women's studies. This is one of the reasons why adult education courses in women's studies are vitally important.

However, this sudden interest in the theme of women and the incorporation of women's studies into many university faculties and specialist centres also holds the danger of coopting women's problems into the system and reducing them to a subject of study. The following quotation describes these dangers well:

"There is a danger that in becoming part of these institutions, women's studies may lose the desire for change which was fundamental to its origins. If that happens, we will have gained nothing. If the problems are not brought into the open, the dangers are twofold. The first is that feminist theory will be hived off into women's studies options, leaving unchallenged the bulk of knowledge produced by academics and presented to students. Women's studies thus runs the risk of becoming another quirky subsection of sociology rather than a radical challenge to the whole of patriarchal learning. The second danger is that women's studies will become increasingly remote from the women's movement. If such issues as the political implications of theory, the "objectivity" of academic standards and the ways in which assessment creates hierarchies are treated as unproblematic, feminists themselves may soon come to regard women's studies as irrelevant to the liberation of women, and as easily accommodated within the status quo. The women's liberation movement has given rise to an enormous amount of intellectual activity over the past few years; it would be a pity if the knowledge thus gained lost its usefulness to, and its connection with, the movement that mothered it."[16]

In fact, such courses on women's studies run by the traditional educational institutions, could serve the goals of feminism if they are not isolated, but rather linked to courses making women-centred knowledge. According to Dale Spender,

"If women control women's studies and use it to produce new knowledge about women, then it is likely that women's studies will be a powerful force in transforming the present inequitable power arrangement in our society. There can be no more radical educational goal than transforming the inferiority of women into independence and autonomy. The potential that adult education affords for the achievement of this goal is great. When women come together and question and query the arrangements under which they are required to live, the basis for the construction of women-centred knowledge is being laid; the learning is obvious, the changes are predictable. This is a form of political resistance in a patriarchal society."[17]

women and popular education

The women's movement has also resulted in changing the methods used in some of the non-formal popular education programmes being run by and for women in developing countries. The aim of popular education is to transform social structures through consciousness-raising and organization of the popular sectors of society (the people). This is especially important for women since they are already calling for lasting social change. In brief, this type of education presupposes the construction of a new society and a new culture.

In Latin America, a variety of groups and organizations are working in the field of popular education with women in the poorest sectors of society. The main object of most of these organizations is to organize women in the ongoing process of liberation. They are trying to achieve this central object through education and the building up of women in their capacity as leaders and their ability to analyze and denounce reality by investigating women's problems and finding solutions to the immediate problems. To try and achieve this, many women are using the methods of Paulo Freire. This includes discussion about one's own reality, with or without the aid of other material such as publications, the use of popular techniques in communication, such as social drama, puppets, audiovisuals, etc. They also organize courses on specific themes such as nutrition and health.

This type of education takes as its starting point the need for women first to investigate the social sector to which they belong and to examine their own problems and organization.

An example of one such popular education programme is the project "Research education for women" carried out by the Centro Dominicano de Estudios de la Educación of Santo Domingo. The following is an extract from the methodological part of this project report:

II Method

1) Introduction

"The result of our research is not meant to be a definitive statement on the position of women in this country. It is a piece of work on education which leaves a lot of questions open for further study. This project uses a method whereby those who make up the OBJECT of research become its SUBJECT, so they themselves assimilate and profit from the research, criticising, perfecting and complementing it. In the end, they transform the KNOWLEDGE OF THEIR REALITY INTO ACTION IN ORDER TO TRANSFORM IT.

2) Central aspects of the method used can be summarized as follows:

a. Taking into account the context of the Dominican Republic as a dependent capitalist country with its own specific conditions, the project has come close to the reality of WOMEN (workers, peasants, housewives, domestic servants), starting from their perception of their own reality.

b. This research should be handed back to WOMEN from these same sectors of society which gave rise to their testimonies.

c. The material was structured in a certain way so as to serve women, give them deeper knowledge of their reality and

Rural Literacy Centre organized and run by the Union de Recintos 25th of July, a group formed by the peasants themselves in Tres Postres, Guayas province, Ecuador.

also provide one more element they could use in their task of organizing.

3) Procedure employed:

a. The whole project was based on direct recordings: of women's testimonies as well as photographic documentation of the situations being described.

b. Recordings were transcribed in their entirety.

c. The material was then codified and labelled.

d. Testimonial statements were elaborated on the basis of this material. Furthermore, the same material was used in the work of the Cuadernos de Reflexion, an audiovisual programme and a play.

e. This material was first returned to its original source before a group of 50 women, most of them representative of the groups studied, i.e., workers and housewives from urban and rural areas and domestic workers.

We did it in a workshop as a form of COLLECTIVE AP–PRENTICESHIP, the collective work being the work which would direct the practical application of this project material."

feminist response to the traditional media

Women in the women's movement have realized how important it is for us to try and change the image of women as portrayed in the traditional media, to create a space where women could speak for and about ourselves. The following two sections entitled "A Strategy for Change" and "Feminist Publications and Networks," by Marilee Karl, give a good account of how women are trying to create our own alternative communication networks. She also deals with the different ways that women could act in order to overcome the negative influence of the traditional media on the image of women.

a strategy for change

"Women must devise an overall strategy for change in the information and communication order of the world. Our goals are clear: we want media which are responsive to our needs as women, which enable us to communicate with each other about our lives and experiences, which give us the information we need to make choices and decisions, which do not distort,

189

belittle or demean women or confine us to stereotyped behaviour and roles; media in which women participate and share in determining the content, in decision making and control.

How can we obtain these goals? Is it possible to obtain them through the reform of existing mass media structures or will we need to radically change these structures? Or should we try to create and strengthen alternative structures, such as independent women's networks and publications? Is it desirable and possible to work on several levels at once? Some voices are now calling for women's participation in the new international information order in what seems to be a process similar to that of 'integrating women into development', i.e., integrating women into the information and communication systems of the world. This call has been raised mainly because of two interrelated factors: the **pressure** exerted by women and women's groups on the information and communication circles and the growing recognition of the **need** for women's participation if a new order is to succeed. The implications of integrating women into either present communication structures or a new order to be created must be carefully analyzed. Otherwise women may end up being 'integrated' into a new international information order as detrimental to themselves as their 'integration' into much of 'development' has been...

The massive presence of women might be helpful in bringing about changes in the media's treatment of women. However, the 'integration' or participation of women in a male-dominated system is not sufficient. Other basic changes are needed as well.

Another approach being taken is that of trying to get more media coverage about women, more stories and positive images of women, especially in the press. The goal is to help change attitudes about women among the public and the self-images of women themselves. This is certainly a goal to be pursued, but again, attention must be given to the quality of the cover-

age as well as to the quantity. The media could very easily increase the amount of information about women without becoming any more responsive to the needs of the vast majority of women. Even the increase of positive images of women in the news will not by itself be very helpful. A few success stories of women who have made it in a basically oppressive society will do nothing to change that society which keeps most women in chains. This approach must give careful consideration to the content of media coverage.

Closely tied to efforts to increase women's participation in the media industries and media coverage of women is the pressure being exerted from outside to influence or force the media to discontinue those practices most damaging to women. Here and there some small victories have already been won through the pressure and action of women's groups: sexist advertisements have been removed from a magazine, editorial policy changed in a local paper, guidelines handed down on the use of non-sexist language in journalism, more attention given to women in programming. Yet, by and large, these represent only a small dent in the huge anti-women bias of the media.

Hand in hand with these efforts is the patient work of research and documentation of the anti-women bias of the media and the collection of data on the negative images of women in the media, on the lack of appropriate information, on the discrimination of women in media jobs. This is the new material for consciousness-raising and changing public opinions. So often these images are taken for granted and accepted even by women themselves, who have incorporated these into their own self-image. Awareness of this is a first step for enlisting support and organizing to bring changes in the media's treatment of women.

All of the approaches described here could be carried out within either a strategy for reform of the present media struc-

Women participants in national metalworkers' strike, Italy 1971. Banners read: We want to produce, we want to work. No sackings.

Eduardo Simoes/Agencia F4

Women demonstrate against the imprisonment of metalworkers, Brazil 1980.

tures or in a strategy which aims at radical restructuring of the present media system. If they remain at the level of reforms, they could result in increased participation of women in the media and improved coverage of women without changing the basic structures... The very same reforms could be much more effective carried out within a long-term strategy for basic change. Women currently organizing around these issues must give more thought to developing a long-term strategy and to involving more women...

feminist publications and networks

If we opt for strengthening the independent women's press and communication networks, great efforts will have to be made to move out of the 'ghetto' and into a wider circulation. We must try to avoid the dangers of becoming marginalized or restricted to a small circle, a new elite. We must find ways to make a greater impact on the rest of the mass media. There are no easy solutions to this. On the other hand, if we choose to work within existing media structures, we must be constantly vigilant to avoid all the danger involved, not the least of which is cooptation...

The upsurge in feminist publications and communications networks reflects the reawakening and renewal of a militant feminist movement in many parts of the world. Although still young, these networks have already succeeded in carrying out some effective international actions. Some examples are the spread of information about the harmful side effects of depoprovera, an injectable contraceptive; the sharing of knowledge

of alternative health measures; investigation and mobilization of support for women in the textile and electronic industries in southeast Asia. Women are beginning to share their experiences and knowledge without distorting intermediaries of the establishment mass media...

These feminist publications and networks suffer from lack of money and technological resources. However, since they are independent of male-dominated organizations, they do not have to compromise their positions or content. Their circulation and reach are as yet tiny compared to the transnational media systems, but they are beginning to act as a leaven among women around the world."[18]

women's culture

Women have begun to challenge the truth of traditional patriarchal beliefs and practices by creating our own positive alternatives in the form of women's knowledge through women studies, women's music, women's art and literature, touching every aspect of life. All this we see as contributing to the creation of a women's culture which is essential for the development of a more human culture and society. We conclude by presenting one of the most fascinating definitions and descriptions of women's culture, given by Robin Morgan in the book *Women's Culture: The Women's Renaissance of the Seventies*, edited by Gayle Kimball, 1981.

She defines women's culture as a "new women's renaissance," arising from the feminist movement, revolutionary and vital for the preservation of the planet. It expresses the half of human experience not much heard of previously with "tremen-

Marc Van-Appelghem/WCC

dous energy, passion and a quality of daring to speak the unspeakable."

She feels that the obsession with love that has been women's reality should not change, but hopes that it is catching to men: "... unless the whole species begins to be obsessed with it on a philosophical as well as a practical level, we're doomed." She speaks of a fierce, cleansing, purgative, revolutionary kind of love that demands change — profound change.

With regard to men, she feels that women's culture will of necessity go through a period where it is separatist. It is necessary in order that we discover and develop our own voices and that we try to unlearn what Honor Moore has called the "Male Approval Desire Syndrome." She expresses the hope, however, that "I do hope this is a phase though, mainly because I think that what women have to say as artists, as cultural beings and as political sensibilities is capable of transforming the entire species, and has to. There comes a sort of suicidal point if we insist only on talking to ourselves and on leaving outside and unaffected all those who happen to have power, money, munitions, "matériel" and the means of ending the planet ... ultimately we will be speaking to — not as primary audience but as an addendum audience — men as well as women."

She sees the feminist revolution as the next step in human evolution, as the state that will finally propel the human species into another evolutionary curve.

More concretely, she says it is also going to take arm twisting in the back rooms of legislatures, it's going to take getting out on the streets again, it's going to take arrests, it's going to take its own form of real confrontation. It is, after all, a battle about power. But power in all senses of that term and not the way the male left or right settles for power.

Footnotes

1   *Report of the International Workshop on Feminist Ideology and Structure in the First Half of the Decade for Women, June 24-30, 1979* (Kuala Lumpur: Asian and Pacific Center for Women and Development, 1979).

2   Vivian Lowery Derrek, *The Comparative Functionality of Formal and Non-formal Education for Women — Final Report* (Washington: United States Agency for International Development, 1979), pp. 60-65.

3   Ibid.

4   Mallica Vajrathon, "Toward Liberating Women: A Communications Perspective," *Women and World Development* (Washington: Overseas Development Council, 1976), p. 95.

5   Ibid.

6   "La Mujer en la Sociedad y en la Iglesia," *Mision Abierta,* vol. 73, no. 3 (June 1980).

7   Vajrathon, *Women and World Development,* pp. 95 and 96.

8   Margaret Gallagher, *The Portrayal and Participation of Women in the Media* (Paris: UNESCO, 1979), p. 5.

9   Marilee Karl, "Alternative World Communication?", *ISIS International Bulletin,* no. 18 (1981), p. 26.

10   Roxanne Claire, "Women and Pornography," *ISIS International Bulletin,* no. 18 (1981), p. 24.

11   "Media as Manipulation," *ISIS International Bulletin,* no. 18 (1981), pp. 18-21.

12   Dale Spender, "Learning to Create our own Knowledge," *Convergence,* vol. 8, no. 1-2 1980 pp. 15-16.

13   Ibid.

14   Ibid.

15   "Women's Studies Part II," *Broadsheet,* no. 87 (March 1981), p. 24.

16   Ibid., p. 54.

17   Dale Spender, *Convergence,* vol. 8, no. 1-2, p. 22.

18   Marilee Karl, "Alternative World Communication?", *ISIS,* no. 18, (1981), pp. 27-29.

education

resources for research & organizing

women's centres

Asian Women's Institute
c/o Lucknow Publishing House, 37 Cantonment Road, Lucknow, India.

An institute which coordinates nine centers for women's studies in Lebanon, Iran, Korea, India, Pakistan, India and Japan. It is an "organization for growth equality and justice for all Asian Women", with three main activities: documentation, research and communications. The nine colleges are coordinated to ensure the sharing of ideas and plans. The Institute publishes a quarterly newsletter informing of its activities. It is especially supported by the Association of North American Co-operating Agencies of Overseas Women's Christian Colleges.

"Proyecto de Investigación-Educación para Mujeres"
CEDEE, Juan Sanchez Ramirez 41, Santo Domingo, Dominican Republic. 1979.

This project, presented in a pamphlet, is an elaboration of educational material for women in the sectors being researched. In the context of the Dominican Republic (capitalist, dependent country) the project tries to come closer to the reality of women of the working class (laborers, peasants, housewives, domestic workers) in the perspective that it is these women who know what reality is. The project consists of four parts: (1) a series of 9 testimonials on what it is like to be a Dominican woman; (2) Women and Society: comprising a four-part dossier on a) the situation of Dominican women, b) invisible work of housewives, c) factory workers, d) organisation; (3) Audiovisual on the situation of women; and (4) a play — "Women in this country".

La Mujer y La Organización/Bolivia

Centro de Estudios "Elsa Bergamaschi"
Via della Colonna Antonina 41, Roma, Italy.

This centre has been operating for 12 years as a training and study centre on women's issues. It carries out research on themes such as "women in the cooperative movement", "women and university". Has extensive documentation available for public use. Organises seminars, debates, workshops and has a library which is also a meeting place for women to work and have discussions.

Centro Culturale "Virginia Woolf"
Via del Governo Vecchio 39, Roma, Italy.

This centre was started in January 1980 by a group of ten "historical" feminists who also call it the "women's university". It is self-financing, with a registration fee of 10,000 Lire (US$10) per year. Most of the classes are conducted after 5 p.m. The aim is to focus on traditional courses on history, anthropology, economics, literature, psychology etc. from a feminist perspective. It also organises study groups, research, conferences.

Centre for Research on Women in Higher Education and the Professions
Wellesley College, 828 Washington Street, Wellesley, Massachusetts 02181, USA.

The centre is co-sponsored by the Federation of Organizations for Professional Women at Wellesley College, focussing on policy studies relating to women's needs. It is committed to developing research and innovative programs which will expand the range and quality of education and work open to women. It focuses on 3 areas: patterns of paid and unpaid work, higher education, and intersections between work, education and family, in the lives of women.

Centre for Women's Studies and Services
908 "E" Street, San Diego, California 92101, USA.

Begun in 1969 this centre is a non-profit, multifaceted organisation whose aim is to bring to the fore issues of women's rights, exposing all the factors involved in women's oppression. It has four sections:

1. The academic part which takes place on the Campus of the State University of San Diego. It was the first official women's studies programme in the USA.
2. A centre providing a wide variety of services to women, developing non-traditional activities and work programmes for women, helping battered wives, giving "emergency services" — legal aid, employment and professional advice, information on educational programmes about women's benefits at work etc. One of the most important services is individual and group therapy on themes like pregnancy, abortion, drugs, family problems or other crisis situations.
3. Educational and cultural parts: the Centre organizes a large number of activities aimed at re-establishing women's lost heritage. For example, the annual festivals of women's art, monthly feminist forums, talks in schools, universities and clubs, cultural meetings twice a week.
4. Communication: publication and distribution of a wide variety of material on and by women, amongst which are the **CWSS Bulletin** (monthly), and **The Longest Revolution: news and views of progressive feminism** (weekly).

In addition, the Centre offers some special programmes like the free feminist university which takes place three times a year with voluntary professors, and a feminist library.

Centro de Estudios de la Mujer
Bulnes 2591, Planta Alta, Buenos Aires 1425, Argentina.

The group conducts interdisciplinary meetings and seminars of topics related to women. For instance women and work, sexuality, pediatric and obstetrical practices, female psychology, motherhood.

GRIF Université des Femmes
Place Quételet 1a, 1030 Bruxelles, Belgium.

Bimonthly bulletin of the Women's University in Bruxelles, giving information on courses and workshops as well as other activities of the University, documentation centre, books and periodicals available.

Non-sexist Information Centre
N.S.W. Department of Education, Teaching Resources, P.O. Box 4439, North Sydney 2060, Australia.

Deals with problems such as the different opportunities available in the education system for young boys and girls; isolation of teachers; scarce information on sexism, women's issues, women's history etc. The centre has a bookshop of non-sexist material, manifestos, pamphlets, non-sexist books for children, feminist literature. Also has audiovisual material and provides speakers for schools and colleges to introduce films and other teaching materials.

National Women's Education Centre
728 Sugaya, Ranzan-machi, Hiki-gun, Saitama-ken, Japan.

This institution deals with education outside school, encouraging women to take up positions of leadership in society. It also carries out investigations in the field of female education. The centre is a place of study, research and exchange for women concerned with education, both inside and outside Japan. The centre is used by individual women, as well as feminist organisations.

periodicals & articles

Al-Raida
University of Beirut, Lebanon.

A bulletin dealing mainly with the work and research of the Institute for Women's Studies in the Arab World of the University of Beirut. Frequently touches on the theme of education — analysis of the image of women in Lebanese text books, access of women to university education, women artists, sex-role stereotyping in schools.

"Capacitación: para qué y para quién?"
Elisabeth Dasso, **Mujer y Sociedad** no. 3, Jr. Manuel Moncloa 2654, Of. 401, Lima, Peru.

A brief article dealing with training poor women at different levels. Training is seen as a process with specific objectives and as something which should help women's organisations develop towards fighting for their basic rights and social recognition.

Convergence
P.O. Box 250, Station F, Toronto, Canada M4Y 2L5.

An international adult education journal. It is written in English, but the most important articles are summarised in French and Spanish. It forms part of the information network of the International Council for the Education of Adults, a non-governmental association formed in 1973 and which now includes more than 55 educational organisations from all over the world. The journal includes articles on the most important themes, practices and new developments in the field of education.

A special issue on women and adult education called "Women speaking and learning for ourselves", came out in 1980 (vol. XIII no. 1-2). It is a collection of articles from all over the world on women and adult education, which reflects different understandings and attitudes to the subject. The articles cover topics such as the need for women's studies programmes, women in development programmes for western women, specific needs of third world women, lessons learnt from women's organizations. The articles reflect well the different international viewpoints on the topic and thus makes useful reading.

"Education and Community Self-Reliance"
Assignment Children, no. 51/52, Autumn 1980, Unicef, Villa Le Bocage, Palais des Nations, CH-1211 Genève 10, Switzerland.

Assignment Children is a multidisciplinary publication which deals with social problems related to development with special reference to children, women and youth. This issue is devoted to how people's educational needs can be fulfilled. There is an analysis of the main problems in the education crisis: increase in educational needs, quality and importance of education, inequality and disparity in education, lack of resources to invest in education systems, education and employment, new problems arising from linking informal and formal education, relationship between education, culture and politics including the problem of language.

Gives examples through case studies on: pre-school communities in Panama, half-time in primary schools in India, other studies on Nepal, Bangladesh, Honduras, Tanzania, Somalia. Also includes a list of material on the subject.

"Education—Women: A Critical Study"
Swarna Yayaweera, **Pacific and Asian Women's Network**, PAWF, 529 Bauddhaloka Mawata, Colombo 8, Sri Lanka.

This short article discusses the theme of women's education from two angles: 1) access to education, and 2) the impact of education on their lives and quality of life. It presents both positive and negative aspects, and deals with the reasons why women in Sri Lanka enjoy a relatively favourable position in the field of education compared with other sectors and with women in other developing countries, even though they are disadvantaged in so many other ways. Includes statistics.

Equal Treatment of the Sexes
Guidelines for Educational Materials, Resource Centre, YWCA of Canada, 571 Jarvis St., Toronto, Ontario M4Y 2J1, Canada.

Pamphlet prepared by The Provincial Advisory Committee on Sex Discrimination of the Department of Education Victoria and reproduced by YWCA of Canada. "The Provincial Advisory Committee on Sex Discrimination concerns itself with the principle of equality of educational opportunity for both sexes. Where social customs and outdated stereotypes negate the principle, change is necessary."

The pamphlet includes guidelines for evaluating sexism in arts materials, literature, different types of textbooks, in music and home economics, how to change this trend and recommendations for avoiding sexist language.

It is an excellent pamphlet for the orientation of teachers and other people interested in providing an equal treatment of the sexes.

C. Christina Johanson

"The Image of Women in Lebanese Arabic Textbooks"
Dr. Ilham Kallab, **Al-raida**, June 1978, Institute for Women's Studies in the Arab World, P.O. Box 11-4080, Beirut University College, Beirut, Lebanon.

Brief article, an excerpt from a longer study, in which the image of women in arabic books is analyzed. The author maintains that in developing countries in which there is an interest in reorganizing the education system, modernizing the curriculum and training teachers, textbooks ought to be considered an instrument of the highest importance, principally in elementary education, the stage at which children acquire the images of the world around them which will influence their future life. This study is limited to the images and concepts referring to the condition of men and women in school textbooks.

"Mujeres y Educación"
ISIS Boletín Internacional no. 6, Via S. Maria dell'Anima 30, 00186 Roma, Italy.

This issue of ISIS presents an analysis of the ways in which women encounter and adapt to educational problems. School systems above all restrict women's possibilities. Female illiteracy and drop-out rates are much higher than for boys, and there are less women in professions and universities, except in those areas specifically designated as female – nursing, obstetrics and primary education. From infancy on women are bombarded with a series of norms, prejudices and styles of behaviour which are in line with a certain image of the archetypal female.

The Bulletin reproduces articles which show how education is riddled with sexist values, and that there is a difference between the ways in which values and ideas about men and those about women are transmitted in school.

Also reproduced are examples of popular education using alternative methods directed at changing social structures through awareness building and organising of the working classes in Latin America.

"The Right Time to Be a Woman"
Hilka Pietila, **Intercambio Overseas Education Fund**, year 13, no. 1, 1730 M Street, N.W., Washington D.C., 20036, USA.

The author maintains that profound cultural changes are necessary in order to liberate men and women, including profound changes in education. Equal access to education cannot be the sole objective. The content and attitudes of education have to be changed. The false images of men and women presented in literature, the arts, film and magazines have to be analyzed and new ones created. This article is in Spanish.

Women and Education
24 St. Brendan's Road, Withington, Manchester 20, U.K.

A newsletter brought out by a group of feminists who between them have practical experience of all levels of education, as mothers, students and teachers. The newsletter is termly and is a digest of information for students and others developing an awareness of how the education system discriminates against women and girls.

"Women in Religion: Past, Present, and Future"
Boletín Documental sobre las Mujeres, vol. II, no. 1, CIDHAL, Rio Fuerte N. 3, Apartado 42-A, Cuernavaca, Mexico.

The struggle of women within the Church has become an interesting phenomenon. Will it be possible for religion – an alienating mechanism in the majority of cases – to be converted into an important form of liberation and one of the more prominent fronts of struggle for feminism? The material on this theme is vast. The **Boletín** contains articles on the role of women in the Scriptures, and in various religions, analyses of women and religion from different perspectives, and conclusions on the emphases in theological reflection in relation to the nature and role of women in society. The importance of popular religiosity and the role of the Virgin in establishing the traditional role of women in Latin America is emphasised.

"Women in Society and the Church"
Mision Abierta, vol. 73, no. 3, June 1980, Fernandez de los Rios, 2–3 a izquierda, Madrid 15, Spain.

Open Mission (Mission Abierta) is a Christian publication in Spanish. This particular issue is dedicated to the problems of women. It describes the different aspects of the problems from the search for women's own identity to a critique of the patriarchal and capitalist system. The principal interest of the magazine however is the role of women in society and the Church.

This publication contains opinions of feminist collectives, articles on the oppression of women, the images of women in the Church and in the Bible, and articles on "women clergy", the mass media, and antimilitarism.

Women's Collective Newsletter
Northwestern University Library, Evanston, Illinois 60201, USA.

Bulletin of the Northwestern University Library which includes a list of new acquisitions with a brief résumé, recent important events such as conferences, research, new books.

Women's Educational Equity Communications Network (WEECN)
Women's Educational Equity Act Program, U.S. Department of Education, 1100 Donahue Building, 400 Maryland Avenue SW, Washington D.C. 20202, USA.

A newsletter which contains book reviews, research reports on women and education, news and other useful information.

books and studies

Comparative Analysis of Schooling and Illiteracy in Women and Men
UNESCO, 7 Place de Fontenoy, 75700 Paris, France. 1980.

The two studies presented in this document summarize and analyse the inequality between men and women in the two key aspects of education: illiteracy and schooling. Both studies conclude that although the situation in general for women in developing countries and in Latin America is improving, the inequalities continue in Africa and South Asia. Study of interest to those who want statistical data on this theme.

La Educación Popular con Mujeres en América Latina
CEDEE – CELADEC, Juan Sanchez Ramirez 41, Santo Domingo, Dominican Republic.

Extensive report on a meeting of women's groups from Colombia, Dominican Republic and Mexico held in Santo Domingo in March 1981, on the subject of popular education and women, in which all participating groups were active. Population and natalist policies, women and the mass media, the role of women and change processes, were the three major themes dealt with.

Also included is the work of Michèle Mattelart on women and liberation processes, based on the ideas of Agnes Heller with the notion of socialism founded in self-management.

Non-Formal Education for Women – The Grihini Training Programme
Jessie Tellis-Nayak, The Indian Social Institute, Department of Publications, Lodi Road, New Delhi 110003, India.

An interesting book focusing on a unique non-formal educational programme for women and girls. The first part of the book highlights the need of education for women and girls. Four different training approaches are analysed. A step by step account of planning such a programme follows. The second part of the book is devoted to practical aids that will assist in planning these programmes.

Role of the University in the Women's Movement
Eva I. Shipstone and Norah Shipstone (Eds.), Asian Women's Institute, 37 Cantonment Road, Lucknow, India. 1979.

This book is an anthology of papers presented at a seminar entitled "Asian Scholar" which was organised by the Institute of Asian Women in Seoul, Korea, in 1978. The global theme of the seminar was the role of the university in the women's movement. Some of the arguments dealt with were: Asian Universities as an ideological force for the women's movement; the imposition of sex-role stereotypes in higher education, the introduction of courses reflecting a feminist perspective in the university curriculum.

Women for Women
Women and Education, Bangladesh Books International Ltd, Ittefaq Building, 1, R.K.Mission Road, Dacca 3, Bangladesh. 1978.

The book traces the social attitudes towards women's roles and status and its relation to the type of education received by women in Bangladesh. It goes on to examine the participation of women in the various stages of formal education, both as students and teachers. The last part of the book deals with the question of women and non-formal education.

"Women for Women" gives us a good idea of the relationship between the social status of Bangladesh women and their participation in the education system. It emphasises the need to involve women in development education in order to "tap" the resources of one half of society.

La Mujer y la Organización/Bolivia

Women's Culture: The Women's Renaissance of the Seventies
Gayle Kimball (Ed.), The Scarecrow Press, Inc., Matuchen, New Jersey, USA. 1981.

An excellent collection of essays, and interviews on different aspects of women's culture. Divided into six sections, it starts with the evolution of the various definitions of women's culture, and goes on to examine the visual arts — women's imagery, women's art, language, humour, goddess imagery in ritual, women's theatre, women's images in film, women and fashion.

Subsequent sections cover women's music including composition, literature and dreams, religion including feminist theology, goddess worship, and finally a part on organisations — feminist therapy, feminist women's health centres, institutions of women's culture.

This book is a valuable source of information and very stimulating to read. It goes beyond the usual critique of a woman's place in society, and the tales of every woman, to study the emerging women's culture which has been evolving as a potential source of revolutionary change to human society.

Women's "True" Profession
Nancy Hoffman, Feminist Press, Box 334 Old Westbury, New York 11568, USA.

This is the first book in a series about the history of woman's participation in development education in the USA. In an anthology of letters, personal diaries, journals, autobiographies, government information, short stories and photographs, the author provides a comprehensive analysis of women's position in the field of education during the 19th and 20th centuries.

bibliographies

Feminist Resources for Schools and Colleges
Edited by Merle Froschl and Jane Williamson

A complete bibliography listing more than 500 books, pamphlets, articles, audio-visual materials etc., aimed at teachers and students of all ages.

Inequality in Female Access to Education in Developing Countries: a Bibliography
C. Epskamp, CESO (Centre for Studies in Education in Developing Countries), Badhuisweg 251, The Hague, Netherlands. 1979.

Bibliography of literature published mainly between 1968 and 1978. It is divided into three broad sections: a general bibliography, publications of various United Nations agencies, and documents published by other organisations and individuals.

Non-Sexist Resources
Lynn Berberich, Non Sexist Education Studies Services, Metropolitan West, P.O. Box 62 Wentworthville, Australia.

An excellent list of non-sexist books, films and other materials which are very useful for understanding and changing the sexist language of education.

Women in Development: A Selected Annotated Bibliography and Resource Guide
Linda Gire Vavrus, Ron Cadieux and the Staff of the Non-formal Education Information Centre, Institute for International Studies in Education, Michigan State University, 513 Erickson Hall, East Lansing, Michigan 48824, USA. 1980.

The bibliography has a section on women and education, containing a list of annotated documents dealing with the education of women for development.

women's studies

Canadian Women's Studies / les Cahiers de la Femme
Centennial College Women's Studies, 651 Warden Avenue, Scarborough, Ontario, M1L 3Z6, Canada.

Publishes articles where women describe the obstacles they meet in their efforts to improve their lot. A very useful bi-lingual journal (english/french) containing lots of information relevant to, for example, women and work, day care, unions.

Institut d'Action Culturelle (IDAC)
27 chemin des Crets, 1218 Grand-Saconnex, Genève, Switzerland.

The research centre formed by Professor Paulo Freire in 1974, concentrates on education and development through research as well as workshops, courses, and seminars. Publishes a quarterly – **Documents IDAC** on different themes. No. 21 "Féminin Pluriel" is on education and women.

International Journal of Women's Studies
Eden Press Women's Publications, Inc., 245 Victoria Avenue, Suite 12, Montreal, Quebec, Canada H3Z 2M6; and P.O. Box 51, St. Albans, Vermont, USA 05478.

Publishes 5 issues a year, each issue containing articles of scholarly research, critical analysis and speculative studies on women. Also contains substantial reviews on books about women. A valuable source of information.

Women's Studies International Quarterly
Pergamon Press, Inc., Maxwell House, Fairview Park, Elmsford, New York 10523, USA or Pergamon Press Ltd., Headington Hill Hall, Oxford, OX3 OBW, UK.

This Journal has been established to aid the rapid dissemination of important works of scholarship and criticism in the multidisciplinary area of women's studies. It reflects the international nature of the subject, the wide variety of disciplines represented and the extensive range of interests of those involved. It presents multidisciplinary work of academic excellence related to the field of women's studies and includes such disciplines as: anthropology, archaeology, art, communication, economics, education, health, history, law, linguistics, literature, the media, philosophy, political science, psychology, religion, science, sociology and urban studies.

Women's Research and Resource Centre
190 Upper Street, London N1, UK.

Collects information about women's studies, research and education, and publishes a women's studies newsletter. They have also produced a book, **Women's Studies Courses in the UK, 1980.**

Workers Education Association
9 Upper Berkeley Street, London W1, UK.

Produces a WEA Women's newsletter and also conducts many local women's studies courses.

the media: women's groups

Affirm – Alliance for Fair Images and Representation in the Media

c/o Women's Arts Alliance, 10 Cambridge Terrace News, London NW1, UK.

Acts as a central body through which British women can channel complaints. AFFIRM – like many of the American organizations – issues a newsletter, **Women's Media Action Bulletin**, and provides information on which particular agencies to address complaints on media imagery, as well as providing advice on how to lodge them. It was instrumental in bringing about the redesign of a particularly offensive popular book cover in 1979. Also produces stickers which can be used on advertisements – "This degrades women" and "This exploits women".

Association internationale des journalistes de la presse féminine et familiale (AIJPF)

Boulevard Charlemagne 1 – Bte 54, B-1041 Bruxelles, Belgium.

Recently started taking up the issue of the way in which women are treated by the media, and published a survey in 1978, "How the Press Treats Women", covering France, Hungary, Israel, Italy, Netherlands, Canada, Great Britain and Switzerland.

Cine Mujer

Apartado Aereo 2758, Bogota, Colombia.

Cine Mujer is an organisation of professional women who make films with the prime concern of promoting a different image of women in all ways. Among the themes which interest this organisation are: education of women from childhood, the roles women play, women whom history has overlooked, prostitution, machismo, themes related to women and health (e.g. reproduction and abortion). Their aim is to raise consciousness about the situation of women in Colombia and Latin America.

The group was started at the end of 1979 by Eulalia Carrizosa and Sara Bright who were later joined by two others: Rita Escobar and Dora Cecilia Ramirez. Their first film was called "A primera vista" (at first glance) – a documentary dealing with the daily life of a woman and the contradiction between this image and the images presented by advertising. It's a film full of humour, where the structure is clear: daily life is in black and white while advertising is in colour.

Deutscher Frauenrat

Augustastrasse 42, D-5300 Bonn – Bad Godesberg 1, Federal Republic of Germany.

Also working for better presentation and representation of women in the media, the German women's council recently launched an appeal to all media directors to stop programmes where women and men are presented as stereotypes, and where women are presented as luxury products. They are encouraging women to write as often as possible to producers and editors whenever women are presented as caricatures.

Federation of African Media Women Newsletter

Abigail Ngara, c/o Zimbabwe Inter-Africa News Agency, P.O. Box 8166, Causeway, Harare, Zimbabwe.

The Federation of African Media Women was formed to provide a forum for joint planning and action, a channel through which media women can share news and information about developments within the media and among media women. As the newsletter of this organisation, the FAMWN will carry information on training and employment opportunities, ideas on how to improve the image of women in the media, and any views, ideas and concerns that members of the FAMW wish the newsletter to carry. Published in French and English, the first issue carried stories on the launching of FAMW, a workshop on African Women Features Service, and women and the media in Kenya.

Medienkartie

c/o Rita Schmidt, Hauptstrasse 97, 1 Berlin 62, West Germany.

Has files on everything pertaining to media, particularly addresses of women working in video, film, photo and theatre

Through the Looking Glass

Voice of Women

16/1, Don Carolis Road, Colombo 5, Sri Lanka.

"The Voice of Women group has for the past year been conducting a campaign against sexism in advertising. By this we mean the use of women as sex symbols to advertise all kinds of products such as whisky, fans, tiles, tin foods, leather and rubber goods. These products are totally unrelated to the women in the advertisements whose only role is to attract the eye of the reader to the advertisements.

We have felt it necessary to start such a campaign as sexist trends in advertising have been on the increase. In our first letter to Lanka Walltiles Ltd., we expressed our regret that a subsidiary of a government corporation like Ceylon Ceramics should indulge in vulgar advertisements. Our campaign was successful and this advertisement was withdrawn. Next we sent a letter of protest to a firm advertising a packaging service, which had taken a large half-page advertisement figuring a girl tied in ropes and dumped in a packing case. We sent copies of this letter to other firms indulging in similar advertising and copies to all advertising agents in our country, calling their attention to this type of advertising which we said was "vulgar and degrading". In all these letters we also indicated that a copy was addressed to the President of the Republic.

We received no replies to our letters but were pleased to note that many of these advertisements disappeared from our daily papers. We were also heartened to note that one Sunday newspaper reproduced our protest on the front page.

However we are continuously monitoring the press, for we realise that vigilance and sustained effort is needed in a campaign of this kind. The Voice of Women calls upon all womens' organisations and other groups to protest against sexism in the media, whether it be in advertising, news reporting or in the publication of stories and reports which are directed against women."

books, articles & periodicals

Women in Media
22 Torbay Road, London NW6, UK.

Originally set up in 1970, this is a group of women working within the media in Britain. Their first campaigns were mainly directed at the BBC (British Broadcasting Corporation) since it is the biggest television channel and the images are created predominantly by men. They aim not only to monitor women's presentation in the media, but especially to push for more women working in responsible media positions, and to support each other in this.

In 1972 they mounted a successful campaign to ban advertising for vaginal deodorants on commercial television. In 1976 they organized a workshop on advertising, bringing together leading advertisers, media women and political figures to discuss this particular problem. Their report, "The Packaging of Women" has been widely circulated in Britain. Members of the group have also published a book containing their analyses of images of women as they are presented in the media: **Is This Your Life? Images of Women in the Media**, by Josephine King and Mary Scott, Virago/Quartet, London, 1977.

In 1979 they represented women's interests while the fourth television channel was developed. They particularly pushed for budgets for training and retraining women, and were successful.

Women's Press Bookclub
124 Shoreditch High Street, London E1 6JE, UK.

"The Women's Press Bookclub was launched to ensure that around 50 books a year — our own and other publishers' — reach readers at realistic prices and that worthwhile books can continue to be published. We offer savings of between 25–50% off the published price. Through our quarterly catalogues we offer around 50 book choices each year. We concentrate on the areas of fiction, feminist politics, art history and physical and mental health, as well as offering books, posters and calendars from publishers outside the UK."

Membership is available to people living outside the UK. Two selections from the latest catalog are Adrienne Rich's "Dream of a Common Language" and Anais Nin's Journal IV-VI. Write above address for further membership information and current book list.

"Graphically Speaking" Everywoman's Almanac

"19 Sprecher und fünfmal Dagmar Berghoff"
Courage no. 1, Jan. 1981, Bleibtreustr. 48, 1 Berlin 12, Federal Republic of Germany.

Report of a women's media meeting in Cologne (called "Frauen Medien Treffen") in 1980, on two different aspects of the women and media theme: women in the media and how women are represented by media. On the first, examples are given of there being 68 women journalists against 406 men at the West German Radio Station, but 91 women cutters and only 6 men cutters, or 312 secretaries and no men among them. On the second theme, it was emphasized that men are still the detectives and women the victims, or men the doctors and women the nurses.

There is also a self-criticism on "how women report on women", and a booby prize for the most misogynous television transmission. The choice was so wide they had to give some consolation prizes.

"Frau und Fernsehen – International"
Fernsehen und Bildung – Internationale Zeitschrift für Medienpsychologie und Medienpraxis. Jrg. 14, Nr. 1/2, 1980, Projectgruppe Sturm-Grewe am Bayerischen Rundfunk, Rundfunkplatz 1, 8000 München 2, Federal Republic of Germany.

A realistic, if rather bleak, survey of women's position in the most modern of media — television. It points out the horizontal and vertical segregation women journalists are submitted to, the way non-occupational factors (such as being mothers) interact with their work, the "quiet (and sometimes not so quiet) way" of assigning to the traditional stereotypes of "women's interests".

The articles collected in this issue are written by highly qualified women professionals and come from different countries of the world (FRG, UK, USA, Australia, France), but contents are similarly depressing and reach the same conclusion: the "symbolic annihilation of women", that is their systematic absence both in TV from the "serious" programs such as network news, and from the "hard news" section of newspapers.

Specialized bibliography, which lists a great number of titles, from around the world.

Femmes Suisses
Mensuel Féminin Indépendant, B.P. 194, 1227 Carouge, Genève, Switzerland.

Alas, nothing's new under the sun! Even if the trade-mark image of Swiss women is one of efficiency and prosperity, they are (mis)represented by local media along the usual lines of dumb-housewifery and eternal seduction. To those who want to know more on the subject, the issue of October 1980 of "Femmes Suisses", the oldest Swiss feminist newsletter in French, founded in 1912 in Geneva, will give some information about the image of Swiss women in their media and their participation as professionals in the news-making business.

Fraue-Zitig
Nr. 21 Dezember 1980/Februar 1981, c/o Angela Koller, Spitalgasse 8, CH-8001 Zürich, Switzerland.

This number contains various articles on women and film, and films made by and about women (mostly Swiss). The films mentioned are: "Regarde, elle a les yeux grand-ouverts" on abortion and birth, "Il valore della donna è il suo silenzio" about migrant women in Germany and their problems in daily life, and "Dienstjahre sind keine Herrenjahre" about Swiss-German girls going to work for one year as au-pairs in French-speaking Switzerland. There is an interview with four of the film directors.

Killing Us Softly — Advertising's Image of Women
Jean Kilbourne, Cambridge Documentary Films, Inc., P.O. Box 385, Cambridge, Massachusetts 02139, USA.

A half-hour 16 mm. colour film in which, using hundreds of advertisements from magazines, newspapers, album covers and storefront windows, the author has produced a concise and important analysis of a US$40 billion industry that preys on the fears and insecurities of every consumer.

La cultura de la opresión femenina
Michèle Mattelart, ERA, Mexico D.F. 1977.

Three essays in Spanish based on the author's studies and experiences during her stay in Chile. The first essay entitled, "Remarks on modern life: a review of women's magazines", analyzes the image of "novelty" and "the modern" presented in these magazines and directed towards women. The author shows how these values only serve to obscure an ideology which they in fact sustain and which defends traditional values.

The second and longest essay, "Fotonovelas, reality pushed aside", is an analysis of this medium which is so popular in Latin culture. An examination of the contents of the "fotonovelas" (picture novels) reveals a message charged with the most conventional values and a constant polarization between rich and poor. At the same time it presents reality with conflicts only of an emotional kind, where injustice is something personal, without social dimensions.

The third essay, "When women of the bourgeoisie take to the streets", analyses the manipulation of women by dominant groups which use them as a reserve force, only to send them back to their traditional roles afterwards.

L'invenzione della donna — miti e tecniche di uno sfruttamento
Maria Rosa Cutrufelli, Edizioni Mazzotta, Milano, Italy. 1974.

Written in 1974 by one of the most prominent and militant Italian feminists, Maria Rosa Cutrufelli, this strong political essay, now in its third reprint, can already be considered a classic of feminism. It demonstrates, through a series of examples referring both to European and American "imperialist" societies and extracted from the most popular media of the two continents, the "making" of woman, and the ways in which such an image is exploited. Unfortunately, we must say, nothing has changed and the book is still very much up-to-date.

Media Report to Women
c/o Women's Institute for Freedom of the Press, 3306 Ross Place N.W., Washington D.C. 20008, USA.

This monthly publication is packed full of information about the extent and progress of women's media nationally and internationally. It also includes facts about existing media (monitoring studies, statistics, etc.), about changes being made (legal actions, agreements negotiated between media and women's organizations, the founding of new periodicals and media business and products like films and records, etc.). Also covers ideas and philosophies as to what media should do (for example, defining "news" to include all people, differences between male and female journalism, women's thinking on increasing the effectiveness of media in keeping the public informed, etc.). Beginning its ninth year, it is still the only source of this kind of information. **The Media Report to Women** is one of the publications of the Women's Institute for Freedom of the Press. Other publications by the same organization are:

The Index / Directory of Women's Media
Consists of a five year collection of annotated indices of media activities and research by indexing the pages of **Media Report to Women**, and thus recording for history the progress of women in increasing communication both with each other and with the general public.

The Directory of Women's Media, which appears annually, is a listing of about 500 women's groups (periodicals, presses, film, video, music, multi-media, art, etc.) and covers 600 media women and media-concerned women. Entries include addresses, phone numbers, contact people, and descriptions written by the groups or individuals themselves.

Syllabus Source Book on Media and Women
Outlines reading lists and other data such as where courses are currently being taught, where students and teachers can find documents, special collections in the field, resource people and speakers.

Spare Rib/England

"A Generation of Problem Pages"
Spare Rib no. 101, 27 Clerkenwell Close, London EC1R OAT, UK.

Witty analysis of the evolution of women's magazine mentality through the letters and answers of **Woman's Own's** "problem page" from 1960 to the present. Marriage, sexuality, abortion, women's work and later on social problems are the issues brought up by these letters, but in the answers the emphasis slowly shifts from finding the man (usually the husband) always in the right, to urging women to be more independent. A revealing approach to how women's roles are portrayed by the media.

The Impact of Sex-role Acquisition: Mass Media Research

Linda J. Busby, Telecommunicative Arts, Iowa State University, Ames, Iowa 50011, USA. (no date).

Study on the role that the mass media plays in shaping individual sex roles. It particularly deals with the media in the United States, but recognises that media impact is world wide. It is particularly interesting for the information given on the role of children's programmes on television in sex role socialization of children. Has an extensive bibliography, divided into three sections: media effects — sex role socialization; media content; and personal and social impact of sex-role acquisition.

The Media Game

Manushi, May/June 1980, Cl/202 Lajpat Nagar, New Delhi 110024, India.

A critical study of 3 popular women's magazines in an attempt to understand their influence or impact on women, and the social role that these magazines have come to perform, in reinforcing traditional values and attitudes about women. The way they manipulate women is also revealed in the study.

Unequal Opportunities: the Case of Women and the Media

Margaret Gallagher, UNESCO Press, 7 Place de Fontenoy, 75700 Paris, France. 1981.

An extremely important book. Based on worldwide analysis of research and action programmes in the area of women and media, this study examines the two very interrelated factors — portrayal and participation of women in the media — seeing them as mutually reinforcing elements of the wider problem of access to knowledge and control in society. The author shows that the overall picture is remarkable only for its consistency from one country to another, both in the lack of women's participation in media, and in the stereotypical portrayal. The author goes on to examine some of the alternatives women have started creating, in new communication patterns and media structures through which their authentic voices may be heard.

The book includes a valuable reference section, with a very full bibliography and a long list of feminist publications, groups, journals, etc. throughout the world.

"Women and the Media"

ISIS International bulletin no. 18, 1981, ISIS-Switzerland, C.P. 50, 1211 Geneva 2, Switzerland.

Presents a good selection of articles and resources on women and the media. The bulletin is a critical review of the role of media and its influence on the status of women. It also has a section on how the women's movement has responded to the negative influence of the traditional media through campaigns to counter it as well as the development of positive alternatives, by women and women's groups.

Steve Bredner

L. Saenz

UNESCO women's features service

With the aim of increasing the flow of news and information on women in society and "to help remove prejudices and stereotypes reflected in the mass media and thus to speed up women's full equality with men", a women's features service was set up in Latin America in 1978. Sponsored by UNESCO (United Nations Education, Scientific and Cultural Organisation) the idea of the features service was to create a network of women correspondents in the region who would write articles concerning women. These would then be disseminated through the Third World wire service — Inter Press Service (IPS). IPS distributes the articles to newspapers and radio stations, and by March 1979, 235 features had appeared in 19 Latin America daily newspapers.

Since then, two other features services have been set up — the Caribbean Women's Features Syndicate (CWFS), and Depth News Women's Features Services (DNWFS) (covering Asia). These, however, do not use the IPS wire, but a postal distribution system. Two more are currently being set up, in the Arab States and in Africa.

Features cover a very wide variety of topics from women and development, economics and politics, to women and the law, illiteracy, infant malnutrition, etc. They also deal with women and the media from time to time: the CFS in September 1980 distributed a piece entitled "The Impact of broadcast media on values of Jamaican women", which looks at the way communication media, particularly radio, reflect the values of women in recently urbanized society, and shows how television and advertisements in particular still present women in stereotyped roles aimed at consumption. A DNWFS story of December 1980 reports on a "women and media" seminar held in Kuala Lumpur (Malaysia) the previous month, where resolutions were made for improving portrayal and participation of women in media.

The services are currently funded by UNFPA (United Nations Fund for Population Activities), which means their future is precarious since the funding will not continue forever. There may be ways in which such services can be made self-sufficient ultimately, but problems arise in that it is not clear there is a guaranteed market for "women's" stories. Whatever happens, these features services are an interesting initiative which can be built upon.

Addresses of the different services:

African Women's Features Service
P.O. Box 74536
Nairobi
Kenya

Carribbean Women's Features Syndicate
P.O. Box 159
Bridgetown
Barbados

Depth News Women's Features Services
P.O. Box 1843
Manila
Philippines

Officina Informativa de la Mujer
c/o Inter-Press Service
Via Panisperna 207
Rome
Italy   (for Latin America)

Coordinating office:
Population Division
UNESCO
7, place de Fontenoy
75700 Paris
France

women and religion

Christian Women's Information and Resource Service (CWIRS)
c/o Blackfriars, St Giles, Oxford, UK.

Publishes a feminist newsletter.

Glastonbury Goddess Group
c/o Gothic Image, 7 High St., Glastonbury, Somerset, UK.

Journal of women and religion
c/o Centre for Women and Religion of the Graduate Theological Union, 2465 LeConte Avenue, Berkeley, California 94709, USA.

A bi-annual publication, containing articles on feminism and religion — a feminist analysis of the different religions, etc.

Roman Catholic Feminists
c/o 33 Arlow Road, London N21, UK.

pornography

Take Back the Night. Women on Pornography
Laura Lederer, ed., Morrow Quill, 105 Madison Ave, New York, New York 10016, USA.

Probably the most important book available on women and pornography; it contains examinations of the political content of pornography; reports on the latest research on harmful effects of pornography; discussion on the First Amendment, freedom of speech, and pornography. Articles entitled "What is Pornography" has a good definition of pornography (at least for 'hardcore' porn). Also an excellent bibliography. However, perhaps the best description of the book is found within the book itself, in the afterword written by Adrienne Rich: that **Take Back the Night** deepens one's "perception not only of pornography itself and its omnipresence in our lives, but of the dynamics among racism, woman-hating, and compulsory heterosexuality; of the powerful economic interests which comprise the pornography empire and which are ranged against even the most moderate demands of women; of the institutional misogyny that underlies apparent permissiveness or tolerance towards feminism." Price: US$7.95 paperback, $14.95 hardbound.

Off Our Backs/USA

migration and tourism

This chapter examines migration and tourism, especially sex-tourism, as development problems with often disastrous effects on the lives of the women they uproot. After an overview of the issues, it offers a short account of international actions taken by the women's movement to counter this exploitation. This is followed by a bibliography of resource materials.

This chapter was written by Roxanne Claire and Jane Cottingham.

migration and tourism: an overview

Roxanne Claire & Jane Cottingham

Why do tens of thousands of women leave their homes and often their families every year to migrate to another country or region? Sometimes it is for reasons of religious or political persecution, more often it is out of the sheer economic necessity resulting from high rates of unemployment, being pushed off land, or the increasing need for money in societies shifting to cash economies. Yet migration resists any simple explanation. Unfortunately, migration has been such a time-honored tradition that it is only comparatively recently that there has been any economic analysis of the patterns of migration, although the patterns themselves — from Greece to Canada, Malaysia to Singapore, India to Kuwait, Mexico to the USA, or simply from rural to urban areas within a single country — are clear. And it is only more recently that an examination of the impact of migration upon people's lives has included a recognition that migration affects the women who remain behind as well as those who leave, and that migrant workers themselves are often women.

Rural women in Panama, for example, usually migrate to urban areas because they have had to sell their land, which through lack of seed, fertilizer and resources no longer produces even a subsistence living. Or they might be following their husbands to the city where he will try and find work as a gardener, mason, or hired hand in a sugar mill or banana company.[1]

Filipinas, trained as nurses, teachers, or secretaries, often leave their country because they can't find work, or because the pay for work available is abysmally low — although the minimum wage is about $1.35, many work for as little as $.70.[2]

Thus workers migrate in the hopes of finding jobs and improved pay and living conditions. What they find are higher costs of living, discrimination, exploitation, and problems caused by cross-cultural differences. Discrimination described in real terms means that migrant workers occupy the most strenuous, monotonous, dirtiest, and lowest paid jobs. They pay more for lower quality housing, and are accorded fewer political rights and educational and job opportunities. Prob-

lems of crossing cultural lines, of language and of new values such as consumerism range from difficulty in finding and communicating with a doctor to feelings of isolation. This isolation may be exacerbated by illiteracy which eliminates letters or newspapers as means of keeping contact with home, and the absorption, especially of children, into the alien culture. Often too this threat of losing cultural identity results in a strong defense of the traditions of the migrants' own culture, which then often oppresses the women more than in their own countries.

Perhaps the best known aspect of migration is exploitation. Given the hopes pinned to escaping conditions left behind, the migrant's fear of losing her job or being deported makes her ripe for scandalously low pay, overwork, unsafe working conditions, and sexual harassment.

factory work

In an earlier section (see women and multinationals) the exploitation of women working in Asian electronics factories was described. Yet this phenomenon is far from limited to Asia alone. Similar conditions exist in factories in Mexico, Britain, Canada, and the USA.

Maria M., 40, is a sewing machine operator who used to work for a Montreal sportswear contractor on piece-work rates. During her first week, she was asked to work from seven in the morning until seven at night to fill rush orders. She should have earned about $220. However, her employer gave her $125 and told her she should be grateful because of high unemployment. Two months later she was still working the same hours for the same pay. When the foreman discovered she was thinking of complaining, she was fired with no cheque for her final week's work.

Teresa V., 35, is a Toronto hosiery worker. When she first joined the factory, the piece-work rate for her job was ten cents a dozen. However, as the women increased their speed, the employer lowered the rate until it is now seven cents a dozen. Teresa works at breakneck speed putting in ten hour days with no coffee breaks and just ten minutes for lunch. However, she makes barely above the minimum wage.[3]

In the United States the proliferation of "sweatshops" has even come to the attention of Federal investigators of the US Labor Department. Common violations of the labor laws, as these investigators report, include failure to pay minimum wage or overtime pay (1 1/2 times the regular hourly rate for work beyond 40 hours per week), child labor regulation (children between the ages of 10 and 12 are commonly employed in garment factories), and health and safety laws — a not unusual situation includes bare dangling light bulbs, crowded, filthy working conditions, and one toilet for perhaps 40 to 80 workers.[4]

home work

For many migrant women barriers of language and lack of childcare facilities, often added with a cultural expectation that women should not work outside the home, prevent them from seeking jobs in factories. For these women, a solution has been presented in the form of factory work coming to them. Homework, also called outwork, while solving child care problems and providing flexible working hours, actually provides many more benefits for the employer than to the woman worker. Employers avoid costs related to capital, machinery and running costs (garment makers, for example, are expected to buy and keep in working order the sewing machines necessary for their work), power and cleaning, insurance, and holiday and sick pay. It goes without saying that homeworkers are poorly paid. Moreover, their wages are not just low, they are also irregular and unpredictable. Based on a seasonal market, there are several periods during the year when production is slowed down or halted. When homeworkers don't work, they

don't get paid. On the other hand, there are also peak periods when work begins in the early morning and continues into late night, often for six or seven days a week.

Doreen, for example, has been sewing and packaging shower caps for the past two years. The sewing takes 11 seconds per cap, packing takes another five. Bundling the caps in bunches of five takes more time and Doreen often persuades her children to help with that work... The employer pays $15 per 1,000 caps. When there is a rush job — a big order for a hotel — Doreen works seven days a week. There are also slack times, such as when her employer ran out of elastic thread which had to be ordered from San Francisco. For two weeks, Doreen had no work and no pay.[5]

Mrs. Hunt started working at home six years ago, just after the birth of her first and only child. He is now old enough to go to nursery school, but there are no facilities in the nearby villages and anyway the bus services are infrequent. Her job is to package Christmas cards individually for a well-known local company. Each plastic packet has to have a card, an envelope, a greetings slip and then be sealed with the appropriate price tag. Mrs. Hunt earns £14.30 a week for a 30-hour week, which works out at 47 1/2 p. per hour. In addition, she has to pay heating and lighting overhead — and provide storage space for the cards, at considerable inconvenience for her family.[6]

The physical isolation of these women, and the distance caused by culture and language differences, plus the situation where it is often their husbands who are the employers, makes their organizing difficult. Unions have not paid a great deal of attention to the homeworker. They have been either resentful of her, seeing her as acting to depress wages, or they have ignored her, seeing homework as "women's work" and therefore not "real" work. In some places, this has begun to change. However, because the supply outstrips the demand, a woman who joins a union or criticises her pay or working conditions will usually risk losing her job.

agricultural work

Like work in electronics factories, work in agricultural fields is noted for its hazards to worker health. High on the list of factors responsible is contact with pesticides and fertilizers. The low quality housing provided for migrant workers — no heating or plumbing, contaminated water — contributes to ill health, as does malnutrition and lack of health care. Migrant workers have neither the time, money, nor means of transportation for seeking medical attention. In the USA alone, maternal and infant mortality rates — a key index of overall health care — are reported to be more than 100 percent higher among migrants than the national US average. And, as for all women workers, migrant women agricultural workers put in full 10 hour days, picking in the fields, often next to their husbands, and once home, while the husband rests or visits friends, the woman bathes the babies, cooks, and cleans.[7]

domestic work

While domestic work is often the easiest kind of job for women to find once they've migrated, domestic positions are

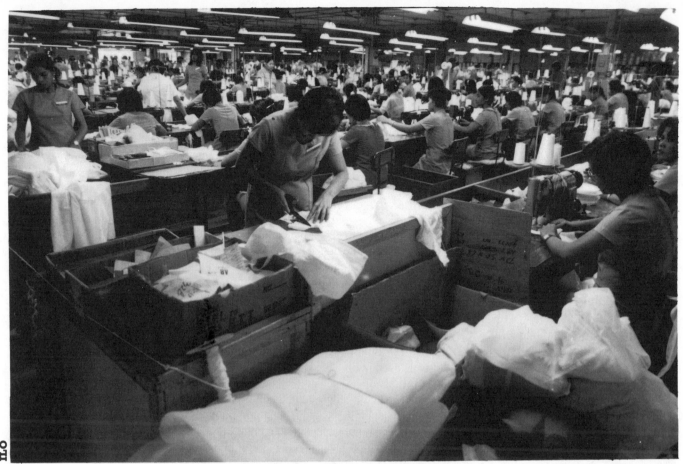

In the cities women often find work in big factories like these Filipino textile workers.

also heavily "recruited." That is, agencies entice women to leave their countries with promises of good paying jobs, then make a small fortune from each woman with charges for airfare, false passports and medical certificates, and non-existent work permits. Women are usually told that the airfare is paid for by the employer, only to be told by the employer upon reaching her new job that this cost will be deducted from her monthly salary. This means in effect that the woman must work for up to a year in order to pay off her "debt" to her employer, before she can begin earning any money for herself.

The peculiar position of the domestic worker, living with her employer, makes her especially vulnerable to exploitation. Without a set schedule for work and leisure, she may be on call virtually 24 hours a day. Her work day usually begins around 5:30 a.m. and continues into the late night hours. Without a defined job description, she cooks, cleans, babysits... stays home evenings to answer the phone, does yard work, and wipes up after the dog. Sons and husbands often expect her to provide sexual services as well.

She is usually without medical benefits, unemployment insurance or retirement plan. Her isolation in the home and the language barrier not only contribute to her loneliness, but make it difficult for her to be aware of the illegality of her situation or make contact with those who might be able to help her fight back or get out.[8]

street sellers

Often migrant women are obliged to turn to the "informal" sector to earn money. As street sellers, these women are often seen with babies on their backs and their other children gathered around them. They sell fruit, cakes, various grains and sometimes chewing gum.

They work all day, without protection from the weather or access to running water and are subject to attacks from small shopkeepers, who resent their competition and the fact that they do not have to pay taxes. There is no social insurance or medical help available, no statutory hours of work or holidays. Sometimes these women are picked up by the police and forced to spend the night in the police station, along with their children.[9]

women who stay

The migration of husbands, fathers, or sons, leaving the women behind, can cause a serious strain on the family structure, especially when the absence becomes prolonged over several years. Not only does the separation create a distance between the migrant and his wife and family, but the ties between remaining family members break down. For example, in many cultures, brothers-in-law responsible for helping their brother's wife no longer do so.[10]

There is also the burden the woman must take on of performing not only her own work, but that of her absent husband as well. The woman often cannot bear up under the weight of this double burden, and so falls back to subsistence farming. This in turn creates a problem if there is a need for cash and the migrant sends back little or no remittance. At some point it may become necessary for the woman too to

Philippines.

migrate, abandoning the farm and perhaps leaving the children with relatives.

One South African woman, after many hungry months without receiving money from her husband, left her children with relatives and borrowed money to go looking for her husband. When she found that he had begun living with another woman, her shame and penniless state kept her from returning home. Unable to go back home, and illegally in the city, she was forced to "take boyfriends" in order to survive.[11]

prostitution and tourism

For many women, like this South African woman, who migrate from rural areas to the city, prostitution is the final, and for some the only, means of survival. The story of Noi from Thailand speaks for others in her situation as well as for herself. Noi is twenty years old, and looks for clients independently in the evenings in the cafes while working in a battery factory during the day. "I get 25 baht per day but this is not enough to cover my expenses. How could this be enough to pay for my rent, my food, my bus tickets and other expenses, and I can tell you, I am thrifty." Noi's eight brothers and sis-

ters live with their parents, peasants from Yutthaya, whose only means of sustenance comes from Noi. "I have to find work at night so that I can send money to my parents. I don't live in a brothel so that I can be free to go to work during the day."[12]

Often women who have fled rural poverty only to be forced into prostitution by urban unemployment, are also victims of the double standard. Women who have been raped, jilted, or taken advantage of no longer fit the chaste wife-mother-sister ideal and are ostracized by nearly all sectors of society.

The vulnerable position of the hundreds of thousands of such women has not passed unnoticed. In many Asian countries, especially the Philippines, Thailand, South Korea, Indonesia, and Sri Lanka, an entire industry — sex tourism — has sprung up to exploit it to the fullest.

Thailand is a world full of extremes and the possibilities are limitless. Anything goes in this exotic country. Especially when it comes to girls. Yet visitors to Thailand cannot always find the exciting places where they can indulge in unknown pleasures. It is frustrating to have to ask the hotel receptionist in broken English where you can pick up pretty girls. Rosie Travel has come up with the answer. For the first time in history you can book a trip to Thailand with erotic pleasure included in the price...[13]

In Japan all the big travel agencies handle large tours, especially to South Korea, where "kisaeng" (meaning prostitute)

From report on tourism workshop, Manila 1980. Christian Conference of Asia

FOREIGN EXCHANGE ?

DOES TOURISM EARN FOREIGN EXCHANGE ?

RESTAURANT X — FOOD FROM AUSTRALIA

SUN & SEX HOTEL

LIGHTING FROM HOLLAND

CURTAINS FROM FRANCE

ELEVATORS FROM JAPAN

CARPET FROM NEW ZEALAND

FIRE CONTROL SYSTEM FROM ITALY

INTER-COM FROM BRITAIN

FURNITURE FROM SWEDEN

COMPUTER FROM U.S.A.

SLIDING DOORS FROM BELGIUM

WHISKEY FROM SCOTLAND & VODKA FROM RUSSIA

AIR-CON FROM CANADA.

VAN FROM GERMANY

AN AMERICAN TOUR PARTY (FOR EXAMPLE) PAYS THE OPERATOR IN USA, TRAVELS PAN AM, STAYS IN AN AMERICAN-OWNED HOTEL, EATS ONLY AMERICAN FOOD AND TRAVELS IN AMERICAN PLANES, CARS & SHIPS.

WHO PROFITS MOST?

get even this much, because club management imposes fines for improper dress, smoking, drinking, tardiness, and other arbitrary infractions.[14]

And there are others who profit from the sex tourism industry. In the Philippines alone in 1977 over 200,000 Japanese visitors spent an average of nearly $55 a day on food, drink, shopping, and lodging. Further, in this last category, hotels charge not only for rooms but under a "joiner pass" system require payment of $10 for the right to bring a woman into these rooms. One source reports that a major hotel in the Philippines has admitted to making 40 percent of its gross income from the "joiner" system.[15]

Clearly the industry is a very lucrative one. The World Tourism Organisation estimates the income from international tourism in 1980 at US$75 billion — a sum which represents the highest figure of world trade. In Thailand tourism is the third highest source of currency earnings, bringing in more than US$220 million. Rice provides US$290 million and sugar US$260 million. The present estimate of income from tourism in South Korea is nearly US$300 million. In the Philippines the tourist industry has grown from a negligible dollar earner in the 1960's to the fourth largest source of foreign exchange in the late 1970's. In 1977 tourism brought in over US$300 million, US$262 million more than in 1972. For these countries tourism is seen as a major source of foreign currency which they so desperately need.[16]

A parallel can be drawn here with the remittances which

parties are automatically included in the price. Small and medium-sized companies send their employees on "rest and recreation" holidays there, and the number of male Japanese tourists to South Korea has nearly trebled in the last 10 years.

Another factor in the growth of the sex tourism industry is the presence of US military bases in the South East Asian region. One example is the Subic Bay Naval Base in the Philippines. While city officials and business operators claim that the R & R (rest and recreation) industry is plain entertainment, a number of city ordinances and other forms of collaboration by the city, clearly reveal organized prostitution taking place. For example, the city government maintains and operates a social hygiene clinic which certifies whether or not an entertainer is free from VD and other communicable diseases. In addition, there is an anti-streetwalking ordinance which considers soliciting customers in the streets punishable, but not soliciting customers inside the clubs. This assures business operators the incomes from various fees involved in selling women — "ladies drinks," the price of the company of a woman in the bar and "bar fines," the price of taking her out of the club.

Bar fines, however, are only a fraction of the money generated by the sale of women to foreign tourists. Sources in the business report that the men on tour pay an average of $60 for one night with a woman. A rough breakdown looks like this: clubowners — $15, tour operator — $15, local guide — $10, Japanese guide — $10, the women themselves receive between $4.25 and $5.75 from the owner's share. Often they do not

PROSTITUTION IN MANILA

THE JAPANESE TOURIST WANTS A GIRL FOR ONE NIGHT. HE WILL PAY THE HOTEL THE SUM OF US $12

AND HE PAYS THE TOUR OPERATOR $50, SOME OF WHICH GOES UNDER THE COUNTER.

THE TOUR OPERATOR GIVES THE LOCAL PIMP $20.

AND THE PIMP PAYS THE GIRL (WHO DOES THE WORK) THE SUM OF $8!

A KIND OF LEGALISED GANG-RAPE

Japanese tourist photographing Masai woman at special "tourist village" in Kenya.

Margaret Murray

migrant workers send back to their families. In 1978 remittances sent back to the Philippines totaled $374.3 million, second only to the $620 million earned that year from coconut oil, and was estimated to have reached a billion dollars by the end of 1979.[17]

For the women involved, however, the money they earn is vital. Often it is used to support whole families. In a study of 50 "Masseuses" in Thailand, it was found that the majority sent back nearly one-half of their earnings to support their families, pay school fees for brothers and sisters to "get a better start" and find a reasonable job. And most of them also tried to save in order to eventually get out of prostitution and find training for themselves. Others, however, simply graduated to becoming agents for other masseuses.[18]

The situation does not stop there, though. Asian women have been seen as "good produce" for the European market, both as prostitutes and as "nice, docile wives." Businessmen have been quick to set up mechanisms for bringing Thai and other women to many European countries for use in nightclubs and hotels. The women being desperate for money and offered the promise of "a better life," are duped, exploited and left even more isolated in a country where they probably don't speak the language or have any real human contact. The marriage business is just as bad: European, Australian and Japanese agencies make catalogues with "eligible" women, touting their beauty, docility and sexiness as in a cattle market. Prices for such a wife can be anything from US$5,000—8,000, none of which goes to the woman, who must consider as her payment the acquisition of a "faithful, understanding" husband. The marriage bureaux, on the other hand, are mushrooming.[19]

development perspective

The fundamental economic and political problems which cause patterns of migration and lead to urban slums, overcrowding, unemployment, exploitation, and impoverished land development, are complex and not easy to deal with. It is clear, though, that for many governments it is both convenient and even advantageous to leave the situation as it is or at worst even encourage it. For a poor, overcrowded country, a population which emigrates abroad in large numbers has definite advantages: discontent over unemployment is diffused, and much-needed foreign currency is brought in. Bad as the rural-urban migration is within the country, as long as women can be sexually exploited there are also advantages: the tourist industry — great source of foreign exchange — flourishes, and there is no need to provide social benefits or infrastructure to the slum-dwellers or rural inhabitants since the women are providing this with their meagre earnings.

For the richer countries whose populations are diminishing, a marginal workforce of immigrant laborers who have no political rights and cost little in social benefits is just what is needed for industrial growth and consumerism. When economic recession looms, migrant workers can be sent back home, and immigration laws tightened up. Travel agencies in these countries can continue to flourish by capitalising on the market provided by the economic needs and vulnerability of poorer nations.

While considerable attention has been focussed over the past decade on the problem of rapidly growing cities and the attendant problems mentioned above, most development agencies "have not confronted international migration either as a problem requiring careful study or as a programatic concern."[20] In addition, the smattering of projects specifically aimed at migrant workers often neglect to take the situation of women into account in the special hardships they confront as mothers, isolated domestic workers, low-skilled factory workers, or agricultural workers left behind. For example, a project designed to create jobs for men to enable them to earn a living in Guatemala rather than migrating to Mexico, assumes that working men will alleviate the hardship of their families. This ignores the existing inequality between women and men and the vital nature of women's contribution to supporting their families. It also implies that women should become dependent upon men.

Commission for Filipino Migrant Workers

Filipino migrant workers organize in Italy, 1981. Banners read: Workers unite against marginalization and cultural and social isolation.

Likewise, although recommendations have been made for increasing agricultural production in an attempt to counter migration to urban areas, these recommendations fail to take women specifically into account. For example, no efforts have been made to clearly set forth the status of landless women in land redistribution schemes. Furthermore, proposals for overcoming rural unemployment rely heavily on intensive production methods, demanding an increase in hours worked, which means an additional burden on already overworked women. Many rural development programmes to date, combined with massive emphasis on centralised industrial growth, have in fact been at least partially responsible for the massive displacement of people from rural to urban areas. (See chapter on Rural Development for detailed elaboration of this point.)

Recognition of the problems of domestic workers and especially prostitutes and the sex tourism industry is only just beginning. It is probably fair to say that in no way have development planners seriously considered these issues. The case of the sex tourism industry encapsulates the problems which are fundamental to women and development: women's lack of economic and educational opportunity; their role as sole in-

come-earner for whole families and thus the imperative of earning something however it is done; their incredibly vulnerable position in a society which abuses women sexually and makes money from this and yet where women are left entirely and often solely responsible for children; the impossibility for women to organise effectively because they have to resort to work which is illegal and because they are already overworked and have no extra time. One writer even comments: "for the women whose bodies provide the balance of payments in such a development model, there is almost no concern."[21] Many of the same observations may be made about domestic work, where, in addition to being isolated and providing essential but unrecognised labour, women are frequently sexually harrassed too.

It is not by chance that these issues have only recently surfaced and that development planners have overlooked them. The point made throughout this book is that development is mostly male-oriented and therefore short-sighted and totally inadequate to respond to such fundamental problems.

The women's movement has been largely responsible for bringing these issues to public attention, and it is women who are actively organising to combat this with all the means at their disposal. Examples of migrant women organising, forming unions and associations to fight for their rights, are multiplying: in Canada, Australia, some European countries and the USA, strong movements of migrant women workers now exist, and in our resources for this chapter we list and describe just some of them.

To close this chapter, however, we think it important to relate in more detail the actions which women have been taking on the sex tourism issue.

women's action

"You have money and you feel strong. You think you can use us as you like. Japanese men treat Korean women like sexual slaves." With these bitter words and an appeal of the South Korean Church Women United to their Japanese sisters, an international campaign against prostitution tourism was launched in the summer of 1973.[22]

Three months later the women's division of the Christian Council of Japan published a position paper condemning the abuse of South Korean women by Japanese men, and this started a public awareness campaign. In December of the same year there was a demonstration at Haneda Airport in which many different women's groups participated against "kisaeng" (Korean word come to mean prostitution) tourism. Parallel demonstrations in South Korea where the kisaeng tour planes landed, strengthened the growing movement against sex tourism and by 1977 several groups formed the Asian Women's Association (AWA). AWA started publishing a magazine **Aji to josei Kaiho** (Asian Women's Liberation) and participated in trade union activities against the policies of Japanese businesses in South East Asia. In 1980 AWA published a special number of the magazine devoted entirely to sex tourism, based on considerable research and contacts with women in the countries most concerned (South Korea, Taiwan, Philippines, Thailand). This document was presented to the United Nations Women's Conference in Copenhagen in July 1980.

In September 1980 the Christian Conference of Asia sponsored an International Workshop on Tourism. It was held in

Manila, Philippines, in recognition of the perverse direction of the tourist industry there, and encouraged by the fact that the Assembly of the World Tourism Organization was to take place there later that month. One outcome of this meeting was a series of synchronized protest actions against organized sex tours in Asia, at the time of Japanese Premier Zuko Suzuki's visit to ASEAN countries in January 1981. Beginning in the Philippines, organizations of local and national scope endorsed a letter of protest addressed to Premier Suzuki. Groups in other countries followed suit. The letter urged Premier Suzuki firstly to make an official statement banning the organization in Japan of all sex tours, and secondly to take concrete measures against those who are party to these organized sex tours: Japanese companies and businessmen, airlines, hotels, travel agencies and tour operators.

Massive demonstrations took place throughout his tour, and the groups involved in each country began to feel a tremendous solidarity in their action. They sent support telegrams to each other and their joint action came to be known as the Third World Movement Against the Exploitation of Women (TW-MAE-W). The group went on to send a letter to the Pope before his visit to the Philippines in February 1981, asking him to denounce the degradation of women through sex tours and to recognise the link with militarization (the naval military bases which foster prostitution). A copy was sent to Messrs Reagan, Suzuki and Marcos. Actions and publicity continue, and already TW-MAE-W reports that their actions have led to the following tangible results:

- According to the statistics of the Japan Immigration Bureau, the number of male Japanese tourists who visited the Philippines declined sharply, from 14,699 to 11,998 or 18% in March, 19.7% in April, and 24.6% in May, compared to figures of the previous year. (Depthnews, 17 Sep 81)
- In Thailand, there was a drastic decline of 94% or from 20,803 to 1,249 in May. (Depthnews, 17 Sep 81)
- The sharp decline in Japanese "sex tours" has forced Japan Airlines (JAL) to reduce flights to Manila from November on. Passengers from Nagoya, Osaka, and Fukuoka in the April-June period decreased by 14%, 21.4%, and 34% respectively. Drops were remarkable in package tours that have been actively used by people who wanted to make love cheaply. (AFP telex)
- The advertisements for Southeast Asian tours in the Tokyo dailies no longer make allusions to the beautiful ladies of Manila or Chiang Mai but instead feature seashores and mountains, meant to be read by office ladies rather than male customers. (Daily Express, 17 Sep 81)
- Big hotels are facing financial difficulties because of the big drop in room occupancy. (DE, 18 Sep 81)
- Restaurants and cocktail lounges in the so-called tourist belt in Ermita have reported low income. (DE, 18 Sep 81)
- Suspected fronts for prostitution have temporarily closed shop for lack of business. These are beauty parlors, exclusive night clubs, which actually are pick-up points for prostitutes. (DE, 18 Sep 81)[23]

Action cannot stop at attempting to end sex tours, however. The problem is much more complex, and any campaign against prostitution tourism can so easily be transformed into a moralistic campaign against prostitution in general – thus putting the blame back onto women in general and Asian women in particular. One woman from the TW-MAE-W group, speaking to European women points to another aspect: "There is obviously something radically wrong with **your** society when your sex problems have to be exported to the Third World. You can support our struggle by publicizing what your men are doing and by taking action against the travel agencies involved."[24]

Some West German women's groups have taken up the challenge. In February 1980 two religious groups – the Evangelical Women of Germany and the German Catholic Women's Society wrote an open letter to German travel agencies, with copies to journalists, suggesting that they were carrying out a racist and sexist form of exploitation with their package tours. The Women's World Day of Prayer collected more than 120,000 signatures protesting against sex tourism. They demanded that (1) German money for development be allocated to constructing alternative ways of earning money for Thai women, (2) an end to the body business in Thai women within the Federal Republic of Germany, and (3) condemnation of German travel agencies organising sex tours to Thailand.

This is just a beginning. Much more needs to be done to attack the roots of the problem, but at least there is some public awareness of the issue. As women we will have to continue relentlessly, and perhaps if this issue is taken up as a major development question the fundamental issues of global sexism can be addressed.

Footnotes

1 *Migration Today*, no. 25, 1979, p. 7.

2 *Filipina Workers* (Geneva: World Council of Churches, 1980), p. 7.

3 *Women*, issue on migrant women, 1979, p. 25.

4 *U.S. News and World Report*, 14 January 1980, p. 73.

5 *Perception*, September/October 1979, p. 34.

6 *New Statesman*, 21 - 28 December 1979, p. 972.

7 *ISIS International Bulletin*, no. 14, 1980, p. 22.

8 *Filipina Workers*, p. 7.

9 Danda Prado, "Women and Migration in Latin America," *ISIS* no. 14, 1980, p. 15.

10 Elsa Chaney, *Women in International Migration* (Washington DC: Agency for International Development, 1980), p. 14.

11 *Migration Today*, no. 24, p. 26.

12 *Bangkok Post*, 27 August 1977.

13 From an advertisement for Rosie Reisen (Rosie Travel) cited in *ISIS* no. 13, 1979, p. 9.

14 A. Lin Neumann, "Hospitality Girls in the Philippines," *ISIS* no. 13, 1979, p. 14.

15 Ibid.

16 Jane Cottingham, "Sex Included," *Development Forum*, vol. 9 no. 5, June 1981.

17 *Filipina Workers*, p. 47.

18 Pasuk Phongpaichit, *Rural Women in Thailand: from Peasant Girls to Masseuses* (Geneva: International Labour Office, 1980).

19 Ekkehard Launer, "Asiatinnen auf Abzahlung," *Entwicklungspolitische Korrespondenz*, no. 5, 1981, pp. 18-22.

20 Elsa Chaney, *Women in International Migration*, p. 28.

21 Renate Wilke, "Sexuelle Abenteuerferien," *Entwicklungspolitische Korrespondenz*, no. 5, 1981, p. 3. This entire issue is entitled "Sexploitation: das Geschäft mit asiatischen Frauen," and is one of the sources used as a basis for the section below on "women's action," especially the article by Renate Wilke entitled "'Wir brauchen Eure Wut'– Widerstand gegen Prostitutionstourismus."

22 Ibid., p. 12. See also *TW – MAE – W Action Bulletin*, which deals entirely with the issue of sex tourism and women's action against it.

23 *TW – MAE – W Action Bulletin*, no. 5, November 1981, p. 1.

24 *Entwicklungspolitische Korrespondenz*, no. 5, 1981, p. 14.

resources for research & organizing

women's groups
sex tourism

Asian Women's Association
Poste Restante, Shibuya Post Office, Tokyo, Japan.

One of the major groups involved in campaigns against sex-tourism, they produce a newspaper, *Asian Women's Liberation*, in which they continually bring the issue to the fore, and report on actions taking place.

Concerned Asian Women
p/a MIAC, Voor Clarenburg 10, Utrecht, Netherlands.

This group of Asian women in the Netherlands was recently set up to draw attention to the sex-tourism industry in Europe and to give support to their sisters struggling in the South-East Asian countries where the industry flourishes. In a statement made at the time of a demonstration they organised at Schiphol airport in the Netherlands, 21 March 1982, they said,

"Sex-tourism is a logical consequence of the exploitative nature of the relations between the rich and powerful and the poor and powerless. It is also a consequence of the unequal relations between men and women.

"The problem of sex-tourism is most acute in Thailand, the Philippines, South Korea and Sri Lanka. In these countries the ruling elites, whether civil or military, are undemocratic and repressive. The governments are selling out their countries and peoples in their efforts to increase and consolidate their power. They have sold out the natural resources of their countries. They have offered young people, especially women, as cheap and docile labour to the profit-hunting multinationals. Now, they are allowing young women and children to be used as objects of perverted pleasure by foreign and local tourists.

"The rich and developed nations also have their part in the exploitation and oppression of Asian peoples. They support and collaborate with the oppressive Asian regimes by giving military aid. They continue to exploit the natural and human reserves of Asian countries economically through their multinational corporations. They condone the organization of sex-tours to Asia.

"Women and children have always been the most subdued and manipulated group in society. In the modern system of international cooperation and relations, Asian women and children are being scandalously manipulated and victimised on both the international labour market and the international and local sex-market.

"We call on all people to:

EXPRESS   their solidarity with the women and children of Asia

CONDEMN   – the repressive Asian governments and their foreign collaborators who prevent the organization and development of Asian peoples
  – the exploitative investment practices of multinationals which provide the economic backing for the repressive regimes in Asia and aggravate the problems of the people
  – the tourist and other agencies in Asia and Europe which organise, operate and profit from the 'sex-industry'.

SUPPORT   the struggles of all Asian people and especially the struggles of Asian women to organize themselves and fight for a just and humane existence in their various societies."

Evangelische Frauenhilfe
Alte Landstrasse 121, 4000 Düsseldorf, Federal Republic of Germany.

Katholische Frauengemeinschaft
Prinz Georg Strasse 44, 4000 Düsseldorf, Federal Republic of Germany.

These two groups have been very active in West Germany in denouncing the sex-tourism industry, and in campaigning to get German travel agencies to stop their sex-tours. They have also been waging a large publicity campaign.

Third World Movement Against Exploitation of Women (TW-MAE-W)
P.O. Box 1434, Manila 2800, Philippines.

An organisation which came into being as a result of concerted action and demonstrations at the time of Premier Suzuki of Japan's visit to ASEAN countries in January 1981. The group spreads across Philippines, Thailand, Taiwan, Indonesia, South Korea and Japan, and continues to work to stop sex-tourism and the exploitation of women in many different ways. They produce a bi-monthly newsletter, **TW-MAE-W Action Bulletin** which reports on the latest actions of the group and the links and activities around the world on the issue.

Women's World Day of Prayer
Deutenbackerstr. 1, D-8504 Stein-über-Nürnberg, Federal Republic of Germany.

Have carried out a signature campaign, demanding that German development money be spent on finding alternative employment possibilities for South-East Asian women who are currently exploited by the sex-tourism industry.

Other groups involved in action are:

Institute of Religion and Culture
P.O. Box EA 131, Ermita, Manila, Philippines.

Nippon Christian Academy Kansai Seminar House
23 Takenouchi-cho, Ichijoji, Sakyo-ku, Kyoto 606, Japan.

Christian Conference of Asia
480 Lorong 2, Tao Payoh, Singapore 12.

They have also produced a document, "Tourism: The Asian Dilemma", a useful resource.

bibliography
sex tourism

"Hospitality Girls in the Philippines"
A. Lin Neumann, **South East Asia Chronicle**, no. 66, January/February 1979, South East Asia Resource Center, P.O. Box 4000D, Berkeley, California 94704, USA.

This article, which has been reproduced in many different journals and magazines, is an important study of the way in which the entire prostitution tourism industry operates in the Philippines, giving details of money earned by the various parties involved, the government attitude, the tourists and, most importantly, considerable attention to the women involved. The article is based on considerable research and interviews with many people in the Philippines.

Multinational Sex: Feminist Roots of the South Korean Crisis
Carl Cronstadt and Eli Tov, c/o Yamagushi, 3-5-27 Asagaya Kita, Suginami-ku, Tokyo 166, Japan. 1978.

This 224 page manuscript is a very interesting and comprehensive examination of the *kisaeng* (sex tourism) industry in South Korea. The authors examine this topic from three different perspectives: the historical background leading up to and condoning such an industry; an overview of the situation from a feminist point of view including an exploration of the liberation and reunification of South Korea and the elimination of the *kisaeng* industry; and finally suggestions of feminist tactics appropriate for achieving these goals.

This last section suggests strategies for feminist tactics. The authors suggest that the US women's movement should take steps to promote international solidarity and support with the Korean liberation struggle. Targets for activists could be US and Japanese corporations and banks. Companies like American Airlines depend upon *kisaeng* and encourage this industry by investing in hotels, transportation systems and tourist bureaux that exploit them. Other companies and banks to be targeted are: (US interests): Motorola Corporation, Gulf Oil

Corporation, Chase Manhattan Bank; (Japanese interests): Mitsubishi Corporation, Marubeni Corporation, Matsushita Corporation; (umbrella organisations): US-Korea Economic Council and the World Bank. Suggested demands for targeted business include: 1. pay South Korean women a humane wage; 2. eliminate all sexist practices including discrimination in promotion, training opportunities, forced early retirement, retirement at marriage, sexual threats and hassles, etc.; 3. adhere to the "Declaration of Workers' Human Rights". (This document, signed by a group of workers in Seoul in 1977 is reproduced in the text.)

While the effectiveness of the entire campaign depends on mass participation by ordinary people, there are certain groups whose mobilization is especially important. The influence of organized prostitutes and women activists in both industrialised and Third World countries would be explosive, destroying powerful forces in traditional power structures.

Multinational Sex provides information and valuable insight into the problem. The study is well researched, and includes a useful bibliography and list of sources, but suffers from redundancy and poor organization. This does not however detract from its importance. As the authors point out, exploitation is not only a problem of the *kisaeng* or of South Korean women or Asian workers. It is an international problem.

Olongapo's Rest and Recreation Industry
Asian Social Institute, 1518 Leon Guinto St., Malate, Manila, Philippines.

A slide film. Once a small fishing village in the Philippines, Olongapo today is a city based on the rest and recreation industry. A network of 503 clubs, bars, hotels, restaurants, sauna baths, massage clinics and other recreational and entertainment centers services the "needs" of visiting military and civilian personnel from the adjacent US Naval Base in Subic Bay. An estimated average of 7,000 servicemen and civilian personnel come to Olongapo everyday for "rest and recreation" where some 9,056 registered hostesses and other entertainment employees are waiting to serve them.

This slide show, produced by Leopoldo Moselina, illustrates the operations of the industry and its causes. Most of the women who are exploited by the industry come from poverty stricken areas and many of them were victims of rape or abandonment. The film concludes that prostitution at Olongapo is not a "moral" problem but a constituent part of an exploitative economic system.

Moss Side Community Press Women's Coop

Prostitution Tourism
Sister Mary Soledad Perpinan, P.O. Box 1434, Manila 2800, Philippines.

A 19 page paper presented at the Church and Tourism Conference held in November 1981 sponsored by the Church of Sweden and the World Council of Churches. Sister Soledad examines many aspects of the prostitution tourism issue in her country, and relates the activities of the Third World Movement Against Exploitation of Women. She emphasizes the link with militarization – describing the prostitution circles which have been set up in Olongapo as a result of the US Subic Naval Base. "We have to stress that a nuclear disaster looms wherever military installations are. If we work towards their abolishment, we likewise shoo away men who abuse our women. In other words, the fight against militarization is also a fight against prostitution which it proliferates."

· "Sex Included"
Jane Cottingham, **Development Forum** vol. 9 no. 5, June 1981, Department of Economic and Social Information, C-527, United Nations, 1211 Geneva, Switzerland.

An article tracing the history of the sex-tourism industry in South East Asia, showing the growth and magnitude of the industry today, and examining more closely the situation of the women who are abused and exploited by it. Also describes action which has been taken by women's, church and other groups to combat this enormous industrial complex.

"Sexploitation: Das Geschäft mit asiatischen Frauen"
Entwicklungspolitische Korrespondenz, no. 5, December 1981, Postfach 2846, 2000 Hamburg 19, Federal Republic of Germany.

The entire issue of this excellent bi-monthly magazine is devoted to sex-tourism in South East Asia, and the extension of that – the imported prostitution and "marriage business" in Asian women within Europe. Nineteen articles cover all aspects of the issue with a clear, well-researched analysis, which includes an examination of free trade zones in Asia, and the exploitation of migrant workers in Europe. A basic document on the issues.

Shameful Japanese: Prostitution Tourism
Ms. Takahashi Kikue, c/o Fuijn-Kyofukai, 2-23-5 Hyakunin-cho, Shinjuku-ku, Tokyo 160, Japan.

A slide film sponsored by the Women's Christian Temperance Union of Japan, exposing exploitative tourism. It shows Japanese tour groups composed almost entirely of men, which inevitably include prostitute buying. In Korea, part of tour package deals include what is advertised as "Kisaeng Party". Prostitute buying is, in many guises or openly, advertised in tour brochures and guide books.

Many very young girls are forced into prostitution because of poverty. The double jeopardy committed is realized when the aggressive rise in economic activity of the Japanese in these same countries is understood as one contributing factor to why the people of these countries involved remain in poverty. The Japanese, once labelled the "economic animal" has now come to be called the "sexual animal".

In the Korean situation, centuries-old superior attitudes and discriminatory practices by Japanese toward Korean people compound the feelings of resentment of the past into the present.

Many women's groups in Japan and Korea have started action: researching, protest action to government and tour agencies, and demonstrating and passing out leaflets at Haneda and Kimpo airports respectively.

These slides with text in English and Japanese are available for rent or sale.

Nancy Szabo/Woman Becoming

"Tourism and Prostitution"
ISIS International Bulletin no. 13, 1979, ISIS, C.P. 50, 1211 Geneva 2, Switzerland.

A collection of articles on many aspects of the sex-tourism phenomenon both in general and with specific articles on Thailand, the Philippines, and South Korea. In order to better place the issue within the scope of sexual abuse against women, there are also articles on prostitution as a whole and feminist thinking about this – the way in which women have always been considered either "madonna" or "whore". Prostitutes in industrialised countries have been organising themselves against abuse and illegal status for the past few years. The **Bulletin** shows the clear link in the abuse and exploitation of women across the globe, and describes how women in different parts of the world are organising.

"Women's Predicament: Why I oppose Kisaeng Tours: Unearthing a structure of economic and sexual aggression"
Matsui Yayori, **Japanese Women Speak Out**, June 1975, c/o PARC, P.O. Box 5250, Tokyo International, Japan.

This is an eight-page article describing Kisaeng tourism (well-advertised tours for Japanese men to come to South Korea for a "sex" holiday) giving some of the historical growth and clearly showing government involvement. Briefly describes some of the actions which women and other groups are taking to stop Kisaeng. A very impassioned article by a Japanese woman. The whole volume **Japanese Women Speak Out** is an impressive anthology of articles on different aspects of women's oppression not only in Japan, but in South Korea, Thailand, and other South East Asian countries, including ways in which women are building solidarity in their struggles.

women's groups
migration

Commission for Filipino Migrant Workers (CFMW)
Via Capo d'Africa 37/int. 2, 00184 Roma, Italy; and St. Francis Community Centre, Pottery Lane, London W11, U.K.

CFMW was established in September 1979 by a group of concerned Filipinos and missionaries who have worked in the Philippines. The general objectives of the CFMW are: 1. to help form autonomous and self-reliant organizations of Filipino migrant workers in order to protect their rights and promote their welfare; 2. to promote a sense of responsibility for and participation in the social struggle and development taking place in the Philippines.

They produce pamphlets and a newsletter, *Kabisig,* available from either of the above addresses. The May 1982 issue of this newsletter gives an "update" on Filipino migrant organisation in different countries of Europe. "At present Italy is the country where we are closest to building a genuine and truly Filipino migrant organisation. From the beginning the Filipinos got the strong support of the Italian trade unions... who have given consistent support and made available many facilities for the Filipino migrants. The unions have also helped Filipinos to hold conferences and meetings for a better understanding of the society and laws of Italy and helped them draft recommendations for better laws on migrants." Activities of Filipino migrant workers in Britain, France, the Netherlands, Germany, Sweden and Belgium are also described.

Korean Women's Group in West Germany
c/o Won-Hea Feussner-Kang, Adlzereiterstr. 15, 8000 München 2, Federal Republic of Germany.

A group of mainly nurses who started to organise when, in 1977, they were threatened with expulsion from West Germany. They carried out a signature campaign which was supported by many groups including colleagues in hospitals, representatives of Protestant and Catholic churches, the trade unions and women's groups. They held a two-day meeting in May 1978, and presented to the Government demands for unlimited permission to reside and work in the Federal Republic with the right to continue to work, even for those of them who had not been in the country for five years. Part of this demand was later recognised. They continue to work for the rights of South Korean people in European countries.

Reaching Out/India

cpf

Labour Rights for Domestic Servants
704-82 Warren Road, Toronto M4V 2R7, Canada.

"I have worked the 80 hour a week jobs, receiving only $250 a month, a bare room to live in, and left-overs for my meals. I have been fired on the spot for questioning my hours of work, with my employer refusing to pay me my back wages... Domestic work was the only type of work I could perform legally while I was in this country. If I was fired or unhappy with my job, I would first have to consult immigration officials and receive their permission to seek new employment. Without their permission I would have to leave Canada, or as many domestics do, work illegally.

"I knew that I was not the only exploited domestic in Toronto... I had heard stories about other domestic workers which made my worst jobs seem terrific. I decided to try to do something about the general exploitation which faced all my fellow domestic workers. I called a very small meeting to discuss what could be done with regard to domestic workers in our province... We decided to draft a petition which called on the Ontario Government to include domestic workers under the Provincial Employment Standards Act (minimum wage, 44 hour work week, vacation pay, overtime pay). The petition was called 'Slavery Today?'. On January 15, 1979 we took the name Labour Rights for Domestic Servants (LRDS)."

So writes Mirjana Vukman-Tenebaum, originally from Yugoslavia, in an article published in **Resources for Feminist Research/Documentation sur la Recherche Feministe** Vol. 10 No. 2 July 1981. She goes on to explain how the petition received wide support from many community, political, women's and labour organizations. LRDS had much publicity and by March 1979 over 80 domestic workers had joined the organisation. They decided that LRDS should not only lobby the Government, but also find ways of helping domestics with their day-to-day problems like collecting back-wages, obtaining or renewing employment visas, finding lodgings for temporarily unemployed domestics. In fact, they began to operate as a Domestic Workers' Union.

They also set up a legal counselling service, and started a monthly newsletter, **The Domestic Worker.** But their major problem was funding. Since June 1980 LRDS has been trying to become the first Domestic Workers Union under the charter of the Canadian Labour Congress and the Ontario Federation of Labour. A Union Charter would give LRDS exclusive rights to organize domestic workers in Ontario and would also entitle them to permanent funding. "If we are given this charter we would open a hiring hall from which we could place domestics. With the money received from the employers for finding them help and our membership dues, we believe that we could support ourselves after one or two years of operation." The final decision on this charter has not yet been taken.

In the meantime, LRDS counts more than 500 members, and because of their work, domestics are now entitled to the minimum wage and to statutory holidays and vacation pay.

Migrant Women Speak
Published for the Churches Committee on Migrant Workers by Search Press Limited, 2-10 Jerdan Place, London SW6 5PT, U.K. and World Council of Churches, 150 route de Ferney, 1211 Geneva 20, Switzerland. 1978.

This is a really fundamental book on the question of migrant women. The result of several years of inquiries, research and practical work with women migrant workers and housewives living in major urban centres in the different regions of Europe, it presents a series of personal accounts by these women, based on extensive interviews by a group of researchers. Not only do these first-hand accounts present a vivid picture of all the problems faced by migrant women, but they show how very strong these women are, giving examples of how they have organised and what they need to improve their situation. Accounts included are: North African women in Marseille (France), migrant women in Belgium (from Italy, Spain, Morocco, Greece, Turkey and Poland), Portuguese women in France, Italian and Spanish women in Switzerland and Germany. Especially noteworthy is the **Women Migrants' Manifesto** reproduced here from the migrant women's meeting held in Switzerland in 1974. It is a very outspoken and still relevant document.

Fem/Mexico

fem.

Migration of Mexican Campesinos
Ed Krueger, American Friends Service Committee, Mexico-US Border Program, 1501 Cherry St., Philadelphia, PA 10102, USA.

A 21 page paper examining the causes of migration of agricultural workers and peasants in Mexico. It looks at Mexico City's phenomenal growth in the past few years to its becoming the largest city in the world, and points to deliberate government policy of growth and centralised industrialisation as a main factor. It also examines the de-stabilization of agriculture and the deterioration of rural life, the other side of the migration coin, and gives considerable space to details on multinational companies involved in this entire process.

The American Friends Service Committee is an important source of material on migration, especially concerning Mexico and the USA.

Migration Today no. 24, 1979, World Council of Churches, 150 route de Ferney, 1211 Geneva 20, Switzerland.

Produced jointly with the Women's Desk of the World Council of Churches, this issue of this excellent publication of the Migration Desk is devoted entirely to women migrants. It not only covers the situation of migrant women in many different parts of the world — Asian women in Britain, Italian and Spanish women in Switzerland, Italian women in Australia, Indian women in Kuwait, Turkish women in Norway, Filipina women in Italy, migrant women in Canada and South Africa — but also gives good examples of positive action and organisation by migrants. Available in English, French, and Spanish. Highly recommended.

Minority Rights Group
Benjamin Franklin House, 36 Craven Street, London WC2N 5NG, U.K.

An international research and information unit which works to secure justice for minority or majority groups suffering discrimination, by investigating their situation and publicising the facts as widely as possible, to educate and alert public opinion throughout the world. Publishes regular reports on minorities in different parts of the world, from the Kurds or the Namibians to the Aborigines or the Basques. There are currently 42 reports based on considerable research and analysis. No. 27 is on **Arab Women**, and No. 28 on **Western Europe's Migrant Workers**, both in English and French. £0.75 each.

Multiculturalism vol. 11, no. 4, 1979
Faculty of Education, University of Toronto, 371 Bloor St. West, Toronto Ontario M5S 2R7, Canada.

This issue on "Immigrant Women" is an excellent production on the very varied aspects of immigrant women's situations in Canada, drawing for the most part on first-hand interviews with Portuguese, East Indian, Chinese, Greek, St. Lucia and Hungarian women. The main emphasis is on labour force participation and work within the family, with special emphasis on programs particularly designed for immigrant women — looking at what is practically available in the different regions of Canada, and listing centres and organisations of immigrant women. An extensive annotated resource guide is given.

"People on the Move"
Aprodicio A. Laquian, **Populi** vol. 7 no. 3, 1980, United Nations Fund for Population Activities, 485 Lexington Avenue, New York, New York 10017, USA.

A lengthy article describing patterns and consequences of migration internationally in a recent historical perspective, and an important elaboration of policies which have been taken to try to influence internal migration. These are classified as: 1) stop the flow of migrants by encouraging people to stay in the rural areas (rural development), 2) creating "resettlements", "growth poles" and "new cities", 3) restricting movements of population by legal measures, 4) accommodating to existing migration patterns by providing services in urban areas. The author clearly criticises the first three and shows where and why they have failed. In opting for the fourth policy, however, he entirely by-passes any examination of the enormous emphasis on centralised industrialisation which many Third World countries have endorsed and which contributes in part to the massive rural-urban migration patterns. Nowhere is there any specific mention of women.

This whole issue of **Populi** deals with "population and the urban future".

Organisation of Women of Asian and African Descent (OWAAD)
1 Cambridge Terrace, London NW1, U.K.

An organisation founded in 1980 to promote and fight for the interests of Asian, African and West Indian women in Britain, many of whom have been living in Britain for more than one generation. They produce a newsletter, **FOWAAD**, dealing with issues like immigration laws, race discrimination, sex discrimination and the overall treatment of migrant working women in Britain.

Working Women's Centre
Majorca Building, 1st Floor, 258 Flinders Lane, Melbourne 3000, Victoria, Australia.

Among its many services, the Working Women's Centre gives emphasis to helping migrant women. It has established a multilingual newspaper, "Women at Work" which is distributed through unions to workers on the job, and contains information about unions, occupational health, child care and other matters which particularly concern women who work outside their homes. They give information, help and advice on a wide range of problems, including discrimination in pay, promotion etc. training and retraining, child care, workers' compensation, health, safety, exploitative piecework conditions, and enquiries for employment. They also run seminars and discussion groups, and supply speakers.

bibliography
migration

Bolivian Information Bulletin/Belgium

Filipina Workers: A Case of Exported Women Workers
Migration Secretariat, World Council of Churches, 150 route de Ferney, 1211 Geneva 20, Switzerland. 1980.

A selection of documents which describe the lives of Filipina workers in England, Spain, Italy, Belgium and Canada, the exploitation by their employers and by "job agencies", and the economics of international migration, explained in terms of the Philippines. Also contains a section on sexual exploitation — prostitution and tourism. A guide for "study and action", it includes useful addresses for further information and support and solidarity campaigns.

Filipina Workers is the sixth in a series of documents for "study and action" published by the Migration Secretariat of the World Council of Churches. Other publications in the series include "Migrant Workers in the Dominican Republic", "Migrant Workers in South Africa: Question of Rights and Racism", and "Migrant Workers and Expatriates of the Middle East". All represent excellent resources on the different aspects of migration.

Finding a Voice: Asian Women in Britain
Amrit Wilson, Virago Ltd., 5 Wardour Street, London W1V 2HE, U.K. 1978.

Amrit Wilson explains why she wrote this book: "I felt that Asian women had so much to tell, I wanted to write a book in which they could express their opinions and feelings. There have been things written about Asian women which show them always as a group who can't speak for themselves. They are just treated as objects — nothing more. That they have any feelings about their own lives or that they can analyse their own lives never comes up. I wanted to show how Asian women are quite capable of speaking for themselves."

Based on hundreds of first-hand accounts of Asian women working in Britain, this book gives a vivid and personal picture of what it is like to be an Asian migrant there. The material presented shows how Asian women come at the bottom of the heap — being given jobs which used to be done by Asian men or white women. It shows how, as these women start "finding a voice" they are beginning to recognise the injustice against them and to start organising.

"I Thought There Was No More Slavery in Canada!"
Canadian Women's Studies, vol. II, no. 1, 1980, 651 Warden Avenue, Scarborough Ontario M1L 3Z6, Canada.

This article describes the lives of West Indian women working as domestics in Canada, and their efforts in organising against exploitation. Includes short list of groups in Canada.

Mexican Border Industrialization, Female Labor Force, Participation and Migration
Maria Patricia Fernandez Kelly, Graduate Dept. of Anthropology, Livingstone College, Rutgers University, USA.

This 26 page study examines the connections among gender, class and family structure and occupational alternatives for both men and women along the Mexican border in the context of its recent industrialization. The author interprets the statistics and shows the various factors which make the options of the women migrant workers significantly different than those of male migrants. There is a good bibliography of material on migration in Latin America, particularly having to do with the US-Mexico border industries. This unpublished manuscript is available from the American Friends Service Committee (AFSC), Aurora Schmidt, Mexico-US Border Program, 1501 Cherry St., Philadelphia, PA 19102, USA.

"Migrant Women"
ISIS International Bulletin, no. 14, 1980, ISIS, C.P. 50, 1211 Geneva 2, Switzerland.

The articles in this **ISIS Bulletin** cover many aspects of the problems of migrant women — low paid, low skilled work, alienation, insecurity, language problems, sexual harassment — on a broad spectrum, from domestics in Latin America to outworkers in Australia. Presented as well are women organising to improve their situation such as the Korean Women's Group in West Germany. Also included is an extensive bibliography.

Vrouwen te Gast
Feminist Press Sara, Plantage Muidergracht 149, Amsterdam, Netherlands.

A photographic report on migrant women in the Netherlands by Bertien van Manen, published by the feminist press Sara. In the last 15 years more than ten thousand women from southern Europe, North Africa and Turkey have come to the Netherlands as migrants. The photographs in this book illustrate many aspects of the lives of these women at home and at work.

"Women and Trade Unions"
Resources for Feminist Research/Documentation sur la Recherche Féministe vol. 10, no. 2, July 1981, Ontario Institute for Studies in Education, 252 Bloor Street West, Toronto, Ontario, M5S 1V6 Canada.

A valuable issue on all aspects of women within trade unions, but particularly interesting for the section on "Domestic workers — organizing strategies". Gives ample resources both of literature and groups. This is always an excellent publication, and invaluable to anyone concerned with women's studies and women and development.

Women in International Migration. Issues in Development Planning
Elsa M. Chaney, Office of Women in Development, USAID, Washington DC, USA.

An overview of the issues of women and international migration — problems faced by the women who stay behind as well as those faced by women who themselves migrate. Also includes a description of women and migration activities in various development-oriented agencies, as well as an extensive bibliography. Contains interesting information, and offers some insight into the perspectives of development planners.

Women in Struggle
Box 50, Rising Free Bookshop, 182 Upper Street, London N1, U.K.

An excellent collection of articles put together by the Poster Film Collective based on a three week event in Feb-March 1978 under the title "Women in Struggle". All the contributions come from women or women's groups which organize independently but at the same time situate themselves firmly within the context of the broader struggle for people's liberation. Articles from: Zimbabwe, South Africa, Eritrea, Latin America, Chile, the Philippines, China, Malaya, Ireland, India, and also dealing with the Britain-Africa-Caribbean triangle, the Grunwick women's strike, Malaysian Nurses in the UK, and several London women's groups. It is well produced and provides an excellent resource on women in liberation struggles. No price or date mentioned.

ISIS is an international women's information and communication service, with a resource and documentation centre. It was established in 1974 in response to demands from women in many countries for an organisation to facilitate global communication among women and to gather and distribute internationally materials and information produced by women and women's groups.

Over the years we have built up an extensive pool of documentation and information comprising:

- a network of 10,000 contacts in 130 countries.
- 50,000 items — periodicals, newsletters, pamphlets, books, manuscripts, information about films, projects, groups — by and about women from all over the world.

The information covers a vast variety of topics from health, education, food, nutrition and appropriate technology to communication, media, violence against women, employment, and theories of feminism.

From this wealth of information ISIS provides many services:

* **Direct information services** in answer to written and telephone requests, on any aspect of the women's movement internationally and topics of concern to women in different parts of the world. Our users include school students, university students and graduates, professional women, planners and producers of television and radio programmes, women's groups, church organisations, national and international organisations, and non-governmental organisations. Visitors come to our offices to do research or consult our information. We also refer our users directly to other groups and resources.

* **ISIS Women's International Bulletin** in English and Spanish: a quarterly publication bringing together documentation on themes of particular concern to women, reflecting action and resources from around the world. Among the themes covered since No. 1 was published in 1976 are: health, the mass media, violence against women, nuclear power and militarization, women, land and food production, migrant women, tourism and prostitution, women in national liberation movements.

* **ISIS News Service**: a monthly news bulletin of all the latest women's events, comments and activities in different parts of the world, distributed through an international wire service to developing countries, to women's groups and publications in many parts of the world.

* **Resource Guides** are more in-depth publications on certain subjects. Three Guides published to date are: **Bottle Babies** — a guide to the baby food issue, the **International Women and Health Guide**, and the **Resource Guide on Women and Development**.

* **Documentation packets and bibliographies** prepared on request. Packets and bibliographies are on very specific themes of burning concern to women, such as women and peace, aging, the new technology, films — any issue where groups, individuals and organisations need collected information rapidly for conferences, seminars etc.

Facing page: UNESCO

* **The International Feminist Network (IFN)** which mobilizes international support for women who are being persecuted on the grounds of their sex. Recent cases for IFN support have included women political prisoners in Brazil, and a women's centre threatened with closure in India. This service is open to all women everywhere.

* **Technical assistance** in communication skills and information management. Many women's groups starting information/documentation centres request our skills in helping them set these up. Others ask for help in publishing, layout, editing and networking.

* **Training** at our offices in women's communication, information management, publishing and research. Each year two or three women from different parts of the world work with us on some aspect of women's communication.

* **Exchange programme** for women activists to live for a time in another culture, learning and sharing skills in areas of crucial concern to women such as health, legal aid, crisis centres, communication, agriculture.

* **Conference organisation.** In June 1981 ISIS organised jointly with the Women's Health Centre of Geneva, an International Women and Health meeting in which 500 women from nearly 40 countries attended.

ISIS is an independent, non-profit organisation financed by subscriptions and sales of its publications, and by donations from women's groups, non-governmental and development organisations.
The work is carried out by an international team of women from four continents.

Our services are open to you — please call us. For more details on any of these services, our publications and information available, write to:

ISIS Italy   or   ISIS Switzerland
Via S. Maria dell'Anima 30   Case Postale 50 (Cornavin)
00186 ROMA   CH-1211 Geneva 2
Italy.   Switzerland.

Tel: 06/65 65 842   Tel: 022/33 67 46

LIST OF PUBLICATIONS AND ORDERING INFORMATION

RESOURCE GUIDES

Bottle Babies: a guide to the baby food issue
1976, 44 pp. in English, German
Spanish edition updated and printed 1981
Price: US$ 5.-surface, US$ 8.- airmail

International Women and Health Resource Guide
A joint project of ISIS and the BOSTON WOMEN'S HEALTH
BOOK COLLECTIVE (a multi-lingual guide)
1980, 175 pages, English, French, German, Spanish
Price: US$ 5.- surface, US$ 8.- airmail

Women in Development: A resource guide
1983, 240 pages, English.
Price: US$ 12 (includes surface postage, add $7 for airmail).
Bulk rates available on request.

ISIS WOMEN'S INTERNATIONAL BULLETINS

In English:

1976
No. 1 The International Tribunal on Crimes
       Against Women
No. 2 Women in the Daily Press*

1977
No. 3 Women in Liberation Struggles*
No. 4 Battered Women and the Refuges
No. 5 Feminism and Socialism Part I

1978
No. 6 Feminism and Socialism Part II*
No. 7 Women and Health Part I*
No. 8 Women and Health Part II
No. 9 Women in Southern Africa

1979
No. 10 Women and Work
No. 11 Women, Land, and Food Production
No. 12 Organizing Against Rape
No. 13 Tourism and Prostitution*

1980
No. 14 Women and Migration
No. 15 Nuclear Power and Militarization
No. 16 The Feminist Press in Western Europe
No. 17 International Feminist Network (IFN)

1981
No. 18 Women and the Media
No. 19 Women in National Liberation Struggles
No. 20 3rd International Women and Health
        Meeting
No. 21 News from the Women's Movement

1982
No. 22 1st Latin American and Caribbean Feminist
        Meeting
No. 23 Motherhood
No. 24 Women and New Technology
No. 25 Sexuality

In Spanish:

1980
No. 1 Mujer: Problemas y Perspectivas*
No. 2 Mujeres y Salud*
No. 3 Prensa Feminista en Europa
No. 4 Mujeres y Medios de Comunicación

1981
No. 5 Mujeres Latinoamericas en Europa
No. 6 Mujeres y Educación
No. 7 Mujeres y Movimientos de Liberación
       Nacional

No. 8 Tercer Encuentro Internacional de Mujeres
       y Salud

1982
No. 9 Primero Encuentro Feminista Latinoame-
       ricano y del Caribe
No. 10 Mujeres y Maternidad
No. 11 Mujeres, Trabajo y
and 12 Multinacionales

* Out of Print

SUBSCRIPTIONS

Beginning January each year:

For 1 year

Individual/ women's groups	US$	15.—	surface
	US$	20.—	airmail
Institutions	US$	25.—	surface
	US$	30.—	airmail

For 2 years

Individual/ women's groups	US$	28.—	surface
	US$	35.—	airmail
Institutions	US$	45.—	surface
	US$	55.—	airmail

Back copies

Individual	US$	4.50	surface
	US$	6.—	airmail
Institutions	US$	6.50	surface
	US$	8.—	airmail

Cheques or money orders to ISIS, P.O. Box .50 (Cornavin), 1211 Geneva 2, Switzerland. Bank transfers to C1.605.667/0 at Société de Banque Suisse, Geneva, Switzerland. Currency equivalents accepted. Special reductions to women's and alternative bookstores and for bulk orders.

resources for research & organizing

rural development

Binhi Agricultural Resource Foundation
P.O. Box SM-132, Manila, Philippines.

A non-governmental resource center, Binhi promotes and assists peasant organizations and self-reliant, ecological farming. It has assisted the development of many small, functional rural women's groups with a wide range of organizational, educational and socio-economic activities. Binhi emphasizes the need to get at the root causes of the poverty and exploitation of peasants, the need to organize, and the need to improve traditional agriculture and appropriate grassroot technologies to make it competitive with so-called modern agriculture. A number of publications are available on these issues.

Center for Women Resources (CWR)
Room 403 FMSG Building, New York Street, corner E. Rodriguez Sr. Boulevard, Quezon City, Philippines.

Founded in 1981, CWR is a non-governmental resource center for women and women's groups in the Philippines. It assists women peasants and workers, feminist groups and others concerned with women through the provision of documentation and resources, training programs, seminars, speakers, curricula and educational materials for grassroots women to assist them in mobilizing and organizing themselves. CWR also serves to link up women's groups in the Philippines and to link with women's groups internationally. It has available a number of case studies and information on women in the Philippines.

Farmers Assistance Board Inc. (FAB)
P.O. Box AC-623, Quezon City, Philippines.

A non-governmental organization assisting peasant organizations, FAB has recently given special attention to the situation of rural women. FAB aims to promote self-awareness and the mobilization and organization of women themselves, especially the most exploited and oppressed. Among its publications is the result of a participatory research project, **The Struggle Toward Self-Reliance of Organized Resettled Women in the Philippines: A Case Study**. It also produces material for use by rural women, such as **Herbal and other Local Remedies.**

KANITA Project
School of Social Sciences, Universiti Sains Malaysia, Penang, Malaysia.

A research program on women and children initiated in 1978, KANITA is carrying out action-oriented research on basic issues and problems of women to aid in drawing up development policies and programs. It has produced a number of critical evaluations of development projects for women in Malaysia, including **Status of Rural Women in Relation to Labour and State Modernisation Processes** by Maznah Mohammad and **Income Generating Activities for Women: A Case Study of Malaysia** by Vasanthi Ramachandran and James Lochhead. The **KANITA Papers**, published occasionally, bring together the research and studies of the project. Of particular interest are issues no. 3 (April 1981) and no. 4 (July 1982) which explain and evaluate KANITA's experiences in conducting participatory research with rural women. These articles point out the constraints and implications of this methodology and some of the lessons learned.

Women in Southeast Asia: A Bibliography
Fan Kok Sim, Institute of Advanced Studies, University of Malaya, Kuala Lumpur, Malaysia. Available from G.K. Hall and Co., 70 Lincoln Street, Boston, Massachusetts, USA. 1982.

This extensive bibliography with about 4000 entries is divided by subject area and covers a wide range of topics from women workers, marriage, rural development to feminist literature in Southeast Asia. While it is not annotated, it is a useful compilation of what has been written on women in this part of the world.

appropriate technology

Women's Research Centre in Social Science
H.C. Andersens Boulevard 38, Mezz. DK-1553 Copenhagen V Denmark.

The monthly newsletter produced by this group, **Women and the Labour Market** reports on up-coming seminars and conferences concerning women, especially in Europe. It also contains extensive resources on specific themes, such as women and the new technology, giving annotated listings of projects, literature, summaries of reports etc., and news about ongoing research projects on women, studies of public policies, studies of new patterns of women's work, and recent literature.

education

Kvinfo
Leaderstraede 15, 2 Sal. DK-1201 Copenhagen K Denmark.

An information service whose aim is to support and promote women's studies and gender research on a broad, interdisciplinary basis. Kvinfo coordinates Danish research on women and related topics. It also has a reading room and collection of catalogues, handbooks, bibliographies and files which encompass the registration of academic research and sources of women's expertise outside the universities. It has a photography and slide collection on loan, containing an extensive catalogue of contact prints of old photographs displaying women's lives at work, at school, at play and at home. The slides include paintings, graphics, handicrafts and sculpture by Danish artists.

WAYS TO SELF RULE:
BEYOND MARXISM AND ANARCHISM
by George Fischer

How democratic self rule transforms science, school, and community, and how it offers our best alternative to the modern authoritarianism of "1984." Carol Ascher, feminist author: "A lovely book by a much loved professor."

244 pages. Hardbound. $14.95

DESPAIRWORK: AWAKENING TO THE
PERIL AND PROMISE OF OUR TIME
by Joanna Macy

"What we urgently need is to break the taboo against expressions of despair for our world—to validate these feelings of rage and grief, realize their universality, and experience in them the mutual support that can empower us to act. To do despair work is, in a real sense, to wake up—both to the peril and the promise."

32 pages. 1982. $2.45

MOVING TOWARD A NEW SOCIETY
by Susanne Gowan, George Lakey, William Moyer and Richard Taylor.

Move from doomsday ideology to a joyous celebration of struggle. A bold analysis of current social and political conditions, coupled with an exciting vision of a new democratic, decentralized and caring social order, and a nonviolent revolutionary strategy.

"A must for any serious social change activist."
—*Peacework*

296 pages. $5.00

A MODEL FOR NONVIOLENT
COMMUNICATION
by Marshall Rosenberg

This groundbreaking work in interpersonal relations helps us more fully open ourselves to give and receive information, share feelings, and overcome blocks to effective communication. It is filled with illuminating examples.

40 pages. 1983. $3.95

A MANIFESTO FOR NONVIOLENT
REVOLUTION
by George Lakey

Original 1972 working paper analyzing problems of contemporary society, presenting visions of a new society, and a nonviolent strategy for getting there. Excellent for initiating group dialogue.

26 pages. Large format. $1.75

HANDBOOK FOR SATYAGRAHIS:
A MANUAL FOR VOLUNTEERS OF
TOTAL REVOLUTION
by Narayan Desai

India's foremost trainer in nonviolent action presents an integrated, practical approach to training for radical social change, growing out of the experience of the Gandhian movement.

57 pages. $3.95

To Order: send check or money order to New Society Publishers, 4722 Baltimore Avenue, Philadelphia, PA 19143. For postage and handling: add $1.50 for the first book and 40¢ for each additional book.

More Resources From New Society Publishers

**NO BOSSES HERE! A MANUAL ON
WORKING COLLECTIVELY AND
COOPERATIVELY**
by Karen Brandow, Jim McDonnell, and
Vocations for Social Change

The title says it all! Down-to-earth, simply written,
easy to use. Great for small businesses, co-ops, organizations, church groups.

120 pages. Second edition. $5.95

**CLEARNESS: PROCESSES FOR
SUPPORTING INDIVIDUALS AND
GROUPS IN DECISION-MAKING**
by Peter Woodrow

Having trouble making personal decisions? Feeling
isolated, alone? Don't know how to utilize other people's good thinking effectively? Handy resource for
helping you think about things with the people around,
develop trust, tap new resources for support, help
people joining new groups. Sample agendas.

32 pages. $2.45

A MANUAL FOR GROUP FACILITATORS
Center for Conflict Resolution

Get your group to work together more effectively. A
working manual for learning to communicate well,
doing effective planning, solving problems creatively,
dealing with conflict, and moving groups toward ful-
fillment of their own goals.

88 pages. Large format. Illustrated. $6.00

**RESOURCE MANUAL FOR A
LIVING REVOLUTION**
by Virginia Coover, Ellen Deacon, Charles Esser
and Christopher Moore

The practical tools you need for everything from consciousness raising, working in groups, and developing
communities of support to education, training, and
organizing skills. Used by women's groups, disarma-
ment and antinuclear activists, and community organizers worldwide. 25,000 copies in print. An activist's
dream!

330 pages. Agendas. Exercises. New edition. 1981.
$19.95 (hardbound): $7.95 (paperback)

**BUILDING UNITED JUDGEMENT:
A HANDBOOK FOR CONSENSUS
DECISION MAKING**
Center for Conflict Resolution

Reach group unity and make your decision-making
structure work for *you*. Maximize cooperation and
fully use the creativity of all members of your group.
Learn to recognize conflict as a source of growth.
Handle common group problems practically.

124 pages. Large format. Illustrated. $6.95

**LEADERSHIP FOR CHANGE:
TOWARD A FEMINIST MODEL**
by Bruce Kokopeli and George Lakey

Reject authoritarian and paternalistic forms of leadership. Making practical use of feminist perspectives,
break leadership functions down into their component
parts to be shared and rotated, empowering all.

33 pages. Illustrated. $2.45

**MEETING FACILITATION:
THE NO MAGIC METHOD**
by Berit Lakey

Plan and carry out consistently productive meetings.
Easy steps to help a group help itself.

11 pages. 50¢

To Order: send check or money order to New Society Publishers, 4722 Baltimore Avenue, Philadelphia PA 19143. For postage and handling: add $1.50 for the first book and 40¢ for each
additional book.

THE EYE OF THE CHILD
by Ruth Mueller

A brilliant healing myth for a world gone mad!

"Of all the creatures to whom the great mother had given birth all were a part, not apart, but one. Yes all but one flowed as she flowed, born of her womb, dying in her bosom, struggling, true, but never against their own life support. One, only one, capable of standing apart, imagining self above and outside, turning to rend, turning to overpower, to subdue, to conquer the vessel of life itself, creation's own embodiment. Had she not labored for aeons to give birth to a triumph of joy and beauty as fair as dawn, a creature of light to share the glowing consciousness of the whole, one of understanding as deep as her deeps are deep, of laughter as divine as tears and of tears as cleansing as laughter, one who was no alien to mercy, capable of new visions above predation, a familiar to the art of healing, above all a creature of tongues, creation itself no longer mute to express—to express—

"What had gone wrong?"

Ecological speculative fiction of the highest order.

240 pages. 1984
Paperback: $7.95

A MANUAL ON NONVIOLENCE AND CHILDREN
Compiled and edited by Stephanie Judson
Foreword by Paula J. Paul, Educators for Social Responsibility

"As adults we now have the responsibility to inspire in our children the determination to resolve conflicts without the use of weapons. A world in which our children can become sophisticated in the skills of problem-solving, dialogue, and negotiation is a world in which we are educating our children for survival."
— *Paula J. Paul,*
Educators for Social Responsibility

Exercises, games, agendas. Anecdotes by teachers, parents. Annotated bibliography. Illustrated. Large format. 160 pages. 1984.
Paperback $9.95
Hardcover $24.95

NO TURNING BACK: LESBIAN AND GAY LIBERATION FOR THE '80s
by Gerre Goodman, George Lakey, Judy Lashof and Erika Thorne; Foreword by Malcolm Boyd

"*No Turning Back* fulfills a long felt need for a progressive analysis and pragmatic sourcebook for lesbians, gays and others concerned with replacing patriarchal oppression with a more human alternative. I was quite pleased by the integration of personal statements and experiences into the more theoretical discussion, and by the inclusion of practical and feasible proposals for individual and collective action."
—Larry Gross, Professor, Annenberg School of Communications, University of Pennsylvania, and Co-Chair, Philadelphia Lesbian and Gay Task Force

Recommended for public libraries by *Library Journal.*

168 pages.
Hardcover: $16.95
Paperback: $7.95

TWO ESSAYS: ON ANGER and NEW MEN, NEW WOMEN Some Thoughts on Nonviolence
by Barbara Deming

Thought-provoking essays adding new depth to the slogan that 'the personal is political'. Modern classics in the literature of nonviolent struggle, challenging us to recreate ourselves even as we attempt to recreate our world. Originally appeared in Barbara Deming's *We Can Not Live Without Our Lives.*

32 pages. 1982. $2.45

OFF THEIR BACKS...AND ON OUR OWN TWO FEET
by Men Against Patriarchy

This pamphlet addressed to men includes three essays: "More Power Than We Want: Masculine Sexuality and Violence," "Understanding and Fighting Sexism," and "Overcoming Masculine Oppression in Mixed Groups."

32 pages. 1983. $2.45

To Order: send check or money order to New Society Publishers, 4722 Baltimore Avenue, Philadelphia PA 19143. For postage and handling: add $1.50 for the first book and 40¢ for each additional book.